W9-BYJ-346

Rick Steves'
LONDON
2003

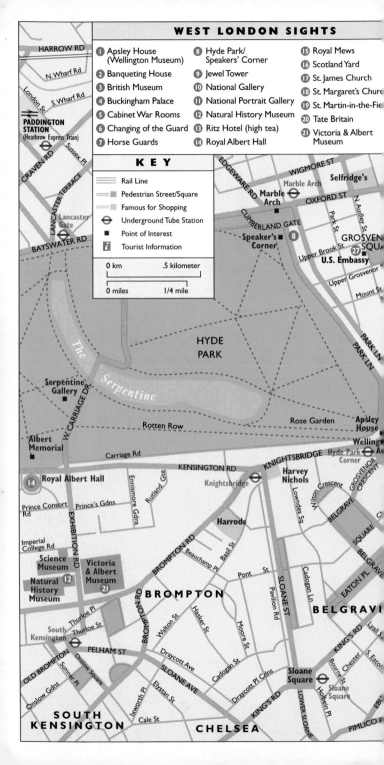

WEST LONDON SIGHTS

1. Apsley House (Wellington Museum)
2. Banqueting House
3. British Museum
4. Buckingham Palace
5. Cabinet War Rooms
6. Changing of the Guard
7. Horse Guards
8. Hyde Park/ Speakers' Corner
9. Jewel Tower
10. National Gallery
11. National Portrait Gallery
12. Natural History Museum
13. Ritz Hotel (high tea)
14. Royal Albert Hall
15. Royal Mews
16. Scotland Yard
17. St. James Church
18. St. Margaret's Churc
19. St. Martin-in-the-Fie
20. Tate Britain
21. Victoria & Albert Museum

KEY

- Rail Line
- Pedestrian Street/Square
- Famous for Shopping
- ⊖ Underground Tube Station
- ■ Point of Interest
- 𝒊 Tourist Information

0 km   .5 kilometer

0 miles   1/4 mile

HARROW RD

N. Wharf Rd

S. Wharf Rd

London St

Sussex Pl

PADDINGTON STATION
(Heathrow Express Train)

Craven Rd

LANCASTER TERRACE

Lancaster Gate

BAYSWATER RD

EDGEWARE RD

WIGMORE ST

Marble Arch

Selfridge's

Marble ⊖ **Arch**

OXFORD ST

CUMBERLAND GATE

Park St

N. Audley St

GROSVEN

Speaker's ■ **Corner**

8

Upper Brook St

SQUA

27

U.S. Embassy

Upper Grosvenor

Mount St

The

PARK LN

PARK LN

HYDE PARK

Serpentine Gallery ■

The Serpentine

W. CARRIAGE DR

Rotten Row

Rose Garden

Apsley House

Welling

Albert Memorial

Carriage Rd

KENSINGTON RD

KNIGHTSBRIDGE

Hyde Park Ar Corner

GROSVENOR CRESCENT

14 **Royal Albert Hall**

Prince Consort Rd

Prince's Gdns

Ennismore Gate

Rutland Gate

⊖ **Knightsbridge**

Harvey Nichols

Milton Crescent

Lowndes Sq

BELGRAVE

Imperial College Rd

EXHIBITION RD

Science Museum

Natural History Museum

12

Victoria & Albert Museum

21

Beauchamp Pl

Basil St

Harrods

BROMPTON RD

BROMPTON

Pont St

Sloane St

Cadogan Ln

BELGRAVE SQUARE

EATON PL

BELGRAVI

South Kensington

⊖ Thurloe Pl

Thurloe St

Walton St

Hasker St

Moore St

Pavilion Rd

Cadogan Ln

KING'S RD

Lyall S

Chester

S. Eato

OLD BROMPTON

Sumner Pl

PELHAM ST

Onslow Square

Draycott Ave

SLOANE AVE

Draycott Pl Gdns

Sloane Square ⊖

Bourne St

Holbein Pl

EB1

Onslow Gdns

Ixworth Pl

Elystan St

Cale St

KING'S RD

LOWER SLOANE

Sloane Square

SOUTH KENSINGTON

CHELSEA

PIMLICO R

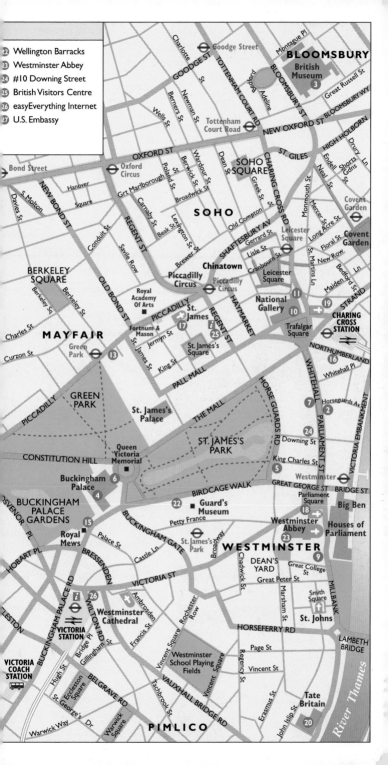

22	Wellington Barracks
23	Westminster Abbey
24	#10 Downing Street
25	British Visitors Centre
26	easyEverything Internet
27	U.S. Embassy

BLOOMSBURY

British Museum

Goodge Street

Montague Pl

Charlotte St
GOODGE ST
TOTTENHAM COURT RD
BLOOMSBURY ST
Bedford
Adeline
Great Russell St
BLOOMSBURY WY

Wells St
Berners St
Newman St

Tottenham Court Road
NEW OXFORD ST
ST. GILES
HIGH HOLBORN

Bond Street
OXFORD ST
Oxford Circus

Endell St
Shorts Gdns
Neal St
Drury Ln
Monmouth St
Mercer St

Hanover Square
Grt Marlborough St
Wardour St
Poland St
Berwick St
Broadwick St
Dean St
Greek St
CHARING CROSS RD
SOHO SQUARE
SOHO

Davies St
S. Molton St
NEW BOND ST

Covent Garden

Conduit St
Savile Row
REGENT ST
Carnaby St
Beak St
Lexington St
Brewer St
Old Compton St
SHAFTESBURY AV
Gerrard St
Lisle St
Cranbourn St
Leicester Square
St Martins Ln
Floral St
New Row
Bedford St
Long Acre
Maiden Ln
Covent Garden

BERKELEY SQUARE

Berkeley Sq
OLD BOND ST
Royal Academy Of Arts
PICCADILLY
Chinatown
Piccadilly Circus
Piccadilly Circus
11
National Gallery
10
19
STRAND
CHARING CROSS STATION

Charles St
MAYFAIR
Curzon St
Green Park
13
Fortnum & Mason
St. James St
Jermyn St
St. James
17
St James's Square
King St
25
Haymarket
REGENT ST
Trafalgar Square
NORTHUMBERLAND
16
Whitehall Pl

PICCADILLY
GREEN PARK
St. James's Palace
THE MALL
PALL MALL
ST. JAMES'S PARK
HORSE GUARDS RD
WHITEHALL
7
Horseguards Av
2

CONSTITUTION HILL
Queen Victoria Memorial
24
Downing St
King Charles St
5
Westminster

Buckingham Palace
6
4
BIRDCAGE WALK
GREAT GEORGE ST
BRIDGE ST
Parliament Square
Big Ben

BUCKINGHAM PALACE GARDENS
15
22
Guard's Museum
Petty France
BUCKINGHAM GATE
St. James's Park
Broadway
18
Westminster Abbey
23
Houses of Parliament

Royal Mews
Palace St
Castle Ln
WESTMINSTER
DEAN'S YARD
9
Great College St
Great Peter St
Marsham St
Smith Square
St. Johns

HOBART PL
BRESSENDEN
GROSVENOR PL
VICTORIA ST
26
Ambrosden Av
Westminster Cathedral
Francis St
Rochester Row
Chadwick St
HORSEFERRY RD
LAMBETH BRIDGE

VICTORIA STATION
BUCKINGHAM PALACE RD
WILTON RD
Bridge St
Gillingham St
Vincent Square
Westminster School Playing Fields
Page St
Regency St
Vincent St
VAUXHALL BRIDGE RD

VICTORIA COACH STATION
Hugh St
St. George's Dr
Eccleston Square
BELGRAVE RD
Warwick Square
Tachbrook St
PIMLICO
Erasmus St
John Islip St
Tate Britain
20
River Thames

Warwick Way

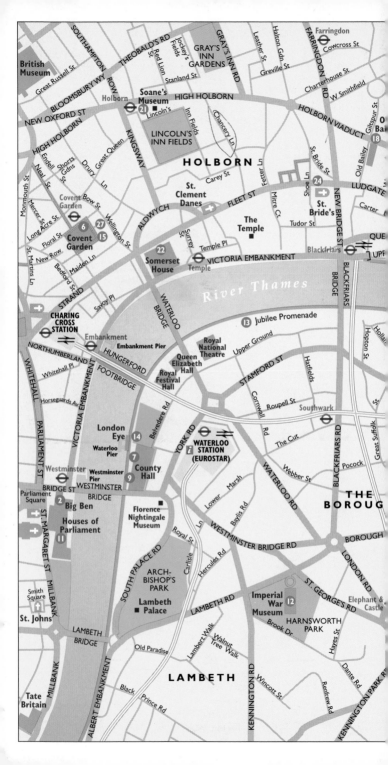

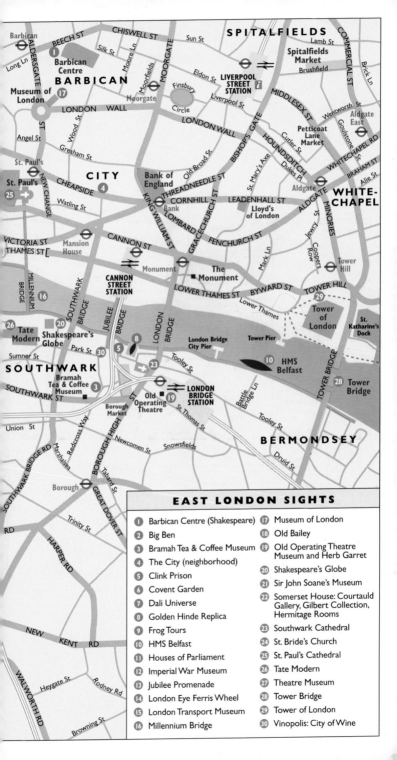

EAST LONDON SIGHTS

1. Barbican Centre (Shakespeare)
2. Big Ben
3. Bramah Tea & Coffee Museum
4. The City (neighborhood)
5. Clink Prison
6. Covent Garden
7. Dali Universe
8. Golden Hinde Replica
9. Frog Tours
10. HMS Belfast
11. Houses of Parliament
12. Imperial War Museum
13. Jubilee Promenade
14. London Eye Ferris Wheel
15. London Transport Museum
16. Millennium Bridge
17. Museum of London
18. Old Bailey
19. Old Operating Theatre Museum and Herb Garret
20. Shakespeare's Globe
21. Sir John Soane's Museum
22. Somerset House: Courtauld Gallery, Gilbert Collection, Hermitage Rooms
23. Southwark Cathedral
24. St. Bride's Church
25. St. Paul's Cathedral
26. Tate Modern
27. Theatre Museum
28. Tower Bridge
29. Tower of London
30. Vinopolis: City of Wine

UNDERGROUND

Bakerloo	District
Central	East London
Circle	Hammersmith & City

Hatched lines represent peak hours only

London Travel Information
020 7222 1234
24 hours

Textphone
020 7918 3015

www.transportforlondon.gov.uk

LTM FA(a) 03.01

© Transport for London

Jubilee
Metropolitan
Northern
Piccadilly
Victoria
Waterloo & City
DOCKLANDS LIGHT RAILWAY
National Rail

High Barnet
Totteridge & Whetstone
Woodside Park
West Finchley
Finchley Central
East Finchley
Highgate
Archway
Tufnell Park
Mill Hill East
Cockfosters
Oakwood
Southgate
Arnos Grove
Bounds Green
Wood Green
Turnpike Lane
Manor House
Epping
Theydon Bois
Debden
Loughton
Buckhurst Hill
Roding Valley †
Chigwell †
Grange Hill †
Hainault
Fairlop
Barkingside
Newbury Park
Woodford
South Woodford
Snaresbrook
Wanstead
Gants Hill
Redbridge
Upminster
Upminster Bridge
Hornchurch
Elm Park
Dagenham East
Dagenham Heathway
Becontree
Upney
Barking
East Ham
Upton Park
Plaistow
West Ham
Gospel Oak
Kentish Town West
Kentish Town
Holloway Road
Caledonian Road
Arsenal
Finsbury Park
Seven Sisters
Blackhorse Road
Tottenham Hale
Walthamstow Central
Camden Road
Camden Town †
Mornington Crescent
King's Cross St. Pancras
Euston
Angel
Caledonian Road & Barnsbury
Highbury & Islington
Canonbury
Dalston Kingsland
Hackney Central
Homerton
Hackney Wick
Leyton
Leytonstone
Stratford
Euston Square
Farringdon
Barbican
Old Street
Liverpool Street
Bethnal Green
Mile End
Pudding Mill Lane
Russell Square
Moorgate
Shoreditch †
Bow Road
Bow Church
Bromley-by-Bow
Devons Road
Chancery Lane
St. Paul's
Holborn
Covent Garden
Cannon Street †
Mansion House
Bank
Aldgate East
Aldgate
Whitechapel
Stepney Green
All Saints
Poplar
East India
Canning Town
Royal Victoria
Custom House for ExCeL
Prince Regent
Royal Albert
Beckton Park
Cyprus
Gallions Reach
Beckton
Monument
Tower Hill
Tower Gateway
Shadwell
Wapping
Limehouse
Westferry
Blackwall
Blackfriars
Temple
Embankment
Charing Cross
London Bridge
Rotherhithe
Bermondsey
Canada Water
West India Quay
Canary Wharf
Heron Quays
South Quay
Crossharbour & London Arena
Mudchute
Island Gardens
North Greenwich
Silvertown
North Woolwich
Southwark
Waterloo East
Lambeth North
Borough
Elephant & Castle
Surrey Quays
New Cross Gate
New Cross
Cutty Sark for Maritime Greenwich
Greenwich
Deptford Bridge
Elverson Road
Lewisham
River Thames

Interchange stations
Connections with National Rail
Connections with National Rail within walking distance
Connections with riverboat services
Connection with Tramlink
Airport interchange
Closed Sundays
Served by Piccadilly line trains early morning and late evening
For opening times see poster journey planners. Certain stations are closed on public holidays.

Reg. user No. 02/3720

Rick Steves'
LONDON
2003

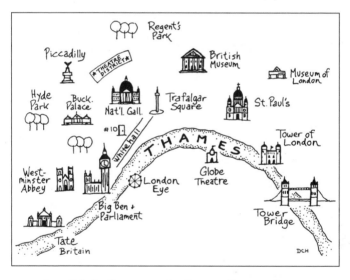

by Rick Steves & Gene Openshaw

AVALON
TRAVEL

Other ATP travel guidebooks by Rick Steves

Rick Steves' Best of Europe
Rick Steves' Europe 101: History and Art for the Traveler (with Gene Openshaw)
Rick Steves' Europe Through the Back Door
Rick Steves' Mona Winks: Self-Guided Tours of Europe's Top Museums
  (with Gene Openshaw)
Rick Steves' Postcards from Europe
Rick Steves' France (with Steve Smith)
Rick Steves' Germany, Austria & Switzerland
Rick Steves' Great Britain
Rick Steves' Ireland (with Pat O'Connor)
Rick Steves' Italy
Rick Steves' Scandinavia
Rick Steves' Spain & Portugal
Rick Steves' Amsterdam, Bruges & Brussels (with Gene Openshaw)
Rick Steves' Florence (with Gene Openshaw)
Rick Steves' Paris (with Steve Smith and Gene Openshaw)
Rick Steves' Rome (with Gene Openshaw)
Rick Steves' Venice (with Gene Openshaw)
Rick Steves' Phrase Books: French, German, Italian, Portuguese, Spanish, and
  French/Italian/German

Avalon Travel Publishing, 1400 65th Street, Suite 250, Emeryville, CA 94608

Text © 2003, 2002, 2001, 2000, 1999 by Rick Steves.
Paris chapter coauthored with Steve Smith, excerpted from *Rick Steves' France 2003*.
Maps © 2003 by Europe Through the Back Door. All rights reserved.

Printed in the U.S. by R.R. Donnelley. First printing January 2003
Distributed by Publishers Group West

Portions of this book were originally published in *Rick Steves' Mona Winks* © 2001,
1998, 1996, 1993, 1988 by Rick Steves and Gene Openshaw; and in *Rick Steves' France,
Belgium & the Netherlands* © 2002, 2001, 2000, 1999, 1998, 1997, 1996 by Rick Steves
and Steve Smith.

ISBN 1-56691-455-8 • ISSN 1522-3280

For the latest on Rick's lectures, books, tours, and television series, contact Europe
Through the Back Door, Box 2009, Edmonds, WA 98020, tel. 425/771-8303, fax
425/771-0833, www.ricksteves.com, e-mail: rick@ricksteves.com.

Europe Through the Back Door Managing Editor: Risa Laib
Europe Through the Back Door Editors: Jill Hodges, Cameron Hewitt
Avalon Travel Publishing Series Manager & Editor: Laura Mazer
Copy Editor: Kate McKinley
Research Assistance: Colleen Cox
Production & Typesetting: Kathleen Sparkes, White Hart Design
Cover and Interior Design: Janine Lehmann
Maps and Graphics: David C. Hoerlein, Rhonda Pelikan, Zoey Platt
Photography: Leo de Wys Inc. provided p. 29 (Steve Vidler), p. 279 (Sylvain Grandadam);
all others: Rick Steves, Dominic Bonuccelli, Gene Openshaw, and Elizabeth Openshaw
Front matter color photos: p. i, Tower Bridge and River Thames, © Laurence Parent;
  p. viii, Guards outside Buckingham Palace, © Dominic Bonuccelli
Cover Photo: Big Ben; London, England; Leo de Wys Inc./Dave & Les Jacobs

*Although the author and publisher have made every effort to provide up-to-date information,
they accept no responsibility for loss, injury, mushy peas, or inconvenience sustained by readers.*

CONTENTS

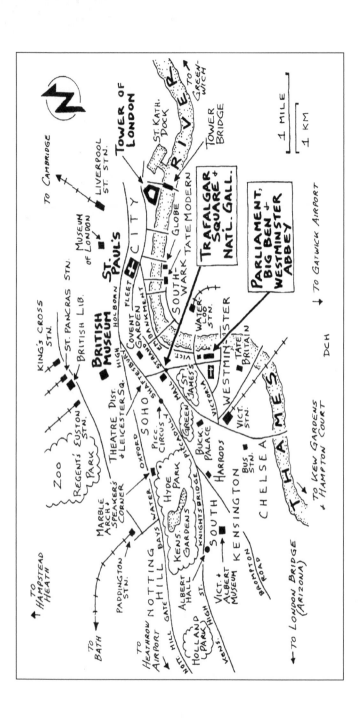

INTRODUCTION

Blow through the city on the open deck of a double-decker orientation tour bus and take a pinch-me-I'm-in-Britain walk through the West End. Ogle the crown jewels at the Tower of London, hear the chimes of Big Ben, and see the Houses of Parliament in action. Hobnob with the tombstones in Westminster Abbey, duck WWII bombs in Churchill's underground Cabinet War Rooms, and stand in awe over the original Magna Carta at the British Library. Cruise the Thames River and take a spin on the London Eye Ferris Wheel. Visit with Leonardo, Botticelli, and Rembrandt in the National Gallery. Whisper across the dome of St. Paul's Cathedral and rummage through our civilization's attic at the British Museum. And sip your tea with pinky raised and clotted cream all over your scone.

Enjoy some of Europe's best people-watching at Covent Garden and snap to at Buckingham Palace's Changing of the Guard. Just sit in Victoria Station, Piccadilly Circus, or a major Tube station and observe. Spend one evening at a theater and the others catching your breath. Sip a pint in a pub with a yacky local, and experience British Invasion rock in its birthplace.

London is more than its museums and landmarks. It's a living, breathing, thriving organism . . . a coral reef of humanity. The city has changed dramatically in recent years, and many visitors are surprised to find how "un-English" it is. Whites are now a minority in major parts of the city that once symbolized white imperialism. Arabs have nearly bought out the area north of Hyde Park. Chinese take-outs outnumber fish-and-chips shops. Many hotels are run by people with foreign accents (who hire English chambermaids), while outlying suburbs are home to huge communities of Indians and Pakistanis. With the English Channel Tunnel complete and union with Europe inevitable, many locals see even more holes in their bastion of Britishness. London is learning—sometimes fitfully—to live as a microcosm of its formerly vast empire.

This Information Is Accurate and Up-to-Date

This book is updated every year. Most publishers of guidebooks that cover a city from top to bottom can afford an update only every two or three years. Since this book is selective, covering only the places we think make the top week or so in and around London, we can update it each summer. Even with an annual update, things change. But if you're traveling with the current edition of this book, we guarantee you're using the most up-to-date information available in print (for the latest, visit www.ricksteves.com/update). This book will help you have an inexpensive, hassle-free trip. Use this year's edition. Saving a few bucks by traveling on old information is not smart. If you're packing an old book, you'll learn the seriousness of your mistake...in London. Your trip costs at least $10 per waking hour. Your time is valuable. This guidebook saves you lots of time.

Welcome to Our London City Guide

This book is organized in the following way:

London Orientation includes tourist information and public transportation. The "Planning Your Time" section offers a suggested schedule with thoughts on how best to use your limited time.

Sights provides a succinct overview of London's most important sights, arranged by neighborhood, with ratings: ▲▲▲—Don't miss; ▲▲—Try hard to see; ▲—Worthwhile if you can make it; No rating—Worth knowing about.

The **Westminster Walk** takes you on a personal tour through downtown London, from Big Ben to Trafalgar Square.

The **Bankside Walk** connects the sights on London's once-gritty, now-trendy South Bank, from London Bridge through Shakespeare's world to the Tate Modern.

The **Self-Guided Museum Tours** lead you through the British Museum, National Gallery, National Portrait Gallery, Tate Britain, Tate Modern, British Library, Westminster Abbey, St. Paul's Cathedral, Courtauld Gallery, Theatre Museum, and the Tower of London.

Day Trips chapters cover nearby destinations: Windsor, Greenwich, Cambridge, Bath, and even Paris.

Sleeping is a guide to our favorite good-value hotels, mainly in four pleasant London neighborhoods.

Eating offers a wide assortment of restaurants ranging from fun, inexpensive eateries to classy splurges.

Tips for Tackling Our Self-Guided Tours

Our self-guided tours are designed to help make your visits to London's finest museums meaningful, fun, fast, and painless. To make the most of our tours, read the tour the night before your visit.

When you arrive at the sight, use the overview map to get the lay of the land and the basic tour route. Expect a few changes—paintings can be on tour, on loan, out sick, or shifted at the whim of the curator. Even museum walls are often moved. To adapt, pick up any available free floor plans as you enter, ask an information person to glance at this book's maps to confirm they're current, or if you can't find a particular painting, just ask any museum worker. If the person doesn't recognize the title, show the photograph in this book.

We cover the highlights. You might want to supplement with an audioguide (about $5, provides dry-but-useful recorded descriptions of the art), or a guided tour (usually $6 or more). The quality of a tour depends on the guide's knowledge, fluency, and enthusiasm.

Museums have their rules; if you're aware of them in advance, they're no big deal. Keep in mind that many sights have "last entry" times 30 to 60 minutes before closing. Guards usher people out before the official closing time.

Cameras are normally allowed in museums, but no flashes or tripods (without special permission). A hand-held camera with ASA-400 film and an F-2 aperture will take a fine picture (or you can buy slides at the museum bookstore). Video cameras are usually allowed.

For security reasons, you're often required to check even small bags. Every museum has a free checkroom at the entrance. They're safe. Prepare to stash anything that you can't bear to part with in a purse or pocket.

At the museum bookshop, thumb through the biggest guidebook (or scan its index) to be sure you haven't overlooked something that is of particular interest to you. If there's an on-site cafeteria, it's usually a good place to rest and have a snack or light meal. Museum WCs are free and generally clean.

London with Children includes my top recommendations for keeping your kids (and you) happy in London.

Shopping offers tips on shopping painlessly and enjoyably, without letting it overwhelm your vacation or ruin your budget.

Entertainment is a guide to evening fun, including museums, music and theater.

Transportation Connections covers connections by train (including the Eurostar to Paris) and by plane (with detailed information on London's two major airports), laying the groundwork for your smooth arrival and departure.

London History, which gives the background of this historic city, includes a timeline and a *Who's Who* list of British notables.

The **appendix** includes telephone tips, a climate chart, and a fun British/Yankee dictionary.

Throughout this book, when you see a ✪ in a listing, it means that the sight is covered in much more depth in a self-guided walk or one of our museum tours—a page number will tell you just where to look to find more information.

Browse through this book and choose your favorite sights. Then have a great trip! You'll become your own guide with our self-guided walks and museum tours. Traveling like a temporary local, you'll get the absolute most out of every mile, minute, and dollar. You won't waste time on mediocre sights because, unlike other guidebooks, this one covers only the best. Since your major financial pitfall is lousy, expensive hotels, we've worked hard to assemble the best accommodations values.

Trip Costs

Five components make up your trip costs: airfare, surface transportation, room and board, sightseeing/entertainment, and shopping/miscellany.

Airfare: Don't try to sort through the mess. Find and use a good travel agent. A basic, round-trip, United States–London flight costs $500 to $1,000 (even cheaper in winter), depending on where you fly from and when.

Surface Transportation: For a typical one-week visit, allow about $35 for Tube tickets (for a 1-week pass or 2 *carnets* for 20 single rides). The cost of round-trip trains to day-trip destinations ranges from $10 for Greenwich (cheaper by Tube), $20 for Cambridge, and $50 for Bath, to about $140 (one-way second-class Leisure Ticket) for Paris on the Eurostar. (Save money by taking buses instead of trains, and see the Transportation Connections chapter for tips on how to get the cheapest Eurostar tickets.) Add $100 if you plan to take a couple of taxi rides between

London's Heathrow Airport and your hotel (or save money by taking the Tube, train, or airport bus).

Room and Board: You can thrive in London on $90 a day per person for room and board. A $90-a-day budget allows $10 for lunch, $20 for dinner, and $60 for lodging (based on 2 people splitting the cost of a $120 double room that includes breakfast). That's doable. Students and tightwads do it on $50 a day ($30 for bed-and-breakfast, $20 for groceries). But budget sleeping and eating require the skills and information covered below (and in greater detail in *Rick Steves' Europe Through the Back Door*).

Sightseeing and Entertainment: Many of the best sights in London are free: the British Museum, National Gallery, Tate Britain, Tate Modern, British Library, Imperial War Museum, Natural History Museum, and the Victoria and Albert Museum. Figure on paying $7–18 for the major sights that charge admission (Westminster Abbey-$9, Tower of London-$18), $8 for guided walks, and $20 for bus tours and splurge experiences (plays range from $12 to $60). An average of $20 a day works for most. Don't skimp here. This category directly powers most of the experiences all the other expenses are designed to make possible.

The British Heritage Pass, which gets you into more than 500 British Heritage and National Trust properties, doesn't make sense for a London visit, but is worth considering if you'll be traveling extensively throughout Britain (£35/$52 for 7 days, £46/$70 for 15 days, £60/$90 for 30 days; sold at Heathrow Airport TI and the Britain Visitors Centre on Regent Street in London; don't get the pass for kids, since they get discounts on admissions but not on the pass).

Shopping and Miscellany: Figure $1 per postcard, tea, or ice-cream cone, and $2 per beer. Shopping can vary in cost from nearly nothing to a small fortune. Good budget travelers find that this category has little to do with assembling a trip full of lifelong and wonderful memories.

Exchange Rate

We list prices in pounds (£) throughout this book.

> 1 British pound (£1) = about $1.50

While the euro is now the currency of most of Europe, Britain is sticking with its pound sterling. The British pound (£), also called a "quid," is broken into 100 pence (p). Pence means "cents." You'll find coins ranging from 1p to £2 and bills from £5 to £50. To convert pounds to dollars, add 50 percent to British prices: £6 is about $9, £3 is about $4.50, and 80p is about $1.20.

Prices, Times, and Discounts

The prices in this book, as well as the hours and telephone numbers, are accurate as of mid-2002. The economy is flat and inflation is low, so these prices should be pretty accurate in 2003. But Britain is always changing, and we know you'll understand that this, like any other guidebook, starts to yellow even before it's printed.

In Britain, you'll be using the 24-hour clock. After 12:00 noon, keep going—13:00, 14:00, and so on. For anything over 12, subtract 12 and add p.m. (so 14:00 is 2:00 p.m.).

This book lists year-round hours for sights. While we don't list discounts (called "concessions" in Britain), nearly all British sights are discounted for seniors (loosely defined as anyone retired or willing to call themselves a "senior"), youths (ages 8–18), students, groups of 10 or more, and families (with 2 full-fare parents, kids go for about half price).

When to Go

July and August are the peak-season months—our favorite time—with very long days, the best weather, and the busiest schedule of tourist fun. Prices and crowds don't go up as dramatically in Britain as they do in much of Europe. Still, travel during "shoulder season" (May, early June, September, and early October) is easier and a bit less expensive. Shoulder-season travelers get minimal crowds, decent weather, and the full range of sights and tourist fun spots. Winter travelers find absolutely no crowds and soft room prices, but shorter sightseeing hours. The weather can be cold and dreary, and nightfall draws the shades on sightseeing well before dinnertime. While England's rural charm falls with the leaves, London's sights are fine in the winter.

Plan for rain no matter when you go. Just keep going and take full advantage of "bright spells." Conditions can change several times in a day, but rarely is the weather extreme. Daily averages throughout the year range between 42 and 70 degrees Fahrenheit. Temperatures below 32 or over 80 degrees cause headlines (see the climate chart in the appendix). July and August are not much better than shoulder months. May and June can be lovely. While sunshine may be rare, summer days are very long. The summer sun is up from 6:30 to 22:30 (10:30 p.m.). It's not uncommon to have a gray day, eat dinner, and enjoy hours of sunshine afterward.

Red Tape and VAT Refunds

You need a passport, but no visa or shots, to travel in Britain.

VAT Refunds for Shoppers: Wrapped into the purchase price of your British souvenirs is a Value Added Tax (VAT) that's generally about 15 percent. If you make a purchase of more than £30 at a store that participates in the VAT refund scheme, you're entitled to get most of that tax back. Personally I've never felt that VAT refunds are worth the hassle, but if you do, here's the scoop.

If you're lucky, the merchant will subtract the tax when you make your purchase (this is more likely to occur if the store ships the goods to your home). Otherwise, here's what you'll need to do:

Get the paperwork. Have the merchant completely fill out the necessary refund document, called a "Tax-Free Shopping Cheque." You'll have to present your passport at the store.

Have your cheque(s) stamped at the border at your last stop in the European Union by the customs agent who deals with VAT refunds. It's best to keep your purchases in your carry-on for viewing, but if they're too large or dangerous to carry on, then track down the proper customs agent to inspect them before you check your bag. You're not supposed to use your purchased goods before you leave. If you show up at customs wearing your new kilt, officials might look the other way—or deny you a refund.

To collect your refund, you'll need to return your stamped documents to the retailer or its representative. Many merchants work with a service, such as Global Refund or Cashback (also called Vatback), which have offices at major airports, ports, or border crossings. These services, which extract a 4 percent fee, can refund your money immediately in your currency of choice or credit your card (within two billing cycles). If you have to deal directly with the retailer, mail the store your stamped documents and then wait. It could take months.

Banking
Throughout Britain, cash machines are the way to go. Bring an ATM or debit card (with a PIN code) to withdraw funds from cash machines as you travel, and carry some American cash as a backup. Since fees are charged per exchange, and most ATM screens top out at £200, save money by pushing the "other amount" button and asking for a higher amount. Bring a second debit card in case the first is lost, stolen, or mysteriously demagnetized. Check in with your bank before leaving for your trip so they won't question the sudden international activity on your account.

Bring a credit card, handy for booking rooms and theater and transportation tickets over the phone, and necessary for renting a car. For cash advances, you'll find that Barclays, National Westminster, and places displaying an Access or Eurocard sign accept MasterCard. Visa is accepted at Barclays and Midland banks. In general, Visa is far more widely accepted than American Express.

Traveler's checks work fine in Britain, but banks commonly charge a commission fee of £2 to £4, or even more.

Even in jolly olde England, you should use a money belt (order online at www.ricksteves.com or call 425/771-8303 for our free newsletter/catalog). Thieves target tourists. A money belt provides peace of mind. You can carry lots of cash safely in a money belt—and, given the high bank fees, you should.

Bank holidays bring most businesses to a grinding halt on New Year's Day, Good Friday, Easter Monday, the first and last Mondays in May, the last Monday in August, Christmas, and December 26.

Travel Smart

A smart trip is a puzzle—a fun, doable, and worthwhile challenge. Reading this book before you leave, and rereading as you travel, will enhance your enjoyment and save you time and money. The British Museum is much more enjoyable, for instance, if you've boned up on mummies the night before.

Buy a phone card and use it for reservations and confirmations. You speak the language; use it! Enjoy the friendliness of the local people. Ask questions. Most locals are eager to point you in their idea of the right direction. Pack along a pocket-size notebook to organize your thoughts. Plan ahead for banking, laundry, post-office chores, and picnics. Every traveler needs slack days. Pace yourself. Assume you will return.

Design an itinerary that enables you to hit the various sights at the best possible times. For example, if you like to free up your busy days, note that Westminster Abbey is open and empty Wednesday evenings. Visit The City (London's old center) during the day on weekdays when it's lively, not at night and on weekends when it's dead. The two-hour orientation bus tour is best on Sunday morning (when some sights are closed). There are no plays on Sunday nights.

Trip Tips and Travel Arrangements

If you're planning to stay in Bath as well as London, consider a gentler, small-town start in Bath (the ideal jet-lag pillow), and visit London afterward, when you're rested and accustomed to travel in Britain. Heathrow Airport has direct connections to Bath and other cities.

Consider making these travel arrangements and reservations before your trip:

• Reserve your room. For our recommended hotels, see the "Sleeping" chapter.

• If you want to book a play, you can call from the United

States as easily as from London, using your credit-card number to pay for your tickets. For the current schedule and phone numbers, visit www.officiallondontheatre.co.uk or photocopy your hometown library's London newspaper theater section. For simplicity, we book plays while in London. For more information, see the Entertainment chapter.

• If you want to attend the pageantry-filled Changing of the Keys in the Tower of London, write for tickets (details in Sights chapter, under "East London").

• Gather tourist information before you depart. Britain's national tourist office in the United States is responsive to individual needs and offers a wealth of meaty material. Contact the **British Tourist Authority** to ask for the Britain Vacation Planner, free maps of London and Britain (the same maps are sold for £1.40 each at tourist offices in Britain), and schedules of upcoming festivals (551 Fifth Avenue, 7th floor, New York, NY 10176, tel. 800/462-2748, fax 212/986-1188, www.travelbritain.org, e-mail: travelinfo@bta.org.uk). For a list of London's events, browse the Web: www.timeout.co.uk, www.thisislondon.com, and www.londontown.com.

• If you'll be day-tripping to Paris on the Eurostar train, consider ordering a ticket in advance (or buy in Britain); for details, see the Transportation Connections chapter.

Recommended Guidebooks

For most travelers, this book is all you need. But racks of fine London guidebooks are sold at bookstores throughout London. The *Michelin Green Guide to London*, which is somewhat scholarly, and the more readable Access guide for London, are both well-researched. *Let's Go London* is youth-oriented, with good coverage of nightlife, hosteling, and cheap transportation deals. Tourist offices (abbreviated as TI in this book) in London hand out a useful, free, monthly *London Planner* (includes a listing of sights and lots of London tips). Newsstands sell the excellent *Time Out*, which has good maps and a concise and opinionated run-down on sightseeing, shopping, entertainment, eats, and sleeps (£2, www.timeout.co.uk). If you'll be traveling elsewhere in Britain, consider *Rick Steves' Great Britain 2003*.

Rick Steves' Books and Videos

Rick Steves' Europe Through the Back Door 2003 gives you budget travel skills, such as minimizing jet lag, packing light, planning your itinerary, traveling by car or train, finding beds without reservations, changing money, avoiding rip-offs, outsmarting thieves, staying healthy, taking great photographs, using cell phones, and much more. The book also includes chapters on 35 of Rick's favorite Back Doors, six of which are in Great Britain.

Rick Steves' **Country Guides** are a series of eight guide-books covering the Best of Europe; Great Britain; Ireland; France; Italy; Spain and Portugal; Scandinavia; and Germany, Austria & Switzerland. All are updated annually and come out in December and January.

Rick's **City Guides** feature Rome, Venice, Florence, Paris, London, and—new for 2003—*Rick Steves' Amsterdam, Bruges & Brussels.* These practical guides offer in-depth coverage of the sights, hotels, restaurants, and nightlife in these grand cities along with illustrated tours of their great museums. They're up-dated annually and come out in December and January. With the sleek Eurostar train, Paris is just three hours from London. Consider combining these two exciting cities (and city guides) for a great visit.

Rick Steves' Europe 101: History and Art for the Traveler (with Gene Openshaw, 2000) gives you the story of Europe's people, history, and art. Written for smart people who were sleeping in their history and art classes before they knew they were going to Europe, *101* really helps Europe's sights come alive. However, this book has far more coverage of the European continent than of Britain.

Rick Steves' Mona Winks (with Gene Openshaw, 2001) provides fun, easy-to-follow, self-guided tours of Europe's top 25 museums. All of the *Mona Winks* chapters on London are included in this London guidebook. But if you'd like similar coverage for the great museums in Paris, Amsterdam, Madrid, Venice, Florence, and Rome, *Mona*'s for you.

Rick's new PBS-TV series, *Rick Steves' Europe*, keeps churning out shows. Of 82 episodes (in the new series plus *Travels in Europe with Rick Steves*), two shows are on London and eight are on other parts of Great Britain. These air nationally on public television and the Travel Channel. They are also available in information-packed home videos and DVDs (order online at www.ricksteves.com or call us at 425/771-8303 for our free newsletter/catalog).

Rick Steves' Postcards from Europe (1999), Rick's autobio-graphical book, packs more than 25 years of travel anecdotes and insights into the ultimate 2,000-mile European adventure. Through his guidebooks, Rick shares his favorite European discoveries with you. *Postcards* introduces you to Rick's favorite European friends.

All Rick Steves' books are published by Avalon Travel Publishing (www.travelmatters.com).

Maps

The maps in this book, designed and drawn by Dave Hoerlein, are concise and simple. Dave, who is well-traveled in London and Britain, has designed the maps to help you quickly orient and painlessly get to where you want to go. In London, buy a detailed city map at any newsstand (Bensons Mapguide, £2.25, is excellent, better than the TI map and the vending-machine maps sold in Tube stations), and you're ready to travel.

For a longer trip, consider our new Rick Steves' Britain Planning Map. Designed for the traveler, it lists sightseeing destinations prominently. Showing Britain on one side and London on the other, it's a good value (order online at www.ricksteves.com or call 425/771-8303 for our free newsletter/catalog).

Tours of London and Britain

Travel agents will tell you about all the normal tours of London and Britain, but they won't tell you about ours. At Europe Through the Back Door, we organize and lead one-week getaway tours of London (departures March–Oct, max 20 people). We also offer 17-day tours of Britain featuring just the right mix of thatch-happy villages and big-city thrills. Our Britain tours depart each year from May through September, are limited to 24 people per group, and have two great guides and a big roomy bus. For details, call 425/771-8303 or check www.ricksteves.com.

Transportation

Transportation concerns within London are limited to the Tube (subway), buses, and taxis, all of which are covered in the Orientation chapter. If you have a car, stow it. You don't want to drive in London. Transportation to day-trip destinations is covered in the Day Trips and Transportation Connections chapters.

For all the specifics on transportation throughout Great Britain by train or car, see *Rick Steves' Great Britain 2003*.

Telephones, Cell Phones, Mail, and E-mail

London is a big city. Always use the telephone to confirm tour times, book theater tickets, or make reservations at fancy restaurants. If you call before heading out, you'll travel more smoothly.

Public Pay Phones: The British telephone system is great. Easy-to-find public phone booths take coins and phone cards. Phones clearly list which coins they'll take (usually from 10p to £1), and a display shows how your money supply's doing. Only completely unused coins will be returned, so put in biggies with caution. (If money's left over, rather than hanging up, push the "make another call" button.)

To avoid the hassle of carrying enough coins, buy a BT (British Telecom) Phone Card Plus—sold at newsstands, post offices, and some tourist offices. You can make a call with a Plus card by either inserting it into a phone and dialing away, or by dialing an access number and PIN (a scratch-off personal identification number listed on the card). You can recharge a Plus card using your credit or debit card by calling the operator's number listed on the phone card, and you can use the card on any phone, including the one in your hotel room.

The only tricky public payphones you'll use are the expensive, Mickey Mouse, coin-op ones in bars and B&Bs. Some require money before you dial, while others wait until after you're connected. Many have a button you must push before you begin talking. But all have clear instructions.

Calling Long Distance within Britain: First dial the area code (which starts with 0), then dial the local number. Area codes are listed by city on phone-booth walls or are available from directory assistance (dial 192, free from phone booths). It's most expensive to call from 8:00 to 13:00 and cheapest from 17:00 to 8:00. Still, a short call across the country is inexpensive; don't hesitate to call long distance.

Making International Calls: For a listing of **international access codes and country codes,** see the appendix.

When making an international call to Britain, first dial the international access code of the country you're in (011 from the United States or Canada, 00 if you're calling from Europe), then Britain's country code (44), then the area code (without its initial 0) and the local number. For example, London's area code is 020. To call one of our listed London B&Bs from the United States, dial 011 (U.S. international access code), 44 (Britain's country code), 20 (London's area code without its initial 0), then 7730-8191 (the B&B's number).

To call my office from Britain, I dial 00 (Britain's international access code), 1 (U.S. country code), 425 (Edmonds' area code), then 771-8303.

International Calling Cards: The easiest, cheapest way to make international calls from Britain (under 20 cents a minute to the United States) is with an international calling card. There are many different brands, so just ask for an "international calling card" (sold for £5, £10, and £20 at most newsstands, exchange bureaus, and minimarts; Unity has a reputation for having the cheapest per-minute rates). Because cards are occasionally duds, avoid the high denominations. (A BT Phone Card Plus also works for making international calls, but at a higher per-minute rate than these cheapie phone cards).

Since you don't insert international calling cards into the phone, you can use them from any phone, including the one in your hotel room. To use a card, scratch off the back to reveal your PIN (personal identification number). Then dial the toll-free access number listed on the card. At the prompt, enter your PIN, then just dial the number you want to call. (To call the U.S., dial 00+1+area code+local number. For calls within Britain, dial area code+local number; when using an international calling card, the area code must be dialed even if you're calling across the street.) These cards work only within the country of purchase (so one bought in Britain won't work in France, for example).

To make numerous calls with an international calling card without having to redial the long access number each time, press the keys (see instructions on card) that allow you to launch directly into your next call.

Calling Cards from American Companies: Calling cards offered by AT&T, MCI, and Sprint used to be a good value until direct-dialing rates dropped and international calling cards appeared. It's now much cheaper to dial direct using coins, BT Phone Card Plus, or any international calling card.

Cell Phones: You can buy inexpensive cell phones—about $70 on up—to make local and international calls. The cheapest phones work only in the country where they're sold; the pricier phones work throughout Europe (but it'll cost you about $40 per country to outfit the phone with the necessary chip and prepaid phone time). Because of their expense, cell phones are most economical for travelers staying in one country for two weeks or more. If you're interested, stop by one of the ubiquitous phone shops or at a cell-phone counter in a department store. Confirm with a clerk whether the phone works only in Britain or throughout Europe. Make sure the clerk shows you how to use the phone—practice making a call to the store or, for fun, to the clerk's personal cell phone. You'll need to pick out a policy; different policies offer, say, better rates for making calls at night or for calling cell phones rather than fixed phones. I get the basic fixed rate: a straight 30 cents per minute to the United States and 15 cents per minute to any fixed or cell phone in the home country at any hour. Receiving calls is generally free. When you run out of calling time, buy more time at a newsstand. Upon arrival in a different country, purchase a new chip (which comes with a new phone number). If you're on a tight budget, skip cell phones and buy phone cards instead.

Mail: Get stamps at the neighborhood post office, newsstands within fancy hotels, and some minimarts and card shops. To arrange for mail delivery, reserve a few hotels along your route in advance and give their addresses to friends, or use American

Express mail services (free to AmEx cardholders and a minimal fee for others). Allow 10 days for a letter to arrive. Phoning is so easy that we've dispensed with mail stops altogether.

E-mail: E-mail is getting more common among hoteliers. We've listed e-mail addresses where possible. Internet service providers can change with alarming frequency, so if your e-mail message to a hotel bounces back, search for the hotel's name in a search engine such as Google (www.google.com) to see if it has a new Web site. If that doesn't work, fax or call the hotel.

Cybercafés are easy to find in London (the huge easyEverything company has branches at popular spots such as Victoria Station; for more information, see "Helpful Hints" in the "Orientation" chapter). If the extension .com at the end of a Web address doesn't work, try .co.uk or org.uk.

If you're planning to log on from your laptop in your hotel room, you'll need an Internet service provider that has local phone numbers for each country you'll visit. While an American modem cable plugs into British and European phone jacks, you may have to tweak your settings to make your computer recognize a pulse instead of the U.S. dial tone. Bring a phone jack tester that reverses line polarity as needed.

Tipping

Tipping in Britain isn't as automatic and generous as it is in the United States, but for special service, tips are appreciated, if not expected. As in the United States, the proper amount depends on your resources, tipping philosophy, and the circumstance, but some general guidelines apply.

Restaurants: At pubs where you order at the counter, don't tip. At a pub or restaurant with wait staff, check the menu to see if the service is included; if not, tip around 10 percent (for details, see page 285).

Taxis: To tip the cabbie, round up. For a typical ride, round up to a maximum of 10 percent (to pay a £4.50 fare, give £5; or for a £28 fare, give £30). If the cabbie hauls your bags and zips you to the airport to help you catch your flight, you might want to toss in a little more. But if you feel like you're being driven in circles or otherwise ripped off, skip the tip.

Special Services: Tour guides at public sites might hold out their hands for tips after they give their spiel; if I've already paid for the tour, I don't tip extra, though some tourists do give a pound, particularly for a job well done. I don't tip at hotels, but if you do, give the porter about 50 pence for carrying bags and leave a pound in your room at the end of your stay for the maid if the room was kept clean. In general, if someone in the service industry does a super job for you, a tip of a pound or two is appropriate ... but not required.

When in doubt, ask. If you're not sure whether (or how much) to tip for a service, ask your hotelier or the TI; they'll fill you in on how it's done on their turf.

Stranger in a Strange Land

We travel all the way to Europe to enjoy differences—to become temporary locals. You'll experience frustrations. There are certain truths that we find God-given and self-evident, such as cold beer, ice in drinks, bottomless coffee cups, "the customer's always right," easy shower faucets, and driving on the right-hand side of the road. One of the benefits of travel is the eye-opening realization that there are logical, civil, and even better alternatives. A willingness to go local ensures that you'll enjoy a full dose of English hospitality.

Send Us a Postcard, Drop Us a Line

If you enjoy a successful trip with the help of this book and would like to share your discoveries, please fill out the survey at the end of this book and send it to me at Europe Through the Back Door, Box 2009, Edmonds, WA 98020. We personally read and value all feedback. Thanks in advance—it helps a lot.

For our latest travel information, tap into our Web site: www.ricksteves.com. To check on any updates for this book, visit www.ricksteves.com/update. Rick's e-mail address is rick@ricksteves.com. Anyone can request a free issue of our newsletter.

Judging from the happy postcards we receive from travelers, it's safe to assume you'll enjoy a great, affordable vacation— with the finesse of an experienced, independent traveler. From this point on, "we" (your co-authors) will shed our respective egos and become "I". Thanks, and happy travels!

BACK DOOR TRAVEL PHILOSOPHY
From *Rick Steves' Europe Through the Back Door*

Travel is intensified living—maximum thrills per minute and one of the last great sources of legal adventure. Travel is freedom. It's recess, and we need it.

Experiencing the real Europe requires catching it by surprise, going casual . . . "Through the Back Door."

Affording travel is a matter of priorities. (Make do with the old car.) You can travel—simply, safely, and comfortably—anywhere in Europe for $80 a day plus transportation costs. In many ways, spending more money only builds a thicker wall between you and what you came to see. Europe is a cultural carnival and, time after time, you'll find that its best acts are free and the best seats are the cheap ones.

A tight budget forces you to travel close to the ground, meeting and communicating with the people, not relying on service with a purchased smile. Never sacrifice sleep, nutrition, safety, or cleanliness in the name of budget. Simply enjoy the local-style alternatives to expensive hotels and restaurants.

Extroverts have more fun. If your trip is low on magic moments, kick yourself and make things happen. If you don't enjoy a place, maybe you don't know enough about it. Seek the truth. Recognize tourist traps. Give a culture the benefit of your open mind. See things as different but not better or worse. Any culture has much to share.

Of course, travel, like the world, is a series of hills and valleys. Be fanatically positive and militantly optimistic. If something's not to your liking, change your liking. Travel is addictive. It can make you a happier American, as well as a citizen of the world. Our Earth is home to six billion equally important people. It's humbling to travel and find that people don't envy Americans. They like us, but, with all due respect, they wouldn't trade passports.

Globetrotting destroys ethnocentricity. It helps you understand and appreciate different cultures. Travel changes people. It broadens perspectives and teaches new ways to measure quality of life. Many travelers toss aside their hometown blinders. Their prized souvenirs are the strands of different cultures they decide to knit into their own character. The world is a cultural yarn shop. And Back Door travelers are weaving the ultimate tapestry. Come on, join in!

ORIENTATION

London is more than 600 square miles of urban jungle. With nine million struggling people—many of whom speak English—it's a world in itself and a barrage on all the senses. On my first visit, I felt extremely small. To grasp London comfortably, see it as the old town in the city center without the modern, congested sprawl.

The River Thames runs roughly west to east through the city, with most of the visitor's sights on the north bank. Mentally—maybe even physically, using scissors—trim down your map to include only the area between the Tower of London (to the east), Hyde Park (west), Regent's Park (north), and the Thames (south). (This is roughly the area bordered by the Tube's Circle Line.) This three-mile stretch between the Tower and Hyde Park (about a 90-minute walk) holds 80 percent of the sights mentioned in this book.

London is a collection of neighborhoods that bleed together:

The City: Shakespeare's London was a walled town clustered around St. Paul's Cathedral. Today that's the modern financial district.

Westminster: This neighborhood includes Big Ben, Parliament, Westminster Abbey, and Buckingham Palace, the grand government buildings from which Britain is ruled.

The West End: Lying between Westminster and The City (that is, at the "west end" of the original walled town), this is the center of London cultural life. Trafalgar Square has major museums. Piccadilly Circus and Leicester Square host tourist traps, cinemas, and nighttime glitz. Soho and Covent Garden house the theater district, as well as restaurants, pubs, and boutiques.

Residential neighborhoods to the west: Though they lack major tourist sights, Mayfair, South Kensington, Notting Hill, Chelsea, and Belgravia are home to London's wealthy and trendy, as well as many shopping streets and nice restaurants.

With this focus and a good orientation, you'll find London manageable and even fun. You'll get a good taste of the city's top sights, history, and cultural entertainment, as well as its ever-changing human face.

Planning Your Time

London's a great one-week getaway. Its sights can keep even the most fidgety traveler well entertained for a week. After considering London's major tourist sights, I've covered just my favorites. You won't be able to see all of these, so don't try. You'll keep coming back to London. After dozens of visits myself, I still enjoy a healthy list of excuses to return.

Here's a suggested schedule:

Day 1: 9:00–Tower of London (Crown Jewels first, then Beefeater tour, then White Tower), 12:30–Munch a sandwich on the Thames while cruising from Tower to Westminster Bridge, 14:00–Tour Westminster Abbey, coffee in the cloisters, 15:30–Follow the self-guided Westminster Walk.

Day 2: 9:00–Take double-decker hop-on, hop-off London sightseeing bus tour (start at Victoria Street and hop off for the Changing of the Guard—11:30 at Buckingham Palace; guards change daily April–Aug and generally every even-numbered day Sept–March), 13:00–Covent Garden for lunch, shopping, and people-watching (consider following the self-guided West End Walk and popping into the Theatre Museum), 15:00–Tour British Museum. Have a pub dinner before a play, concert, or evening walking tour.

Day 3: Tour British Library, St. Paul's Cathedral (following The City Walk), and Museum of London. See Shakespeare play at Shakespeare's Globe (14:00 or 19:30). Take the recommended "Food is Fun" Dinner Crawl tonight (or any night; see Eating chapter).

Day 4: 10:00–National Gallery, fun and lunch on or near Trafalgar Square, National Portrait Gallery, 14:00–Follow the self-guided Bankside Walk. Cap the day with a ride on the London Eye Ferris Wheel (reserve in advance).

Day 5: Spend the morning at an antique market and visit a famous London department store. In the afternoon, depending upon your interests, choose from Tate Britain, Tate Modern, the Imperial War Museum, or Kew Gardens (cruise to Kew, return to London by Tube). Take in a play, go on a guided walk, or watch a concert tonight (for ideas, see Entertainment chapter).

Day 6: Cruise to Greenwich, tour the town's salty sights, then Tube back to London. With extra time in the afternoon, drop by the Victoria and Albert Museum.

Daily Reminder

Sunday: Some sights don't open until noon (Museum of London). The Tower of London is especially crowded today. Hyde Park Speakers' Corner rants from early afternoon until early evening. These are closed: Banqueting House, Sir John Soane's Museum, and legal sights (Houses of Parliament, Old Bailey, The City is dead). Evensong is at 15:00 at Westminster Abbey (plus organ recital at 17:45 for a fee) and 15:15 at St. Paul's (plus free organ recital at 17:00); both churches are open during the day for worship but closed to sightseers. Many stores and theaters are closed. Street markets flourish: Camden Lock, Spitalfields, Greenwich, and Petticoat Lane.

Monday: Virtually all sights are open except for Apsley House, the Theatre Museum, Sir John Soane's Museum, and a few others. The St. Martin-in-the-Fields church offers a free 13:05 concert. At Somerset House, the Courtauld Gallery is free until 14:00. Vinopolis is open until 21:00.

Tuesday: All sights are open; the British Library is open until 20:00. St. Martin-in-the-Fields has a free 13:05 concert.

Wednesday: All sights are open, plus evening hours at Westminster Abbey (until 19:45), the National Gallery (until 21:00), and Victoria and Albert Museum (until 22:00).

Thursday: All sights are open, British Museum until 20:30 (selected galleries), National Portrait Gallery until 21:00. St. Martin-in-the-Fields hosts a 19:30 evening concert (for a fee).

Friday: All sights are open, British Museum until 20:30 (selected galleries only), National Portrait Gallery until 21:00, Tate Modern until 22:00. Best street market: Spitalfields. St. Martin-in-the-Fields offers two concerts (13:05–free, 19:30–fee).

Saturday: Most sights are open except legal ones (Old Bailey; Houses of Parliament—open summer Sat for tours only; skip The City). Vinopolis is open until 20:00, Tate Modern until 22:00. Best street markets: Portobello, Camden Lock, Greenwich. Evensong is at 15:00 at Westminster Abbey, 17:00 at St. Paul's. St. Martin-in-the-Fields hosts a concert at 19:30 (fee).

Notes: Evensong occurs daily at St. Paul's (Mon–Sat at 17:00 and Sun at 15:15) and daily except Wednesday at Westminster Abbey (Mon–Tue and Thu–Fri at 17:00, Sat–Sun at 15:00). London by Night Sightseeing Tour buses depart Victoria Station every evening at 20:00, 21:00, and 22:00. The London Eye Ferris Wheel spins nightly until 22:00 in summer, until 20:00 in winter (closed Jan).

Day 7: For a one-week visit to London, I'd spend a day or two side-tripping. To keep an English focus, side-trip out to Windsor, Cambridge, or Bath for one day. For maximum travel thrills, consider a Paris getaway. With the zippy English Channel train, Paris is only three hours away and can even be worth a long day trip. To pull this off, see the Day Trip to Paris chapter.

Arrival in London

By Train: London has eight train stations, all connected by the Tube (subway) and all with exchange offices and luggage storage. From any station, ride the Tube or taxi to your hotel.

By Bus: The bus station is one block southwest of Victoria Station, which has a TI and Tube entrance.

By Plane: For more detailed information on getting from London's airports to downtown London, see the Transportation Connections chapter.

Tourist Information

The **Britain Visitors Centre** is the best tourist information service in town (Mon–Fri 9:00–18:30, Sat–Sun 10:00–16:00, phone not answered after 17:00 Mon–Fri and not at all Sat–Sun, booking service, just off Piccadilly Circus at 1 Lower Regent Street, tel. 020/8846-9000, www.visitbritain.com). It's great for London information; buy your city map here. Bensons Mapguide for £2.25 is the best (also sold at newsstands), although bargain-hunters may prefer the London Smart Saver Street Map, which gets you a 20 percent discount at many attractions, including Tower Bridge and the Cabinet Rooms.

If you're traveling beyond London, take advantage of the Centre's well-equipped London/England desk, Wales desk (tel. 020/7808-3838), Ireland desk (tel. 020/7808-3841), and Scotland desk. At the center's extensive bookshop, gather whatever guidebooks, hostel directories, maps, and information you'll need. For trips through Britain, consider the *Michelin Green Guide to Britain* (£9.25; Green Guide just for London also available), the Britain road atlas (£10), and Ordnance Survey maps for areas you'll be exploring by car. The Visitors Centre has a travel agency upstairs, plus computers displaying only its Web site: www.visitbritain.com.

Nearby you'll find the **Scottish Tourist Centre** (mid-June–mid-Sept Mon–Fri 9:00–18:00, Sat 10:00–17:00, off-season Mon–Fri 9:30–17:30, Sat 12:00–16:00, Cockspur Street, tel. 0131/472-2035, www.visitscotland.com) and the slick **French National Tourist Office** (Mon–Fri 10:00–18:00, Sat until 17:00, closed Sun, 178 Piccadilly Street, tel. 0906-824-4123).

Unfortunately, **London's Tourist Information Centres**

(TIs) are now owned by the big hotels' exchange bureaus and are simply businesses selling advertising space to companies with fliers to distribute. They are reasonably helpful but biased. Locations include Heathrow Airport's Tube station, which serves Terminals 1, 2, and 3 (daily 8:00–18:00, most convenient and least crowded); Victoria Station (daily 8:00–20:00, crowded and commercial); and Waterloo International Terminal Arrivals Hall (daily 8:30–22:30, serving trains from Paris; if you arrive by train when the TI is mobbed, skip it, buy city map at newsstand upstairs in station lobby, then return downstairs to catch the Tube or a taxi to your hotel).

At any of the TIs, bring your itinerary and a checklist of questions. Pick up these publications: *London Planner* (a great free monthly that lists all the sights, events, and hours), walking-tour schedule fliers, a theater guide, "Central London Bus Guide," and the Thames River Services brochure.

TIs sell BT phone cards, long-distance bus tickets and passes, British Heritage Passes, and tickets to plays (20 percent booking fee). They also book rooms (avoid their £5 booking fee by calling hotels direct).

The **London Pass** gives free entrance to most of the city's sights, but since many museums are free and a pass can add cluttery decisions to your trip (should I go here, there, or everywhere . . . ?), it's worthwhile only for fervent sightseers (£22/1 day, £39/2 days, £49/3 days, £69/6 days, includes 128-page guidebook, buy at any London Transport Info Centre including Heathrow, Victoria, and Paddington, www.londonpass.com). London does have many mildly interesting sights worth a quick look but not their steep £6 admission fee. With this pass, you can just go crazy.

TIs also sell **Fast Track tickets** to some of London's attractions (at no extra cost), allowing you to skip the queue at the sights. They're worthwhile for places notorious for long ticket lines, such as the Tower of London, London Eye Ferris Wheel, and Madame Tussaud's Wax Museum.

Helpful Hints
U.S. Embassy: 24 Grosvenor Square (for passport concerns, open Mon–Fri 8:30–11:30 plus Mon, Wed, Fri 14:00–16:00, Tube: Bond Street, tel. 020/7499-9000).

Theft Alert: The Artful Dodger is alive and well in London. Be on guard, particularly on public transportation and in places crowded with tourists. Tourists, considered naive and rich, are targeted.

Over 7,500 handbags are stolen annually at Covent Garden alone. Thieves paw you so you don't feel the pickpocketing.

Changing Money: ATMs are the way to go. For changing traveler's checks, standard transaction fees at banks are £2 to £4. American Express offices offer a fair rate and change any brand of traveler's checks for no fee. Handy AmEx offices are at Heathrow's Terminal 4 Tube station (daily 7:00–19:00) and near Piccadilly (June–Sept Mon–Fri 9:00–18:00, Sat 9:00–18:30, Sun 10:00–17:00; Oct–May Mon–Sat 9:00–17:30, Sun 10:00–17:00; 30 Haymarket, tel. 020/7484-9600; refund office 24-hr tel. 0800/521-313). Marks & Spencer department stores give good rates with no fees.

Avoid changing money at exchange bureaus. Their latest scam: They advertise very good rates with a same-as-the-banks fee of 2 percent. But the fine print explains that the fee of 2 percent is for buying pounds. The fee for *selling* pounds is 9.5 percent. Ouch!

What's Up: For the best listing of what's happening (plays, movies, restaurants, concerts, exhibitions, protests, walking tours, shopping, and children's activities) and a look at the trendy London scene, pick up a current copy of *Time Out* (£2, www.timeout.co.uk) or *What's On* at any newsstand. The TI's free, monthly *London Planner* lists sights, plays, and events at least as well. For a chatty, *People Magazine*–type Web site on London's entertainment, theater, restaurants, and news, visit www.thisislondon.com. For plays, go to www.officiallondontheatre.co.uk.

Sights: Free museums include the British Museum, British Library, National Gallery, National Portrait Gallery, Tate Britain (British art), Tate Modern (modern art), Imperial War Museum, Natural History Museum, Victoria and Albert Museum, and the Royal Air Force Museum Hendon. Special exhibitions cost extra.

Telephoning first to check hours and confirm plans, especially off-season, when hours can shrink, is always smart.

Internet Access: The astonishing easyEverything offers up to 500 computers per store, 24 hours daily. Depending on the time of day, a mere £2 ticket buys anywhere from 80 minutes to six hours of computer time. The ticket is valid for four weeks and multiple visits at any of their five branches: Victoria Station (across from front of station, near taxis and buses, long lines), Trafalgar Square (456 Strand), Tottenham Court Road (9–16 Tottenham Court Road), Oxford Street (358 Oxford Street, opposite Bond Street Tube station), and Kensington High Street (160–166 Kensington High Street). EasyEverything also sells 24-hour, seven-day, and 30-day passes (www.easyeverything.com).

Travel Bookstores: Stanfords Travel Bookstore is good and stocks current editions of my books at Covent Garden (Mon–Fri 9:00–19:30, Sat 10:00–19:00, Sun 12:00–18:00, 12 Long Acre, tel. 020/7836-1321) and 156 Regent Street (tel. 020/7434-4744). There are two impressive Waterstone's bookstores: the biggest in Europe on Piccadilly (Mon–Sat 10:00–23:00, Sun 12:00–18:00, 203 Piccadilly, tel. 020/7851-2400) and one on the corner of Trafalgar Square (Mon–Sat 9:30–21:00, Sun 12:00–18:00, next to Coffee Republic café, tel. 020/7839-4411).

Beatles: Fans of the still–Fabulous Four can take one of the Beatles walks (5/week, offered by Original London Walks, see "Tours of London," below), visit the Beatles Shop (231 Baker Street, next to Sherlock Holmes Museum, Tube: Baker Street), or go to Abbey Road and walk the famous crosswalk (at intersection with Grove End, Tube: St. John's Wood).

Left Luggage: As security concerns heighten, train stations have replaced their lockers with left-luggage counters. Each bag must go through a scanner (just like at the airport), so lines can be long. Expect up to a 20-minute wait to pick up your bags, too (each item–£5/24 hrs, daily 7:00–24:00). You can also check bags at the airports (£3.50/day). If leaving London and returning later, you may be able to leave a box or bag at your hotel for free— assuming you'll be staying there again.

Getting Around London

London's taxis, buses, and subway system make a private car unnecessary. To travel smart in a city this size, you must get comfortable with public transportation. For Tube and bus information 24 hours a day, call 020/7222-1234 (www.transportforlondon.gov.uk).

By Taxi: London is the best taxi town in Europe. Big, black, carefully regulated cabs are everywhere. I never met a crabby cabbie in London. They love to talk, and they know every nook and cranny in town. I ride in one each day just to get my London questions answered. Rides start at £1.50 and cost about £1.50 per Tube stop. Connecting downtown sights is quick and easy and will cost you about £4 (e.g., St. Paul's to the Tower of London). For a short ride, three people in a cab travel at Tube prices. Groups of four or five should taxi everywhere. If a cab's top light is on, just wave it down. (Drivers flash lights when they see you.) They have a tiny turning radius, so you can wave at cabs going in either direction. If waving doesn't work, ask someone where you can find a taxi stand. While telephoning a cab gets one in minutes, it's generally not necessary and adds to the cost. London is such a great wave-'em-down taxi town that most cabs don't even have a radio phone. Don't worry about meter cheating. British cab meters come with a sealed computer chip and clock that ensures you'll get the regular tariff #1 most of the time, tariff #2 during "unsociable hours" (18:00–6:00 and Sat–Sun), and tariff #3 only on holidays.

All extra charges are explained in writing on the cab wall. The only way a cabbie can cheat you is to take a needlessly long route. There are alternative cab companies driving normal-looking, non-metered cars that charge fixed rates based on the postal codes of your start and end points. These are generally honest and can actually be cheaper when snarled traffic drives up the cost of a metered cab. Tip a cabbie by rounding up (maximum 10 percent).

By Bus: London's extensive bus system is easy to follow. Just pick up a free "Central London Bus Guide" map from a TI or Tube station. Signs at stops list routes clearly. There are two kinds of buses—those without a conductor (pay the driver as you enter) and those with a conductor (just hop on, take a seat, relax, and sooner or later the conductor will come by and collect £1). Any ride in downtown London costs £1. (The best views are upstairs.) If you have a Travel Card (see below), get in the habit of hopping buses for quick little straight shots, even just to get to a Tube stop. During bump-and-grind rush hours (8:00–10:00 and 16:00–19:00), you'll go faster by Tube. Consider two special bus deals: all day for £2 and a ticket six-pack for £4.

By Tube: London's subway is one of this planet's great people-movers and the fastest—and cheapest—long-distance transport in town (runs Mon–Sat about 5:00–24:00, Sun about 7:00–23:00). Any ride in the Central Zone (on or within the Circle Line, including virtually all my recommended sights and hotels) costs £1.60. You can avoid ticket-window lines in Tube stations by buying tickets from coin-op machines; practice on the punchboard to see how the system works (hit Adult Single and your destination). Again, nearly every ride will be £1.60. (These tickets are valid only on the day of purchase.) Beware: Overshooting your zone nets you a £10 fine.

At the front of this book, you'll find a complete Tube map with color-coded lines and names (you can also pick up a free Tube map at any station window). Each line has a name (such as Circle, Northern, or Bakerloo) and two directions (indicated by end stop). In stations, you'll have a choice of two platforms per line. Navigate by signs leading to the platforms (usually labeled North, South, East, or West) that clearly list the stops served by each line, or ask a local or a blue-vested staff person for help. All city maps have north on top. If you know the general direction in which you're heading, Tube navigation suddenly becomes easier. Some tracks are shared by several lines, and electronic signboards announce which train is next and the minutes remaining until various arrivals. Each train has its final destination or line name above its windshield. Depending on the particular line, trains run roughly every 3 to 10 minutes. Bring something to do to make your wait productive. The system is fraught with construction delays and breakdowns (pay attention to signs and announcements explaining necessary detours, etc). The Circle Line is notorious for problems. And always . . . mind the gap.

You can't leave the system without feeding your ticket to the turnstile. Save time by choosing the best street exit (look at the maps on the walls or ask any station personnel). "Subway" means "pedestrian underpass" in "English."

London Tube and Bus Passes: Consider using these passes, valid on both the Tube and buses (all passes are available for more zones and are purchased as easily as a normal ticket at any station):

One-Day pass: If you figure you'll take three rides in a day, a day pass is a good deal. The One Day Travel Card, covering Zones 1 and 2, gives you unlimited travel for a day, starting after 9:30 on weekdays and anytime on weekends (£4.10). The all-zone version of this card costs £5 (and includes Heathrow Airport). The One Day LT Card, covering six zones (including Heathrow) with no time restriction, costs £7.90. Families save with the One Day Family Travel Card (price varies depending on number in family). For details, including a handy journey planner, see www.thetube.com.

Weekend pass: The Weekend Travel Card, covering Saturday, Sunday, and Zones 1 and 2 for £6.10, costs 25 percent less than two one-day cards.

Seven-Day pass: The 7-Day Travel Card costs £19.30, covers Zones 1 and 2, and requires a passport-type photo (cut one out of any snapshot and bring it from home). If you have no photo, the TI at Heathrow Airport sells a similar Visitors' Card for about the same price without requiring a photo.

Ten rides: If you want to travel a little each day or if you're part of a group, an £11.50 *carnet* is a great deal: You get 10 separate tickets for Tube travel in Zone 1 (£1.15 per ride rather than £1.60). Wait for the machine to lay all 10 tickets.

Group deals: Groups of 10 or more can travel all day on the Tube for £3 each (not on buses).

Tours of London

▲▲▲**Hop-on, Hop-off Double-Decker Bus Tours**—Two competitive companies (Original and Big Bus) offer essentially the same tours with buses that have live (English-only) guides, as well as some marked buses with a tape-recorded, dial-a-language narration. This two-hour, once-over-lightly bus tour drives by all the famous sights, providing a stressless way to get your bearings and at least see the biggies. You can sit back and enjoy the entire two-hour orientation tour (a good idea if you like the guide and the weather) or hop on and hop off at any of the nearly 30 stops and catch a later bus. Buses run about every 10–15 minutes in summer, every 20 minutes in winter. It's an inexpensive form of transport as well as an informative tour. Grab one of the maps from a TI and study it. Buses run daily (from about 9:00 until early evening in summer, until late afternoon in winter) and stop at Victoria Street (1 block north of Victoria Station), Marble Arch, Piccadilly Circus, Trafalgar Square, and elsewhere.

Each company offers a core two-hour overview tour, two other routes, and a narrated Thames boat tour covered by the same ticket (buy ticket from driver, CC accepted at major stops such as Victoria Station, ticket good for 24 hrs, bring a sweater and extra film). Note: If you start at Victoria Station at 9:00, you'll finish near Buckingham Palace in time to see the Changing of the Guard (at 11:30); ask your driver for the best place to hop off. Sunday morning—when the traffic is light and many museums are closed— is a fine time for a tour. The last full loop leaves Victoria at 18:00. Both companies have entertaining and boring guides. The narration is important. If you don't like your guide, jump off and find another. If you like your guide, settle in for the entire loop.

Original London Sightseeing Bus Tour: Live guided buses have a Union Jack flag and a yellow triangle on the front of the bus. If the front has many flags or a green or red triangle, it's a tape-recorded multilingual tour—avoid it, unless you have kids who'd enjoy the entertaining

recorded kids' tour (£15, £2.50 discount with this book, limit 2 discounts per book, they'll rip off the corner of this page—raise bloody hell if they don't honor this discount, ticket good for 24 hrs, CC, tel. 020/8877-1722, www.theoriginaltour.com). Your ticket includes a 50-minute-long round-trip boat tour from the London Eye (departs hourly, tape-recorded narration).

Big Bus Hop-on, Hop-off London Tours: These are also good. For £16, you get the same basic tour plus coupons for four different one-hour London walks and the scenic and usually entertainingly guided Thames boat ride (normally £5) between Westminster Pier and the Tower of London. The pass and extras are valid for 24 hours. Buses with live guides are marked in front with a picture of a blue bus; buses with tape-recorded spiels display a picture of a yellow bus and headphones. While the price is steeper, Big Bus guides seem more dynamic than the Original guides (daily 8:30–18:00, July–Aug until 19:00, winter until 16:30,

office a block from Victoria Station at 48 Buckingham Palace
Road, tel. 020/7233-9533, www.bigbus.co.uk).

At Night: The London by Night Sightseeing Tour runs
basically the same circuit as the other companies, but after hours.
While the narration is pretty lame (the driver does little more
than call out the names of famous places as you roll by), the views
at twilight are grand (£9.50, pay driver or buy tickets at Victoria
Station or Paddington Station TI, April–Oct only, 2-hr tour with
live guide, can hop on and off, departs at 19:00, 20:00, and 21:00
from Victoria Station, Taxi Road, at front of station near end of
Wilton Road, tel. 020/8646-1747, www.londongeneral.co.uk).

▲▲**Walking Tours**—Many times a day, top-notch local guides
lead (often big) groups through specific slices of London's past.
Schedule fliers litter the desks of TIs, hotels, and pubs. *Time Out*
lists many, but not all, scheduled walks. Simply show up at the
announced location, pay £5, and enjoy two chatty hours of
Dickens, the Plague, Shakespeare, Legal London, the Beatles,
Jack the Ripper, or whatever is on the agenda. Original London
Walks, the dominant company, lists its extensive daily schedule
in a beefy, plain black-and-white *The Original London Walks*
brochure. They also run **Explorer day trips,** a good option for
those with limited time and transportation (different trip daily:
Stonehenge/Salisbury, Oxford/Cotswolds, York, Bath, and so
on; walks offered year-round—even Christmas, get schedule at
hotel or TI, private tours for £90, tel. 020/7624-3978, recorded
information 020/7624-9255, www.walks.com).

Standard rates for London's registered **guides** are £85
for four hours, £136 for eight hours (tel. 020/7403-2962,
www.touristguides.org.uk). Robina Brown leads tours with
small groups in her Toyota Previa (£185/3 hrs, £270–400/
day, tel. 020/7228-2238, www.driverguidetours.com, e-mail:
robina@driverguidetours.com). Brit Lonsdale, an energetic
mother of twins, is another registered London guide (£89/half-
day, £142/full day, tel. 020/7386-9907).

▲▲**Cruises**—Boat tours with entertaining commentaries sail
regularly from **Westminster Pier** (at the base of Westminster
Bridge under Big Ben). For pleasure and efficiency, consider
combining a one-way cruise (to Kew, Greenwich, wherever)
with a Tube ride back.

From Westminster Pier, you can sail to the **Tower of
London** (£5.20 one-way, £6.30 round-trip, one-way included
with Big Bus London tour; covered by £8.50 "River Red Rover"
ticket that includes Greenwich—see next paragraph; 3/hr during
June–Aug daily 9:40–20:40, 2/hr and shorter hours rest of year,
30 min, City Cruises).

To get from Westminster Pier to **Greenwich,** you can choose between two companies: City Cruises (£6.50 one-way, £8 round-trip; or get their £8.50 all-day, hop-on, hop-off "River Red Rover" ticket to have option of getting off at London Eye and Tower of London; June–Aug daily 9:40–18:00, less off-season, every 40 min, 70 min to Greenwich, usually narrated only downstream—to Greenwich, tel. 020/7930-9033, www.citycruises.com) and Thames River Services (£6.30 one-way, £7.80 round-trip, April–Oct daily 10:00–16:00, July–Aug until 17:00, 2/hr, 50 min, has shorter hours and runs every 40 min rest of year, usually narrated only to Greenwich, tel. 020 /7930-4097, www.royalriverthames.com).

Boats sail daily from Westminster Pier to **Kew Gardens** (£9 one-way, £15 round-trip, 4/day, generally departing 10:00–14:00, 90 min, narrated for 30 min, Westminster Passenger Services Association, tel. 020/7930-2062, www.wpsa.co.uk). Some boats continue on to **Hampton Court Palace** for an additional £3.

Westminster isn't the only pier in town. Fifty-minute **round-trip cruises** of the Thames leave hourly from the Waterloo Pier at the base of the London Eye, (£7.50, included with Original London Bus tour—listed above, tape-recorded narration, Catamaran Circular Cruises, tel. 020/7839-3572).

From the Embankment Pier (at Charing Cross Station), you can catch a boat to the Tower of London and Greenwich; or if you're at the Tower of London pier, you can hop a boat heading west to Westminster Pier or going east to Greenwich.

Consider exploring London's canals by taking a cruise on historic **Regent's Canal** in north London. Jenny Wren offers round-trips from Walker's Quay in Camden Town to Little Venice, including 90-minute canal boat cruises (£6, March–Oct daily 12:30, 14:30, Sat–Sun also 10:30, 16:30) and three-hour *My Fair Lady* cruises featuring gourmet spreads (£19 for Sunday lunch at 13:00 year-round, £33 for 3-course dinner at 20:00— book in advance, CC, Walker's Quay, 250 Camden High Street, Tube: Camden Town, tel. 020/7485-4433 or 020/7485-6210, www.walkersquay.com). While in Camden Town, stop by the popular Camden Lock Market to browse through trendy arts and crafts (daily 10:00–18:00, busiest on weekends, a block from Walker's Quay, tel. 020/7284-2084, www.camdenlock.net).
Frog Tours—A bright-yellow amphibious vehicle takes you street-side past some famous sights (Big Ben, Buckingham Palace, Piccadilly Circus), then splashes into the Thames for a 30-minute cruise (£15, daily 10:00–18:00, 70 min, live commentary, these book up in advance, departs from Belvedere Road behind County Hall near London Eye Ferris Wheel, Tube: Waterloo or Westminster, tel. 020/7928-3132, www.frogtours.com, e-mail: enquiries@frogtours.com).

SIGHTS

These sights are arranged by neighborhood for handy sight-seeing. When you see a ✪ in a listing, it means the sight is covered in much more depth in my self-guided walk or one of the museum tours.

From Westminster Abbey to Trafalgar Square

✪ These sights are linked by the Westminster Walk chapter on page 53.

▲▲▲**Westminster Abbey**—The greatest church in the English-speaking world, Westminster Abbey is the place where England's kings and queens have been crowned and buried since 1066 (£6, Mon–Fri 9:00–16:45, Wed also 18:00–19:45, Sat 9:30–14:45, last admission 60 min before closing, closed Sun to sightseers but open for services, evensong at 17:00 on Mon, Tue, Thu, and Fri, and at 15:00 on Sat and Sun, organ recital for a fee on Sun at 17:45, photography prohibited at all times, coffee in cloister, Tube: Westminster or St. James' Park, tel. 020/7222-7110).
✪ See Westminster Abbey Tour, page 186.

▲▲**Houses of Parliament (Palace of Westminster)**—This neo-Gothic icon of London, the royal residence from 1042 to 1547, is now the meeting place of the legislative branch of government. Tourists are welcome to view debates in either the bickering House of Commons or the genteel House of Lords (when in session—indicated by a flag flying atop the Victoria Tower). While the actual debates are generally extremely dull, it is a thrill to be inside and see the British government inaction (House of Commons: Mon–Wed 14:30–22:30, Thu 11:30–19:30, Fri 9:30–15:00, generally less action and no lines after 18:00, use St. Stephen's entrance, Tube: Westminster, tel. 020/7219-4272 for schedule, www.parliament.uk). The House of

Central London

Lords has more pageantry, shorter lines, and less interesting
debates (Mon–Wed 15:00 until they finish, Thu from 15:00 on,
sometimes Fri from 11:00 on, tel. 020/7219-3107 for schedule).
If there's only one line outside, it's for the House of Commons.
Go to the gate and tell the guard you want the Lords. You may
pop right in—that is, after you've cleared the security gauntlet.
Once you've seen the Lords (hide your HOL flier), you can often
slip directly over to the House of Commons and join the gang
waiting in the lobby. Inside the lobby, you'll find an announcement board with the day's line-up for both houses.

Just past security to the left, study the big dark **Westminster
Hall,** which survived the 1834 fire. The hall was built in the 11th
century, and its famous self-supporting hammer-beam roof was
added in 1397. The Houses of Parliament are located in what was
once the Palace of Westminster, long the palace of England's
medieval kings, until it was largely destroyed by fire in 1834. The
palace was rebuilt in Victorian Gothic style (a move away from
neo-classicism back to England's Christian and medieval heritage,
true to the Romantic Age). It was completed in 1860.

Houses of Parliament tours are offered in August and

September (£7; 75 min, Mon, Tue, Fri, and Sat 9:15–16:30; Wed and Thu 13:15–16:30; to avoid waits, book in advance through First Call, tel. 0870/906-3773, www.firstcalltickets.com, no booking fee). Meet your Blue Badge guide (at the Sovereign's Entrance—far south end) for a behind-the-scenes peek at the royal chambers and both Houses.

The **Jewel Tower** is the only other part of the old Palace of Westminster to survive (besides Westminster Hall). It contains a fine little exhibit on Parliament (first floor—history, second floor—Parliament today) with a 25-minute video and lonely, picnic-friendly benches (£1.60, daily April–Sept 10:00–18:00, Oct 10:00–17:00, Nov–March 10:00–16:00, closed Dec 24–26 and Jan 1, across street from St. Stephen's Gate, tel. 020/7222-2219).

Big Ben, the clock tower (315 feet high), is named for its 13-ton bell, Ben. The light above the clock is lit when the House of Commons is sitting. The face of the clock is huge—you can actually see the minute hand moving. For a hip view of it, walk halfway over Westminster Bridge.

▲▲**Cabinet War Rooms**—This is a fascinating walk through the underground headquarters of the British government's fight against the Nazis in the darkest days of the Battle for Britain. The 21-room nerve center of the British war effort was used from 1939 to 1945. Churchill's room, the map room, and other rooms are just as they were in 1945. For all the blood, sweat, toil, and tears details, pick up an audioguide at the entry and follow the included and excellent 45-minute tour; be patient— it's worth it (£5.80, daily April–Oct 9:30–18:00, Nov–March 10:00–18:00, last entry 45 min before closing, on King Charles Street 200 yards off Whitehall, follow the signs, Tube: Westminster, tel. 020/7930-6961, www.iwm.org.uk). For a nearby pub lunch, try the Westminster Arms (food served downstairs, on Storey's Gate, a couple of blocks south of War Rooms).

Horse Guards—The Horse Guards change daily at 11:00 (10:00 on Sun), and there's a colorful dismounting ceremony daily at 16:00. The rest of the day, they just stand there— terrible for camcorders (on Whitehall, between Trafalgar Square and #10 Downing Street, Tube: Westminster). While Buckingham Palace pageantry is canceled when it rains, the horse guards change regardless of the weather.

▲**Banqueting House**—England's first Renaissance building was designed by Inigo Jones around 1620. It's one of the few London landmarks spared by the 1666 fire and the only surviving part of the original Palace of Whitehall. Don't miss its Rubens ceiling, which, at Charles I's request, drove home the doctrine of the legitimacy of the divine right of kings. In 1649—divine right ignored—Charles I was beheaded on the balcony of this building by a Cromwellian parliament. Admission includes a restful 20-minute audiovisual history, which shows the place in banqueting action; a 30-minute tape-recorded tour—interesting only to history buffs; and a look at the exquisite banqueting hall (£4, Mon–Sat 10:00–17:00, closed Sun, last entry at 16:30, subject to closure for government functions, aristocratic WC, immediately across Whitehall from the Horse Guards, Tube: Westminster, tel. 020/7930-4179). Just up the street is Trafalgar Square.

Sights—Trafalgar Square

▲▲**Trafalgar Square**—London's central square is a thrilling place to simply hang out. Lord Nelson stands atop his 185-foot-tall fluted granite column, gazing out to Trafalgar, where he lost his life but defeated the French fleet. Part of this 1842 memorial is made from his victims' melted-down cannons. He's surrounded by giant lions, hordes of people, and—until recently—even more pigeons. London's new mayor, nicknamed "Red Ken" for his passion for an activist government, decided that London's "flying rats" were a public nuisance and evicted the venerable seed salesmen. This high-profile square is the climax of most marches and demonstrations (Tube: Charing Cross).

▲▲▲**National Gallery**—Displaying Britain's top collection of European paintings from 1250 to 1900—including works by Leonardo, Botticelli, Veláz-quez, Rembrandt, Turner, van Gogh, and the Impressionists—this is one of Europe's great galleries (free, daily 10:00–18:00, Wed until 21:00, free 1-hour overview tours daily at 11:30 and 14:30 plus Wed at 18:30, closed Dec 24–26, Jan 1, and Good Friday, photography prohibited, on Trafalgar Square, Tube: Charing Cross or Leicester Square, tel. 020/7747-2885, www.nationalgallery.org). ✪ See National Gallery Tour, page 116.

▲▲**National Portrait Gallery**—Put off by halls of 19th-century characters who meant nothing to me, I used to call this "as interesting as someone else's yearbook." But a selective walk through this 500-year-long *Who's Who* of British history is quick and free and puts faces on the story of England (free, daily 10:00–18:00, Thu–Fri until 21:00, entry 100 yards off Trafalgar Square, around corner from National Gallery, opposite Church of St. Martin-in-the-Fields, tel. 020/7306-0055). ✪ See National Portrait Gallery Tour, page 135.

▲**St. Martin-in-the-Fields**—This church, built in the 1720s with a Gothic spire atop a Greek-type temple, is an oasis of peace on the wild and noisy Trafalgar Square (free, donations welcome, open daily, www.stmartin-in-the-fields.org). St. Martin cared for the poor. "In the fields" was where the first church stood on this spot (in the 13th century), between Westminster and The City. Stepping inside, you still feel a compassion for the needs of the people in this community. A free flier provides a brief yet worth-while self-guided tour. The church is famous for its concerts. Consider a free lunchtime concert (Mon, Tue, and Fri at 13:05) or an evening concert (£6–16, Thu–Sat at 19:30, CC, box office tel. 020/7839-8362, church tel. 020/7766-1100). Downstairs, you'll find a ticket office for concerts, a gift shop, a brass-rubbing center, and a fine support-the-church cafeteria (see Eating chapter).

More Top Squares: Piccadilly, Soho, and Covent Garden

For a "Food Is Fun" dinner crawl from Covent Garden to Soho, see page 286.

▲▲**Piccadilly Circus**—London's most touristy square got its name from the fancy ruffled shirts—*picadils*—made in the neighbor-hood long ago. Today the square is surrounded by fascinating streets swimming with youth on the rampage. For overstimulation, drop by the extremely trashy **Pepsi Trocadero Center**'s "theme park of the future" for its Segaworld virtual-reality games, nine-screen cinema, and thundering IMAX theater (admission to Troca-dero is free; individual attractions cost £2–8; before paying full price for IMAX, look for a discount ticket at brochure racks at TI or hotels; between Coventry and Shaftesbury, just off Piccadilly). Chinatown, to the east, has swollen since Hong Kong lost its inde-pendence. Nearby Shaftesbury Avenue and Leicester Square teem with fun-seekers, theaters, Chinese restaurants, and street singers.

Soho—North of Piccadilly, seedy Soho is becoming trendy and is well worth a gawk. Soho is London's red-light district, where "friendly models" wait in tiny rooms up dreary stairways and voluptuous con artists sell strip shows. While venturing up a stairway to check out a model is interesting, anyone who goes into any one of the shows will be ripped off. Every time. Even a £5 show in a "licensed bar" comes with a £100 cover or minimum (as it's printed on the drink menu) and a "security man." You may accidentally buy a £200 bottle of bubbly. And suddenly, the door has no handle. By the way, telephone sex is hard to avoid these days in London. Phone booths are littered with racy fliers of busty ladies "new in town." Some travelers gather six or eight phone booths' worth of fliers and take them home for kinky wallpaper.

London's Top Squares

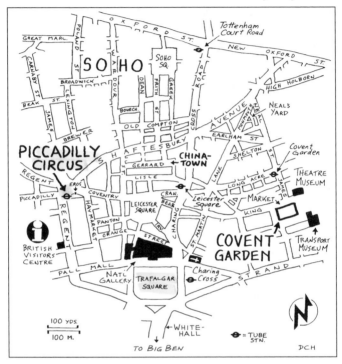

▲▲**Covent Garden**—This boutique-ish shopping district is a people-watcher's delight, with cigarette eaters, Punch-and-Judy acts, food that's good for you (but not your wallet), trendy crafts, sweet whiffs of marijuana, two-tone hair (neither natural), and faces that could set off a metal detector (Tube: Covent Garden). For better Covent Garden lunch deals, walk a block or two away from the eye of this touristic hurricane (check out the places north of the Tube station along Endell and Neal Streets).

Museums near Covent Garden

▲▲**Somerset House**—This grand 18th-century civic palace offers a marvelous public space, three fine art collections, and a riverside terrace (between the Strand and the Thames). The palace once housed the national registry that records Britain's births, marriages, and deaths ("where they hatched 'em, latched 'em, and dispatched 'em"). Step into the courtyard to enjoy the fountain. Go ahead . . . walk through it. The 55 jets get playful twice an hour.

Surrounding you are three small and sumptuous sights: the Courtauld Gallery (paintings), the Gilbert Collection (fine arts), and the Hermitage Rooms (the finest art of czarist Russia). All three are open the same hours (daily 10:00–18:00, buy a ticket at one gallery and get a £1 discount off admission to either or both of the other two on the same day, easy bus #6, #9, #11, #13, #15, or #23 from Trafalgar Square, Tube: Temple or Covent Garden, tel. 020/7848-2526 or 020/7845-4600, www.somerset-house.org.uk). The Web site lists a busy schedule of tours, kids' events, and concerts. The riverside terrace is picnic-friendly (deli inside lobby).

The **Courtauld Gallery** is less impressive than the National Gallery, but its wonderful collection of paintings is still a joy. The gallery is part of the Courtauld Institute of Art, and the thoughtful description of each piece of art reminds visitors that the gallery is still used for teaching. You'll see medieval European paintings and works by Rubens, the Impressionists (Manet, Monet, Degas, Seurat), Post-Impressionists (such as Cézanne), and more (£5, free Mon until 14:00, last admission 17:15, downstairs cafeteria, cloak room, lockers, and WC). ✪ See Courtauld Gallery Tour, page 202.

The **Hermitage Rooms** offer a taste of Romanov imperial splendor. As Russia struggles and tourists are staying away, someone had the bright idea of sending the best of its art to London to raise some hard cash. These five rooms host a different collection every six months, with a standard intro to the czar's winter palace in St. Petersburg (£6, includes unmissable live video of the square, last admission 17:00, tel. 020/7420-9410). The excellent audioguide offered for some collections costs £3 . . . consider it charity for Russia.

The **Gilbert Collection** displays 800 pieces of the finest in European decorative arts, from diamond-studded gold snuffboxes to intricate Italian mosaics. Maybe you've seen Raphael paintings and Botticelli frescoes . . . but this lush collection is refreshingly different (£5, includes free audioguide with a highlights tour and a kid-friendly tour, free after 16:30, last admission 17:30).

▲**London Transport Museum**—This wonderful museum is a delight for kids. Whether you're cursing or marveling at the buses and Tube, the growth of Europe's biggest city has been made possible by its public transit system. Watch the growth of the Tube, then sit in the simulator to "drive" a train (£6, kids under 16 free, Sat–Thu 10:00–18:00, Fri 11:00–18:00, 30 yards southeast of Covent Garden's marketplace, tel. 020/7379-6344).

Theatre Museum—This earnest museum, traces British theater from Shakespeare to today (free, Tue–Sun 10:00–18:00, closed Mon, free guided tours at 11:00, 12:00, and 16:00, a block east of Covent Garden's marketplace down Russell Street, tel. 020/7943-4700, www.theatremuseum.org). ✪ See Theatre Museum Tour, page 205.

Sights—North London

▲▲▲**British Museum, Great Court, and Reading Room**—
Simply put, this is the greatest chronicle of civilization . . . anywhere. A visit here is like taking a long hike through Encyclopedia Britannica National Park (free, £2 donation requested, daily 10:00–17:30, Thu–Fri until 20:30—but only a few galleries open after 17:30, tours offered nearly hourly, least crowded weekday late afternoons, Great Russell Street, Tube: Tottenham Court Road, tel. 020/7323-8000 or recorded information 020/7388-2227, www.thebritishmuseum.ac.uk). ✪ See British Museum Tour, page 94.

▲▲▲**British Library**—The British Empire built its greatest monuments out of paper. And it's with literature that England made her lasting contribution to civilization and the arts (free, Mon–Fri 9:30–18:00, Tue until 20:00, Sat 9:30–17:00, Sun 11:00–17:00; 60-min tours for £5 usually offered Mon, Wed, and Fri–Sun at 15:00, also Tue 18:30, Sat 10:30, and Sun 11:30; call 020/7412-7332 to confirm schedule and reserve; Tube: King's Cross, turn right out of station and walk a block to 96 Euston Road, library tel. 020/7412-7000, www.bl.uk). ✪ See British Library Tour, page 176.

▲**Madame Tussaud's Waxworks**—This is expensive but dang good. The original Madame Tussaud did wax casts of heads lopped off during the French Revolution (such as Marie Antoinette's). She took her show on the road and ended up in London. And now it's much easier to be featured. The gallery is one big *Who's Who* photo-op—a huge hit with the kind of travelers who skip the British Museum. Don't miss the "make a model" exhibit (showing Jerry Hall getting waxed) or the gallery of has-been heads that no longer merit a body (such as Sammy Davis Jr. and Nikita Khruschev). After looking a hundred famous people in their glassy eyes and surviving a silly hall of horror, you'll board a Disney-type ride and cruise through a kid-pleasing "Spirit of London" time trip (£14.95, children-£10.50, under 5 free, tickets include entrance to the London Planetarium, Jan–Sept daily 9:00–17:30, Oct–Dec Mon–Fri 10:00–17:30, Sat–Sun 9:30–17:30, last entry 30 min before closing, Marylebone Road, Tube: Baker Street). The wax works are popular. Avoid a wait by either booking ahead to get a ticket with an entry time (tel. 0870-400-3000, online at www.madame-tussauds.com for a £2 fee, or at any TI in London at no extra cost) or arriving late in the day—90 minutes is plenty of time for the exhibit.

Sir John Soane's Museum—Architects and fans of eclectic knickknacks love this quirky place (free, Tue–Sat 10:00–17:00, first Tue of the month also 18:00–21:00, closed Sun–Mon, £3 guided tours Sat at 14:30, 5 blocks east of British Museum, Tube: Holborn, 13 Lincoln's Inn Fields, tel. 020/7405-2107).

Buckingham Palace

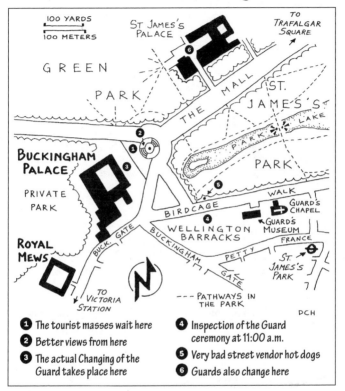

100 YARDS
100 METERS

ST JAMES'S PALACE

TO TRAFALGAR SQUARE

G R E E N

P A R K

THE MALL

ST. JAMES'S

PARK

LAKE

BUCKINGHAM PALACE

PRIVATE PARK

WALK

BIRDCAGE

WELLINGTON BARRACKS

GUARD'S CHAPEL

GUARD'S MUSEUM

FRANCE

ROYAL MEWS

BUCK. GATE

BUCKINGHAM GATE

PETTY

ST. JAMES'S PARK

N

TO VICTORIA STATION

--- PATHWAYS IN THE PARK

DCH

❶ The tourist masses wait here

❷ Better views from here

❸ The actual Changing of the Guard takes place here

❹ Inspection of the Guard ceremony at 11:00 a.m.

❺ Very bad street vendor hot dogs

❻ Guards also change here

Sights—Buckingham Palace

▲**Buckingham Palace**—This lavish home has been Britain's royal residence since 1837. When the queen's at home, the royal standard flies; otherwise the Union Jack flaps in the wind (£11.50 for state apartments and throne room, open early Aug–Sept only, daily 9:00–17:00, only 8,000 visitors a day—to get an entry time, come early or for £1 extra book ahead by phone or online, Tube: Victoria, tel. 020/7321-2233, www.the-royal-collection.com, e-mail: buckinghampalace@royalcollection.org.uk).

Royal Mews—Actually the queen's working stables, the "mews" are open to visitors to wander, talk to the horse-keeper, and see the well-groomed horses. Marvel at the gilded coaches paraded during royal festivals, see fancy horse gear—all well-described— and learn how skeptical the attendants were when the royals first parked a car in the stables, (£5, April–Oct 11:00–16:00, closed

Nov–March, Buckingham Palace Road, book ahead by phone or
online-£1 extra, tel.020/7321-2233, www.the-royal-collection.com,
e-mail: buckinghampalace@royalcollection.org.uk).

▲▲**Changing of the Guard at Buckingham Palace**—The
guards change with much fanfare at 11:30 daily April through
August and generally every even-numbered day September
through March (no band when wet; worth a 50p phone call
any day to confirm that they'll change, tel. 020/7321-2233).
Join the mob behind the palace (the front faces a huge and
extremely private park). You'll need to be early or tall to
see much of the actual Changing of the Guard, but for the
pageantry in the street you can pop by at 11:30. Stake out the
high ground on the circular Victoria Monument for the best
overall view. The marching troops and bands are colorful
and even stirring, but the actual Changing of the Guard is a
nonevent. It is interesting, however, to see nearly every tourist
in London gathered in one place at the same time. Hop into
a big black taxi and say, "Buck House, please." The show lasts
about 30 minutes: Three troops parade by, the guard changes
with much shouting, the band plays a happy little concert, and
then they march out. On a balmy day, it's a fun happening.

For all the pomp with none of the crowds, see the colorful
Inspection of the Guard ceremony at 11:00 in front of the
Wellington Barracks, 500 yards east of the palace on Birdcage
Walk. Afterward, stroll through nearby St. James' Park (Tube:
Victoria, St. James' Park, or Green Park).

Sights—West London

▲**Hyde Park and Speakers' Corner**—London's "Central Park,"
originally Henry VIII's hunting grounds, has more than 600 acres
of lush greenery, a huge man-made lake, the royal Kensington
Palace (not worth touring), and the ornate neo-Gothic Albert
Memorial across from the Royal Albert Hall. Early afternoons
on Sunday (until early evening), Speakers' Corner offers soapbox
oratory at its best (Tube: Marble Arch). "The grass roots of
democracy" is actually a holdover from when the gallows stood
here, and the criminal was allowed to say just about anything he
wanted to before he swung. I dare you to raise your voice and
gather a crowd—it's easy to do.

▲**Apsley House (Wellington Museum)**—Having beaten
Napoleon at Waterloo, the Duke of Wellington was once the
most famous man in Europe. He was given London's ultimate
address, #1 London. His newly refurbished mansion offers one
of London's best palace experiences. An 11-foot-tall marble
statue (by Canova) of Napoleon, clad only in a fig leaf, greets you.

West London

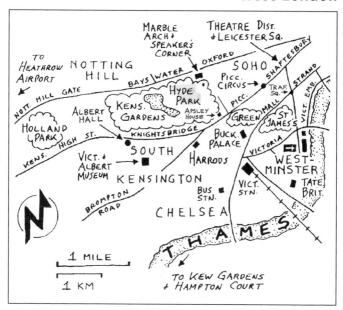

Downstairs is a small gallery of Wellington memorabilia (including a pair of Wellington boots). The lavish upstairs shows off the duke's fine collection of paintings, including works by Velázquez and Steen (£4.50, Tue–Sun 11:00–17:00, closed Mon, well-described by included audioguide, 20 yards from Hyde Park Corner Tube station, tel. 020/7499-5676, www.apsleyhouse.org.uk). Hyde Park's pleasant and picnic-wonderful rose garden is nearby.

▲▲**Victoria and Albert Museum**—The world's top collection of decorative arts (vases, stained glass, fine furniture, clothing, jewelry, carpets, and more) is a surprisingly interesting assortment of crafts from the West as well as Asian and Islamic cultures.

The V&A, which grew out of the Great Exhibition of 1851—that ultimate festival celebrating the Industrial Revolution and the greatness of Britain—was originally for manufactured art, but fine art sculptures (and copies) were soon added. After much support from Queen Victoria and Prince Albert, it was renamed after the royal couple, and its present building was opened in 1909. The idealistic Victorian notion that anyone can be continually improved by education and example remains the driving force behind this museum.

Cost, Hours, and Location: Free, possible fee for special exhibits, daily 10:00–17:45, open every Wed and last Fri of month until 22:00 except mid-Dec–mid-Jan (Tube: South Kensington, a long tunnel leads directly from the Tube station to the museum, tel. 020/7942-2000, www.vam.ac.uk).

Museum Overview and Tours: The museum is large and gangly, with 150 rooms and over 12 miles of corridors. While just wandering works well here, consider catching one of the free 60-minute orientation tours (daily, on the half-hour from 10:30–15:30, also daily at 13:00, Wed at 16:30, and a half-hour version at 19:30) or buying the fine £5 *Hundred Highlights* guide-book, or the handy £1 *What to See at the V&A* brochure (out-lines 5 self-guided, speedy tours).

To tour this museum on your own, grab a museum map and start with these ground-floor highlights:

Near the entrance: The **Medieval Treasury** (room 43) has stained glass, bishops' robes, old columns, and good descrip-tions. Statues by **Antonio Canova** (room 50A)—white, polished, and pretty Greek graces, minotaurs, and nymphs—are rare origi-nals by the neoclassical master.

Southeast corner (to the right of entrance, at the end of the hall): Plaster casts of **Trajan's Column** (room 46A) are a copy of Rome's 140-foot spiral relief telling the story of the conquest of Romania. (The V&A's casts are copies made for the benefit of 19th-century art students who couldn't afford a railpass.) Plaster casts of **Renaissance sculptures** (room 46B) let you compare Michelangelo's monumental *David* with Dona-tello's girlish *David;* see also Ghiberti's bronze Baptistery doors that inspired the Florentine Renaissance. The hall of **Great Fakes and Forgeries** (room 46) chronicles concocted art and historical objects passed off as originals.

Southwest corner (left of entrance, end of hall): **Raphael's "cartoons"** (room 48A) are seven huge watercolor designs by the Renaissance master for tapestries meant for the Sistine Chapel. The cartoons were sent to Brussels, cut into strips (see the lines), and placed on the looms. Notice that the scenes, the Acts of Peter and Paul, are the reverse of the final product (lots of left-handed saints). The **Dress Gallery** (in room 40) has 400 years of English fashion corseted into 40 display cases. The **Musical Instruments** section displays lutes, harpsichords, early flutes, big violins, and strange, curly horns—some recognizable, some obsolete (room 40A, up the staircase in the center of the Dress Gallery).

The rest of the ground floor: Room 41 has the finest col-lection of **Indian** decorative art outside India. There's medieval **stained glass** in room 28 (and much more upstairs).

To make a thorough, **chronological trip** through European

arts from medieval to modern, start at the entrance: Medieval Treasury (room 43), exiting to Europe 1100–1450 (room 23), then turn left and loop counterclockwise (through rooms 22, 21, then downstairs to rooms 2–7), ending up back at the entrance.

Upstairs you can walk through the **British Galleries** for centuries of British furniture, clothing, glass, jewelry, and sculpture.

▲**Natural History Museum**—Across the street from the Victoria and Albert Museum, this mammoth museum is housed in a giant and wonderful Victorian, neo-Romanesque building. Built in the 1870s specifically to house the huge collection (50 million specimens), it presents itself in two halves: the Life Galleries (creepy-crawlies, human biology, the origin of species, "our place in evolution," and awesome dinosaurs) and the Earth Galleries (meteors, volcanoes, earthquakes, and so on). Exhibits are wonderfully explained, with lots of creative interactive displays. Pop in, if only for the wild collection of dinosaurs and the roaring *T. rex*. Free 45-minute tours occur daily about every hour from 11:00 to 16:00 (free, possible fee for special exhibits, Mon–Sat 10:00–17:50, Sun 11:00–17:50, last entrance 15:30, a long tunnel leads directly from South Kensington Tube station to museum, tel. 020/7942-5000, exhibit info and reservations tel. 020/7942-5011, www.nhm.ac.uk).

Sights—East London: The City

▲▲**The City of London**—When Londoners say "The City," they mean the one-square-mile business, banking, and journalism center that 2,000 years ago was Roman Londinium. The outline of the Roman city walls can still be seen in the arc of roads from Blackfriars Bridge to Tower Bridge. Within The City are 24 churches designed by Christopher Wren, mostly just ornamentation around St. Paul's Cathedral. Today, while home to only 5,000 residents, The City thrives with over 500,000 office workers coming and going daily. It's a fascinating district to wander on weekdays, but since almost nobody actually lives there, it's dull in the evenings and on Saturday and Sunday. ❂ See The City Walk chapter, page 78.

▲**Old Bailey**—To view the British legal system in action—lawyers in little blond wigs speaking legalese with a British accent—spend a few minutes in the visitors' gallery at the Old Bailey (free, no kids under 14, Mon–Fri 10:00–13:00 and 14:00–17:00 most weeks, reduced hours in Aug; no bags, cell phones, or cameras, but small purses OK; you can check your bag at SPAR grocery across the street for £1—or try travel agency or bagel shop; 1; Tube: St. Paul's, 2 blocks northwest of St. Paul's on Old Bailey Street, follow signs to public entrance, tel. 020/7248-3277).

The City

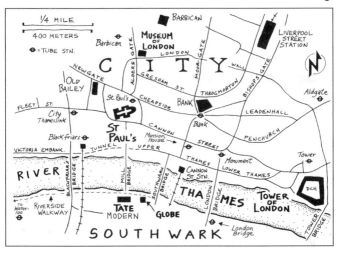

▲▲▲**St. Paul's Cathedral**—Wren's most famous church is the great St. Paul's, its elaborate interior capped by a 365-foot dome (£6, Mon–Sat 8:30–16:30, last entry 16:00, closed Sun except for worship, no photography allowed, tours available, cheery café in crypt, Tube: St. Paul's, tel. 020/7236-4128). The **evensong** services are free, but nonpaying visitors are not allowed to linger afterward (Mon–Sat at 17:00, Sun at 15:15, 40 min). On Sunday, there's an organ recital at 17:00. ✪ See St. Paul's Tour, page 194.

▲**Museum of London**—London, a 2,000-year-old city, is so littered with Roman ruins that when a London builder finds Roman antiquities, he doesn't stop work. He simply documents the finds, moves the artifacts to a museum, and builds on. If you're asking, "Why did the Romans build their cities underground?" a trip to the creative and entertaining London Museum is a must. Stroll through London history from pre-Roman times through the Blitz up to today. This regular stop for the local school kids gives the best overview of London history in town (free, Mon–Sat 10:00–18:00, Sun 12:00–18:00, Tube: Barbican or St. Paul's, tel. 020/7600-3699).

Geffrye Decorative Arts Museum—Walk through English front rooms from 1600 to 1990 (free, Tue–Sat 10:00–17:00, Sun 12:00–17:00, closed Mon, Tube: Liverpool Street, then bus #149 or #242 north, tel. 020/7739-9893).

▲▲▲**Tower of London**—The Tower has served as a castle in wartime, a king's residence in peace time, and, most notoriously, as the prison and execution site of rebels (£11.50, 1-day

combo-ticket with Hampton Court Palace–£19, March–Oct
Mon–Sat 9:00–18:00, Sun 10:00–18:00; Nov–Feb Tue–Sat
9:00–17:00, Sun–Mon 10:00–17:00; last entry 60 min before
closing, the long but fast-moving ticket line is worst on Sun, no
photography allowed of jewels or in chapels, Tube: Tower Hill,
tel. 020/7709-0765, recorded info: 020/7680-9004, booking:
0870-756-7070). You can avoid the long lines by picking up your
ticket at any London TI or the Tower Hill Tube station ticket
office. ★ See Tower of London Tour, page 210.

Ceremony of the Keys—Every night at 21:30, with
pageantry-filled ceremony, the Tower of London is locked
up (as it has been for the last 700 years). To attend this free
30-minute event, you need to request an invitation at least two
months before your visit. Write to Ceremony of the Keys,
H.M. Tower of London, London EC3N 4AB. Include your
name; the addresses, names, and ages of all people attending
(up to 7 people, nontransferable, no kids under 8 allowed);
requested date; alternative dates; and an international reply
coupon (buy at U.S. post office—if your post office doesn't
have the $1.75 coupons in stock, they can order them; the
turn-around time is a few days). If you don't manage to score
an invite ahead of time, inquire with a Yeoman about last-
minute cancellations—there might be a spot available.

Sights next to the Tower—The best remaining bit of London's
Roman Wall is just north of the tower (at the Tower Hill Tube
station). The impressive Tower Bridge is freshly painted and
restored; for more information on this neo-Gothic maritime
gateway to London, you can visit the **Tower Bridge Experience**
for its 1894–1994 history exhibit (£4.50, family–£14 and up, daily
9:30–18:30, last entry at 17:00, good view, poor value, tel. 020/
7403-3761). The chic **St. Katherine Yacht Harbor,** just east of
the Tower Bridge, has mod shops and the classic old Dickens Inn,
fun for a drink or pub lunch. Across the bridge is the South Bank,
with the upscale Butlers Wharf area, museums, and promenade.

Sights—South London, on the South Bank

The South Bank is a thriving arts and cultural center tied together
by a riverside path. This trendy, pub-crawling walk—called the
Jubilee Promenade—stretches from the Tower Bridge past
Westminster Bridge, where it offers grand views of the Houses
of Parliament. (The promenade hugs the river except just east of
London Bridge, where it cuts inland for a couple of blocks.)

★ The Bankside Walk (on page 64) connects these sights
(described below): Shakespeare's Globe, Tate Modern, Millennium
Bridge, Old Operating Theatre Museum, and Vinopolis.

The South Bank

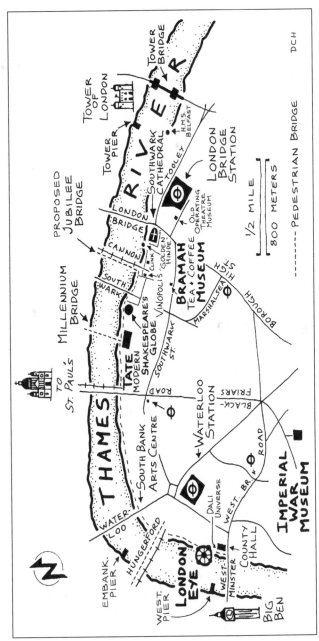

▲▲▲**London Eye Ferris Wheel**—Built by British Air, the wheel towers above London opposite Big Ben. This is the world's highest observational wheel, giving you a chance to fly British Air without leaving London. Designed like a giant bicycle wheel, it's a pan-European undertaking: British steel and Dutch engineering, with Czech, German, French, and Italian mechanical parts. It's also very "green," running extremely efficiently and virtually silently. Twenty-five people ride in each of its 32 air-conditioned capsules for the 30-minute rotation (each capsule has a bench, but most people stand). From the top of this 450-foot-high wheel—the highest public viewpoint in the city—Big Ben looks small. You only go around once; save a shot on top for the glass capsule next to yours.

A big hit with Londoners and tourists alike, the ride gets booked up fast, especially on weekends. To save time and guarantee a spot, reserve a time slot a day ahead—at a London TI, in person at the office near the base of the wheel, at the Big Bus Information Centre (daily 8:30–17:30, 48 Buckingham Palace Road, a block from Victoria Station), possibly through your hotel (ask), or online at www.ba-londoneye.com. You can also book by phone, but allow at least five days before your ticket is available (pick up ticket at wheel office, 50p charge, automated booking tel. 0870-500-0600). Whether you book ahead or just stand in line, you'll be assigned—or you can request—a half-hour time slot. You must arrive at the wheel during this time (earlier is better) to ensure getting on. Advance booking, which costs little or nothing extra, allows you to skip the queue to buy tickets. But you'll still have to stand in the second queue, the ticket-holders' line to get on the wheel (line starts forming 10 min before your half-hour time slot begins; listen for announcement). Freewheeling types who don't care for lines or prebooking can usually avoid the line by riding early (before 11:00) or at night. It's open until 22:00 in peak season (last boarding 21:30). If you're lucky, you can waltz right on (£10.50, daily 9:30–22:00, mid-Sept–March 9:30–20:00, closed Jan for maintenance, shop with binoculars for rent at County Hall, Tube: Waterloo or Westminster, www.ba-londoneye.com). Skip the £30 Fast Track ticket sold here; it gets you on the wheel without a wait, but you pay triple the price.

Dalí Universe—Cleverly located next to the hugely popular London Eye Ferris Wheel, this exhibit features 500 works of mind-bending art by Salvador Dalí. While pricey, it's entertaining if you like Surrealism and want to learn about Dalí (£7, daily 10:00–17:30, generally summer eves until 20:00, tel. 020/7620-2720).

▲▲**Imperial War Museum**—This impressive museum covers the wars of the last century, from heavy weaponry to love notes and Varga Girls, from Monty's Africa campaign tank to

Schwartzkopf's Desert Storm uniform. You can trace the development of the machine gun, watch footage of the first tank battles, see one of over a thousand V2 rockets Hitler rained on Britain in 1944 (each with over a ton of explosives), hold your breath through the gruesome WWI trench experience, and buy WWII–era toys in the fun museum shop. The "Secret War" section gives a fascinating peek into the intrigues of espionage in World Wars I and II. The section on the Holocaust is one of the best on the subject anywhere. Rather than glorify war, the museum does its best to shine a light on the powerful human side of one of mankind's most persistent traits (free, daily 10:00–18:00, 90 min is enough time for most visitors, Tube: Lambeth North or bus #12 from Westminster, tel. 020/7416-5000).

The museum is housed in what was the Royal Bethlam Hospital. Also known as "the Bedlam asylum," the place was so wild it gave the world a new word for chaos: "bedlam." Back in Victorian times, locals—without trash-talk shows and cable TV—came here for their entertainment. The asylum was actually open to the paying public on weekends.

Bramah Tea and Coffee Museum—Aficionados of tea or coffee will find this small museum fascinating. It tells the story of each drink almost passionately. The owner, Mr. Bramah, comes from a big tea family and wants the world to know how the advent of commercial television, with breaks not long enough to brew a proper pot of tea, required a faster hot drink. In came the horrible English instant coffee. Tea countered with finely chopped leaves in tea bags, and it's gone downhill ever since (£4, daily 10:00–18:00, closed only Dec 25–26, 40 Southwark Street, 2 blocks south of Jubilee pedestrian bridge, Tube: London Bridge plus 3-min walk, tel. 020/7403-5650, www.bramahmuseum.org). Its café, which serves more kinds of coffees and teas than cakes, is open to the public (same hours as museum).

▲▲**Shakespeare's Globe**—The original Globe Theater has been rebuilt—half-timbered and thatched—as it was in Shakespeare's time. (This is the first thatched roof in London since they were outlawed after the great fire of 1666.) The Globe originally accommodated 2,000 seated and another 1,000 standing. (Today, leaving space for reasonable aisles, the theater holds 900 seated and 600 groundlings.) Its promoters brag that the theater melds "the three A's"—actors, audience, and architecture—with each contributing to the play. Open as a museum and a working theater, it hosts authentic old-time performances of Shakespeare's plays. The theater can be toured when there are no plays. The Globe's exhibition on Shakespeare is the world's largest, with interactive displays and film presentations, a sound lab, a script factory, and costumes (£8; mid-May–Sept Mon–Sat 9:30–12:00, Sun 9:30–11:30, free 30-min tour offered

Crossing the Thames on Foot

You can cross the Thames on any of the bridges that carry car traffic over the river, but pedestrian bridges are more fun. The **Millennium Bridge**, connecting the sedate St. Paul's Cathedral and the great Tate Modern, is now open, apparently for good. The proposed **Jubilee Bridge**, two bridges east of the Millennium Bridge, may be built in 2003; it was supposed to open last year to commemorate the Queen's Jubilee Year, but funding didn't materialize in time. The new **Hungerford Bridge** (consisting of two walkways that flank a railway trestle) just opened, connecting bustling Trafalgar Square on the North Bank with the London Eye Ferris Wheel and Waterloo Station on the South Bank. Replacing an old, rundown bridge, the Hungerford Bridge—well lit with a sleek, futuristic look—makes this popular route safer and more popular.

on the half hour; also open daily 12:30–16:00 but for disappointing virtual tours only; Oct–mid-May daily 10:30–17:00, free 30-min tour offered on the half hour; on the South Bank directly across Thames over Southwark Bridge from St. Paul's; Tube: London Bridge plus a 10-min walk; tel. 020/7902-1500; www.shakespeares-globe.org). For details on seeing a play, see Entertainment chapter, page 301). The Globe Café is open daily (10:00–18:00, tel. 020/7902-1433).

▲▲▲**Tate Modern**—Dedicated in the spring of 2000, this striking museum across the river from St. Paul's opened the new century with art from the old one. Its powerhouse collection of Monet, Matisse, Dalí, Picasso, Warhol, and much more is displayed in a converted power house (free, fee for special exhibitions, daily 10:00–18:00, Fri–Sat until 22:00—a good time to visit, audioguide-£1, free guided tours from 11:00–12:00 and 14:00–15:00, call for schedule, view café on top floor; cross the Millennium Bridge from St. Paul's, or Tube: Southwark plus a 10-min walk; tel. 020/7887-8008, www.tate.org.uk). ✪ See Tate Modern Tour, page 164.

▲**Millennium Bridge**—This pedestrian bridge links St. Paul's Cathedral and the Tate Modern across the Thames. This is London's first new bridge in a century. When it first opened, the $25 million bridge wiggled when people walked on it, so it promptly closed for a $7 million stabilization; now it's stable and back open (free). Nicknamed "a blade of light" for its sleek minimalist design—370 yards long, four yards wide, stainless steel with teak planks—it includes clever aerodynamic handrails to deflect wind over the heads of pedestrians.

Jubilee Bridge—When completed, this pedestrian bridge (two bridges east of the Millennium Bridge) will provide another feet-friendly way to connect the North and South banks. It may be finished late in 2003 and will be attached to the Cannon Street Railway Bridge.

▲▲**Old Operating Theatre Museum and Herb Garret**— Climb a tight and creaky wooden spiral staircase to a church attic where you'll find a garret used to dry medicinal herbs, a fascinating exhibit on Victorian surgery, cases of well-described 19th-century medical paraphernalia, and a special look at "anesthesia, the defeat of pain." Then you stumble upon Britain's oldest operating theater, where limbs were sawed off way back in 1821 (£3.75, daily 10:30–17:00, Tube: London Bridge, 9a St. Thomas Street, tel. 020/8806-4325, www.thegarret.org.uk). ✪ For more information, see Bankside Walk, page 64.

▲▲**Vinopolis: City of Wine**—While it seems illogical to have a huge wine museum in London, Vinopolis makes a good case. Built over a Roman wine store and filling the massive vaults of an old wine warehouse, the museum offers an excellent audioguide with a light yet earnest history of wine. Sipping various reds and whites, ports, and champagnes—immersed in your headset as you stroll—you learn about the libation from its Georgian origins to Chile, including a Vespa ride through Chianti country in Tuscany. Allow some time, the audioguide takes 90 minutes—the sipping can slow things down wonderfully (£11.50 with 5 tastes, £14 with 10, don't worry . . . for £2.50 you can buy 5 more tastes inside, daily 11:00–18:00, Sat until 20:00, Mon until 21:00, last entry 2 hours before closing, Tube: London Bridge, between the Globe and Southwark Cathedral at 1 Bank End, tel. 0870-241-4040 or 020/7940-8301, www.vinopolis.co.uk).

More South Bank Sights, in Southwark

These sights are mediocre but worth knowing about. The area stretching from the Tate Modern to London Bridge, known as Southwark (pron. SUTH-uck), was for centuries the place Londoners would go to escape the rules and decency of the city and let their hair down. Bear-baiting, brothels, rollicking pubs and theater—you name the dream, and it could be fulfilled just across the Thames. A run-down warehouse district through the 20th century, it's been gentrified with classy restaurants, office parks, pedestrian promenades, major sights (such as the Tate Modern and Shakespeare's Globe), and this colorful collection of lesser sights. The area is easy on foot and a scenic—though circuitous—way to connect the Tower of London with St. Paul's. ✪ You'll find more information on these sights (except for HMS *Belfast*) in the Bankside Walk chapter).

Southwark Cathedral—While made a cathedral only in 1905, this has been the neighborhood church since the 13th century and comes with some interesting history (Mon–Sat 10:00–18:00, Sun 11:00–17:00, last admission 30 min before close, evensong services weekdays at 17:30, Sun at 15:00, audioguide-£2.50, tel. 020/7367-6711).The adjacent church-run **Long View of London Exhibition** tells the story of Southwark (£3, same hours as church).

The Clink Prison—Proudly the "original clink," this was where law-abiding citizens threw Southwark troublemakers until 1780. Today, it's a low-tech torture museum filling grotty old rooms with papier-mâché gore. Unfortunately, there's little to seriously deal with the fascinating problem of law and order in Southwark, where 18th-century Londoners went for a good time (overpriced at £4, daily 10:00–18:00, 1 Clink Street, tel. 020/7378-1558, www.clink.co.uk).

Rose Theatre—This slight sight may be closed or open only by appointment in 2003; call ahead if you're interested (tel. 020/7593-0026). In the basement of an 11-story office building are the scant remains of the 16th-century theater that once stood here. The Rose Theatre was built in 1587, 12 years before the original Globe, and excavated in 1989. In this barren site, you view a 25-minute video on the history of theater in the days of Shakespeare (£4).

Golden Hinde **Replica**—This is a full-size replica of the 16th-century warship in which Sir Francis Drake circumnavigated the globe from 1577 to 1580. Commanding this ship, Drake earned the reputation as history's most successful pirate. The original is long gone, but this boat has logged more than 100,000 miles, including its own voyage around the world. While the ship is fun to see, its interior is not worth touring (£2.50, daily 9:30–17:30, may be closed if rented out for birthday parties, school groups, or weddings, tel. 0870/011-8700, www.goldenhinde.co.uk).

HMS *Belfast*—"The last big-gun armored warship of World War II" clogs the Thames just upstream from the Tower Bridge. This huge vessel—now manned with wax sailors—thrills kids who always dreamed of sitting in a turret shooting off their imaginary guns. If you're into WWII warships, this is the ultimate... otherwise it's just lots of exercise with a nice view of the Tower Bridge (£6.20, daily March-Oct 10:00–18:00, Nov–Feb 10:00–17:00, tel. 020/7940-6300).

Sights—South London, on the North Bank

▲▲**Tate Britain**—One of Europe's great art houses, Tate Britain specializes in British painting from the 16th century through the 20th, including Pre-Raphaelites (free, daily 10:00–17:50, last admission 17:00, closed Dec 24–26, fine £3 audioguide, free tours: 11:30—Turner, 14:30 and 15:30—British Highlights,

call to confirm schedule, no photography allowed, Tube: Pimlico, then 7-min walk; or arrive directly at museum by taking bus #88 from Oxford Circus or #77A from National Gallery, tel. 020/7887-8000, recorded info tel. 020/7887-8008, www.tate.org.uk).
★ See Tate Britain Tour, page 149.

Sights—Greater London

▲Kew Gardens—For a fine riverside park and a palatial greenhouse jungle to swing through, take the Tube or the boat to every botanist's favorite escape, Kew Gardens. While to most visitors the Royal Botanic Gardens of Kew are simply a delightful opportunity to wander among 33,000 different types of plants, to the hardworking organization that runs the gardens, it's a way to promote understanding and preservation of the botanical diversity of our planet. The Kew Tube station drops you in an herbal little business community a two-block walk from Victoria Gate (the main garden entrance). Pick up a map brochure and check at the gate for a monthly listing of best blooms.

Garden-lovers could spend days exploring Kew's 300 acres. For a quick visit, spend a fragrant hour wandering through three buildings: the Palm House, a humid Victorian world of iron, glass, and tropical plants built in 1844; a Waterlily House that would impress Monet; and the Princess of Wales Conservatory, a modern greenhouse with many different climate zones growing countless cacti, bug-munching carnivorous plants, and more (£6.50, £4.50 at 16:45 or later, Mon–Fri 9:30–18:30, Sat–Sun 9:30–19:30, until 16:30 or sunset off-season, galleries and conservatories close at 17:30, consider £2.50 narrated floral joyride on little train departing from 11:00–15:30 from Victoria Gate, Tube: Kew Gardens, tel. 020/8332-5000). For a sun-dappled lunch, walk 10 minutes from the Palm House to the Orangery (£6 hot meals, daily 10:00–17:30).

▲Hampton Court Palace—Fifteen miles up the Thames from downtown (£15 taxi ride from Kew Gardens) is the 500-year-old palace of Henry VIII. Actually, it was the palace of his minister, Cardinal Wolsey. When Wolsey, a clever man, realized Henry VIII was experiencing a little palace envy, he gave the mansion to his king. The Tudor palace was also home to Elizabeth I and Charles I. Sections were updated by Christopher Wren for William and Mary. The stately palace stands overlooking the Thames and includes some impressive Tudor rooms, including a Great Hall with magnificent hammer-beam ceiling. The industrial-strength Tudor kitchen was capable of keeping 600 schmoozing courtesans thoroughly—if not well—fed. The sculpted garden features a rare Tudor tennis court and a popular maze.

Greater London

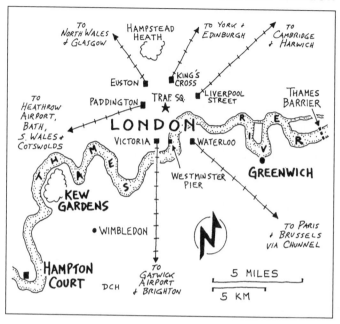

The palace, fully restored after a 1986 fire, tries hard to please, but it doesn't quite sparkle. From the information center in the main courtyard, visitors book times for tours with tired costumed guides or pick up audioguides for self-guided tours of various wings of the palace (all free). The Tudor Kitchens, Henry VIII's Apartments, and the King's Apartments are most interesting. The Georgian Rooms are pretty dull. The maze in the nearby garden is a curiosity some find fun (maze free with palace ticket, otherwise £3). The train (2/hr, 30 min) from London's Waterloo station drops you just across the river from the palace (£11, 1-day combo-ticket with Tower of London–£19, Mon 10:15–18:00, Tue–Sun 9:30–18:00, Nov–March until 16:30, tel. 020/8781-9500).

Royal Air Force Museum Hendon—A hit with aviation enthusiasts, this huge aerodrome and airfield contain planes from World War II's Battle of Britain up through the Gulf War. You can climb inside some of the planes, try your luck in a cockpit, and fly with the Red Arrows in a flight simulator (free, daily 10:00–18:00, café, shop, parking, Tube: Colindale—top of Northern Line Edgware branch, Grahame Park Way, tel. 020/8205-2266, www.rafmuseum.org.uk).

Disappointments of London

The venerable BBC broadcasts from the Broadcasting House. Of all its productions, its "BBC Experience" tour for visitors is among the worst. On the South Bank, the London Dungeon, a much-visited but amateurish attraction, is just a highly advertised, overpriced haunted house—certainly not worth the £11 admission, much less your valuable London time. It comes with long and rude lines. Wait for Halloween and see one in your hometown to support a better cause. "Winston Churchill's Britain at War Experience" (next to the London Dungeon) wastes your time. The Kensington Palace State Apartments are lifeless and not worth a visit.

WESTMINSTER
WALK

From Big Ben to Trafalgar Square

London is the L.A., D.C., and N.Y. of Britain. This walk starts with London's "star" attraction, continues to its "Capitol," passes its "White House," and ends at its "Times Square" . . . all in about an hour.

Just about every visitor to London strolls the historic White-hall Boulevard from Big Ben to Trafalgar Square. This quick eight-stop walk gives meaning to that touristy ramble. Under London's modern traffic and big-city bustle lie 2,000 fascinating years of history. You'll get a whirlwind tour as well as a practical orientation to London.

Start halfway across Westminster Bridge (Tube: Westminster; take the Westminster Pier exit).

1. On Westminster Bridge

Views of Big Ben and the Parliament

• *First look south (upstream), toward the Parliament. (Note that, though the Thames runs generally west-to-east, here it makes a jog to the north.)*

Ding dong ding dong. Dong ding ding dong. Yes, indeed, you are in London. **Big Ben** is actually "not the clock, not the tower, but the bell that tolls the hour." However, since the 13-ton bell is not visible, everyone just calls the whole works Big Ben. Ben (named for a fat bureaucrat) is scarcely older than my great-grandmother, but it has quickly become the city's symbol. The tower is 320 feet high, and the clock faces are

Westminster Walk

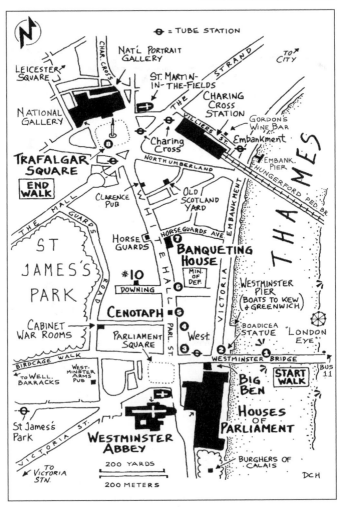

⊕ = TUBE STATION

NAT'L PORTRAIT GALLERY

LEICESTER SQUARE

NATIONAL GALLERY

TRAFALGAR SQUARE

END WALK

ST MARTIN-IN-THE-FIELDS

Charing Cross

NORTHUMBERLAND

CHARING CROSS STATION

GORDON'S WINE BAR

Embankment

EMBANK. PIER

THE STRAND

TO CITY

VILLIERS ST.

HUNGERFORD PED. BR.

THAMES

THE MALL

ST JAMES'S PARK

CLARENCE PUB

HORSE GUARDS

OLD SCOTLAND YARD

HORSEGUARDS AVE.

BANQUETING HOUSE

MIN. OF DEF.

WESTMINSTER PIER (BOATS TO KEW & GREENWICH)

#10 DOWNING

CENOTAPH

CABINET WAR ROOMS

PARLIAMENT SQUARE

West.

BOADICEA STATUE

"LONDON EYE"

BIRDCAGE WALK

TO WELL. BARRACKS

WEST-MINSTER ARMS PUB

WESTMINSTER BRIDGE

BUS 11

START WALK

St James's Park

TO VICTORIA STN.

VICTORIA ST.

WESTMINSTER ABBEY

BIG BEN

HOUSES OF PARLIAMENT

BURGHERS OF CALAIS

200 YARDS

200 METERS

DCH

23 feet across. The 13-foot-long minute hand sweeps the length of your body every five minutes.

Big Ben is the north tower of a long building, the **Houses of Parliament,** stretching along the Thames. Britain is ruled from this building, which for five centuries was the home of kings and queens. Then, as democracy was foisted on tyrants, a parliament of nobles was allowed to meet in some of the rooms.

Soon, commoners were elected to office, the neighborhood was shot, and the royalty moved to Buckingham Palace. The current building, though it looks medieval with its prickly Flamboyant spires, was built in the 1800s after a fire gutted old Westminster Palace. Its horizontal symmetry is an impressive complement to Big Ben's vertical.

Today, the **House of Commons,** which is more powerful than the queen and prime minister combined, meets in the north half of the building. The rubber-stamp **House of Lords** grumbles and snoozes in the south end of this 1,000-room complex and provides a tempering effect on extreme governmental changes. The two houses are very much separate: Notice the riverside tea terraces with the color-coded awnings—royal red for lords, common green for commoners. If a flag is flying from the Victoria Tower, at the far south end of the building, Parliament is in session.

Views of the London Eye Ferris Wheel, The City, and the Thames

• *Now look north (downstream).*
Built in 2000 to celebrate the millennium, the London Eye—known to some as "the London Eyesore"—stands 443 feet tall and slowly spins 32 capsules, each filled with 25 visitors, up to London's best viewpoint (up to 25  miles on a rare clear day; for more on the London Eye, see page 43). Aside from Big Ben, Parliament, St. Paul's Cathedral, and the wheel itself, London's skyline is not overwhelming; it's a city that wows from within.

Next to the wheel sprawls the huge former **County Hall building,** now a hotel and tourist complex. Shut down a decade ago, this bastion of London liberals still seems to snarl across the river at the home of the national government.

The London Eye marks the start of the **Jubilee Promenade,** a pleasant one-hour riverside walk along the "South Bank" of the Thames, through London's vibrant, gentrified arts and cultural zone. Along the way, you have views across the river of St. Paul's stately dome and The City. (See the Bankside Walk, page 64.)

London's history is tied to the **Thames,** the 210-mile river highway linking the interior of England with the North Sea. The city got its start in Roman times as a trade center along this watery highway. As recently as a century ago, large ships made their way upstream to the city center to unload. Today, the major port is 25 miles downstream.

Look for the piers on the Thames. A 50-minute round-trip **cruise** geared for tourists departs from the pier near the base of the Ferris wheel. On the other side of the river, at **Westminster Pier,** boats leave for the Tower of London, Greenwich, and Kew Gardens (see page 27).

Lining the river, beneath the lamp posts, are little green copper **lions' heads** with rings for tying up boats. Before the construction of the Thames Barrier in 1982 (the world's largest movable flood barrier, downstream near Greenwich), high tides from the nearby North Sea made floods a recurring London problem. The police kept an eye on these lions: "When the lions drink, the city's at risk."

Until 1750, only London Bridge crossed the Thames. Then a bridge was built here. Early in the morning of September 3, 1803, William Wordsworth stood where you're standing and described what he saw:

> *This city now doth like a garment wear*
> *The beauty of the morning; silent, bare,*
> *Ships, towers, domes, theaters, and temples lie*
> *Open unto the fields, and to the sky;*
> *All bright and glittering in the smokeless air.*

• *Walk to Big Ben's side of the river. Near Westminster Pier is a big statue of a lady on a chariot (nicknamed "the first woman driver"...
no reins).*

2. Boadicea, Queen of the Iceni

Riding in her two-horse chariot, daughters by her side, this Celtic Xena leads her people against Roman invaders. Julius Caesar had been the first Roman to cross the Channel, but even he was weirded out by the island's strange inhabitants, who worshiped

trees, sacrificed virgins, and went to war painted blue. Later, Romans subdued and civilized them, building roads and making this spot on the Thames—"Londinium"— into a major urban center.

But Boadicea refused to be Romanized. In A.D. 60, after Roman soldiers raped her daughters, she rallied her people and "liberated" London, massacring its 70,000 Romanized citizens. However, the brief revolt was snuffed out, and she and her family took poison rather than surrender.

• *There's a civilized public toilet down the stairs behind Boadicea. Continue past Big Ben, one block inland to the busy intersection of Parliament Square.*

3. Parliament Square

To your left is the orange-hued **Parliament.** If Parliament is in session, the entrance is lined with tourists and staked out by camera crews interviewing Members of Parliament (M.P.s). Kitty-corner across the Square, the two white towers of **Westminster Abbey** rise above the trees. And broad Whitehall (here called Parliament Street) stretches to your right up to Trafalgar Square.

This is the heart of what was once a suburb of London—the medieval City of Westminster. Like Buda and Pest, London is two cities that grew into one. The City of London, centered near St. Paul's Cathedral and the Tower of London, was the place to live. But King Edward the Confessor decided to build a church (minster) and monastery (abbey) here, west of the city walls— hence Westminster. And to oversee its construction, he moved his court here and built a palace. The palace gradually evolved into a meeting place for debating public policy, which is why to this day the Houses of Parliament are known to the Brits as the "Palace of Westminster."

Across from Parliament, the cute little church with the blue sundials, snuggling under the Abbey "like a baby lamb under a ewe," is **St. Margaret's Church.** Since 1480, this has been *the* place for politicians' weddings—such as Churchill's.

Parliament Square, the small park between Westminster Abbey and Big Ben, is filled with statues of famous Brits. The statue of **Winston Churchill,** the man who saved Britain from Hitler, shows him in the military overcoat he wore as he limped victoriously onto the beaches of Normandy after D-Day. According to tour guides, the statue has a current of electricity running through it to honor Churchill's wish that if a statue were made of him, his head shouldn't be soiled by pigeons.

In 1868, the world's first traffic light was installed on the corner here where Whitehall now spills double-decker buses into the square. And speaking of lights, the little yellow lantern atop the concrete post on the street corner closest to Parliament says "Taxi." When an M.P. needs a taxi, this blinks to hail one.

• *Consider touring Westminster Abbey (see page 186). Otherwise, turn right (north), walk away from the Houses of Parliament and the abbey, and continue up Parliament Street, which becomes Whitehall.*

4. Walking along Whitehall

Today, Whitehall is choked with traffic, but imagine the effect this broad street must have had on out-of-towners a century ago. In your horse-drawn carriage, you'd clop along a tree-lined boulevard past well-dressed lords and ladies, dodging street urchins. Gazing left, then right, you'd try to take it all in, your eyes dazzled by the bone-white walls of this man-made marble canyon.

Whitehall is now the most important street in Britain, lined with the ministries of finance, treasury, and so on. You may see limos and camera crews as an important dignitary enters or exits. Notice the security measures. Iron grates seal off the concrete ditches between the buildings and sidewalks for protection against explosives. London was terrorist-conscious long before September 2001. As the N.Y., L.A., and D.C. of Britain, London is also seen as the "Babylon" of a colonial empire whose former colonies sometimes resent its lingering control.

The black, ornamental arrowheads topping the iron fences were once colorfully painted. In 1861, Queen Victoria ordered them all painted black when her beloved Prince Albert ("the only one who called her Vickie") died. Possibly the world's most determined mourner, Victoria wore black for the standard two years of mourning—and tacked on 38 more.

• *Continue toward the tall, square, concrete monument in the middle of the road. On your right is a colorful pub, the Red Lion. Across the street, a 700-foot detour down King Charles Street leads to the **Cabinet War Rooms**, the underground bunker of 21 rooms that was the nerve center of Britain's campaign against Hitler (£5.80, April–Oct daily 9:30–18:00, Nov–March 10:00–18:00; also see page 31).*

5. Cenotaph

This big white stone monument (in the middle of the boulevard) honors those who died in the two events that most shaped modern Britain—World Wars I and II. The monumental devastation of these wars helped turn a colonial superpower into a cultural colony of an American superpower.

The actual cenotaph is the slab that sits atop the pillar—a tomb. You'll notice no religious symbols on this memorial. The dead honored here came from many creeds and all corners of Britain's empire. It looks lost in noisy traffic, but on each Remembrance Sunday (closest to November 11), Whitehall is closed off to traffic, the royal family fills the balcony overhead in the foreign ministry, and a memorial service is held around the cenotaph.

It's hard for an American to understand the impact of the Great War (WWI) on Europe. It's said that if all the WWI dead from the British Empire were to march four abreast past the cenotaph, the sad parade would last for seven days.

Eternally pondering the cenotaph is an equestrian statue up the street. Earl Haig, commander-in-chief of the British army from 1916 to 1918, was responsible for ordering so many brave and not-so-brave British boys out of the trenches and onto the killing fields of World War I.

• *Just past the cenotaph, on the other (west) side of Whitehall, is an iron security gate guarding the entrance to Downing Street.*

6. #10 Downing Street and the Ministry of Defense

Britain's version of the White House is where the current prime minister— Tony Blair—and his family live, at #10 (in black-brick building 300 feet down blocked-off street, on the right). It looks modest, but the entryway does open up into fairly impressive digs. Blair is a young, Clinton-esque politician who prefers persuasive charm to rigid dogma. There's not much to see here unless a VIP happens to drive up. Then the bobbies (police officers) snap to and check credentials, the gates open, the traffic barrier midway down

the street drops into its bat cave, the car drives in, and . . . the bobbies go back to mugging for the tourists.

The huge building across Whitehall from Downing Street is the **Ministry of Defense** (MOD). This bleak place looks like a Ministry of Defense should. In front are statues of illustrious defenders of Britain. "Monty" is **Field Marshal Montgomery** of WWII. Monty beat the Nazis in North Africa (defeating "the Desert Fox" Rommel at El Alamein) and gave the Allies a jumping-off point to retake Europe. Along with Churchill, Monty breathed confidence back into a demoralized British army, persuading them they could ultimately beat Hitler.

Nearby, the statue of **Walter Raleigh** marks the spot where he was presented in glory to Queen Elizabeth after returning from America. Nothing marks the spot—a few hundred yards back toward Big Ben—where he was beheaded for plotting against James I, her successor, a few years later.

You may be enjoying the shade of London's **plane trees.** They do well in polluted London: roots that work well in clay, waxy leaves that self-clean in the rain, and bark that sheds and regenerates so the pollution doesn't get into its vascular system.

• *At the equestrian statue, you'll be flanked by the Welsh and Scottish government offices. At the corner (same side as the MOD), you'll find the Banqueting House.*

7. Banqueting House

The Banqueting House is just about all that remains of what was once the biggest palace in Europe—Whitehall Palace, stretching from Trafalgar Square to Big Ben. Henry VIII started it when he moved out of the Palace of Westminster (now the Parliament) and into the residence of the archbishop of York. Queen Elizabeth I and other monarchs added on as

England's worldwide prestige grew. Finally, in 1698, a roaring fire destroyed everything at Whitehall except the name and the Banqueting House.

The kings held their parties and feasts in the Banqueting House's grand ballroom on the first floor.

At 112 feet wide by 56 feet tall and 56 feet deep, the Banqueting House is a perfect double cube. Today, the exterior of Greek-style columns and pediments looks rather ho-hum, much like every other white, marble, neoclassical building in London. But in 1620, it was the first, a highly influential building by architect Inigo Jones that sparked London's distinct neoclassical look.

On January 27, 1649, a man dressed in black appeared at one of the Banqueting House's first-floor windows and looked out at a huge crowd that surrounded the building. He stepped out the window and onto a wooden platform. It was King Charles I. He gave a short speech to the crowd, framed by the magnificent backdrop of the Banqueting House. His final word was "Remember." Then he knelt and laid his neck on a block as another man in black approached. It was the executioner—who cut off the King's head.

Plop—the concept of divine monarchy in Britain was decapitated. But there would still be kings after Cromwell. In fact, the royalty was soon restored, and Charles' son, Charles II, got his revenge here in the Banqueting Hall...by living well. His elaborate parties under the chandeliers of the Banqueting House celebrated the Restoration of the monarchy. But, from then on, every king knew that he ruled by the grace of Parliament.

Charles I is remembered today with a statue at one end of Whitehall (in Trafalgar Square at the base of the tall column), while his killer, Oliver Cromwell, is given equal time with a statue at the other end (at the Houses of Parliament).

• *Cross the street for a close look at the **Horse Guards**, dressed in Charge-of-the-Light-Brigade cavalry uniforms and swords. Until the Ministry of Defense was created, the Horse Guards was the headquarters of the British army. It's still the home of the queen's private guard. (Changing of the guard Mon–Sat 11:00, 10:00 on Sun, dismounting ceremony daily at 16:00.)*

*Continue up Whitehall, dipping into the guarded entry court of the next big building (probably covered with scaffolding) that has the too-long Ionic columns. This holds the offices of the **Old Admiralty**, headquarters of the British Navy. Ponder the scheming that must have gone on behind these walls as the British Navy built the greatest empire the world has ever seen. Across the street, behind the old Clarence Pub (serves lunch only, no dinner), stood the original **Scotland Yard**, headquarters of London's crack police force in the days of Sherlock Holmes. Finally, Whitehall opens up into the grand, noisy, traffic-filled...*

8. Trafalgar Square

London's "Times Square" bustles around the monumental column where Admiral Horatio Nelson stands 170 feet tall in the crow's nest. Nelson saved England at a time as dark as World War II. In 1805, Napoleon (the Mussolini of his day) was poised on the other side of the Channel, threatening to invade England. Meanwhile, more than 900 miles away, the one-armed, one-eyed, and one-minded Lord Nelson attacked the French fleet off the coast of Spain at Trafalgar. The French were routed, Britannia ruled the waves, and the once-invincible French army was slowly worn down, then defeated at Waterloo. Nelson, while victorious, was shot by a sniper in the battle. He died, gasping, "Thank God, I have done my duty."

At the top of Trafalgar Square sits the domed National Gallery, and to the right, the steeple of St. Martin-in-the-Fields, built in 1722, inspiring the style of many town churches in New England (for concert information, see page 33). In between is a small statue of America's George Washington, looking veddy much the English gentleman he was.

Trafalgar Square

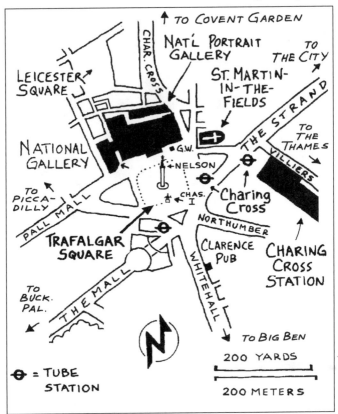

Surrounding Nelson's column are bronze reliefs cast from melted-down enemy cannons, and four huggable lions, dying to have their photo taken with you. The artist had never seen a lion in person, so he used his dog as a model,  giving them doggie paws. In front of the column, Charles I sits on horseback (the oldest such statue in town). Directly behind Charles is a pavement stone marking the center of London.

Trafalgar Square is indeed the center of modern London,

connecting Westminster, The City, and the West End. Spin clock-wise 360 degrees and survey the city:

To the south (down Whitehall) is the center of government, Westminster. Looking southwest, down the broad boulevard called The Mall, you see Buckingham Palace in the distance. (Down Pall Mall is St. James' Palace, where Prince Charles lives when in London.) A few blocks northwest of Trafalgar Square is Piccadilly Circus. Directly north (2 blocks behind the National Gallery) sits Leicester Square, the jumping-off point for Soho, Covent Garden, and the West End theater district.

The boulevard called the Strand takes you past Charing Cross Station, then eastward to The City, the original walled town of London and today's financial center. In medieval times, when people from The City met with the Westminster govern-ment, it was here. And finally, Northumberland Avenue leads southeast to a pedestrian bridge over the Thames. (Along the way, you'll pass the Sherlock Holmes Pub, housed in Sir Arthur Conan Doyle's favorite watering hole, with an upstairs replica of 221-B Baker Street.)

Soak it in. You're smack-dab in the center of London, a thriving city atop thousands of years of history.

BANKSIDE
WALK
From London Bridge to Blackfriars Bridge

Bankside—the neighborhood between London Bridge and Black-friars Bridge—is the historic heart of the newly revamped southern bank of the Thames. For centuries, it was London's red-light district. In the 20th century, it became an industrial wasteland of empty warehouses and street crime. Today, the prostitutes and pickpockets are gone, but it's still interesting, with a riverside prome-nade dotted with pubs, cutesy shops, and historic tourist sights.

Our half-mile walk gives you plenty of history and plenty of sights to choose from—you can see it all, design your own plan, or just enjoy the view of London's skyline across the river.

Orientation
Getting There: Take the Tube to the London Bridge stop to begin the walk. The walk ends near Blackfriars Bridge (closest Tube stops: Blackfriars, just across the bridge on the North Bank, or Southwark, several blocks south of the bridge on the South Bank).

Old Operating Theatre: £3.75, daily 10:30–17:00, 9a St. Thomas Street, tel. 020/8806-4325. www.thegarret.org.uk

Southwark Cathedral: Mon–Sat 10:00–18:00, Sun 11:00–17:00, tel. 020/7367-6711.

***Golden Hinde* Replica:** £2.50, daily 9:30–17:30; note that it may be closed if it's been rented out for weddings or birthday parties.

Clink Prison Museum: £4 (overpriced), daily 10:00–18:00, 1 Clink Street, tel. 020/7378-1558. www.clink.co.uk.

Vinopolis: £11.50 for five tastes, £14 for 10 tastes (for £2.50 you can buy 5 more tastes inside), includes audioguide, daily 11:00–18:00, Sat until 20:00, Mon until 21:00, last entry 2 hours before closing, between the Globe and Southwark Cathedral at 1 Bank End, tel. 0870-241-4040 or 020/7940-8301, www.vinopolis.co.uk.

Rose Theatre: £4, daily 11:00–17:00 (but may be closed without warning, tel. 020/7593-0026).

Shakespeare's Globe: £8, mid-May–Sept daily 9:00–12:00 (best time to visit, free 30-minute tours offered on the half hour) and 12:30–16:00 (open for disappointing virtual tours only), Oct–mid-May 9:30–17:00 (free 30-min tour offered on the half hour, tel. 020/7902-1500, www.shakespeares-globe.org).

Tate Modern: Free (fee for special exhibitions), daily 10:00–18:00, Fri–Sat until 22:00, audioguide-£1, free guided tours, café on top floor, tel. 020/7887-8008, www.tate.org.uk. See page 164 for tour.

Starring: Shakepeare's world, London Bridge, and historic pubs.

1. London Bridge, Griffins, and Nancy's Steps

Start at the south end of London Bridge.

• *From the London Bridge Tube stop, take the Borough High Street exit and turn right (north), walking 100 yards to the bridge.*

The City across the river is to the north, Tower Bridge is east, and the Thames flows from west to east (left to right). Looking to the east (downstream) and turning counterclockwise, you'll see:

• Tower Bridge (the Gothic-towered drawbridge which many Americans mistakenly call London Bridge).

• The HMS *Belfast* (in the foreground, docked on the southern bank), a WWII cruiser open for tourists.

• Canary Wharf (the distant, 800-foot skyscraper with pyramid top and blinking light), built in 1990 on the Isle of Dogs.

• The Tower of London (4 spires and a flag rising above the trees on the North Bank).

• The Monument (directly across London Bridge but buried among modern buildings), a column topped with a shiny bronze knob, marking the start of the Great Fire.

• St. Paul's Cathedral (to the northwest, with a dome like a state capitol and twin spires).

• St. Bride's Church, the pointed, stacked steeple (nestled among office buildings) that supposedly inspired the wedding cake.

• A radio/TV tower.

• Southwark Bridge (the next bridge upstream).

• The Tate Modern art museum (brick smokestack tower on the South Bank).

• Southwark Cathedral (on South Bank, 100 yards away), and . . .

• Borough High Street, the busy street that London Bridge spills into.

The small griffin statues (winged lions holding shields) at the south end of London Bridge guard the entrance to The City. For centuries, they said, "Neener neener" to late-night partiers who got locked out of town when the gates shut tight at curfew.

Nancy's Steps, a simple staircase leading down from the bridge (next to the southwest griffin), will impress fans of Dickens, who set the *Oliver Twist* rendezvous "Meeting on the Bridge" here:

> "'*Come away,' [said Nancy,] 'out of the public road—down yonder!'*
>
> "*The stairs consist of three flights. Just below the second, going down, the stone wall on the left terminates in an ornamental pilaster facing towards the Thames. At this point the lower steps widen . . . .*"

• *The best view of London Bridge is not from the bridge itself, but from the riverbank, 50 yards west, reached by "Nancy's Steps." (Those visiting the Old Operating Theatre and Borough High Street inns may want to see those first, before heading west.)*

2. View of London Bridge

The bridge of today is (at least) the fourth incarnation of this 2,000-year-old river crossing. The Romans (A.D. 50) built the first wooden footbridge to Londinium (rebuilt many times), which was pulled down by English (and Norwegian) boatsmen in 1014 to retake London from invading Danes. (They celebrated with a song passed down to us as "London Bridge is falling down, my fair lady.")

The most famous version—crossed by everyone from Richard the Lionhearted to Henry VIII to Shakespeare to Newton to Darwin—was built around 1200 and stood for more than six centuries, the only crossing point into this major city. Built of stone on many thick pilings, stacked with houses and shops that arched over the roadway and bulged out over the river, with its own chapel and a fortified gate at each end, it was a neighborhood unto itself (pop. 300). Picture Mel Gibson's head boiled in tar and stuck on a stick along the bridge (like the Scots rebel William Wallace in 1305, depicted in the movie *Braveheart*), and you'll capture the local color of that time.

In 1823, the famous bridge was replaced with a more modern (but less impressive) brick one. In 1967, that brick bridge was sold to an American, dismantled, shipped to Arizona, and reassembled (all 10,000 bricks) in Lake Havasu City. (Humor today's Brits, who'd like to believe the American thought he was buying Tower Bridge.)

The current bridge (from 1972) is three spans of boring, traffic-clogged concrete.

• *Those interested—remember, this walk is a pick-and-choose collection of sights—will hike 150 yards south of the bridge (on the left-hand side) to the Old Operating Theatre and the inns along Borough High Street).*

Bankside Walk

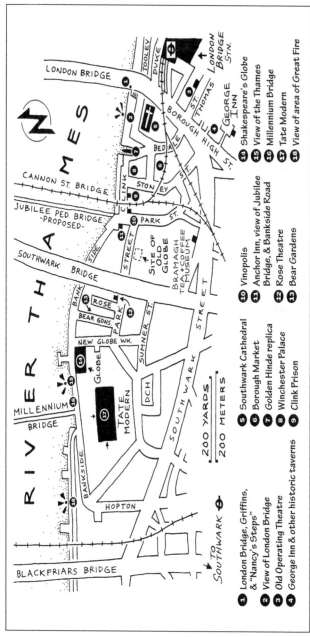

1. London Bridge, Griffins, & "Nancy's Steps"
2. View of London Bridge
3. Old Operating Theatre
4. George Inn & other historic taverns
5. Southwark Cathedral
6. Borough Market
7. Golden Hinde replica
8. Winchester Palace
9. Clink Prison
10. Vinopolis
11. Anchor Inn, view of Jubilee Bridge, & Bankside Road
12. Rose Theatre
13. Bear Gardens
14. Shakespeare's Globe
15. View of the Thames
16. Millennium Bridge
17. Tate Modern
18. View of area of Great Fire

3. Old Operating Theatre

Back when the common cold was treated with a refreshing blood-letting, the Old Operating Theatre—a surgical operating room from the 1800s—was a shining example of "modern" medicine. Today a museum, this is a quirky, sometimes gross, look at that painful transition from folk remedy to clinical health care.

There are three parts to the small museum (reached by a steep, narrow spiral staircase): The Herb Garret displays healing plants used for millennia—different ones for each of the traditional four ailments (melancholic, choleric, sanguine, phlegmatic) to the body's traditional four parts, or "humours" (blood, black bile, yellow bile, and phlegm), corresponding to the earth's traditional four elements (earth, wind, fire, and Ringo). You'll also learn that Florence Nightingale, the nurse famed for saving so many Crimean War soldiers wounded in Turkey, worked here to improve sanitation and to turn nurses from low-paid domestics into trained doctors' assistants.

The medical instruments section shows crude anesthetics (ether, chloroform, 3 pints of ale), surgical instruments by Black & Decker (drills, knives, saws), and a glaring lack of antiseptics—young Dr. Joseph Lister had yet to discover carbolic acid—which resulted in high rates of mortality and halitosis.

The operating theater is the highlight—a semicircular room surrounded by railings for 150 spectators (truly a "theater"), where patients were operated on and med students observed. The patients were poor women, blindfolded for their own modesty. The doctors donated their time to help, practice, and teach (see the motto *Miseratione non Mercede*, "Out of compassion, not for profit"). The surgeries, usually amputations, were performed under very crude working conditions—under the skylight or by gaslight, with no sink, and only sawdust to sop up blood. The wood still bears blood stains. Nearly one in three patients died. The informative (if victim-oriented) 75p pamphlet on *Women, St. Thomas' Hospital and the Old Operating Theatre* draws only a fine line between Victorian male doctors and Jack the Ripper.

• *Farther down Borough High Street (on the left-hand side), you'll find . . .*

4. The George Inn and (faint echoes of) Other Historic Taverns

The George is the last of many "coaching inns" that lined the main highway from London to all points south. Like with Greyhound bus lines, each inn was a terminal for far-flung journeys, since coaches were forbidden inside The City. They offered food, drink, beds, and entertainment for travelers—Shakespeare, as a young actor, likely performed in the George's courtyard.

Along Borough High Street are plaques locating the alleyway ("Yard") of long-gone taverns known to book-lovers: **The White Hart** (north of the George), where Shakespeare and Dickens drank and set scenes; **The Tabard** (now called "Talbot," south of George), where Chaucer's band began its fictional trip south in *Canterbury Tales* ("Befell that in that season on a day/In Southwark at The Tabard as I lay/Ready to wander on my pilgrimage/To Canterbury with full courage"); and **The Queen's Head** (farther south), owned by the mother of John Harvard of University fame.

Fans of Charles Dickens will buy some other guidebook to take them further south to the neighborhood of his David Copperfield childhood. (Marshalsea Debtors' Prison held Dickens' dad, Church of St. George the Martyr is in *Little Dorrit*, and so on.)

• *Southwark Cathedral is near the southwest corner of London Bridge.*

5. Southwark Cathedral

This neighborhood parish church is where Anne Hathaway would drag husband Will and the Shakespeare girls on Sunday mornings. William prayed while brother Edmund rang the bells. The Southwark (pron. SUTH-uck) church dates back to 1207, though the site has had a church for at least a thousand years and inhabitants for 2,500.

1) View down the nave: Clean and sparse, with warm golden stone, the church was recently revamped, a symbol of the urban renewal of the whole Bankside/Southwark area. Its WWII damage has been repaired, with new un-stained glass windows on the right side. The nave bends slightly to the left (the chandelier, ceiling arches, and altar don't line up until you take 2 baby steps left) as a medieval tribute to Christ's bent body on the cross.

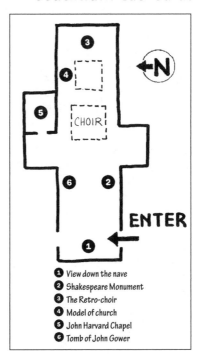

Southwark Cathedral

❶ View down the nave
❷ Shakespeare Monument
❸ The Retro-choir
❹ Model of church
❺ John Harvard Chapel
❻ Tomb of John Gower

2) Shakespeare Monument: William reclines in front of a backdrop of the 16th-century Bankside skyline (view looking north). Find (left to right) the old Globe Theater, Winchester Palace, Southwark Cathedral, and the old London Bridge with its arched gate. Shakespeare seems to be dreaming about the many characters of his plays, depicted in the stained-glass window above. To the right is a plaque to the American actor Sam Wanamaker, who spearheaded the building of a replica of Shakespeare's Globe Theatre (see page 74). Shakespeare's brother Edmund is buried in the church, possibly under a marked slab on the floor of the choir area, near the very center of the church. (The Bard lies buried in his hometown of Stratford-upon-Avon.)

3) The Retro-choir: The 800-year-old crisscross arches and stone tracery in the windows are some of the oldest parts of this historic church.

4) Model of church: Near a reclining stone corpse and a reclining wooden knight, find a model of the church and old Winchester Palace—a helpful reconstruction before we visit the paltry Winchester Palace ruins.

5) John Harvard Chapel: The Southwark-born son of an innkeeper (see the record of baptism near the window) inherited money from the sale of the Queen's Head tavern, got married, and sailed to Boston (1637), where he soon died. The money and his 400-book library funded the start of Harvard University.

6) Tomb of John Gower: The poet and friend of Chaucer (c. 1400) rests his head on his three books, one written in Middle English, one in French, and one in Latin—the three languages from which modern English soon emerged.
• *A block south of Southwark Cathedral, you'll find the . . .*

6. Borough Market

Be here weekdays at 2:00 in the morning, when the first trading starts at this open-air wholesale produce market, and you can knock off by 6:00 for a pint at the specially licensed Globe or Market Porter taverns. Or, if you are not a morning person, come by on Friday afternoon and all day Saturday, when the colorful market opens for retail sales to Londoners seeking trendy specialty foods.

First started a thousand years ago on London Bridge, where country farmers brought fresh goods to the city gates, the market now sits here under a Victorian arcade. Even the railroad rumbling overhead, knifing right through dingy apartment houses (and the Globe Tavern), only adds to the color of London's oldest vegetable market and public gathering spot.
• *Walk to the river, veering left at the Y, on Cathedral Street.*

7. *Golden Hinde* Replica

As we all learned in school, "Sir Francis
Drake circumcised the globe with a
hundred-foot clipper." Or something
like that....

Imagine a hundred men on a boat
this size (yes, this replica is full-size)
circling the globe on a three-year voyage, sleeping on the wave-swept decks,
suffering bad food, floggings, doldrums,
b.o., and attacks from foreigners, exploring unknown waters, paid only from
whatever riches they could find or steal
along the way. (I took a bus tour like that once.)

The *Golden Hinde* (see the female deer—hind—on the
prow and stern) was Sir Francis Drake's flagship as he circumnavigated the globe (1577–80). Drake, a farmer's son who
followed the lure of the sea, hated Spaniards. So did Queen
Elizabeth I, who hired him to plunder rich Spanish vessels
and New World colonies in England's name.

With 164 men on five small ships (the *Hinde* was the largest,
at 100 tons and 18 cannons), he sailed southwest, dipping around
South America, raiding Spanish ships and towns in Chile, and inch-
ing up the coast as far as Canada. By the time it continued across
the Pacific to Asia and beyond, the *Hinde* was so full of booty that
its crew replaced the rock ballast with gold ingots and silver coins.
Three years later, Drake—with only one remaining ship and
56 men—sailed the *Hinde* up the Thames, unloading a fabulously
valuable hoard of gold, silver, emeralds, diamonds, pearls, cloves,
silks, and spices before the Queen. A grateful Elizabeth knighted
Drake on the main deck and kissed him on his *Golden Hinde*.

The *Hinde* was retired gloriously but rotted away from
neglect. Drake received a large share of the wealth, became
enormously famous, and later gained more glory defeating the
Spanish Armada (aided by "the winds of God") in the decisive
battle in the English Channel, off Plymouth (1588), which made
England ruler of the waves.

The galleon replica, a working ship that has itself circled the
globe, is berthed at St. Mary Overie Dock ("St. Mary's over the
river"), a public dock available for free to all Southwark residents.
The Thames river trade that used to thrive even this far upstream
is now concentrated east of Tower Bridge, a victim of WWII
bombing and container ships that require big berths and deep
water. Only a few brick warehouses remain (just west of here),
waiting to be leveled or yuppified.

• *There's a fine view from the riverside. From here, "The Monument" is visible across London Bridge, poking its bristly bronze head above the ugly postwar buildings. Now head west along Clink Street. Twenty-five yards ahead on the left are the excavated ruins of . . .*

8. Winchester Palace .

This was once a lavish 80-acre estate stretching along 200 feet of waterfront, with a palace, gardens, fountains, stables, tennis courts, a working farm, and a fish-stocked lake—but today all that stands is a wall with a medieval rose window. The wall marks the west end of the Great Hall (134 feet by 29 feet), the banquet room for receptions held by the palace's owner, the Bishop of Winchester.

Bishops from 1106 to 1626 lived here as wealthy, worldly rulers of the Bankside area, outside the jurisdiction of The City. They profited from activities illegal across the river, such as prostitution and gambling. They were a law unto themselves, with their own courts and prisons. One famous prison built by the bishops remained on, even after its creators were ousted by a Puritan Parliament—The Clink.

• *Twenty-five yards farther west along Clink Street is . . .*

9. Clink Prison

The prison—now a museum—gave us our expression "thrown in the Clink" from the sound of prisoners' chains. It burned down in 1780, but the underground cells remain, featuring historical information on wall plaques, many torture devices, and a generally creepy, claustrophobic atmosphere.

Originally part of Winchester Palace, it housed troublemakers who upset the smooth running of the bishop's 22 licensed brothels (called "the stews"), gambling dens, and taverns. Bouncers delivered to the Clink drunks who were out of control, johns who couldn't pay, and prostitutes ("women livinge by their bodies") who tried to go freelance or cheated loyal customers. Offending prostitutes had their heads shaved and breasts bared, and were carted through the streets and whipped while people jeered. They might share cells side by side with "heretics"—namely, priests who crossed their bishops.

In 1352, debtors (who'd maxed out their Visa cards) became criminals, housed here among harder criminals in harsh conditions. Prisoners were not fed. They had to bribe guards to get food, to avoid torture, or even to gain their release. (The idea was you'd brought this on yourself.) Prisoners relied on their families for money, prostituted themselves to guards and other inmates, or reached through the bars at street level, begging from passersby. Murderers, debtors, prostitutes, Protestants, priests, and many

innocent people experienced this strange brand of justice... all
part of the rough crowd that gave Bankside such a seedy reputation.
• *Continuing west and crossing under the Cannon Street Bridge,
you'll find...*

10. Vinopolis: City of Wine

This warehouse of wine—
with a splash of France, a
dash of ancient Rome, and a
taste of Italian *vino*—seems
out of place in London, but
no one's complaining. For
more on this wine-tasters'
paradise, see page 48.

• *Switching from wine to beer,
across the street is...*

11. Anchor Inn and Bankside Road

The **Anchor** is the last of the original 22 licensed "inns" (tavern/
brothel/restaurant/nightclub/casino) of Bankside's red-light district
heyday in the 1600s. A tavern has stood here for 800 years. The
big brick buildings behind the inn were once part of the mass-
producing Anchor brewery, with the inn as its brew pub. (Even
back in the 1300s, Chaucer wrote, "If the words get muddled in
my tale/Just put it down to too much Southwark ale.")

In the cozy, maze-like interior are memories of greats who've
drunk here (I did) or indulged in a new drug that hit London in
the 1560s—tobacco. Shakespeare, who may have lived along
Clink Street, likely did, as did Dr. Samuel Johnson, who wrote
much of the famous dictionary that helped codify the English
language and spelling. ("When a man is tired of London," he
belched, "he is tired of life.")

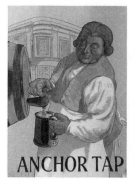

ANCHOR TAP

The Anchor Inn marks the start
of once-notorious **Bankside Road** that
runs along a river retaining wall. In
Elizabethan times (16th century), the
street was lined with "inns" offering
one-stop shopping for addictive personalities. The streets were jammed
with sword-carrying punks in tights
looking for a fight, prostitutes, gaping
tourists from the Borough High Street
coaching inns, pickpockets, river
pirates, highwaymen, navy recruiters
kidnapping drunks, and many proper

ladies and gentlemen who ferried across from The City for
an evening's entertainment. And then there were the really
seedy people . . . actors.
• *Crossing under the green-and-yellow Southwark Bridge, notice the
metal reliefs depicting London's "Frost Fair" of 1564. Because the old
London Bridge was such a wall of stone, the swift-flowing Thames
would back up and even freeze over during cold winters. Emerging
from under the bridge, die-hard theater fans may wish to detour inland
to stop by the site of the Rose Theatre (see map on page 67). It's probably
not open, and if it is, there's not much to see.*

12. The Rose Theatre

When the 2,200-seat Rose first raised its curtain in 1587, it signaled
four decades of phenomenal popularity (centered in Bankside) for
a rapidly evolving form of entertainment—theater. Soon there
were four great theaters in the area: the Rose, the Hope, the Swan,
and . . . the Globe. (Theatrical types can find the unimpressive plaque
marking the site of the original Globe Theater, a half block east of
the Rose—and be as disappointed as Sam Wanamaker, who was
inspired to build the Shakespeare's Globe replica. More on the
Globe when we arrive at the replica.)

It's thought that the young Will Shakespeare, recently arrived
from the country, got his start at the Rose tending theater-goers'
horses ("What?" he said, "and give up show business?!"). Soon,
though, the struggling actor saw his first play *(Henry IV, Part I)*
come to life on the Rose stage.
• *Closer to the river were the . . .*

13. Bear Gardens

Bankside theaters presented everything from serious drama to light
comedy to vaudeville to circus acts to . . . animal fights. Bear-baiting
(especially at the Hope Theatre on Bear Gardens Street) was the
most popular. A bear was chained to a stake while a pack of dogs
(mastiffs) attacked, and spectators bet on the winner. The bears,
often with teeth filed down or jaws wired shut, fought back with their
paws, sweeping dogs into the crowd. Now, that's entertainment.
• *Fifty yards farther west on Bankside is . . .*

14. Shakespeare's Globe— 1997 Replica of the Original Globe Theatre

> *All the world's a stage,*
> *And all the men and women merely players.*
> *They have their exits and their entrances,*
> *And one man, in his time, plays many parts.*
> —As You Like It

By 1599, 35-year-old
William Shakespeare was
a well-known actor, play-
wright, and businessman in
the booming theater trade.
His acting company, the
Lord Chamberlain's Men,
built the 3,000-seat Globe
Theatre, by far the largest
of its day (200 yards from
today's replica, where only

a plaque stands today). The Globe premiered Shakespeare's
greatest works—*Hamlet, Othello, King Lear, Macbeth*—in open-air
summer afternoon performances, though occasionally at night by
light of torches and buckets of tar-soaked ropes.

In 1612, they featured Shakespeare's *All Is True (Henry VIII)*.
During Scene 4, a stage cannon boomed, announcing the arrival
of King Henry, who started flirting with Anne Boleyn. As the two
generated sparks onstage, play-watchers smelled fire. Some stray
cannon wadding had sparked a real fire offstage. Within an hour,
the wood-and-thatch building had burned completely to the
ground, but with only one injury; a man's pants caught on fire,
quickly doused with a bottle of beer.

Built in 1997, the new Globe—round, half-timbered,
thatched, using wooden pegs for nails—is a quite realistic replica,
though slightly smaller (1,500 spectators), and constructed with
fire-repellent materials.

Bankside's theater scene vanished in the 1640s, closed by a
Parliament dominated by Puritans (hard-line Protestants, like
America's Pilgrims). Drama seemed to portray and promote
immoral behavior, and actors—men who also played women's
roles—parodied and besmirched fair womanhood. Bear-baiting
was also outlawed by the outraged moralists (to paraphrase the
historian Thomas Macaulay) not because it caused bears pain,
but because it gave people pleasure.

• *Along the river near the Globe, a plaque gives info about...*

15. The Thames

From the Cotswolds to the North Sea, the river winds eastward
a total of 210 miles. London is close enough to the estuary to be
affected by the North Sea's tides, so the river level does indeed rise
and fall twice a day. However, after centuries of periodic flooding
(spring rains plus high tides), barriers to regulate the tides were
built in 1982, east of Tower Bridge. The barriers also slow down
the once fast-moving river.

The Thames is still a major commercial artery (again, east of Tower Bridge). In the previous two centuries, it ran brown with Industrial Revolution pollution. Today's brown is estuary silt, and the Thames is one of the cleanest rivers in the industrialized world.

• *Fifty yards west of the Globe, spanning the river, is the...*

16. Millennium Bridge

This pedestrian bridge was built in 2000 to connect the Tate Modern with St. Paul's Cathedral and The City. For three glorious days, Londoners made the pleasant seven-minute walk across... before the 25-million-dollar "bridge to the next millennium" started wobbling dangerously (insert your own ironic joke here) and was closed for rethinking. After much work and money, the bridge has reopened. Visually impressive, it's a slender horizontal thread with Y-shaped supports, designed by a three-man team of an engineer, sculptor, and architect. Now stabilized and reopened, it links two revitalized sections of London.

17. Tate Modern

London's large, impressive modern art collection is housed in a former power station—typical of the whole South Bank's move to renovate empty, ugly Industrial Age hulks. Even if you don't tour the collection, pop inside the north entrance (free) to view the spacious interior, decorated each year with a new Industrial-sized sculptural installation by one of the world's top artists.

● See Tate Modern Tour chapter, page 164.

• *Bankside—maybe at the Founder's Arms pub along the river—is a great place to contemplate...*

18. The Great Fire of London, 1666

On Sunday, September 2, 1666, stunned Londoners quietly sipped beers in Bankside pubs and watched their City across the river go up in flames. ("When we could endure no more upon the water," wrote Samuel Pepys in his diary, "we went to a little alehouse on the Bankside.") Started in a bakery shop near The Monument (north end of London Bridge) and fanned by strong winds, the fire swept westward, engulfing the mostly wooden city, devouring Old St. Paul's, moving past what is now Blackfriars Bridge and St. Bride's, to Temple Church and beyond.

In four days, 80 percent of The City was incinerated, including 13,000 houses and 89 churches. The good news? Incredibly, only nine people died, the fire cleansed a plague-infested city, and Christopher Wren was around to rebuild London's skyline.

The fire also marked the end of Bankside's era as London's naughty playground. Having recently been cleaned up by the Puritans, it now served as a temporary refugee camp for those displaced by the fire. And, with the coming Industrial Age, businessmen demolished the inns and replaced them with brick warehouses, docks, and factories to fuel the economy of a world power.

THE CITY
WALK

From Trafalgar Square to London Bridge

In Shakespeare's day, London consisted of a square mile area surrounding St. Paul's. Today, that square mile, the neighborhood known as "The City," is still the financial heart of London, densely packed with history and bustling with business.

This two-mile walk from Trafalgar Square to London Bridge parallels the Thames on the same main road used for centuries. Allow two to three hours, depending on what you visit. Along the way, you'll see sights from The City's storied past, such as St. Paul's Cathedral, the steeples of other Wren churches, historic taverns, a Crusader church, and narrow alleyways with faint remnants of the London of Shakespeare and Dickens.

But you'll also catch today's City in action, especially if you visit on a weekday at lunchtime, when workers spill into the streets and The City is at its liveliest. See lawyers and judges in robes and wigs taking a cigarette break, brokers in pin-striped power suits buying newspapers from Cockneys, and gentlemen with bowler hats and brollies browsing for tailored shirts and Cuban cigars. Sip a pint in the same pub where Dickens did and eavesdrop on a businessmen's power lunch. Use this walk to help resurrect the London that was, then let The City of today surprise you with what is.

Orientation

Getting there: Take the Tube to Charing Cross and head east on The Strand. The walk ends at London Bridge (where the Bankside Walk, page 64, begins).

Somerset House: Courtauld Gallery-£5, free Mon until 14:00; Hermitage Room-£6; Gilbert Collection-£5, free after 16:30; buy one ticket and get a £1 discount on entry to either or both of the other two on the same day; daily 10:00–18:00; Strand, tel. 020/7848-2526. ✪ See Courtauld Gallery Tour, page 202.

St. Clement Danes: Free, Mon–Fri 9:00–16:00, Sat 9:30–15:00, Sun 9:30–15:00 but closed to sightseers during worship.
Royal Courts of Justice: Free, Mon–Fri 9:00–17:00, Strand, tel. 020/7947-7731.
Prince Henry's Room: Free, Mon–Fri 11:00–14:00, 17 Fleet Street, tel. 020/7936-4004.
Temple Church: Free, Wed–Sat 11:00–16:00, Sun 13:00–16:00, closed Mon–Tue, tel. 020/7353-1736.
Dr. Johnson's House: £4, May–Sept Mon–Sat 11:00–17:30, closed Sun, Oct–April Mon–Sat 11:00–17:00, closed Sun, tel. 020/7353-3745.
Old Bailey: Free, public galleries only, most weeks Mon–Fri 10:00–13:00 & 14:00–17:00, no kids under 14, tel. 020/7248-3277.
St. Paul's Cathedral: £6, Mon–Sat 8:30–16:30, last entry 16:00, closed Sun except for worship, tel. 020/7236-4128.
St. Mary-le-Bow: Free, Mon–Thu 6:00–18:00, Fri 6:00–16:00, closed Sat–Sun, Cheapside.
The Monument: £1.50, daily 10:00–18:00, tel. 020/7626-2717.

THE CITY

The City stretches from Temple Church (near Blackfriar's Bridge) to the Tower of London. This was the London of the ancient Romans, of William the Conqueror, Henry VIII, Shakespeare, and Elizabeth I.

But The City has been stripped of its history by the Great Fire (1666), the World War II Blitz (1940–41), and modern economic realities. Today, it's a neighborhood of modern bank buildings and retail stores. Only about 6,000 people actually live here, but every day it's packed with hundreds of thousands of commuting workers. By day, The City is a hive of business activity. At night and on weekends, it's a ghost town.

The route is simple—a two-mile walk east along a single street that changes names as you go. The Strand becomes Fleet Street which becomes Cannon Street.

• *From Trafalgar Square (Tube: Charing Cross), head east on the Strand.*

1. The Strand

This busy boulevard, home to theaters and retail stores, was formerly the high-class riverside promenade, back before the Thames was tamed with retaining walls. **Covent Garden** (see West End Walk, page 90) is just one block left, up Southhampton Street.

Ahead on the right is the drive-up entrance to the **Savoy Hotel and Savoy Theatre,** adorned in green neon. The shiny knight represents the Earl of Savoy who built the original riverside palace here in 1245. See the Rolls-Royces, fancy shops,

The City Walk

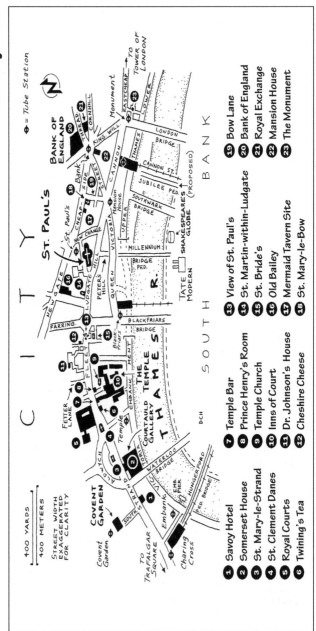

⊖ = Tube Station

400 YARDS
400 METERS
Street width exaggerated for clarity

1 Savoy Hotel
2 Somerset House
3 St. Mary-le-Strand
4 St. Clement Danes
5 Royal Courts
6 Twining's Tea

7 Temple Bar
8 Prince Henry's Room
9 Temple Church
10 Inns of Court
11 Dr. Johnson's House
12 Cheshire Cheese

13 View of St. Paul's
14 St. Martin-within-Ludgate
15 St. Bride's
16 Old Bailey
17 Mermaid Tavern Site
18 St. Mary-le-Bow

19 Bow Lane
20 Bank of England
21 Royal Exchange
22 Mansion House
23 The Monument

Joan-Collins luxury, and the doorman in top hat and tails at one
of London's ritziest locales. Step inside the Art Deco lobby under
the pretext of asking about their afternoon tea (about £25).

The **Somerset House** is the last of the many great riverside
mansions that once lined the Strand. Today it has a people-friendly
courtyard and three separate museums, including the **Courtauld
Gallery.** The Courtauld's small but tasty collection of paintings
includes several famous Impressionist and Post-Impressionist
masterpieces. ✪ See Courtauld Gallery Tour, page 202.

You'll encounter two different
churches left Strand-ed in the middle
of traffic when the road was widened
around them. **St. Mary-le-Strand,**
with its clean white interior lit by blue-
and-green stained glass, is an oasis of
quiet. Charles Dickens' parents got
married here. To the left of the church
is **BBC World Headquarters,** to the
right is the **Government of Gibraltar
Center,** an outpost of one of Britain's
last little "colonies," on the southern
tip of Spain.

St. Clement Danes, built by Christopher Wren (1682),
was Blitzed heavily in World War II. It's now dedicated to the
125,000 Royal Air Force servicemen who gave their lives in both
World Wars.

This is the first of several Wren-built churches we'll see on the
walk, out of 23 that still dot London (from the 51 he originally built).
Despite several renovations since Wren's time, St. Clement Danes
still bears many of his distinct touches: a steeple over the main (west)
entrance; an uncluttered, well-lit interior; neoclassical (Greek-style)
columns; a curved or domed plaster ceiling; geometrical shapes
(e.g., round windows inside a square of columns); and fine carved
woodwork, often by his favorite whittler, Grinling Gibbons.
• *Past St. Clement Danes, on the left side of street are the . . .*

2. Royal Courts of Justice

When former Spice Girls sue tabloids for libel, the trial is likely
to be held here at Britain's highest civil court (criminal cases
down the street at the Old Bailey). The 64 courtrooms in this
neo-Gothic complex are open to the public. At least step into
the lobby to see the vast Gothic entry hall. Submit to a security
check to go farther in. This is just one of several legal buildings
in the neighborhood.
• *Across the street is . . .*

3. Twining's Tea (216 Strand)

When the narrowest store in London first opened its doors in 1706, tea was an exotic concoction from newly explored lands. (The Chinese statues at the entrance remind us that tea came first from China, then India.) In the 1700s, London was in the grip of a coffee craze, and "coffee houses" were everywhere. These were rather seedy places, where "gentlemen" went for coffee, tobacco, and female companionship. Tea offered a refreshing change of pace, and the late-afternoon "cuppa" soon became a national institution.

These days—as you'll see on this walk—coffee is making a comeback in London in the form of modern, Starbucks-style coffee shops.

• *Up ahead, in the middle of the street, is a small statue of a winged dragon.*

4. Temple Bar Monument

The mythological griffin marks the official border between The City of Westminster and The City of London. The Queen, who presides over Westminster, cannot pass this point without permission of The City's Lord Mayor.

• *You can, so leave Westminster and enter The City. Up a few store-fronts, on the right side of the street, find...*

5. Prince Henry's Room (17 Fleet Street)

This half-timbered, three-story, Tudor-style building (1610) is one of the few to survive the Great Fire. In Shakespeare's day, the entire City was packed, rooftop to rooftop, with wood and plaster buildings like this. Many were five and six stories high, with narrow frontage. Little wonder that a small fire could spread so quickly and become the Great Fire of 1666.

The top floor of the house is "Prince Henry's Room" (which you can visit), once an office of King James I's son.

• *Pass underneath the house, through the passageway called Inner Temple Lane that leads a half-block to the exotic...*

6. Temple Church

The round, crenellated, castle-turret roof marks this as a Crusader

church, from the days of King Richard the Lion-hearted. A band of monks, sworn to chastity and the liberation of Jerusalem from the Moslems, built the church (1185) as headquarters for their order, the Knights Templar.

Inside (enter along the side), some honored knights lie face-up on the floor of the unusual circular nave, patterned after the Church of the Holy Sepulchre in Jerusalem. A knight's crossed legs indicate he probably died peacefully at home. Surrounding the serene knights are gargoyle faces (see previous page), perhaps the twisted expressions seen in distant wars.

When the Templars were disbanded (1312), the church and monastery was rented to lawyers who built the Inns of Court around it.

• *Abutting, surrounding, and extending from the Temple Church is a vast complex of buildings covering a full city block between the Strand and the Thames, known collectively as...*

7. The Inns of Court

Wander through the peaceful maze of buildings, courtyards, narrow lanes, nooks, gardens, fountains, and century-old gas lamps, where lawyers take a break from the Royal Courts. The complex is a self-contained city of lawyers, with offices, lodgings, courtrooms, chapels, and dining halls. Law students must live here (and are even required to eat a number of meals here) to complete their legal internship.

You'll see barristers in modern business suits and ties, plus a few in traditional wigs and robes, as they prepare to do legal battle. The wigs are a remnant of French manners of the 1700s, when every European gentleman wore one.

• *Get lost. Don't worry, you'll eventually spill back out onto the busy street. Return to Prince Henry's Room, which marks the spot where the Strand becomes...*

8. Fleet Street

"The Street" was the notorious haunt of a powerful combination—lawyers and the media. In 1500, Wynkyn de Worde moved here with a new-fangled invention, a printing press—making it the center of an early Information Age. In 1702, the first daily newspaper appeared. Soon you had *The Tatler*, *The Spectator*, and many others pumping out both hard news and paparazzi gossip for the hungry masses.

London became the nerve center of a global, colonial empire, and Fleet Street was where every twitch found expression. Hard-drinking, ink-stained reporters gathered in taverns and coffee-

houses, pumping lawyers for juicy pre-trial information, scrambling for that choice bit of must-read gossip that would make their paper number one.

Today, busy Fleet Street bustles with almost every business except newspapers. The industry made a mass exodus in the 1980s for offices elsewhere, replaced by financial institutions. You'll see the former offices of the *Daily Telegraph* (135 Fleet Street) and the *Daily Express* (#121–28). The one major institution that stayed is the Reuters news agency (#85).

• *Continue east on Fleet Street. A half-block past Fetter Lane, turn left (at #167) down a covered alleyway. Follow brown signs directing you to Dr. Johnson's House.*

9. Narrow Lanes—The Great Fire

"Sir, if you wish to have a just notion of the magnitude of this city, you must... survey the innumerable little lanes and courts," said the writer Samuel Johnson to his young friend and biographer, James Boswell (1763). These twisting alleyways and cramped buildings that house urban hobbits give a glimpse of post-fire, 1700s London.

The Great Fire of 1666 started near London Bridge. For three days it swept westward, fanned by hot and blustery weather, leveling everything in its path, until it finally burned itself out near here. (Fetter Lane marks the west border. For more on the fire, see Bankside Walk, page 64.) On this walk, we pass through the entire expanse of the fire zone, a mile long, from here to London Bridge, giving an idea of the scope of the devastation.

After the fire, wood structures were outlawed, but The City was rebuilt along the same medieval street plan, resulting in narrow lanes of brick structures like these.

• *The narrow lanes eventually spill into Gough Square, about a block north of Fleet Street, where you'll find...*

10. Dr. Johnson's House (4 Gough Square)

"When a man is tired of London, he is tired of life," wrote Samuel Johnson, "for there is in London all that life can afford." Johnson (1709–84) loved to wander these twisting lanes, looking for pungent slices of London street life that he could pass along in his weekly columns called "The Rambler" and "The Idler."

At age 28, Johnson arrived in London with one of his former

students, just as the city of half a million was becoming aware of itself. The student, David Garrick, went on to revolutionize London theater, while Doctor Johnson prowled the pubs, brothels, and coffee houses, and the illicit gaming pits where terriers battled cornered rats while men bet on the outcome. Johnson—"tall, stout," "slovenly in his dress"—became a well-known eccentric and man-about-town, though he always seemed to live on the fringes of poverty.

Johnson inhabited this house from 1748 to 1759. He prayed at St. Clement Danes, drank in Fleet Street pubs, and, in the attic of the house, produced his most famous work. In 1755, he published the first great dictionary of the English language, starring Johnson's 41,000 favorite words. It took him and six assistants more than six years of sifting through all the alternate spellings and Cockney dialects of the world's most complex language.

Today, the house is a museum (£4) for hard-core Johnson fans (I met one once), featuring period furniture, pictures of Johnson and Boswell, a video, and a first edition of his dictionary.
* *At the other end of Gough Square, turn right at the cat and head back towards Fleet Street and...*

11. Ye Olde Cheshire Cheese Tavern
Johnson often—and I do mean often—popped round here for a quick one, sometimes with David Garrick and his sleazy actor friends.

"The Cheese" dates from 1667, when it was rebuilt after the Great Fire. It's a warren of small, smoky rooms, each offering different menus, from pub grub to sit-down meals.

Cozy up to the Cheese's fireplace (in the small room along Fleet Street), order a steak and kidney pie and some spotted dick (sponge pudding with currants), and think of others who have sat exactly here— lawyers and reporters taking power lunches, Charles Dickens, Alfred Lord Tennyson, Arthur Conan Doyle, W. B. Yeats, and Mark Twain.
* *Back out on Fleet Street, you're met with a stunning...*

12. View of St. Paul's—the Blitz, the Great Fire, the Plague, and Christopher Wren
If you were standing here on December 30, 1940, the morning after a German Luftwaffe firebomb raid, you'd see nothing but a flat, smoldering landscape of rubble, with St. Paul's rising above it, almost miraculously intact. (For more on the Blitz, see page 199 .)

The Great Fire

The stones of St. Paul's flew like grenades, the lead melting down the streets in a stream.... God grant mine eyes may never behold the like.... Above 10,000 homes all in one flame, the noise and crackling and thunder of the impetuous flames, the shrieking of women and children, the hurry of the people, the fall of the towers, houses and churches was like an hideous storm.

—John Evelyn, eyewitness

Standing here in September 1666, you'd see nothing but smoke and ruins. The Great Fire razed everything, including the original St. Paul's Cathedral. And standing here in 1665, you'd hear "Bring out yer dead!" as they carted away 70,000 victims of bubonic plague. After the double-whammy of plague and fire, the architect Christopher Wren was hired to rebuild St. Paul's and The City.

Even today, we see the view that Wren intended—a majestic dome hovering above the hazy rooftops, surrounded by the thin spires of his lesser churches. Two of Wren's original 51 churches are nearby. In the foreground below St. Paul's is the slender, lead-covered steeple of St. Martin-within-Ludgate, perfectly offsetting the more massive dome. Immediately to your right, a half-block down Carpenter Street, is the stacked-tier steeple of St. Bride's, which inspired a local baker to invent the wedding cake.

The valley in between you and St. Paul's is where the Fleet River—now covered over with concrete—flows southward, crossing underneath Fleet Street on its way to the Thames at Blackfriar's Bridge. In medieval times, the river formed the western boundary of the walled city.

• *Continue on toward St. Paul's, crossing the valley. Look left down Old Bailey Street to see...*

13. The Old Bailey—Central Criminal Court

England's nastiest criminals—from the king-killers of the Civil War to the radically religious William Penn, from the criminally homosexual Oscar Wilde to the Yorkshire Ripper—are tried here in Britain's highest criminal court. On top of the copper dome stands the famous golden Lady who weighs and executes Justice with scale and sword. The Old Bailey is built on the former site of Newgate Prison, with its notorious execution-by-hanging site. Inside, you can visit courtrooms and watch justice doled out the old-fashioned way (see page 41 in Sights chapter). Bewigged barristers argue before stern judges while the accused sits in the dock.

• *Continue up Ludgate Hill to...*

14. St. Paul's Cathedral

✪ See St. Paul's Tour, page 194.

• *From St. Paul's, the most direct route to London Bridge is to continue east on what is now called Cannon Street. But we'll go east on Cheapside, located behind St. Paul's.*

15. Cheapside—Shakespeare's London

This was the main east-west street of Shakespeare's London, which had a population of about 200,000. The wide street hosted The City's marketplace ("cheap" meant market), seen today in the names of the streets that branch off from it: Bread Street, Milk, Honey. Rebuilt after the war, Cheapside today does a different type of business, with concrete-and-glass banks and Ye Olde Starbuckes.

At the intersection of Cheapside and Bread Street, you will not see the **Mermaid Tavern,** Shakespeare's favorite haunt ("What things have we seen/Done at the Mermaid!"), but this is where it stood.

• *A little farther east along Cheapside is...*

16. St. Mary-le-Bow

From London's earliest Christian times, a church has stood here. The steeple of St. Mary-le-Bow (pron. MAR-ly-bo), rebuilt after the fire, is one of Wren's most impressive. Appropriately, he incorporated ribbed arches (a "bow" is an arch) in the steeple's mid-section. Inside the church, see not one but two pulpits, used for point-counterpoint debate of moral issues.

The church's bells chime at the very center of old London. This is the "Cockney" neighborhood of plucky streetwise urchins, where a distinctive Eliza Doolittle dialect is still sometimes spoken. Buy a newspaper and see if the man calls you "guv'nah."

• *Behind Mary-le-Bow church is...*

17. Bow Lane

Today, pedestrian-only Bow Lane features smart clothing shops, sandwich bars, and pubs. The entire City once had narrow lanes like Bow, Watling, and Bread Streets. Explore this area between Cheapside and Cannon Street.

When Shakespeare bought his tights and pointy shoes in Bow Lane, the shops were wood, the streets were dirt, and the bathroom was a ditch down the middle of the road. (The garbage brought rats, and rats brought plagues, like the one in 1665.) You bought your water in buckets carted up from the Thames. And at night, the bellman walked the streets, ringing the hour.

(For more Shakespearean ambience, it's a three-block walk south from St. Paul's to the river, where the Millennium Bridge crosses the Thames to Shakespeare's Globe, a reconstruction of Shakespeare's Globe Theatre. See Bankside Walk, page 64.)
• *Continue east on Cheapside a few blocks to the long, wide intersection where nine streets meet (Tube: Bank).*

18. Bank of England

You're at the center of financial London. Pan left to right to see three neoclassical buildings (with Greek columns and triangular pediments) that sum up The City: the huge Bank of England (at 10 o'clock, with entrance facing onto Threadneedle Street), the Royal Exchange (at 11 o'clock, with entrance facing you), and Mansion House (at 2 o'clock).

The **Bank of England** is the country's national bank. In 1694, it loaned money to the king, and has managed the national debt ever since. It oversees the printing of pounds; serves as the country's Fort Knox, housing stacks of gold bars; and has a free museum inside (enter from far side, on St. Bartholomew Lane).

The **Royal Exchange** was the original stock exchange, back when "stock" meant whatever could be loaded and unloaded onto a boat in the Thames. Remember, London got its start as a river-trading town. Soon, they were gathering here, trading slips of paper and "futures" in place of live goats and chickens. Traders needed money-changers, who needed bankers... and London's financial district boomed. Today, the Stock Exchange has moved a half-block farther east on Threadneedle Street.

Mansion House is the official residence of The City's Lord Mayor. Until recently (when an all-London mayor was elected), each district was self-governing. Even today, the Lord Mayor holds a prestigious office, presiding from this palatial building.
• *From Bank, turn right and head southeast down King William Street, leading to London Bridge. Near the northeast corner of the bridge, find a lone column poking its bristly bronze head above the modern rooftops.*

19. The Monument

The 202-foot hollow column is Wren's tribute to the Great Fire that gave him a blank canvas on which to create modern London. At 2:00 in the morning of September 2, 1666, a small fire broke out in a baker's oven in nearby Pudding Lane. Supposedly, if you tipped The Monument over (to the east), it would fall on the exact spot. Fanned by hot, blustery weather, the fire swept westward, leaping from house to house until The City was a square mile of flame. For three days it burned, leaving a Sodom-and-Gomorrah wasteland that was so hot it couldn't be walked on for weeks.

You can climb the 311 steps up the column for a view that's still pretty good, despite modern buildings.

20. London Bridge

End our walk at The City's beginning. (For the history of London Bridge, see page 66 of the Bankside Walk chapter.)

The City was born as a river-trading town. The Thames carried goods east-to-west, from the interior of England to the open seas. London Bridge, first built by the ancient Romans, established a north-south axis. Soon, goods from every corner of the world were pouring into this, the modern world's first great urban center. Surviving fires, blitzes, and Thatcherism, with its worldwide financial network and cultural heritage, The City thrives.

• *From here, the Tower of London (see page 210) is a 15-minute walk east, down either Eastcheap or Lower Thames Street. The Bankside Walk (page 64) begins across London Bridge. You can return to Trafalgar Square on the Tube (Monument stop nearby) or a sightseeing boat.*

WEST END
WALK

The West End, the area at the west end of the original walled City of London, is London's liveliest neighborhood. Theaters, pubs, restaurants, bookstores, ethnic food, markets, and boutiques attract rock stars, gays, hippies, punks, tourists, and ladies and gentlemen stepping from black cabs for a night on the town.

Allow an hour for this one-mile walk, threading through the heart of the West End and the neighborhood of Soho. From Leicester Square (Tube: Leicester Square), we'll head east to Covent Garden, then north on shop-lined Neal Street, then west along Soho's Old Compton Street, ending at Piccadilly Circus. Use the walk to get the lay of the land, then go explore—especially in the evening, when the neon glitters and London gets funky.

1. Leicester Square

Orient from the top (north) end of sloping Leicester (pron. LES-ter) Square. A few blocks to the west is Piccadilly, to the south is Trafalgar Square (and, way beyond that, Big Ben), to the east is Covent Garden. The neighborhood north of the square is trendy Soho. Gerrard Street, just two blocks north of Leicester Square, is the center of Chinatown, lined with decent-quality, inexpensive Chinese (mostly Cantonese cuisine) restaurants.

Leicester Square itself is, by day, the central clearinghouse for theater tickets. When the neon ignites after dark, it hosts movie premiers and partying teens from the suburbs.

• *To get to Covent Garden, we'll take the most obvious route (though there are more scenic ones). Head east on Cranbourn Street (which becomes Long Street), then turn right on James Street. You'll enter a large square with a covered marketplace in the center.*

West End Walk

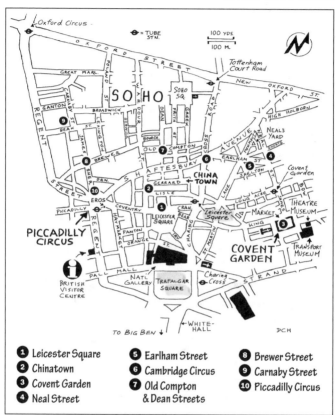

① Leicester Square
② Chinatown
③ Covent Garden
④ Neal Street

⑤ Earlham Street
⑥ Cambridge Circus
⑦ Old Compton
   & Dean Streets

⑧ Brewer Street
⑨ Carnaby Street
⑩ Piccadilly Circus

2. Covent Garden

Originally the produce market for a ritzy housing development
(built in the 1630s by neoclassical architect Inigo Jones), in the
1980s it was converted to boutiques, cafés, and antiques shops. If
you catch a whiff of marijuana smoke, don't call the cops—Britain
recently decriminalized the substance, so (sorry) you can't arrest
the degenerates for possessing small amounts for personal use.

Surrounding the market are street performers, St. Paul's
Cathedral, the London Transport Museum (see page 35), the
Theatre Museum (see page 205), and the Royal Opera House
(entrance on Bow Street). Two blocks east down Russell Street
is one of London's oldest, biggest, and most historic theaters,
the Theatre Royal, on Drury Lane.

• *Head north (uphill) on James Street, which (after a jog to the right) becomes Neal Street.*

3. Neal Street

This busy pedestrian-only street is lined with clothing shops and boutiques. For fun and earthy food (though this walk doesn't go quite that far), check out Neal's Yard, close to where Neal Street intersects Short Gardens Street.

• *From Neal Street, turn left and head west on Earlham Street (the turn is not obvious; it's near where Neal Street intersects Shelton Street).*

4. Earlham Street

You'll pass the recommended Belgo Centraal restaurant (see page 286), cut-flower stands (by day), theaters, shops, and the "Seven Dials" intersection (of seven small streets). You'll emerge into the heavy traffic of the busy, round intersection called...

5. Cambridge Circus

This is the center of the theater district, where Shaftesbury Avenue (running east–west) crosses Charing Cross Road (north–south). The Palace Theatre *(Les Miserables)* is the first of five big theaters stretching west along Shaftesbury. Book-lovers will browse Charing Cross Road, traditional home of bookstores.

• *Cross kitty-corner to the other side of the intersection. Continue west (keeping to the right of the Palace Theatre) on Moor Street, which becomes...*

6. Old Compton Street

Welcome to Soho, which stretches from Charing Cross Road westward to Regent Street, and from Leicester Square and Piccadilly in the south to Oxford Street in the north. ("Soho" was a hunting-cry back when this area consisted of fields.) The restaurants and boutiques here and on adjoining streets are trendy and gay, the kind that attract high society when it feels like slumming it. A right on Frith Street leads to the green lawn of (somewhat-seedy) Soho Square.

Where Old Compton meets Dean Street is perhaps the center of the neighborhood. Just stand and observe the variety of people going by. South of here is Chinatown and Leicester Square, and you're surrounded by the buzz of Soho.

• *Continue west, to where Old Compton Street squeezes down into a narrow alley. Penetrate this sleazy passage, then jog a half-block right and continue west on Brewer Street.*

7. Brewer Street
Sex shops, video arcades, and (illegal) prostitution mingle with
upscale restaurants as we enter the lower-class west Soho.
Berwick Street hosts a daily produce market.
• *At Sherwood Street (also called Lower James Street), a left turn takes
you south to Piccadilly Circus, a block away. But seniors may consider
taking a detour right (north) and walking two blocks to ...*

8. Carnaby Street
In the Swinging '60s, when Pete Townsend needed a paisley
shirt, or John Lennon a Nehru jacket, or Twiggy a miniskirt,
they came here—where those mod fashions were invented.

Today, it looks like everything else from the '60s—sanitized
and co-opted by upscale franchises. (But I do like Lush, a bath-
products store that has somehow spread world-wide while missing
the United States.) From Carnaby Street, it's another block north
to the Oxford Circus Tube station.
• *Back at the intersection of Brewer and Sherwood streets, head south
on Sherwood Street one block to ...*

9. Piccadilly Circus
At night, when neon pulses, the black cabs honk, and people
crowd the attractions, Piccadilly shows off big-city London
at its glitziest.

BRITISH MUSEUM TOUR

In the 19th century, the British flag flew over one-fourth of the world. London was the world's capital, where women in saris walked the streets with men in top hats. And England collected art as fast as it collected colonies. In the British Museum, you'll see much of the world's greatest art from ancient Egypt, Assyria, and Greece.

The British Museum is *the* chronicle of Western civilization. History is a modern invention. Three hundred years ago, people didn't care about crumbling statues and dusty columns. Nowadays, we value a look at past civilizations, knowing that "those who don't learn from history are condemned to repeat it."

The British Museum is the only place I know where you can follow the rise and fall of three great civilizations in a few hours with a coffee break in the middle. And, while the sun never set on the British Empire, it will on you, so on this tour we'll see just the most exciting two hours.

Orientation

Cost: Free, but £2 donation requested. If you can afford it, donate.
Hours: The **British Museum** is open daily 10:00–17:30, plus Thu–Fri until 20:30 (but from 17:30–20:30, only selected galleries and the Reading Room are open). On the first Tuesday of the month, the gallery offers evening tours, lectures, and music (£5, 18:00–21:00). The museum is closed on Good Friday, Dec 24–26, and Jan 1. Rainy days and Sundays always get me down because they're most crowded (the museum is least crowded late on weekday afternoons, particularly on Mon).

The **Great Court**—the grand entrance with eateries, gift shops, an exhibit gallery, and the Reading Room—has longer opening hours than the museum (daily 9:00–18:00, Thu–Sat until 23:00).

The **Reading Room,** located within the Great Court, is free

British Museum Overview

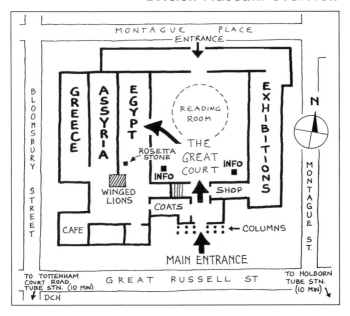

and open to the quiet public (daily 12:30–17:30, Thu–Fri until
20:30, may change opening to 10:30 in 2003). Computer terminals
within the Reading Room offer COMPASS, a database of information about selected museum items; see "Information," below.
The Reading Room viewing area opens at 10:00.

During 2003, the Museum's 250th anniversary, look for
special exhibits in the newly revamped **King's Library,** in the
east wing of the building.

Getting There: The main entrance is on Great Russell Street.
Take the Tube to Tottenham Court Road or Holborn, four blocks
from the museum. You have your choice of buses: #7, #8, #10, #19,
#24, #25, #29, #38, #55, #68, #73, #91, #98, #134, #188, or #242.
Taxis are reasonable if you buddy up.

Information: The information desks just inside the Great Court
sell museum plans for £2.50. For a schedule of the museum's
frequent tours (see "Tours," below), ask at the desk or call the
museum (tel. 020/7323-8000, recorded information 020/7388-
2227, www.thebritishmuseum.ac.uk).

For **books,** consider the main bookstore (just behind the
Reading Room) or The Museum Bookshop (across the street at
36 Great Russell Street).

To take a virtual-reality tour or plot the shortest route to the particular items you want to see, study ahead using COMPASS (www.thebritishmuseum.ac.uk/compass) or access this site online at the terminals in the Reading Room (free). For an educational Web site with some kid appeal, try the museum's www.ancientegypt.co.uk.

Tours: There are three guided tours: Highlights (£8, children under 11 and students with ID £5, 3/day, 90 min), Focus (£5, 1/day, 60 min), and eyeOpeners (free, nearly hrly, 50 min).

There are also three types of audioguide tours: top 50 highlights (90 min, pick up at Great Court information desks), the Parthenon Sculptures (60 min, pick up at desk outside Parthenon Galleries), and the family tour, with themes such as "bodies, boardgames, and beasts" (length varies, pick up at Great Court information desks). To rent an audioguide (£3.50, £2.50 for children under 13), you'll need to leave a photo ID and £10 for a deposit.

Length of Our Tour: 2 hours.

Cloakroom: You can carry a daybag in the galleries, but big backpacks are not allowed. If the line is long and not moving, the cloakroom may be full (£1 per item).

Photography: Photos allowed without a flash. No tripods.

No-no's: No eating, drinking, smoking, or gum-chewing in the galleries.

Cuisine Art: You have three choices inside the complex. In the Great Court, you'll find the Court Café (on the main level) as well as the pricier Court Restaurant (on the upper floor). Within the museum, the Gallery Café is located off Room 12 (the Greek section). There are lots of fast, cheap, and colorful cafés, pubs, and markets along Great Russell Street. No picnicking is allowed inside the Great Court or the museum. Karl Marx snacked on the benches near the entrance and in Russell Square.

Starring: Rosetta Stone, Egyptian mummies, Assyrian lions, and Elgin Marbles.

The Tour Begins

Enter through the main entrance on Great Russell Street. Ahead is the Great Court (with the round Reading Room in the center), providing access to all wings. To the left are the exhibits on Egypt, Assyria, and Greece—our tour. You'll notice that this tour does not follow the museum's numbered sequence of rooms. Instead, we'll try to hit the highlights as we work chronologically.

Enjoy the museum's recent face-lift. The Great Court is Europe's largest covered square, bigger than a football field. This people-friendly court—delightfully out of the London rain—was for 150 years one of London's great lost spaces ...closed off and gathering dust. Now it's the 140-foot-wide glass-domed hub of a two-acre

The Ancient World

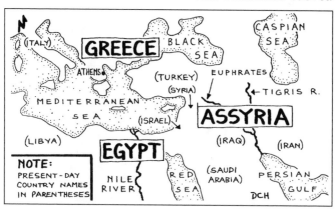

cultural complex. While the vast British Museum wraps around the court, its centerpiece is the stately Reading Room, a study hall for Oscar Wilde, Arthur Conan Doyle, Rudyard Kipling, T. S. Eliot, Virginia Woolf, and W. B. Yeats, and for Karl Marx while formulating his ideas on Communism and writing *Das Kapital*.

• *The Egyptian Gallery is in the West Wing, to the left of the round Reading Room. Enter the Egyptian Gallery and immediately turn left. The Rosetta Stone is at the far end of the gallery.*

EGYPT (3000 B.C.–A.D. 1)

Egypt was one of the world's first "civilizations," that is, a group of people with a government, religion, art, free time, and a written language. The Egypt we think of—pyramids, mummies, pharaohs, and guys who walk funny—lasted from 3000 to 1000 B.C. with hardly any change in the government, religion, or arts. Imagine two millennia of Eisenhower.

The Rosetta Stone (196 B.C.)

When this rock was unearthed in the Egyptian desert in 1799, it caused a sensation in Europe. Picture a pack of scientists (I think of the apes in that scene from *2001: A Space Odyssey*) screeching with amazement and poking curiously with their fingers. This black slab caused a quantum leap in the evolution of history. Finally, Egyptian writing could be decoded.

The writing in the upper part of the stone is known as hieroglyphics. For a thousand years, no one knew how to read this mysterious ancient language. Did a picture of a bird mean "bird"? Or was it a sound, forming part of a larger word, like "burden"? As it

Egypt

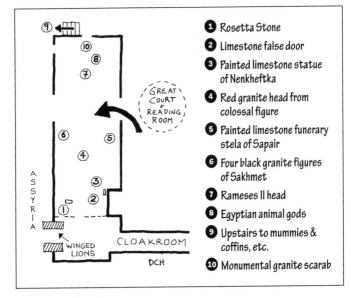

1. Rosetta Stone
2. Limestone false door
3. Painted limestone statue of Nenkheftka
4. Red granite head from colossal figure
5. Painted limestone funerary stela of Sapair
6. Four black granite figures of Sakhmet
7. Rameses II head
8. Egyptian animal gods
9. Upstairs to mummies & coffins, etc.
10. Monumental granite scarab

turned out, hieroglyphics are a complex combination of the two, surprisingly more phonetic than symbolic.

The Rosetta Stone allowed scientists to break the code. It contains a single inscription repeated in three languages. The bottom third is plain old Greek (find your favorite frat or sorority), while the middle is more modern Egyptian. By comparing the two known languages with the one they didn't know, they figured it out.

The breakthrough came from the large oval in the sixth line from the top. They discovered that the bird symbol represented the sound *a*, part of the name Cleo-pa-tra. Simple.

• *On the wall opposite the Rosetta Stone, you'll find the . . .*

Limestone False Door (c. 2400 B.C.)

In ancient Egypt, you could take it with you. They believed that after you died, your soul lived on, enjoying its earthly possessions. This small statue represents the soul of a dead man.

It decorated his tomb, which contained all that he'd need in the next life: his mummified body, a résumé of his accomplishments

on earth, and his possessions—sometimes including his servants, who might be buried alive with their master. The great pyramids, besides being psychic UFO power stations, were also elaborate tombs for the rich and powerful. But most tombs were small rectangular rooms of brick or stone.

"False doors" like this were slapped on the outside of the tomb. The soul of the deceased, like the statue, could come and go through the "door" as it pleased—but grave robbers couldn't. The deceased's relatives placed food outside the door to nourish spirits who woke up in the middle of eternity with the munchies.

• *Just a few steps further down the gallery (as you backtrack toward the entrance), in a glass case on the right, look for the ...*

Painted Limestone Statue of Nenkheftka (2400 B.C.)

After a snack, the soul might wander through the nether lands (somewhere north of Belgium) searching for paradise, meeting strange beings and weird situations. If things got too hairy, the

soul could always find temporary refuge in statues like this one. (The rich scattered statues of themselves everywhere, in case their soul needed a safe resting place.)

This statue, like most Egyptian art, is not terribly lifelike—the figure is stiff, hands at the sides, left leg forward, masklike face with almond eyes, stylized anatomy, and an out-of-date skirt. And talk about uptight—he's got a column down his back! But it does have all the essential features, like the simplified human figures on international traffic signs. To a soul caught in the fast lane of astral travel, this symbolic statue would be easier to spot than a detailed one.

With their fervent hope for life after death, Egyptians created calm, dignified art that seems built for eternity.

• *Head past two tall columns that give a sense of the grandeur of the Egyptian temples. Find a huge head with a hat like a broken bowling pin.*

Red Granite Head from a Colossal Figure of a King (c. 1350 B.C.)

Art also served as propaganda for the pharaohs, kings who called themselves gods on earth. Put this head on top of an enormous

body (which still stands in Egypt), and you have the intimidating image of an omnipotent ruler who demands servile obedience. Next to the head is, appropriately, the pharaoh's powerful fist—the long arm of the law.

The crown is actually two crowns in one. The pointed upper half is the royal cap of Upper Egypt. This rests on the flat, fez-like crown symbolizing Lower Egypt. A pharaoh wearing both crowns together is bragging that he rules a united Egypt.

Egyptian society's two main concerns—church and state— were united in the person of the pharaoh.

• *On the wall to the right of the Red Granite Head, you'll see three painted stelas. The biggest of these is the...*

Painted Limestone Funerary Stela of Sapair

These people walk like Egyptian statues look—stiff. They're flat, like they were just run over by a pyramid. We see his torso from the front and everything else—arms, legs, face—in profile, creating the funny walk that has become an Egyptian cliché.

But the stiffness is softened by a human touch. It's a family scrapbook; snapshots of loved ones from a happy time to be remembered for all eternity. In the upper half, Mr. Sapair worships the god Osiris (with pointed hat). Below, tanned Sapair relaxes with his pale wife while their children prepare a picnic. Their tiny son sniffs a flower, and their daughter crouches beneath her parents—a symbol of protection. When Sapair's winged spirit finally left his body (very top of stela), he could look at this painting on the tomb wall and think of his wife just like this... with her arms around him and a smile on her face.

• *On the opposite wall are four black, lion-headed statues.*

Four Black Granite Figures of the Goddess Sakhmet (1400 B.C.)

This goddess was a good one to have on your side. She looks pretty sedate here, but this lion-headed woman could spring into a fierce crouch when crossed.

The gods ruled the Egyptian cosmos like dictators in a big banana republic (or the American Congress). Egyptians bribed their

gods for favors, offering food, animals, or money, or by erecting statues like these to them.

Notice the ankh that Sakhmet is holding. This key-shaped cross was the hieroglyph meaning "life" and was a symbol of eternal life. Later, it was adopted as a Christian symbol because of its cross shape and religious overtones.

• *Continue on to the eight-foot-tall granite head and torso.*

Upper Half of Colossal Statue of Rameses II of Granite (1270 B.C.)

When Moses told the king of Egypt, "Let my people go!" this was the stony-faced look he got. Rameses II (reigned c. 1290–23 B.C.) was likely in power when Moses freed the Israeli slaves, leading them out of Egypt to their homeland in Israel. According to the Bible, Moses, a former Egyptian prince himself, asked pharaoh to let them go peacefully. When the pharaoh refused, Moses cursed the land with a series of plagues. Finally, the Israelites just bolted with the help of their God, Yahweh, who drowned the Egyptian armies in the Red Sea. Egyptian records don't exactly corroborate the tale, but this Rameses looks enough like Yul Brynner in *The Ten Commandments* to make me a believer.

This statue, made from two different colors of granite, is a fragment from a temple in Thebes. Rameses was a great builder of temples, palaces, tombs, and statues of himself. There are probably more statues of him in the world than there are cheesy fake *David*s. He was so concerned about achieving immortality that he even chiseled his own name on other people's statues. Very cheeky.

Picture what the archaeologists saw when they came upon this: a colossal head and torso separated from the enormous legs and toppled into the sand—all that remained of the works of a once-great pharaoh. Kings, megalomaniacs, and workaholics, take note.

• *Say, "Ooh, heavy," and climb the ramp behind Rameses, looking for animals.*

Various Egyptian Gods as Animals

Before technology made humans the alpha animal on earth, it was easier to appreciate our fellow creatures. Animals were stronger, swifter, or more fierce than puny *Homo sapiens.* The Egyptians worshiped animals as incarnations of the gods.

The powerful ram is the god Amun (king of the gods),

protecting a puny pharaoh under his powerful chin. The clever baboon is Thoth, the god of wisdom. Horus, the god of the living, has a falcon's head. The standing hippo is Tawaret, protectress of childbirth. Her stylized breasts and pregnant belly are supported by ankhs, symbols of life. (Is Tawaret grinning or grimacing in labor?)

• *You can't call Egypt a wrap until you visit the mummies upstairs. If you can handle 72 stairs (if not, return to Rosetta Stone and start Assyria section—below), continue to the end of the gallery past the giant stone scarab (beetle) and up the stairs. At the top, take a left (into Room 61), then a right into Room 62. Browse through Rooms 62 and 63, with glass cases full of...*

Mummies, Coffins, Canopic Jars, and Statuettes— The Egyptian Funeral

To mummify a body, disembowel it, pack the cavities with pitch or other substances, and dry it with natron, a natural form of sodium carbonate (and, I believe, the active ingredient in Twinkies). Then carefully bandage it head to toe with fine linen strips. Let it sit 2,000 years, and...voilà! Or just dump the corpse in the desert and let the hot, dry Egyptian sand do the work—you'll get the same results.

The mummy was placed in a wooden coffin which was put in a stone coffin, which was placed in a tomb. (Remember that the pyramids were just big tombs.)

The result is that we now have Egyptian bodies that are as well preserved as Dick Clark.

The internal organs were preserved alongside in canopic jars, and small-scale statuettes of the deceased were scattered around. Written in hiero-glyphs on the coffins and the tomb walls (see the reconstructed murals on the museum walls) were burial rites from the Book of the Dead. These were magical spells to protect the body and crib notes for the waking soul, who needed to know these passwords to get past the guardians of eternity.

Many of the mummies here are from the time of the Roman occupation, when they painted a fine portrait in wax on the wrapping. X-ray photos in the display cases tell us more about these people.

Don't miss the animal mummies. Cats were incarnations of the goddess Bastet. Worshipped in life, preserved in death, and memorialized with statues, cats were given the adulation they've come to expect ever since.

• *Linger in Room 62 and 63, but remember that eternity is about the amount of time it takes to see this entire museum. In Room 64, in a glass case, you'll find . . .*

"Ginger" (Naturally preserved body)

This man died 5,400 years ago, a thousand years before the pyramids. His people buried him in the fetal position, where he could "sleep" for eternity. The hot sand naturally dehydrated and preserved the body. With him are a few of his possessions: vases, beads, and the flint blade next to his arm. Named "Ginger" by scientists for his wisps of red hair, this man from a distant time seems very human.

• *Head back down the stairs to the Egyptian Gallery, returning to the huge stone beetle in the center of the room near the foot of the stairs.*

Monumental Granite Scarab (200 B.C.)

This species of beetle would burrow into the ground, then reappear—like the sun rising and setting, or dying and rebirth, a symbol of resurrection.

Like the scarab, Egyptian culture was buried—first by Greece, then by Rome. Knowledge of the ancient writing died, condemning the culture to obscurity. But since the discovery of the Rosetta Stone, Egyptology is booming, and Egypt has come back to life.

• *Backtrack to the Rosetta Stone. Next to the Stone are two huge, winged Assyrian lions (with bearded human heads), standing guard over the exhibit halls.*

ASSYRIA (1000–600 B.C.)

Assyria was the lion, the king of beasts of early Middle Eastern civilizations. From its base in northern Mesopotamia (northern Iraq), it conquered and dominated the Middle East—from Israel to Iran—for more than three centuries. The Assyrians were a nation of warriors—hardy, disciplined, and often cruel conquistadors—whose livelihood depended on booty and slash-and-burn expansion.

Assyria

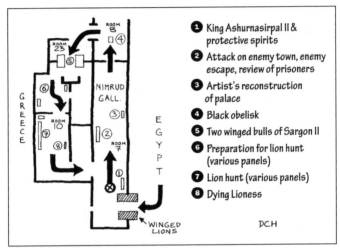

① King Ashurnasirpal II & protective spirits

② Attack on enemy town, enemy escape, review of prisoners

③ Artist's reconstruction of palace

④ Black obelisk

⑤ Two winged bulls of Sargon II

⑥ Preparation for lion hunt (various panels)

⑦ Lion hunt (various panels)

⑧ Dying Lioness

DCH

Two Winged Lions with Human Heads (c. 870 B.C.)

These lions stood guard at key points in Assyrian palaces to intimidate enemies and defeated peoples. With lion body, eagle wings, and human head, these magical beasts—and therefore the Assyrian people—had the strength of a lion, the speed of an eagle, the brain of a man, and the beard of ZZ Top. They protected the palace from evil spirits, and scared the heck out of foreign ambassadors and left-wing newspaper reporters. (What has five legs and flies? Take a close look. These quintupeds, which appear complete from both the front and the side, could guard both directions at once.)

Carved into the stone between the bearded lions' loins, you can see one of civilization's most impressive achievements—writing. This wedge-shaped ("cuneiform") script is the world's first written language, invented 5,000 years ago by the Sumerians and passed down to their less-civilized descendants, the Assyrians.

• *Walk between the lions, glance at the large reconstructed wooden gates from an Assyrian palace, and turn right into the narrow red gallery (Room 7) lined with brown relief panels.*

Nimrud Gallery (Ninth century B.C.)

This gallery is a mini version of the main hall of Ashurnasirpal II's palace. It was decorated with these pleasant sand-colored gypsum relief panels (which were, however, originally painted).

That's Ashurnasirpal himself in the first panel on your right, with braided beard and fez-like crown, flanked by his supernatural hawk-headed henchmen, who sprinkle incense on him with pine-cones. The bulging forearms tell us that Ashurnasirpal was a conqueror's conqueror who enjoyed his reputation as a savage, merciless warrior who tortured and humiliated the vanquished. The room's panels chronicle his bloody career.

The cuneiform inscription running through the center of the panel is Ashurnasirpal's résumé: "The king who has enslaved all mankind, the mighty warrior who steps on the necks of his enemies, tramples all foes and shatters the enemy; the weapon of the gods, the mighty king, the King of Assyria, the king of the world, B.A., M.B.A., Ph.D., etc...."

• *Thirty feet farther down, on your left, you'll find an upper panel labeled...*

Attack on an Enemy Town

Many "nations" conquered by the Assyrians consisted of little more than a single walled city. Here, the Assyrians lay siege with a crude "tank" that shields them as they advance to the city walls to smash down the gate with a battering ram. The king stands a safe distance away behind the juggernaut and bravely shoots arrows.

• *In the next panel to the right, you'll find...*

Enemy Escape

Soldiers flee the slings and arrows of outrageous Assyrians by swimming across the Euphrates, using inflated animal bladders as life preservers. Their friends in the castle downstream applaud their ingenuity.

• *Below, you'll see . . .*

Review of Prisoners

The Assyrian economy depended on booty. Here, a conquered nation is paraded before the Assyrian king, who is shaded by a parasol. Ashurnasirpal sneers and tells the captured chief, "Drop and give me 50." Above the prisoners' heads, we see the rich spoils of war—elephant tusks, metal pots, and so on. The Assyrians depopulated conquered lands by slavery and ethnic cleansing, then repopulated with Assyrian settlers.

• *Notice the painted reconstruction of the palace on the opposite wall, then find the black obelisk in the next room (Room 8).*

Black Obelisk of Shalmaneser III (c. 840 B.C.)

The cruel Assyrians demanded that the vanquished people pay tribute once every year (on April 15, I believe). The obelisk shows people bringing tribute to Shalmaneser from all corners of the empire. The second band from the top shows the Israelites carrying their offerings to the king and prostrating before him. Parts of Israel were under Assyrian domination from the ninth century B.C. on. Old Testament prophets such as Elijah and Elisha constantly warned their people of the corrupting influence of the Assyrian gods.

Also check out the third band, with its parade of exotic animals, especially the missing-link monkeys.

• *Hang a U-turn left (through Room 23) and pause at the entrance of Room 10 to see . . .*

Two Winged Bulls from the Khorsabad Palace of Sargon II (c. 710 B.C.)

These 30-ton marble bulls guarded the entrance of the palace of Sargon II. And, speaking of large amounts of bull, "Sargon" wasn't his real name. It's obvious to savvy historians that Sargon must have been an insecure usurper to the throne, since the name meant "true king."

• *Sneak between these bulls and veer right (into Room 10), where horses are being readied for the big hunt.*

Royal Lion Hunts

Lion-hunting was Assyria's sport
of kings. On the right wall, we see
horses being readied for the hunt.
On the left wall, hunting dogs.
And next to them, lions, resting
peacefully in a garden, unaware
that they will shortly be rousted,
stampeded, and slaughtered.

Lions lived in Mesopotamia up until modern times, and it had
long been the duty of kings to keep the lion population down to
protect farmers and herdsmen. This duty soon became sport as the
kings of men proved their power by taking on the king of beasts.
They actually bred lions so they could stage hunts. As we'll see,
these "hunts" were as sporting as shooting fish in a barrel. The
last Assyrian kings had grown soft and decadent, hardly the raging
warriors of Ashurnasirpal's time.

• *Enter the larger lion-hunt room. Reading the panels like a comic strip,
start on the right and gallop counterclockwise.*

The Lion-Hunt Room (c. 650 B.C.)

They release the lions from
their cages, then soldiers on
horseback herd them into an
enclosed arena. The king has
them cornered. Let the slaugh-
ter begin. The chariot carries
decrepit King Ashurbanipal.
The last of Assyria's great

kings, he's ruled now for 50 years. He shoots the wrong way while
spearmen hold off lions attacking from the rear.

• *At about the middle of the long wall...*

The fleeing lions, cornered by hounds, shot through with
arrows, and weighed down by fatigue, begin to fall, tragically.
The lead lion carries on even while vomiting blood.

This low point of Assyrian cruelty is, perhaps, the high
point of their artistic achievement. It's a curious coincidence that
civilizations often produce their greatest art in their declining
years. Hmm.

• *On the wall opposite the vomiting lion...*

Dying Lioness

A lioness roars in pain and frustration. She tries to run, but her
body is too heavy. Her muscular hind legs, once the source of
her power, are now paralyzed.

Like these brave, fierce lions, Assyria's once-great warrior nation was slain. Shortly after Ashurbanipal's death, Assyria was conquered, sacked, and looted by an ascendant Babylon. The mood of tragedy, dignity, and proud struggle in a hopeless cause makes this Dying Lioness simply one of the most beautiful of human creations.

• *Return to the huge, winged Assyrian lions (near the Rosetta Stone) by exiting the lion-hunt room at the far end. To reach the Greek section, pass between the winged lions and turn right, then right again, into Room 11.*

You'll walk past early Greek Barbie and Ken dolls from the Cycladic period (2500 B.C.). Continue into Room 12 (the hungry can go straight to the Gallery Café) and turn right, into Room 13. Continue to Room 15, then relax on a bench and read, surrounded by statues and vases in glass cases.

GREECE (600 B.C.–A.D. 1)

The history of ancient Greece could be subtitled "making order out of chaos." While Assyria was dominating the Middle East, "Greece"—a gaggle of warring tribes roaming the Greek peninsula—was floundering in darkness. But by around 700 B.C. these tribes began settling down, experimenting with democracy, forming self-governing city-states, and making ties with other city-states. Scarcely two centuries later, they would be a united community and the center of the civilized world.

During its "Golden Age" (500–430 B.C.), Greece set the tone for all of Western civilization to follow. Democracy, theater, literature, mathematics, philosophy, science, art, and architecture, as we know them, were virtually all invented by a single generation of Greeks in a small town of maybe 80,000 citizens.

• *On the long wall, find a . . .*

Map of the Greek World (500–430 B.C.)

Athens was the most powerful of the city-states and the center of the Greek world. Golden Age Greece was never really a full-fledged empire, but more a common feeling of unity among Greek-speaking people.

A century after the Golden Age, Greek culture was spread still further by Alexander the Great, who conquered the Mediterranean world and beyond. By 300 B.C. the "Greek" world stretched from Italy and Egypt to India (including most of what used to be

Early Greece

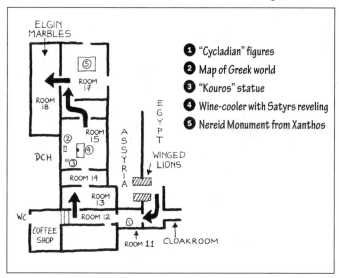

ELGIN MARBLES

ROOM 18
ROOM 17
⑤
ROOM 15
②
④
=③
DCH
ROOM 14
ROOM 13
ROOM 12
WC
COFFEE SHOP
ROOM 11
CLOAKROOM
①
EGYPT
ASSYRIA
WINGED LIONS

❶ "Cycladian" figures
❷ Map of Greek world
❸ "Kouros" statue
❹ Wine-cooler with Satyrs reveling
❺ Nereid Monument from Xanthos

the Assyrian Empire). Two hundred years later, this Greek-speaking "Hellenistic Empire" was conquered by the Romans.
• *There's a nude male to the left of the map.*

Boy *(Kouros)* (490 B.C.)

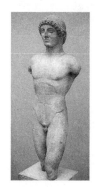

The Greeks saw their gods in human form...and human beings were godlike. With his perfectly round head, symmetrical pecs, and navel in the center, this Boy exemplifies the divine orderliness of the universe. The ideal man was geometrically perfect, a balance of opposites, the "Golden Mean." In a statue, that meant finding the right balance between movement and stillness, between realistic human anatomy (with human flaws) and the perfection of a Greek god. This Boy is still a bit uptight, stiff as the rock from which he's carved. But—as we'll see—in just a few short decades, the Greeks would cut loose and create realistic statues that seemed to move like real humans.
• *Look in the glass case by the map, filled with decorated vases. One in the center is marked...*

Red-Figured Psykter (Wine Cooler) with Satyrs Reveling (490 B.C.)

This clay vase, designed to float in a bowl of cooling water, shows satyrs at a symposium, or drinking party. These half-man/half-animal creatures (notice their tails) had a reputation for lewd behavior, reminding the balanced and moderate Greeks of their rude roots.

The reveling figures painted on this jar are more realistic, more three-dimensional, and suggest more natural movements than even the literally three-dimensional but quite stiff *Kouros* statue. The Greeks are beginning to conquer the natural world in art. The art, like life, is more in balance. And speaking of "balance," if that's a Greek sobriety test, revel on.

• *Carry on into Room 17 and sit facing the Greek temple at the far end.*

Nereid Monument from Xanthos (c. 400 B.C.)

Greek temples (like this reconstruction of a temple-shaped tomb) housed a statue of a god or goddess. Unlike Christian churches, which serve as meeting places, Greek temples were the gods'

homes. Worshipers gathered outside, so the most impressive part of the temple was its exterior. Temples were rectangular buildings surrounded by rows of columns and topped by slanted roofs.

The triangle-shaped roof, filled in with sculpture (reliefs or statues), is called the "pediment." The cross beams that support the roof are called "metopes" (pron. MET-o-pees). Now look through the columns to the building itself. Above the doorway is another set of relief panels running around the building (under the eaves) called the "frieze."

Next, we'll see pediment, frieze, and metope decorations from Greece's greatest temple.

• *Leave the British Museum. Take the Tube to Heathrow and fly to Athens. In the center of the old city, on top of the high, flat hill known as the Acropolis, you'll find . . .*

The Parthenon (447–432 B.C.)

The Parthenon—the temple dedicated to Athena, goddess of wisdom and the patroness of Athens—was the crowning glory

of an enormous urban-
renewal plan during
Greece's Golden Age.
After Athens was ruined
in a war with Persia, the
city—under the bold
leadership of Pericles—
constructed the greatest building of its day. The Parthenon was a
model of balance, simplicity, and harmonious elegance, the symbol
of the Golden Age. Phidias, the greatest Greek sculptor, decorated
the exterior with statues and relief panels.

While the building itself remains in Athens, many of the
Parthenon's best sculptures are right here in the British Museum—
the so-called Elgin Marbles (pronounced with a hard "g"), named
for the shrewd British ambassador who acquired them in the early
1800s. Though the Greek government complains about losing its
marbles, the Brits feel they rescued and preserved the sculptures.
• *Enter through the glass doors labeled The Parthenon Galleries.*

THE ELGIN MARBLES (450 B.C.)
The marble panels you see lining the walls of this large hall are
part of the frieze that originally ran around the exterior of the
Parthenon. The statues at either end of the hall once filled the
Parthenon's triangular-shaped pediments. Near the pediment
sculptures, we'll also find the relief panels known as "metopes."
Let's start with the frieze.

The Frieze
These 56 relief panels show
Athens' "Fourth of July" parade,
celebrating the birth of the city.
On this day, citizens marched up
the Acropolis to symbolically present a new robe to the 40-foot-tall
gold-and-ivory statue of Athena
housed in the Parthenon.

• *Start at the panels to your right (#136) and work counterclockwise.*

Men on horseback, chariots, musicians, animals for sacrifice,
and young maidens with offerings are all part of the grand parade,
all heading in the same direction. Prance on.

Notice the muscles and veins in the horses' legs (#130) and
the intricate folds in the cloaks and dresses. Some panels have
holes drilled in them, where gleaming bronze reins were fitted
to heighten the festive look. Of course, all these panels were originally painted in realistic colors. Despite the bustle of figures posed

Elgin Marbles

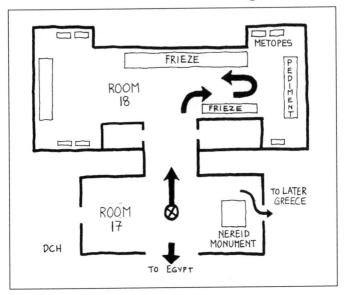

every which way, the frieze has one unifying element—all the people's heads are at the same level, creating a single ribbon around the Parthenon.

• *Cross to the opposite wall.*

A three-horse chariot (#67) cut out of only a few inches of marble is more lifelike and three-dimensional than anything the Egyptians achieved in a freestanding statue.

Enter the girls (#61), the heart of the procession. Dressed in pleated robes, they shuffle past the parade marshals, carrying jugs of wine and bowls to pour out an offering to the thirsty gods.

The procession culmi-
nates (#35) in the presentation
of the robe to Athena. A man
and a child fold the robe for
the goddess, while the rest of
the gods look on. There are
Zeus and Hera (#29), the king
and queen of the gods, seated,
enjoying the fashion show and wondering what length hemlines
will be this year.

• *Head for the set of pediment sculptures at the right end of the hall.*

The Pediment Sculptures

These statues nestled nicely in the triangular pediment above the columns at the Parthenon's east entrance. The missing statues at

the peak of the triangle once showed the birth of Athena. Zeus had his head split open, allowing Athena, the goddess of wisdom, to rise from his brain fully grown and fully armed.

The other gods at this Olympian banquet slowly become aware of the amazing event. The first to notice is the one closest to them, Hebe, the cup-bearer of the gods (tallest surviving fragment). Frightened, she runs to tell the others, her dress whipping behind her. A startled Demeter (just left of Hebe) turns toward Hebe.

The only one who hasn't lost his head is laid-back Dionysus (the cool guy further left). He just raises another glass of wine to his lips. Over on the right, Aphrodite, goddess of love, leans back into her mother's lap, too busy admiring her own bare shoulder even to notice the hubbub. A chess-set horse's head screams, "These people are nuts—let me out of here!"

The scene had a message. Just as wise Athena rose above the lesser gods who were scared, drunk, or vain, so would her city, Athens, rise above her lesser rivals.

This is amazing work-
manship. Compare Diony-
sus, with his natural, relaxed,
reclining pose, to all those
stiff Egyptian statues standing eternally at attention.

Appreciate the folds of
the clothes on the female
figures (on the right half),
especially Aphrodite's clinging, rumpled robe. Some sculptors would first build a nude model of their figure, put real clothes on it, and study how the cloth hung down before actually sculpting in marble. Others found inspiration at the *taverna* on wet T-shirt night.

Even without their heads, these statues, with their detailed anatomy and expressive poses, speak volumes.

Wander behind. The statues originally sat 40 feet above the ground. The backs of the statues, which were never intended to be seen, are almost as detailed as the fronts. That's quality control.

• *The metopes are the panels on the walls to either side. Start with* "*South Metope XXXI*" *on the right wall, center.*

Centaurs Slain Around the World

Dateline 500 B.C.—Greece, China, India: Man no longer considers himself an animal. Bold new ideas are exploding simultaneously around the world. Socrates, Confucius, Buddha, and others are independently discovering a nonmaterial, unseen order in nature and in man. They say man has a rational mind or soul. He's separate from nature and different from the other animals.

The Metopes

In #XXXI, a centaur grabs a man by the throat while the man pulls his hair. The humans have invited some centaurs—wild half-man/half-horse creatures—to a wedding feast. All goes well until the brutish centaurs, the original party animals, get too drunk and try to carry off the women. A battle ensues.

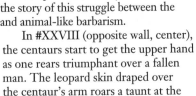

The Greeks prided themselves on creating order out of chaos. Within just a few generations, they went from nomadic barbarism to the pinnacle of early Western civilization. These metopes tell the story of this struggle between the forces of human civilization and animal-like barbarism.

In #XXVIII (opposite wall, center), the centaurs start to get the upper hand as one rears triumphant over a fallen man. The leopard skin draped over the centaur's arm roars a taunt at the prone man. The humans lose face.

In #XXVII (to the left—see photo in sidebar above), the humans finally rally and drive off the brutish centaurs. A centaur, wounded in the back, tries to run, but the man grabs him by the neck and raises his right hand (missing) to finish him off. The man's folded cloak sets off his smooth skin and graceful figure.

The centaurs have been defeated. Civilization has triumphed over barbarism, order over chaos, and rational man over his half-animal alter ego.

Why are the Elgin Marbles so treasured? The British of the 19th century saw themselves as the new "civilized" race, subduing "barbarians" in their far-flung empire. Maybe these rocks made them stop and wonder—will our great civilization also turn to rubble?

THE REST OF THE BRITISH MUSEUM

You've toured only the foundations of Western civilization on the ground floor, West Wing. Upstairs you'll find still more artifacts from these lands, plus Rome and the medieval civilization that sprang from it. Some highlights:

- Lindow Man (a.k.a. the "Bog Man") in Room 50. This victim of a Druid human-sacrifice ritual, with wounds still visible, was preserved for 2,000 years in a peat bog.
- The seventh-century Anglo-Saxon Sutton Hoo Burial Ship (Room 41).
- The only existing, complete cartoon by Michelangelo (Room 90).

But, of course, history doesn't begin and end in Europe. Look for remnants of the sophisticated, exotic cultures of Asia and the Americas (in North Wing, ground floor) and Africa (downstairs)—all part of the totem pole of the human family.

NATIONAL GALLERY TOUR

The National Gallery lets you tour Europe's art without ever crossing the Channel. With so many exciting artists and styles, it's a fine overture to art if you're just starting a European trip and a pleasant reprise if you're just finishing. The "National Gal" is always a welcome interlude from the bustle of London sightseeing.

Orientation

Cost: Free.

Hours: Daily 10:00–18:00, Wed until 21:00, closed on Good Friday, Dec 24–26, and Jan 1. Late afternoons are less crowded.

Getting There: It's central as can be, overlooking Trafalgar Square, a 15-minute walk from Big Ben and 10 minutes from Piccadilly. The closest Tube stop is Charing Cross or Leicester Square. Take your pick of buses: #3, #6, #9, #11, #12, #13, #15, #23, #24, #29, #53, #88, #91, #94, or #109.

Information: The information desk in the lobby offers a free, handy floor plan. Find the latest events schedule and a listing of free lunchtime lectures in the complimentary "National Gallery News" flier. Drop by the Micro Gallery, a computer room even your dad would enjoy (closes 30 min earlier than museum); you can study any artist, style, or topic in the museum, and print out a tailor-made tour map (tel. 020/7839-3321, recorded information tel. 020/7747-2885, www.nationalgallery.org.uk).

Tours: Free one-hour overview tours are offered daily at 11:30 and 14:30 (also Wed at 18:30). Excellent audioguide tours (suggested £4 donation) let you dial up info on any painting in the museum.

Length of Our Tour: 90 minutes.

Cloakroom: Free cloakrooms are at each entrance. You can take in a small bag.

Photography: Photos are strictly forbidden.

Cuisine Art: Crivelli's Garden Café (first floor, Sainsbury Wing) is classy with reasonable prices and a petite menu. The Pret à Manger Café (in basement, near end of this tour, just before Impressionists) is a bustling, inexpensive, self-service cafeteria with realistic salads, Rubens sandwiches, and Gauguin juices. A block away, there's a good cafeteria in the crypt of St. Martin-in-the-Fields church (facing Trafalgar Square). For pub grub, walk a block down Whitehall toward Big Ben and dip into the Clarence. **Starring:** You name it—da Vinci, Raphael, Titian, Rembrandt, Monet, and van Gogh.

The Tour Begins

Of the two entrances that face Trafalgar Square, enter through the smaller building to the left (as you face it) of the main, domed entrance. Pick up the free map and climb the stairs. At the top, turn left and grab a seat in Room 51, facing Leonardo's *Virgin of the Rocks.*

The National Gallery offers a quick overview of European art history. We'll stay on one floor, working chronologically through medieval holiness, Renaissance realism, Dutch detail, Baroque excess, British restraint, and the colorful French Impressionism that leads to the modern world. Cruise like an eagle with wide eyes for the big picture, seeing how each style progresses into the next.

THE ITALIAN RENAISSANCE (1400–1550)

Leonardo da Vinci—
***The Virgin of the Rocks* (1508)**
Mary, the mother of Jesus, plays with her son and little Johnny the Baptist (with cross, at left) while John's mother looks on. Leonardo brings this holy scene right down to earth, sitting among rocks, stalactites, water, and flowering plants. But looking closer, we see that Leonardo has deliberately posed his people into a pyramid shape, with Mary's head at the peak, creating an oasis of maternal stability and serenity amid the hard rock of the earth. Leonardo, who was illegitimate, may have sought, in his art, the young mother he never knew. Freud thought so.

The Renaissance—or "rebirth" of the culture of ancient Greece and Rome—was a cultural boom that changed people's thinking about every aspect of life. In politics, it meant democracy. In religion, it meant a move away from Church dominance and toward the assertion of man (humanism) and a more personal faith. Science and secular learn-ing were revived after centuries of superstition and ignorance. In architecture, it was a return to the balanced columns and domes of Greece and Rome.

In painting, the Renaissance meant realism. Artists redis-covered the beauty of nature and the human body. With pictures of beautiful people in harmonious, 3-D surroundings, they expressed the optimism and confidence of this new age.

• *We'll circle back around to Leonardo in a couple hundred years. But first, turn your back on the Renaissance and cruise through the medieval world in Rooms 52, 53, and 54.*

Medieval and Early Renaissance (1260–1510)

Shiny gold paintings of saints, angels, Madonnas, and crucifixions floating in an ethereal gold never-never land. One thing is very clear: Medieval heaven was different from medieval earth. The holy wore gold plates on their heads. Faces were serene and gen-eric. People posed stiffly, facing directly out or to the side, never in between. Saints are recognized by the symbols they carry (a key, a sword, a book), rather than by their human features.

Middle Ages art was religious, dominated by the Church. The illiterate faithful could meditate on an altarpiece and visualize heaven. It's as though they couldn't imagine saints and angels inhabiting the dreary world of rocks, trees, and sky we live in.

• *One of the finest medieval altarpieces is in a glass case in Room 53.*

Anonymous—*The Wilton Diptych* (c. 1395)

Three kings (left panel) come to adore Mary and her rosy-cheeked baby (right panel), surrounded by flame-like angels. Despite the

gold-leaf background, a glim-mer of human realism peeks through. The kings have distinct, down-to-earth faces. And the back side shows not a saint, not a god, not a symbol, but a real-life deer lying down in the grass of this earth.

Still, the anonymous artist is struggling with reality. John the Baptist (among the kings) is holding a "lamb of God" that looks more like a chihuahua. Nice try. Mary's exquisite fingers hold an anatomically impossible little foot. The figures are flat, scrawny, and sinless, with cartoon features—far from flesh-and-blood human beings.

• *Walking straight through Room 54 into Room 55, you'll leave this gold-leaf peace and find...*

Uccello—*Battle of San Romano* (c. 1450)

This colorful battle scene shows the victory of Florence over Siena—and the battle for literal realism on the canvas. It's an early Renaissance attempt at a realistic, nonreligious, three-dimensional scene.

Uccello challenges his ability by posing the horses and soldiers at every conceivable angle. The background of farm-yards, receding hedges, and tiny soldiers creates an illusion of distance. In the foreground, Uccello actually constructs a grid of fallen lances, then places the horses and warriors within it. Still, Uccello hasn't quite worked out the bugs—the figures in the distance are far too big and the fallen soldier on the left isn't much bigger than the fallen shield on the right.

• *In Room 56, you'll find...*

Van Eyck—*The Arnolfini Marriage* (1434)

Called by some "The Shotgun Wedding," this painting of a simple ceremony (set in Bruges, Belgium) is a masterpiece of down-to-earth details. The solemn, well-dressed couple take their vows, with hands joined in the center.

Van Eyck has built a medieval dollhouse, inviting us to linger over the furnishings. Feel the texture of the fabrics, count the terrier's hairs, trace the shadows generated by the window. Each object is painted at an ideal angle, with the details you'd see if you were standing right in front of it. So, the strings of beads hanging on the back wall are as crystal clear as the bracelets on the bride.

And to top it off, look into the round mirror on the far wall—the whole scene is reflected backward in miniature, showing the loving couple and two mysterious visitors. Is it the concerned parents? The minister? Van Eyck himself at his easel? Or has the artist painted you, the home viewer, into the scene?

National Gallery Highlights

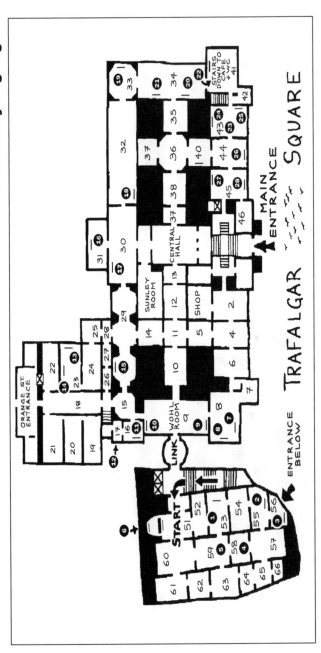

MEDIEVAL & EARLY RENAISSANCE

1 Wilton Diptych
2 UCCELLO Battle of San Romano
3 VAN EYCK Arnolfini Marriage
4 CRIVELLI Annunciation with St. Emidius
5 BOTTICELLI Venus and Mars

HIGH RENAISSANCE

6 LEONARDO DA VINCI Virgin and Child (painting and cartoon)

NATIONAL GALLERY MAIN
BUILDING - HIGH RENAISSANCE

7 MICHELANGELO Entombment
8 RAPHAEL Pope Julius II

VENETIAN RENAISSANCE

9 TITIAN Bacchus and Ariadne
10 TINTORETTO Origin of the Milky Way

NORTHERN PROTESTANT ART

11 VERMEER Young Woman
12 "A PEEPSHOW"
13 REMBRANDT Belshazzar's Feast
14 REMBRANDT Self-Portrait

BAROQUE & ROCOCO

15 RUBENS The Judgment of Paris
16 VAN DYCK Charles I on Horseback
17 VELAZQUEZ The Rokeby Venus
18 CARAVAGGIO Supper at Emmaus
19 BOUCHER Pan and Syrinx

BRITISH

20 CONSTABLE The Hay Wain
21 TURNER The Fighting Temeraire
22 DELAROCHE The Execution of Lady Jane Grey

IMPRESSIONISM & BEYOND

23 MONET Gare St. Lazare
24 MONET The Water Lily Pond
25 MANET The Waitress (La Servante de Bocks)
26 SEURAT Bathers at Asnieres
27 VAN GOGH Sunflowers
28 CEZANNE Bathers

The surface detail is extraordinary, but the painting lacks true Renaissance depth. The tiny room looks unnaturally narrow, cramped, and claustrophobic.

In medieval times (this was painted only a generation after *The Wilton Diptych*), everyone could read the hidden meaning of certain symbols—the chandelier with its one lit candle (love), the fruit on the windowsill (fertility), the dangling whisk broom (the bride's domestic responsibilities), and the terrier (Fido—fidelity).

By the way, she may not be pregnant. The fashion of the day was to wear a pillow to look pregnant in hopes you'd soon get that way. At least, that's what they told their parents.

• *Return to Room 55, turn left into Room 57, then turn right into Room 58.*

Botticelli—*Venus and Mars* (c. 1485)

Mars takes a break from war, succumbing to the delights of love (Venus), while impish satyrs play innocently with the discarded tools of death.

In the early spring of the Renaissance, there was an optimistic mood in the air, the feeling that enlightened Man could solve all problems, narrowing the gap between mortals and the Greek gods. Artists felt free to use the pagan Greek gods as symbols of human traits, virtues, and vices. Venus has sapped man's medieval stiffness, and the Renaissance is coming.

• *Continue to Room 59.*

Crivelli—*The Annunciation with Saint Emidius* (1486)

Mary, in green, is visited by the dove of the Holy Ghost, who beams down from the distant heavens in a shaft of light.

Like Van Eyck's wedding, this is a brilliant collection of realistic details. Notice the hanging rug, the peacock, the architectural minutiae that lead you way, way back, then bam—you have a giant pickle in your face.

It combines meticulous detail with Italian spaciousness. The floor tiles and building bricks recede into the distance. We're sucked right in, accelerating through the alleyway, under the arch, and off into space. The Holy Ghost spans the entire distance, connecting heavenly background with earthly foreground. Crivelli creates an Escher-esque labyrinth of rooms and walkways that we want to walk through, around, and into—or is that just a male thing?

Renaissance Italians were interested in—even obsessed with—portraying 3-D space. Perhaps they focused their spiritual passion away from heaven and toward the physical world. With such restless energy, they needed lots of elbowroom. Space, the final frontier.

• *Just ahead is the Leonardo in Room 51, where we started.*

The High Renaissance (1500)

With the "Big Three" of the High Renaissance—Leonardo, Michelangelo, and Raphael—painters had finally conquered realism. But these three Florence-trained artists weren't content just to copy nature, cranking out photographs-on-canvas. Like Renaissance architects (which they also were), they carefully composed their figures on the canvas, "building" them into geometrical patterns that reflected the balance and order they saw in nature.

• *Enter the small dark cave behind the rocks.*

Leonardo da Vinci—*Virgin and Child with St. John the Baptist and St. Anne* (c. 1499–1500)

At first glance, this chalk drawing, or cartoon, looks like a simple snapshot of two loving moms and two playful kids. The two children play—oblivious to the violent deaths they'll both suffer—beneath their mothers' Mona Lisa smiles.

But follow the eyes: Shadowy-eyed Anne turns toward Mary, who looks tenderly down to Jesus, who blesses John, who gazes back dreamily. As your eyes follow theirs, you're led back to the literal and psychological center of the composition—Jesus—the alpha and omega. Without resorting to heavy-handed medieval symbolism, Leonardo drives home a theological concept in a natural, human way. Leonardo the perfectionist rarely finished paintings. This sketch—pieced together from two separate papers (see the line down the middle)—gives us an inside peek at his genius.

• *Cross to the main building and enter the large Room 9. We'll return to these big, colorful canvases, but first, turn right into Room 8.*

Painting: From Tempera to Tubes

The technology of painting has evolved over the centuries.

1400s: Artists used tempera (pigments dissolved in egg yolk) on wood.

1500s: Still painting on wood, artists mainly used oil (pigments dissolved in vegetable oil such as linseed, walnut, or poppy).

1600s: Artists applied oil paints to canvases stretched across wooden frames.

1850: Paints in convenient, collapsible tubes are invented, making open-air painting feasible.

The Frames: Although some frames are original, having been chosen by the artist, most are selected by museum curators. Some are old frames from another painting, some are Victorian-era reproductions in wood, and some are recent reproductions made of a composition substance to look like gilded wood.

Michelangelo—*Entombment* (unfinished) (c. 1500–01)

Michelangelo, the greatest sculptor ever, proves it here in this "painted sculpture" of the crucified Jesus being carried to the tomb. Like a chiseled Greek god, the musclehead in red ripples beneath his clothes. Christ's naked body, shocking to the medieval Church, was completely acceptable in the Renaissance world, where classical nudes were admired as an expression of the divine.

Renaissance balance and symmetry reign. Christ is the center of the composition, flanked by two equally leaning people who support his body with strips of cloth. They, in turn, are flanked by two more.

Where Leonardo gave us expressive faces, Michelangelo lets the bodies do the talking. The two supporters strain to hold up Christ's body, and in their tension we, too, feel the great weight and tragedy of their dead god. Michelangelo expresses the divine through the human form.

Raphael—*Pope Julius II* (1511)

The new worldliness of the Renaissance reached even the Church. Pope Julius II, who was more a swaggering conquistador than a pious pope, set out to rebuild Rome in Renaissance style, hiring Michelangelo to paint the ceiling of the Vatican's Sistine Chapel.

Raphael gives a behind-the-scenes look at this complex man. On the one hand, the pope is an imposing pyramid of power, with a velvet shawl, silk shirt, and fancy rings boast-ing of wealth and success. But at the same time, he's a bent and broken man, his throne backed into a corner, with an expression that seems to say, "Is this all there is?"

In fact, the great era of Florence and Rome was coming to an end. With Raphael's death in 1520, the Renaissance shifted to Venice.

• *Return to the long Room 9.*

Venetian Renaissance (1510–1600)

Big change. The canvases are bigger, the colors brighter. Madonnas and saints are being replaced by goddesses and heroes. And there are nudes—not Michelangelo's lumps of noble, knotted muscle, but smooth-skinned, sexy, golden centerfolds.

Venice got wealthy by trading with the luxurious and exotic East. Its happy-go-lucky art style shows a taste for the finer things in life.

Titian—*Bacchus and Ariadne* (1523)

Bacchus, the god of wine, leaps from his leopard-drawn chariot, his red cape blowing behind him, to cheer up Ariadne (far left), who has been jilted by her lover. Bacchus' motley entourage rattles cymbals, bangs on tambourines, and literally shakes a leg.

Man and animal mingle in this pre-Christian orgy, with leopards, a snake, a dog, and the severed head and leg of an ass ready for the barbecue. Man and animal also literally "mix" in the satyrs—part man, part goat. The fat, sleepy guy in the background has had too much.

Titian (see his "Ticianus" signature on the gold vase, lower left) uses a pyramid composition to balance an otherwise chaotic scene. Follow Ariadne's gaze up to the peak of Bacchus' flowing cape, then down along the snake handler's spine to the lower-right corner. In addition, he balances the picture with harmonious colors—blue sky on the left, green trees on the right, while the two main figures stand out with loud splotches of red.

Tintoretto—*The Origin of the Milky Way* (c. 1575)

In another classical myth, the god Jupiter places his illegitimate son, baby Hercules, at his wife's breast. Juno says, "Wait a minute. That's not my baby!" Her milk spurts upward, becoming the Milky Way.

Tintoretto places us right up in the clouds, among the gods, who swirl around at every angle. Jupiter appears to be flying almost right at us. An X composition unites it all—Juno slants one way while Jupiter slants the other.

• *Exit Room 9 (just to the right of the Milky Way painting) and turn left into Room 16 for Dutch art.*

NORTHERN PROTESTANT ART (1600–1700)

We switch from CinemaScope to a tiny TV—smaller canvases, subdued colors, everyday scenes, and not even a bare shoulder.

Money shapes art. While Italy had wealthy aristocrats and the powerful Catholic Church to purchase art, the North's patrons were middle-class, hardworking, Protestant merchants. They wanted simple, cheap, no-nonsense pictures to decorate their homes and offices. Greek gods and Virgin Marys were out, hometown folks and hometown places were in—portraits, landscapes, still lifes, and slice-of-life scenes. Painted with great attention to detail, this is art meant not to wow or preach at you, but to be enjoyed and lingered over. Sightsee.

Vermeer—*A Young Woman Standing at a Virginal* (c. 1670)

Inside a simple Dutch home, a prim virgin plays an early piano called a "virginal." We've surprised her and she pauses to look up at us.

Vermeer, by framing off such a small world to look at—from

the blue chair in the foreground to the wall in back—forces us to appreciate the tiniest details, the beauty of everyday things. We can meditate on the shawl, the tiles lining the floor, the subtle shades of the white wall, and, most of all, the pale, diffused light that soaks in from the window. Amid straight lines and rectangles, the woman's billowing dress adds a soft touch. The painting of a nude cupid on the back wall only strengthens this virgin's purity.

• *In Room 17, you'll find...*

A Peepshow

Look through the holes at the ends of this ingenious device to make the painting of a house interior come to three-dimensional life. Compare the twisted curves of the painting with the illusion it creates and appreciate the painstaking work of dedicated artists.

• *Zigzag through Rooms 15, 18, and 24 to Room 23.*

Rembrandt—*Belshazzar's Feast* (c. 1635)

The wicked king has been feasting with God's sacred dinnerware when the meal is interrupted. Belshazzar turns to see the hand of God, burning an ominous message into the wall that

Belshazzar's number is up. As he turns, he knocks over a goblet of wine. We see the jewels and riches of his decadent life.

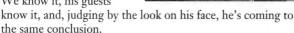
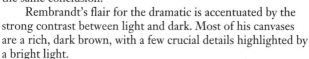

Rembrandt captures the scene at the most ironic moment. Belshazzar is about to be ruined. We know it, his guests know it, and, judging by the look on his face, he's coming to the same conclusion.

Rembrandt's flair for the dramatic is accentuated by the strong contrast between light and dark. Most of his canvases are a rich, dark brown, with a few crucial details highlighted by a bright light.

Rembrandt—*Self-Portrait* (1669)

Rembrandt throws the light of truth on...himself. This craggy self-portrait was done the year he died, at age 63. Contrast it with

one done three decades earlier (hanging nearby). Rembrandt, the greatest Dutch painter, started out as the successful, wealthy young genius of the art world. But he refused to crank out commercial works. Rembrandt painted things that he believed in but no one would invest in—family members, down-to-earth Bible scenes, and self-portraits like these.

Here, Rembrandt surveys the wreckage of his independent life. He was bankrupt, his mistress had just died, and he had also buried several of his children. We see a disillusioned, well-worn, but proud old genius.

• *Backtrack through several rooms to the long Room 29, with mint-green wallpaper.*

BAROQUE (1600–1700)

Rubens

This room holds big, color-ful, emotional works by Peter Paul Rubens and others from Catholic Flanders (Belgium). While Protestant and demo-cratic Europe painted simple scenes, Catholic and aristo-cratic countries turned to the style called Baroque. Baroque art took what was

flashy in Venetian art and made it flashier, gaudy and made it gaudier, dramatic and made it shocking.

Rubens painted anything that would raise your pulse—battles, miracles, hunts, and, especially, fleshy women with dimples on all four cheeks. *The Judgment of Paris*, for instance, is little more than an excuse for a study of the female nude, showing front, back, and profile all on one canvas.

• *Exit Room 29 at the far end. To the left, in Room 31, you'll see the large canvas of . . .*

Van Dyck—*Charles I on Horseback* (c. 1637–38)

King Charles sits a huge horse, accentuating his power. The horse's small head makes sure that little Charles isn't dwarfed. Charles ruled firmly as a Catholic king in a Protestant country until England's Civil War (1648), when his genteel head was separated from his refined body by Cromwell and company.

Kings and bishops used the grandiose Baroque style to impress the masses with their power. Van Dyck's portrait style set the tone for all the stuffy, boring portraits of British aristocrats who wished to be portrayed as sophisticated gentlemen—whether they were or not.

• *For the complete opposite of a stuffy portrait, backpedal into Room 30 for...*

Velázquez—*The Rokeby Venus* (c. 1647–51)

Like a Venetian centerfold, she lounges diagonally across the canvas, admiring herself, with flaring red, white, and gray fabrics to highlight her rosy-white skin and inflame our passion. Horny Spanish kings loved Titian-esque nudes, despite that country's strict Inquisition. This work by the king's personal court painter is the first (and, for over a century, the only) Spanish nude. About the only concession to Spanish modesty is the false reflection in the mirror—if it really showed what the angle should show, Velázquez would have needed two mirrors...and a new job.

• *Turning your left cheek to hers, tango into Room 32.*

Michelangelo Merisi de Caravaggio—*The Supper at Emmaus* (1601)

After Jesus was crucified, he rose from the dead and appeared without warning to some of his followers. Jesus just wants a quiet meal, but the man in green, suddenly realizing who he's eating with, is about to jump out of his chair in shock. To the right, a man spreads his hands in amazement, bridging the distance between Christ and us by sticking his hand in our face.

Baroque took reality and exaggerated it. Most artists amplified the prettiness, but Caravaggio exaggerated the grittiness, using real, ugly, unhaloed people in Bible scenes. Caravaggio's paintings look like a wet dog smells. Reality.

We've come a long way since the first medieval altarpieces that wrapped holy people in gold foil. From the torn shirts to the five o'clock shadows, from the blemished apples to the uneven part in Jesus' hair, we are witnessing a very human miracle.

• *Leave the Caravaggio Room under the sign reading "East Wing, painting from 1700–1900," and enter Room 33.*

FRENCH ROCOCO (1700–1800)

As Europe's political and economic center shifted from Italy to France, Louis XIV's court at Versailles became its cultural hub. Every aristocrat spoke French, dressed French, and bought French paintings. The Rococo art of Louis' successors was as frilly, sensual, and suggestive as the decadent French court. We see their rosy-cheeked portraits and their fantasies: lords and ladies at play in classical gardens where mortals and gods cavort together.

• *One of the finest examples is the tiny . . .*

Boucher—*Pan and Syrinx* (1739)

Curious Pan seeks a threesome, but Syrinx eventually changes to reeds, leaving him all wet.

Rococo art is like a Rubens that got shrunk in the wash—smaller, lighter pastel colors, frillier, and more delicate than the Baroque style. Same dimples, though.

• *Enter Room 34 (the Sackler Room).*

BRITISH (1800–1850)

Constable—*The Hay Wain* (1821)

The more reserved British were more comfortable cavorting with nature than with the lofty gods. Come-as-you-are poets like Wordsworth found the same ecstasy just being outside.

John Constable set up his easel out-of-doors, painstakingly capturing the simple majesty of billowing clouds, billowing trees, and everyday rural life. Even British portraits (by Thomas Gainsborough and others) placed refined lords and ladies amid idealized greenery.

This simple style—believe it or not—was considered shocking in its day. The rough, thick, earth-toned paint and crude country settings scandalized art-lovers used to the highfalutin, prettified sheen of Baroque and Rococo.

• *Take a hike and enjoy the English-country-garden ambience of this room.*

Turner—*The Fighting Téméraire* (before 1839)

Constable's landscape was about to be paved over by the Industrial Revolution. Soon, machines began to replace humans, factories belched smoke over Constable's hay cart, and cloud-gazers had to punch the clock. Romantics tried to resist it, lauding the forces of nature and natural human emotions in the face of technological "progress." But alas, here a modern steam boat symbolically drags a famous but obsolete sailing battleship off into the sunset to be destroyed.

Turner's messy, colorful style gives us our first glimpse into the modern art world—he influenced the Impressionists. Turner takes an ordinary scene (like Constable), captures the play of light with messy paints (like Impressionists), and charges it with mystery (like, wow).

• *London's Tate Britain (see page 149) has an enormous collection of Turner's work. For now, enter Room 41.*

Paul Delaroche—*The Execution of Lady Jane Grey* (1833)

The teenage queen's nine-day reign has reached its curfew. This simple girl, manipulated into power politics by cunning advisors, is now sent to the execution site in the Tower of London. As her friends swoon with grief, she's blindfolded and forced to kneel at the block. Legend has it that the confused, humiliated girl was left kneeling on the scaffold. She crawled around, groping for the chopping block, crying out, "Where is it? What am I supposed to do?"

The executioner in scarlet looks on with as much compassion as he can muster.

Britain's distinct contribution to art history is this Pre-Raphaelite style, showing medieval scenes in luminous realism with a mood of understated tragedy.

• *Exit Room 41, pass the door that leads downstairs to the café and WC, and enter Room 43. The Impressionist paintings are scattered throughout Rooms 43–46.*

IMPRESSIONISM AND BEYOND (1850–1910)

For 500 years, a great artist was someone who could paint the real world with perfect accuracy. Then along came the camera and, click, the artist was replaced by a machine. But unemployed artists refused to go the way of *The Fighting Téméraire*.

They couldn't match the camera for painstaking detail, but they could match it—even beat it—in capturing color, the fleeting moment, the candid pose, the play of light and shadow, the quick impression a scene makes on you. A new breed of artists burst out of the stuffy confines of the studio. They donned scarves and berets and set up their canvases in farmers' fields or carried their notebooks into a crowded café, dashing off quick sketches in order to catch a momentary...impression.

• *Start with the misty Monet train station.*

Monet—
Gare St. Lazare (1877)

Claude Monet, the father of Impressionism, was more interested in the play of light off his subject than the subject itself. He uses smudges of white and gray paint to capture how sun filters through the glass roof of the train station and is refiltered through the clouds of steam.

Monet—
The Water Lily Pond (1916)

We've traveled from medieval spirituality to Renaissance realism to Baroque elegance and Impressionist colors. Before you spill out into the 21st-century hubbub of busy London, relax for a second in Monet's garden at Giverny, near Paris. Monet planned an artificial garden, rechanneled a stream, built a bridge, and planted these water lilies—a living work of art, a small section of order and calm in a hectic world.

Manet—*The Waitress (Corner of a Café-Concert)* (1878–80)

Imagine how mundane (and therefore shocking) Manet's quick "impression" of this café must have been to a public that was raised on Greek gods, luscious nudes, and glowing Madonnas.

• *In Room 44, you'll see . . .*

Renoir—*Boating on the Seine* (1879–80)

It's a nice scene of boats on sun-dappled water. Now move in close. The "scene" breaks up into almost random patches of bright colors. The "blue" water is actually separate brushstrokes of blue, green, pink, purple, gray, white, etc. The rower's hat is a blob of green, white, and blue. Up close, it looks like a mess, but when you back up to a proper distance, voilà! It shimmers. This kind of rough, coarse brushwork (where you can actually see the brush strokes) is one of the telltale signs of Impressionism. Renoir was not trying to paint the water itself, but the reflection of sky, shore, and boats off its surface.

Seurat—*Bathers at Asnières* (1883)

Viewed from about 15 feet away, this is a bright sunny scene of people lounging on a riverbank. Up close it's a mess of dots, showing the Impressionist color technique taken to its logical extreme. The "green" grass is a shag rug of green, yellow, red,

brown, purple, and white brush strokes. The boy's "red" cap is a collage of red, yellow, and blue.

Seurat has "built" the scene dot by dot, like a newspaper photo, using small points of different, bright colors. Only at a distance do the individual brushstrokes blend together. Impressionism is all about color. Even people's shadows are not dingy black, but warm blues greens and purples.

• *In Room 45 . . .*

Van Gogh—*Sunflowers* (1888)

In military terms, van Gogh was the point man of his culture. He went ahead of his cohorts, explored the unknown, and caught a bullet young. He added emotion to Impressionism, infusing his love of life even into inanimate objects. These sunflowers, painted with characteristic swirling brush-strokes, shimmer and writhe in either agony or ecstasy—depending on your own mood.

Van Gogh painted these during his stay in southern France, a time of frenzied creativity, when he him-self hovered between agony and ecstasy, bliss and madness. A year later, he shot himself.

In his day, van Gogh was a penniless nobody, selling only one painting in his whole career. Today, a *Sunflowers* (he did a half dozen versions) sells for $40 million (a salary of about $2,500 a day for 45 years), and it's not even his highest-priced painting. Hmm.

Cézanne—*Bathers (Les Grandes Baigneuses)* (c. 1900-06)

These bathers are arranged in strict triangles à la Leonardo—the five nudes on the left form one triangle, the seated nude

on the right forms another, and even the background trees and clouds are trian-gular patterns of paint.

Cézanne uses the Impres-sionist technique of building a figure with dabs of paint (though his "dabs" are often larger-sized "cube" shapes) to make solid, 3-D geometrical figures in the style of the Renais-sance. In the process, his cube shapes helped inspire a radical new art style—Cube-ism—bringing art into the 20th century.

NATIONAL PORTRAIT GALLERY
TOUR

Rock groupies, book-lovers, movie fans, gossipmongers, and even historians all can find at least one favorite celebrity here. From Elizabeth I to Elizabeth II, from Byron to Bowie, the National Portrait Gallery puts a face on 500 years, making "history" the simple story of flesh-and-blood people. It's a great rainy-day museum for serious students, or a quick (and free) peek at the islands' eccentric inhabitants.

Orientation

Cost: Free.

Hours: Daily 10:00–18:00, until 21:00 on Thursday and Friday.

Getting There: It's at St. Martin's Place, 100 yards off Trafalgar Square (around the corner from National Gallery and opposite Church of St. Martin-in-the-Fields).

Information: Tel. 020/7306-0055, recorded info tel. 020/7312-2463, www.npg.org.uk.

Tours: The audioguide tours are excellent (£3 donation requested); they describe each room (or era in British history) and more than 300 paintings. You'll learn more about British history than art, and actually hear interviews with 20th-century subjects as you stare at their faces.

Length of Our Tour: 90 minutes.

Photography: Photos are not allowed.

Cuisine Art: The elegant Portrait Restaurant on the top floor is pricey but has a fine view. The Portrait Café in the basement is cheaper. The eateries close 30 minutes before the museum closes.

Starring: Royalty (Henry VIII, Elizabeth I, Victoria), writers (Shakespeare, Byron, Wilde), scientists (Newton, Darwin), politicians (Churchill), and musicians (Handel, Bowie).

Overview

The Gallery covers 500 years of history from top to bottom—
literally. Start at the top (second) floor, and work chronologically
down to modern times on the ground floor. Historians will want to
linger at the top; celebrity-hunters will lose elevation quickly to the
contemporary section. There are many, many famous people from
all walks of life, so use this chapter as an overview, then follow your
interests, reading more from the museum's informative labels.

• *Start on the second floor, Room 1, marked "The Early Tudors." Find
the large, black-and-white sketch ("cartoon") of Henry VIII with his
hands on his hips.*

SECOND FLOOR
1500s—DEBUT

The small, isolated island of Britain (pop. 4 million) enters onto
the world stage. The Tudor kings—having already settled family
feuds (the "Wars of the Roses"), balanced religious factions, and
built England's navy—bring wealth from abroad.

Room 1:
Henry VIII (1491–1547), The Whitehall Mural Cartoon

Young, athletic, intense, and charismatic,
with jeweled hands, gold dagger, and
bulging codpiece (the very image of
kingly power), Henry VIII carried
England on his broad shoulders from
political isolation to international power.

In middle age, he divorced his older,
dull-eyed, post-childbearing queen,
Catherine of Aragon (see her portrait
to the left, above eye level), for younger,
shrewd, sparkling-eyed **Anne Boleyn**
(left wall, eye level), in search of love,
sex, and a male
heir. Nine months later, the future Elizabeth I was born, and the Pope excom-
municated adulterous Henry. Defiant,
Henry started the (Protestant) Church
of England, sparking a century-plus of
religious strife between England's Protestants and Catholics.

By the time Henry died—400 pounds
of stinking, pus-ridden paranoia—he had
wed six wives (see #6, sweet young

National Portrait Gallery Second Floor

1 Henry VIII & Wives
2 Edward VI
3 Elizabeth I (3 versions)
4 Shakespeare
5 James I
6 Charles I
7 Cromwell
8 Charles II
9 Newton
10 Locke
11 Wren
12 Handel
13 Garrick
14 Watt
15 George III
16 Washington
17 Nelson
18 Hamilton
19 Wellington
20 The Romantics

Catherine Parr, opposite Henry), executed several of them, killed trusted advisors, pursued costly wars, and produced one male heir, Edward VI.

• *Around the divider is Room 2, with the lo-o-o-ong picture of . . .*

Room 2:
Edward VI (1537–53)
Nine-year-old Edward (son of wife #3, Jane Seymour) ruled for only six years before dying young, leaving England in religious and economic turmoil. (View the optical illusion through the hole at the right end to put the enigmatic boy king into perspective.)

Elizabeth I (1533–1603), Three different portraits on three different walls
Elizabeth I was pale, stern-looking, red-haired (like her father, Henry VIII), and wore big-shouldered power dresses. During her

reign, she kept Protestant/Catholic animosity under control and made England a naval power and cultural capital. The three portraits span her life from age 26 *(Coronation)* to 42 to 60 *(The Ditchley Portrait)*, but she looks ageless, always aware of her public image, resorting to makeup, dye, wigs, showy dresses, and pearls to dazzle courtiers.

The "Virgin Queen" was married only to her country, but she flirtatiously wooed opponents to her side. ("I know I have the body of a weak and feeble woman," she'd coo, "but I have the heart and stomach of a king.") When England's navy sank 72 ships of the Spanish Armada in a single, power-shifting battle (1588), Britannia ruled the waves, feasting on New World spoils. Elizabeth surrounded herself with intellects, explorers, and poets.

Room 3:
William Shakespeare (1564–1616)

Though famous in his day, Shakespeare's long hair, beard, earring, untied collar, and red-rimmed eyes make him look less the celebrity and more the bohemian barfly he likely was. This unassuming portrait (one of only two done in his lifetime) captures 45-year-old Shakespeare just before he retired from his career as actor, poet, and world's greatest playwright. The shiny, domed forehead is a beacon of intelligence.

(I suspect Shakespeare liked this plain-spoken portrait.)

Using borrowed plots, outrageous puns, and poetic language, Shakespeare wrote comedies (c. 1590—*Taming of the Shrew, As You Like It*), tragedies (c. 1600—*Hamlet, Othello, Macbeth, King Lear*), and fanciful combinations (c. 1610—*The Tempest*), exploring the full range of human emotions and reinventing the English language.

• *Pass through the stairwell and into Room 4.*

1600s—RELIGIOUS AND CIVIL WARS

Catholic kings bickered with an increasingly vocal Protestant Parliament until civil war erupted (1642–51), killing thousands, decapitating the king, and eventually establishing Parliament as the main power.

Room 4:
James I (1566–1625) of England and VI of Scotland

When the Virgin Queen died childless, her Catholic cousin—a rough, unkempt, arrogant Scotsman—moved to genteel London and donned the royal robes. Deeply religious, he launched the "King James" translation of the Bible, but he alienated Anglicans (Church of England), harder-line Protest-ants (Puritans), and democrats everywhere by insisting that he ruled by divine right, directly from God. He passed this attitude directly to his son, Charles.

• *Enter Room 5 (the doorway is opposite James) with portraits of Civil War veterans.*

Room 5:
Charles I (1600–49)

Picture Charles' sensitive face (with scholar's eyes and artist's long hair and beard) severed from his elegant body (in horse-riding finery), and you've arrived quickly at the heart of the Civil War. Short, shy, stuttering, and very Catholic Charles had angered Protestants and democrats by dissolving Parliament and raising taxes. Parliament formed an army, fought the king's supporters, arrested and tried Charles, and—outside the Banqueting House on Whitehall—beheaded him. The man responsible was ...

Oliver Cromwell (1599–1658)

Cromwell, with armor, sword, command baton, and a determined look, was the Protestant champion and military leader. The Civil War pitted Parliamentarians (Parliament, Protestant Puritans, industry, and urban areas) against Royalists (King, Catholics, nobles, traditionalists, and rural areas). After Charles' execution, Cromwell led kingless England as "Lord Protector."

Stern Cromwell hated luxury and ordered a warts-and-all portrait (see wart

on his left temple and scar between his eyebrows). He has a
simple, bowl-cut hairstyle, adorning his 82-ounce brain (49 is
average). Speaking of heads, after Cromwell's death, vengeful
royalists exhumed his body, cut off the head, stuck it on a stick,
and placed it outside Westminster Abbey where it rotted publicly
for 24 years.
• *Pass through Room 6 and into Room 7.*

Room 7:
Charles II (1630–85)

After two decades of wars, Cromwell's
harsh rule, and Puritanical excesses (no
dancing, theater, or political incorrectness),
Parliament welcomed the monarchy back
(with tight restrictions) under Charles II.
England was ready to party.

Looking completely ridiculous, with
splayed legs, puffy face, big-hair wig,
garters, and ribbons on his shoes, Charles II
became a king with nothing to do, and he
did it with grace and a sense of humor.
• *Make a U-turn right, doubling back through
Rooms 8 and 10.*

Room 8:
Isaac Newton (1642–1727) and John Locke (1632–1704)
The 1600s, the Age of Enlightenment, saw scientific discoveries
suggesting that the world operates in an orderly, rational way.
Isaac Newton explained the universe's motion with the simplest
of formulas ($F = ma$, etc.), and **John Locke** used human reason
to plan a democratic utopia.

Room 10:
Christopher Wren (1632–1723)
Christopher Wren built St. Paul's Cathedral—a glorious
desmonstration of mathematics in stone.
• *In Room 11, make a U-turn left, entering Room 12, with painters,
writers, actors, and musicians of the 1700s.*

1700s—DOMESTIC STABILITY, WARS WITH FRANCE
Blossoming agriculture, the first factories, overseas colonization,
and political stability from German-born kings (George I, II, III)
allowed the arts to flourish. Overseas, England financed wars
against Europe's #1 power, France.

Room 12:
George Frideric Handel (1685–1729) and David Garrick (1717–79)

In London, an old form of art became something new—modern theater.

Handel, a German writing Italian operas in England, had several smash hits in London (especially with the oratorio *Messiah*, on his desk), making musical theater popular with ordinary folk. Hallelujah.

David Garrick was an enormously popular actor, famed for portraying ordinary, "real" people. (This portrait with his dancer-wife captures his down-to-earth offstage personality.) As a promoter and theater owner, he turned a ragtag entertainment into big business.

Room 13:
James Watt (1736–1819)

Deep-thinking Watt pores over plans to turn brainpower into work power. His steam engines (with a separate condenser to capture formerly wasted heat energy) soon powered gleaming machines, changing England's economy from grains and ships to iron and coal.

• *In Room 14, you'll find George III over your left shoulder and George Washington along the right wall.*

Room 14:
King George III (1738–1820) and George Washington (1732–99)

Just crowned at 23, George gives little hint in this portrait that he will lead England into the drawn-out, humiliating "American War" (Revolutionary War) against a colony demanding independence. George III, perhaps a victim of an undiagnosed disease, closed out the stuffy "Georgian" era (in Percy Shelley's words), "an old, mad, blind, despised, dying king."

Perhaps it was the war that drove him mad, or perhaps it was that his enemy, George Washington, had the same hairdo.

1800s—COLONIAL AND INDUSTRIAL GIANT

Britain defeated France (Napoleon), emerging as the #1 power. With natural resources from overseas colonies (Australia, Canada, India, West Indies, China), good communications, and a growing population of 7 million, Britain became the first industrial power, dotted with smoke-belching factories and laced with railroads.

• *Exit Room 14 into Room 8 and turn right, ending up in Room 17.*

Room 17:
Lord Horatio Nelson (1758–1805); Emma, Lady Hamilton (1761–1815); and Arthur Wellesley, the Duke of Wellington (1769–1852)

Three heroes in the fight against Napoleon's expansion: Wellington on land (the final victory at Waterloo, near Brussels, 1815), Nelson at sea (Battle of Trafalgar, off Spain, 1805), and Lady Hamilton at Nelson's side.

Lady Hamilton, dressed in white with her famously beautiful face tilted coyly, first met dashing Nelson on his way to fight the French in Egypt. She used her husband,

Lord Hamilton's, influence to restock Nelson's ships. Nelson's daring victory *(Nelson Receiving the French Colours)* made him an instant celebrity, though the battle cost him an arm (see sleeveless pose) and an eye (scar above eye). The hero returned home to woo, bed, and impregnate Lady H., with sophisticated Lord Hamilton's patriotic tolerance.

Room 18:
The Romantics

Not everyone worshiped industrial progress. Romantics questioned the clinical detachment of science, industrial pollution, and the personal restrictions of modern life. They reveled in strong emotions, non-Western cultures, personal freedom, opium, and the beauties of nature.

• *Clockwise around the room, you'll see . . .*

John Keats (1795–1821) broods over his just-written ode "To a Nightingale." ("My heart aches, and a drowsy numbness pains/My sense, as though of hemlock I had drunk.")

Samuel Taylor Coleridge (1772–1834), at 23, is open-eyed, open-mouthed, and eager. ("And all should cry, Beware! Beware!/

His flashing eyes, his floating hair!/... For he on honey-dew hath fed,/And drunk the milk of Paradise." —from "Kubla Khan")

Mary Shelley (1797–1851), in telling ghost stories with husband Percy and friend Lord Byron, conceived a story of science run amok—*Frankenstein*—imitated by many. ("Ahhhhhhh, sweet mystery of life, at last I've found you!")

William Wordsworth (1770–1850) "The world is too much with us.../Little we see in Nature that is ours;/We have given our hearts away, a sordid boon!"

Percy Bysshe Shelley (1792–1822), political radical, sexual explorer (involving Mary and a first wife), traveler, and poet. ("O wild West Wind, thou breath of Autumn's being,.../If Winter comes, can Spring be far behind?")

George Gordon, **Lord Byron** (1788–1824), was athletic, exotic, and passionate about women and freedom. Famous and scandalous in his day, he became a Kerouac-ian symbol of the Romantic movement. ("She walks in beauty, like the night/Of cloudless climes and starry skies...")

• *After browsing Rooms 19 and 20, backtrack to Room 15 and head downstairs one flight to the first floor. Turn right at the bottom of the stairs, and you'll enter a long hall lined with busts (Room 22). Start at the far end of the hall in Room 21.*

FIRST FLOOR
THE VICTORIANS—1837–1901

As the wealthiest nation on earth, with a global colonial empire, Britain during Queen Victoria's long reign embraced modern technology, contributing to the development of power looms, railroads, telephones, motor-cars, and electric lights. It was a golden age of science, literature, and middle-class morality, though pockets of extreme poverty and vice lurked in the heart of London itself.

• *To either side of a statue, you'll find paintings of...*

Room 21:
Queen Victoria (1819–1901) and
Prince Albert (1819–61)

Crowned at 18, the short (5 feet), plump, bug-eyed, quiet girl inherited a world empire. The next year, she proposed marriage

National Portrait Gallery First Floor

22 Victoria
23 Albert
24 Florence Nightingale
25 Brontes
26 Tennyson
27 Wilde
28 Disraeli & Gladstone
29 Darwin & Faraday
30 T.E. Lawrence
31 Wallis Simpson & Edward
32 Shaw & Potter
33 Churchill & "Monty"
34 Later 20th Century Arts

(the custom) to the German Prince Albert. They were a perfect match—lovers, friends, partners—a model for middle-class couples. (See the white statue of the pair as genteel knight and adoring lady.) Albert co-ruled, especially when "Vickie" was pregnant with their nine kids. "Bertie" promoted education, science, public works, and the Great Exhibition of 1851 in Hyde Park. When Albert died at 42, a heartbroken Victoria moped for 40 years.

• *Double-back through the long hall lined with stuffy busts of starched shirts (Room 22), browsing around the rooms branching off it, filled with many prominent Victorians. Here are a few...*

Room 23:
Florence Nightingale *(The Mission of Mercy: Florence Nightingale Receiving the Wounded at Scutari)*

Known as "the Lady with the Lamp" for her nightly nursing visits (though she's shown lampless here, in the center, standing, with a piece of paper), Nightingale traveled to Turkey to tend to Crimean War victims. In fact, her forte was not hands-on nursing but efficient hospital administration (sanitation, keeping supplies stocked, transporting wounded) that saved lives and raised public awareness on health issues. To learn more about the Lady with the Lamp, you can visit the Florence Nightingale Museum, just across the Thames from Big Ben (in Gassiot House at 2 Lambeth Palace Road, Tube: Westminster, Waterloo, or Lambeth North).

Rooms 24 and 26: Writers

Anne, Emily, and Charlotte Brontë (left to right, youngest to oldest, painted by brother Branwell), three teenage country girls, grew up to write novels such as *Wuthering Heights* (Emily), about the complex family and love lives of England's rural gentry.

Watch **Alfred, Lord Tennyson** (1809–92; see photos in glass case), evolve from wavy-haired Romantic to grizzled, gray-bearded poet laureate of Victorian earnestness. ("Their's not to reason why,/Their's but to do and die;/Into the Valley of Death/Rode the six hundred.")

Oscar Wilde (1854–1900) satirized Victorian properness with profound-sounding absurdities *(The Importance of Being Ernest)* and scandalized it with his homosexuality. (His dying words, in a cheap hotel room: "Either that wallpaper goes, or I do.")

Room 25: Politicians

The two prime ministers who dominated politics for two decades, with two completely different personalities and beliefs, now face each other— **Benjamin Disraeli,** a flamboyant novelist, dandy (see his billy-goat goatee), and chum of Victoria, and **William Ewart Gladstone,** a righteous moralizer.

Room 27: Science and Technology

Charles Darwin, with bassett-hound eyes and long white beard, looks tired after a lifetime of reluctantly defending his controversial theory of evolution that shocked an entire generation.

Michael Faraday shocked himself from time to time, harnessing electricity as the work force of the next century.

• *The long hall (Room 22) leads directly into Room 30, dedicated to World War I.*

1900s—WORLD WARS

Two devastating World Wars and an emerging U.S. superpower shrank Britain from global empire to island nation. But Britain remained a cultural giant, producing writers, actors, composers, painters, and Beatles.

Room 30: World War I

Fighting Germans from trenches in France, Britain sent a million-man army to the grave. Among **portraits of leaders and victims,** you'll also see a reclining statue of **Thomas Edward Lawrence—**the real-life "Lawrence of Arabia"—looking remarkably like Peter O'Toole.

• *The large Room 31 is divided into four sections. In the first section, find...*

Room 31 (first section):
Wallis, Duchess of Windsor (painting), and Edward, Duke of Windsor (small statue)

The Duchess' smug smile tells us she got her man.

Edward VIII (1894–1972), great-grandson of Queen Victoria, became king in 1936 as a bachelor dating a common-born (gasp), twice-divorced (double gasp), American (oh no!) named Wallis Simpson (1896–1986). Rather than create a constitutional stink, Edward quietly abdicated, married Wallis, and the two moved to the Continent, living happily ever after. They hosted cocktail parties, played golf, and listened to servants call them "Your Majesty"—though they were now just plain Duke and Duchess of Windsor.

(Edward's brother took over as King George VI, married the "Queen Mum"—who died in 2002—and their daughter became Queen Elizabeth II. Elizabeth snubbed her disgraceful aunt and uncle.)

Room 31 (second section): Writers

George Bernard Shaw (bust)—playwright, critic, and political thinker—brought socialist ideas into popular discussion with plays such as *Man and Superman* and *Major Barbara.* **Beatrix Potter** (1866–1943) wrote children's stories starring Peter and Flopsy Rabbit.

Room 31 (third section): World War II

In the darkest days at the beginning of the war, with Nazi bombs raining on a helpless London, **Sir Winston Churchill** (1874–1965, bust) rallied his people with stirring radio speeches from an underground bunker. ("We will fight them on the beaches.... We will never surrender!") Britain's military chief, Field Marshall **Bernard Montgomery, 1st Viscount** (1887–1976, known as "Monty") points out the D-Day beaches of the decisive Allied assault.

Room 31 (last section): Later 20th century

• *Going clockwise, you'll see ...*

Laurence Olivier (bust), movie and stage actor, played everything from romantic leads and Shakespeare heavies to character parts with funny accents. **Noel Coward** continued the British tradition of writing witty, sophisticated comedies about the idle rich. **Henry Moore,** the most famous 20th-century sculptor, combined Michelangelo's grandeur, the raw stone of primitive carvings, and the simplified style of abstract art. **Dylan Thomas** wrote abstract imagery with a Romantic's heart ("Do not go gentle into that good night ... "). American-born poet **T. S. Eliot** (bust and Cubist-style portrait) captured the quiet banality of modern life ("This is the way the world ends—/Not with a bang but a whimper"). And classical music–lovers will recognize the great 20th-century composers, **Ralph Vaughan Williams** and **Benjamin Britten.**

• *Backtrack to the stairs down to the ground floor.*

GROUND FLOOR
Rooms 32–42: 1990 to the Present

London since the Swinging '60s has been a major exporter of

pop culture. The contemporary collection changes often depending on who's hot, but you'll likely find royalty **(Queen Elizabeth, Prince Charles, Princess Di)**, politicians **(John Major, Tony Blair)**, classic-rock geezers **(Sir Paul McCartney, Sir Elton John, David Bowie)**, and actors **(Michael Caine, Hugh Grant)**...as well as those in lower-profile professions (writers, composers, painters, and intellectuals).

We've gone from battles to Beatles, seeing Britain's history in the faces of its major players.

TATE
BRITAIN
TOUR

The Tate Britain has the world's best collection of British art. This is people's art, with realistic paintings rooted in the people, landscape, and stories of the British Isles. You'll see Hogarth's stage sets, Gainsborough's ladies, Blake's angels, Constable's clouds, Turner's tempests, the swooning realism of the Pre-Raphaelites, and the camera-eye portraits of Hockney and Freud. Even if these names are new to you, don't worry. Guaranteed you'll exit the Tate Britain with at least one new favorite.

Orientation
Cost: Free.

Hours: Daily 10:00–17:50, last admission 17:00, closed Dec 24–26.

Getting There: It's on Millbank, on the River Thames, just north of Vauxhall Bridge. Take the Tube to Pimlico (and walk 7 min); or take bus #88 (from Oxford Circus) or #77A (from National Gallery) directly to the museum; or walk 25 minutes south along the Thames from Big Ben. Other alternatives are buses #2, #3, #C10, #159, #185, or #507. The museum has two entrances: on Millbank, facing the Thames, and on Atterbury Street (handicapped-accessible).

Information: Pick up a free map at the information desk (tel. 020/7887-8000, recorded information tel. 020/7887-8008, www.tate.org.uk). The bookshop is great.

Tours: Free tours are offered daily (normally 11:00-Turner, 14:00 and 15:00-British Highlights, call to confirm schedule, tel. 020/7887-8000). Good audioguide tours cost £3. The museum also hosts slide lectures every Saturday at 13:00 and games and activities for children (3–12 years) daily 12:00–17:00 (for location and details, ask at group desk, tel. 020/7887-8759).

Tate Britain Overveiw

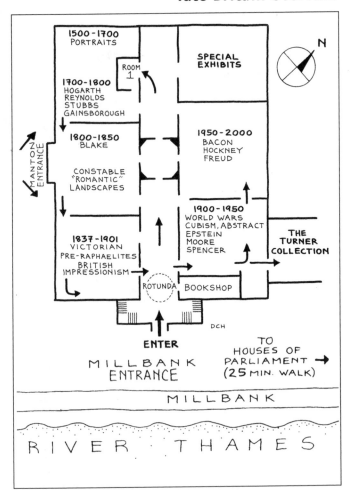

Length of Our Tour: One hour.

Cloakroom: Bag and coat check are free.

Photography: Photos are not allowed.

Cuisine Art: Your two options are a café with an affordable gourmet buffet line (daily 10:00–17:40) and a pricey-but-delightful restaurant (Mon–Sat 12:00–15:00, Sun 12:00–14:00).

Starring: Hogarth, Gainsborough, Reynolds, Blake, Constable, Pre-Raphaelites, and Turner.

The Two Tates

There are two separate Tate museums: The Tate Britain, which
this chapter describes, features British art. The Tate Modern (at
Bankside, on the South Bank of the Thames across from St. Paul's
Cathedral) features modern art (★ see the tour on page 164).

The Tate Britain's large collection of paintings changes
every year, but the basic layout stays the same: A chronological
walk through paintings from 1500–1900 in the west half of the
building, the 20th century in the east, and the works of J. M. W.
Turner in the adjoining Clore Gallery. Since the collection is
constantly in motion, a painting-by-painting tour is impossible.
We'll work chronologically, covering the big picture, seeing the
essence of each artist and style, then let the Tate surprise us with
its grand new wardrobe of paintings.

1500–1700—PORTRAITS

British artists painted people, countrysides, and scenes from daily
life, all done realistically and without the artist passing judgment
(substance over style). What you won't see here are the fleshy
goddesses, naked baby angels, and Madonna-and-child altarpieces
so popular elsewhere. The largely Protestant English abhorred the
"graven images" of the wealthy Catholic world. Many were even
destroyed during the 16th-century Reformation. They preferred
portraits of flesh-and-blood English folk.

Portrait of Lord and Lady Whoevertheyare

Stuffy portraits of a beef-fed society
try to turn crude country nobles into
refined men and delicate women. Men
in ruffled collars clutch symbols of
power. Women in ruffled collars,
puffy sleeves, and elaborately patterned dresses display their lily-white
complexions, turning their pinkies out.

English country houses often had
a long hall built specially to hang
family portraits. You could stroll along
and see your noble forebears looking down their noses at you.
Britain's upper crust had little interest in art other than as a record
of themselves along with their possessions—their wives, children,
jewels, furs, ruffled collars, swords, and guns.

You'll see plenty more portraits in the Tate Britain, right up
to modern times. Each era had its own style. Portraits from the
1500s are stern and dignified. The 1600s brought a more relaxed
and elegant style and more decolletage.

1700s—ART BLOSSOMS

With peace at home (under three king Georges), a strong overseas economy, and a growing urban center in London, England's artistic life began to bloom. As the English grew more sophisticated, so did their portraits. Painters branched out into other subjects, capturing slices of everyday life. The Royal Academy added a veneer of classical Greece to even the simplest subjects.

William Hogarth (1697–1764)

Hogarth loved the theater. "My picture is my stage," he said, "and my men and women my players." The curtain goes up, and we see one scene that tells a whole story, often satirizing English high

society. The London theater scene came into its own (after post-Shakespeare censorship) during Hogarth's generation. He often painted series based on popular plays of the time.

A born Londoner, Hogarth loved every gritty aspect of the big city. You'd find him in seedy pubs and brothels, at the half-price ticket booth in Leicester Square, at prizefights, cockfights, duels, and public executions—sketchbook in hand. An 18th-century Charles Dickens, he exposed the hypocrisy of fat-bellied squires, vain ladies, and gluttonous priests. He also gave the upper classes a glimpse into the hidden poverty of "merry olde England"—poor soldiers with holes in their stockings, overworked servants, and unwed mothers.

Hogarth's portraits (and self-portraits) are unflinchingly honest, quite different from the powdered-wig fantasies of his contemporaries.

Thomas Gainsborough (1727–88)

Thomas Gainsborough showcased the elegant, educated women of his generation. He portrayed them as they wished to see themselves: a feminine ideal, patterned after fashion magazines. The cheeks are rosy, the poses relaxed and S shaped, the colors brighter and more pastel, showing the influence of the refined French culture of the court at Versailles. His ladies tip-toe gracefully towards us, with clear, Ivory-soap complexions that stand out from the swirling greenery of English gardens. Gainsborough worked hard to prettify his subjects, but the results were always natural and never stuffy.

Sir Joshua Reynolds and the "Grand Style" (1723–92)

Real life wasn't worthy of a painting. So said Sir Joshua Reynolds, the pillar of Britain's Royal Academy. Instead, people, places, and things had to be gussied up with Greek columns, symbolism, and

great historic moments, ideally from classical Greece.

In his portraits, he'd pose Lady Bagbody like the Medici Venus, or Lord Milquetoast like Apollo Belvedere. In landscapes, you get Versailles-type settings of classical monuments amid perfectly manicured greenery. Inspired by Rembrandt, he sometimes used dense, clotted paint to capture the look of the Old Masters.

This art was meant to elevate the viewer, to appeal to his rational nature and fill him with noble sentiment. Sir Joshua Reynolds, the pillar of England's art establishment, stood for all that was upright, tasteful, rational, brave, clean, reverent, and . . . and you'll find me in the next room.

George Stubbs—Horses (1724–1806)

Stubbs was the Michelangelo of horse painters. He understood these creatures from the inside out, having dissected them in his studio. He even used machinery to prop the corpses up into life-like poses. He painted the horses first on a blank canvas, then filled in the background landscape around them (notice the heavy outlines that make them stand out clearly from the countryside). The result is both incredibly natural—from the veins in their noses to the freshly brushed coats—and geometrically posed.

1800–1850—THE INDUSTRIAL REVOLUTION

Newfangled inventions were everywhere. Railroads laced the land. You could fall asleep in Edinburgh and wake up in London, a trip that used to take days or weeks. But along with technology came factories coating towns with soot, urban poverty, regimentation, and clock-punching. Machines replaced honest laborers, and once-noble Man was viewed as a naked ape.

Strangely, you'll see little of the modern world in paintings of the time—except in reaction to it. Many artists rebelled against "progress" and the modern world. They escaped the dirty cities to commune with nature (Constable and the Romantics). Or they found a new spirituality in intense human emotions (dramatic scenes from history or literature). Or they left the modern world altogether. Which brings us to ...

William Blake (1757–1827)

At the age of four, Blake saw the face of God. A few years later, he ran across a flock of angels swinging in a tree. Twenty years later, he was living in a run-down London flat with an illiterate wife, scratching out a thin existence as an engraver. But even in

this squalor, ignored by all but a few fellow artists, he still had his heavenly visions, and he described them in poems, paintings, drawings, and prints.

One of the original space cowboys, Blake was also a unique artist who is often classed with the Romantics because

he painted in a fit of ecstatic inspiration rather than by studied technique. He painted angels, not the dull material world. While Britain was conquering the world with guns and nature with machines, and while his fellow Londoners were growing rich, fat, and self-important, Blake turned his gaze inward, illustrating the glorious visions of the soul.

Blake's work hangs in a darkened room to protect the watercolors. Enter his mysterious world and let your pupils dilate opium-wide.

His pen and watercolor sketches glow with an unearthly aura. In visions of the Christian heaven or Dante's hell, his figures have superhero musculature. The colors are almost translucent.

Blake saw the material world as bad, trapping the divine spark inside each of our bodies and keeping us from true communion with God. Blake's prints illustrate his views on the ultimate weakness of material, scientific man. Despite their Greek-god anatomy, his men look noble but tragically lost.

A famous poet as well as painter, Blake summed up his distrust of the material world in a poem addressed to "The God of this World," that is, Satan:

Though thou art worshiped by the names divine
Of Jesus and Jehovah, thou art still
The son of morn in weary night's decline,
The lost traveler's dream under the hill.

John Constable (1776–1837)

While the Royal Academy thought Nature needed makeup, Constable thought she was just fine. He painted the English landscape as it was, realistically, and without idealizing it. With simple earth tones he caught leafy green trees, gathering gray skies, brown country lanes, and rivers the color of the clouds reflected in them.

Clouds are Constable's trademark. Appreciate the effort involved in sketching ever-changing cloud patterns for hours on end—the mix of dark clouds and white clouds, cumulus and stratus, the colors of sunset. A generation before the Impressionists, he actually set up his easel outdoors and painted on the spot, a painstaking process before the invention of ready-made paints-in-a-tube around 1850.

It's rare to find a Constable (or any British) landscape that doesn't have the mark of man in it—a cottage, hay cart, or field hand, or a country road running through the scene. For him, the English countryside and its people were one.

In his later years, Constable's canvases became bigger, the style more "Impressionistic" (messier brushwork), and he worked more from memory than out-of-doors observation.

Constable's commitment to unvarnished nature wasn't fully recognized in his lifetime, and he was forced to paint portraits for his keep. The neglect caused him to ask a friend, "Can it therefore be wondered at that I paint continual storms?"

Other Landscapes

Compare Constable's un-pretentious landscapes with others in the Tate Britain. Some artists mixed land-scapes with intense human emotion to produce huge, colorful canvases of storms, burning sunsets, towering

clouds, and crashing waves, all dwarfing puny humans. Others made supernatural, religious fantasy-scapes. Artists in the Romantic style saw the most intense human emotions reflected in the drama and mystery in nature. God is found within nature, and nature is charged with the grandeur and power of God.

1837–1901—VICTORIAN

In the world's wealthiest nation, the prosperous middle class dictated taste in art. They admired paintings that were realistic (showcasing the artist's talent and work ethic), depicting Norman Rockwell–style slices of everyday life.

We see families and ordinary people eating, working, and relaxing. Some paintings tug at the heartstrings, with scenes of parting couples, the grief of death, or the joy of families reuniting. Dramatic scenes from popular literature get the heart beating. There's the occasional touching look at the plight of the honest poor, reminiscent of Dickens. And many paintings warn us to be good little boys and girls by showing the consequences of a life of sin. Then there are the puppy dogs with sad eyes.

PRE-RAPHAELITES

Millais, Rossetti, Holman Hunt, Waterhouse, Burne-Jones, etc.

You'll see medieval damsels in dresses and knights in tights, legendary lovers from poetry, and even a very human Virgin Mary as a delicate young woman. The women wear flowing dresses and have long, wavy hair and delicate, elongated, curving bodies. Beautiful.

Overdosed with gushy Victorian sentimentality, a band of 20-year-old artists said, "Enough!" and dedicated themselves to less saccharine art. Their "Pre-Raphaelite Brotherhood" (you may see the initials P. R. B. by the artist's signature) returned to a style "pre-Raphael," that is, "medieval" in its simple style, in the melancholy mood, and often in subject matter.

Truth to Nature was their slogan. Like the Impressionists who followed, they donned their scarves, barged out of the stuffy studio, and set up outdoors, painting trees, streams, and people, like scientists on a field trip. Still, they often captured nature with such a close-up clarity that it's downright unnatural. And despite the Pre-Raphaelite claim to paint life just as it is, this is so beautiful it hurts.

This is art from the cult of femininity, worshiping Woman's

haunting beauty, compassion, and depth of soul. (Proto-feminism or nouveau-chauvinism?) The artists' wives and lovers were their models and muses, and the art echoed their love lives. The people are surrounded by nature at its most beautiful, with every detail painted crystal clear. Even without the people, there is a mood of melancholy.

The Pre-Raphaelites hated overacting. Their subjects—even in the face of great tragedy, high passions, and moral dilemmas—barely raise an eyebrow. Outwardly, they're reflective, accepting their fate. But sinuous postures—with lovers swooning into each other, and parting lovers swooning apart—speak volumes. These volumes are footnoted by the small objects with symbolic importance placed around them: red flowers denoting passion, lilies for purity, pets for fidelity, and so on.

The colors—greens, blues, and reds—are bright and clear, with everything evenly lit, so we see every detail. To get the luminous color, some painted a thin layer of bright paint over a pure white, still-wet undercoat, which subtly "shines" through. These canvases radiate a pure spirituality, like stained-glass windows.

Stand for a while and enjoy the exquisite realism and human emotions of these Victorian-era works...real people painted realistically. Get your fill, because beloved Queen Victoria is about to check out, the modern world is coming, and with it, new art to express modern attitudes.

British Impressionism

Realistic British art stood apart from the modernist trends in France, but some influences drifted across the Channel. **John Singer Sargent** (American-born) studied with Parisian Impressionists, learning the thick, messy brushwork and play of light at twilight. **James Tissot** used Degas' snapshot technique to capture a crowded scene from an odd angle. And **James McNeill Whistler** (also born in the United States) composed his paintings like music (see some titles), as collages of shapes and colors that please the eye like a song tickles the ear.

• *To help ease the transition to modern art (in the east half of Tate Britain), first visit the Turner Collection. Pass through the rotunda to the east side of the gallery, and just keep going through a few rooms till you enter "The Clore Gallery/ The Turner Collection."*

THE TURNER COLLECTION

J. M. W. Turner (1775–1851)

The Tate Britain has the world's best collection of Turners. Walking through his life's work, you can trace his progression from a painter of realistic historical scenes, through his wandering years, to Impressionist paintings of color-and-light patterns.

• *Start in Room C9, with biographical info on Turner, his early works, and a display of his paints and brushes.*

Self-Portrait as a Young Man

At 24, Turner has just been elected the youngest Associate of the Royal Academy. The barber's son now dresses like a gentleman. His full-frontal pose and intense gaze show a young man ready to take on the world.

The Royal Academy Years

Trained in the Reynolds school of grandiose epics, Turner painted the obligatory big canvases of great moments in history—*The Battle of Waterloo, Hannibal in the Alps, Destruction of Sodom, The Lost Traveler's Checks, Jason and the Argonauts,* and various shipwrecks. Not content to crank them out in the traditional staid manner, he sets them in expansive landscapes. Nature's stormy mood mirrors the human events, but is so grandiose it dwarfs them.

This is a theme we'll see throughout his works: The forces of nature—the burning sun, swirling clouds, churning waves, gathering storms, and the weathering of time—overwhelm men and wear down the civilizations they build.

Travels with Turner

Turner's true love was nature. And he was a born hobo. Oblivious to the wealth and fame that his early paintings gave him, he set out traveling—mostly on foot—throughout England and the Continent, with a rucksack full of sketch pads and painting gear. He sketched the English countryside, not green, leafy, and placid as so many others had done, but churning in motion, hazed over by a burning sunset.

He found the "sublime" not in the studio or in church,

but in the overwhelming power of nature. The landscapes throb with life and motion. He sets Constable's clouds on fire.

Italy's Landscape and Ruins

Rick Steves' guidebook in hand, Turner visited the great museums of Italy, drawing inspiration from the Renaissance masters. He painted the classical monuments and Renaissance architecture. He copied masterpieces and learned, assimilated, and fused a great variety of styles—a true pan-European vision. Turner's Roman ruins are not grand, they're dwarfed by the landscape around them and eroded by swirling, misty, luminous clouds.

Stand close to a big canvas of Roman ruins, close enough so that it fills your whole field of vision. Notice how the buildings seem to wrap around you. Turner was a master of using multiple perspectives to draw the viewer in. On the one hand, you're right in the thick of things, looking "up" at the tall buildings. Then again, you're looking "down" on the distant horizon, as though standing on a mountaintop.

Venice

I know what color the *palazzo* is. But what color is it at sunset? Or through the filter of the watery haze that hangs over Venice? Can I paint the glowing haze itself? Maybe if I combine two different colors and smudge the paint on....

Venice stoked Turner's lust for reflected, golden sunlight. This room contains both finished works and unfinished sketches...uh, which is which?

Seascapes

The ever-changing sea was his specialty, with waves, clouds, mist, and sky churning and mixing together, all driven by the same forces.

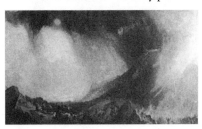

Turner used oils like many painters use watercolors. First he'd lay down a background (a "wash") of large patches of color, then he'd add a few dabs of paint to suggest a figure. The final product lacked photographic clarity but showed the power and constant change in the forces of nature. He was perhaps the most prolific painter ever, with some 2,000 finished paintings and 20,000 sketches and watercolors.

Late Works

The older he got, the messier both he and his paintings became. He was wealthy, but he died in a run-down dive where he'd set up house with a prostitute. Yet the colors are brighter and the subjects less pessimistic than in the dark and brooding early canvases. His last works—whether landscape, religious, or classical scenes—are a blur and swirl of colors in motion, lit by the sun or a lamp burning through the mist. Even Turner's own creations are finally dissolved by the swirling forces of nature.

These paintings are "modern" in that the subject is less important than the style. You'll have to read the title to "get" it. You could argue that an Englishman helped invent Impressionism a generation before Monet and his ilk boxed the artistic ears of Paris in the 1880s. Turner's messy use of paint to portray reflected light "chunneled" its way to France to inspire the Impressionists.

• *The 20th century, found in the east half of the Tate building, starts in Room 19.*

1900–1950

As two World Wars whittled the powerful British Empire down, it still remained a major cultural force.

British art mirrored many of the trends and -isms pioneered in Paris. You'll see Cubism like Picasso's, Abstract art like Mondrian's, and so on. But British artists also continued the British tradition of realistic paintings of people and landscape. (Note: You'll find 20th-century artists' work both here in the Tate Britain and in the Tate Modern.)

World War I, in which Britain lost a million men, cast a long shadow over the land. Artists expressed the horror of war, particularly of dehumanizing battles pitting powerful machines against puny human pawns. **Jacob Epstein's** (1880–1959) gleaming, abstract statues suggest mangled half-human/half-machine forms.

Henry Moore (1898–1986)

Twice a week, young Henry Moore went to the British Museum to sketch ancient statues, especially reclining ones (like in the Parthenon pediment or the Mayan Chac Mool he saw in a photo). His statues—mostly female, mostly reclining—catch the primitive power of carved stone. Moore almost always carved with his own hands (unlike, say, Rodin, who modeled a small clay figure and let assistants chisel the real thing), capturing the human body in a few simple curves, with minimal changes to the rock itself.

The statues do look vaguely like what their titles say, but it's the stones themselves that are really interesting. Notice the texture and graininess of these mini-Stonehenges; feel the weight, the space they take up, and how the rock forms intermingle.

During World War II, Moore passed time in the bomb shelters sketching mothers with babes in arms, a theme found in later works.

Moore carves the human body with the epic scale and restless poses of Michelangelo but with the crude rocks and simple lines of the primitives.

Stanley Spencer (1891–1959)

Spencer paints unromanticized land-scapes, portraits, and hometown scenes. Even the miraculous *Resurrection of the Dead* is portrayed absolutely literally, with the dead climbing out of their Glasgow graves. In fully modern times, Spencer carried on the British tradition of sober realism.

Francis Bacon (1909–92)

With a stiff upper lip, Britain survived the Blitz, the War, and the loss of hundreds of thousands of men—but at war's end, the bottled-up horror came rushing out. Bacon's 1945 exhibition, opening just after Holocaust details began surfacing, stunned London with its unmitigated ugliness.

His deformed half-humans/half-animals—caged in a claus-trophobic room, with twisted, hunk-of-meat bodies and quadri-plegic, smudged-mouth helplessness—can do nothing but scream in anguish and frustration. The scream becomes a blur, as though it goes on forever.

Bacon, largely self-taught, effectively uses "traditional" fig-urativism to express the existential human predicament of being caught in a world that is not of your making—you feel isolated and helpless to change it.

1950–2000

No longer a world power, Britain in the Swinging '60s became a major exporter of pop culture. British art's traditional strengths—realism, portraits, landscapes, and slice-of-life scenes—were redone in the modern style.

David Hockney (b. 1937)

The "British Andy Warhol"— who is bleached blonde, horn-rimmed, gay, and famous— paints Pop-ular culture with photographic realism. Large, airy canvases of L.A. swimming pools, double portraits of his friends in their stylish homes, or mundane scenes from the artist's own life capture the superficial materialism of the '70s and '80s. (Is he satirizing or glorifying it by painting it on a monumental scale with painstaking detail?)

Hockney saturates the canvas with bright (acrylic) paint, eliminating any haze, making distant objects as clear and bright as close ones. This, combined with his slightly simplified "cut-out" figures, gives the canvas the flat look of a billboard.

Lucian Freud (b. 1922)

Sigmund's grandson (who emigrated from Nazi Germany as a boy) puts every detail on the couch for analysis, then reassembles

them into works that are still surprisingly realistic. His subjects look you right in the eye, slightly on edge. Even the plants create an ominous mood. Everything is in sharp focus (unlike in real life, where you concentrate on one thing while your peripheral vision is blurred). Thick brushwork is especially good at capturing the pallor of British flesh.

In the great tradition of British portrait painting, Freud recently did an unflinching (and controversial) portrait of Queen Elizabeth.

Bridget Riley (b. 1931)

The pioneer of Op Art paints patterns of lines and alternating colors that make the eye vibrate (the way a spiral will "spin") when you stare at it. These obscure, scientific experiments in human optics suddenly became trendy in the psychedelic, cannabis-fueled '60s. Like, wow.

Barbara Hepworth (1903–75)

Hepworth's small-scale carvings in stone and wood—like "mini-Moores"—make even holes look interesting. Though they're not exactly realistic, it isn't hard to imagine them being inspired by, say, a man embracing a woman (she called it "sex harmony"), or the shoreline encircling a bay near her Cornwall-coast home, or a cliff penetrated by a cave—that is, two forms intermingling.

Gilbert and George (b. 1943 and 1942)

The Siegfried and Roy of art satirize the "Me Generation" and its shame-less self-marketing by portraying their nerdy, three-piece-suited selves on the monumental scale normally dedicated to kings, popes, and saints.

THE REST OF THE TATE

We've covered 500 years, with social satire from Hogarth to Hockney, from Constable's placid landscapes to Turner's churn-ing scenes, from Blake's inner visions to Pre-Raphaelite fantasies, from realistic portraits to...realistic portraits.

But the Tate's great strength is championing contemporary British art in special exhibitions. There are two exhibition spaces: in the northeast corner of the main floor and the Linbury Gallery downstairs (each usually requiring separate admission). Explore the cutting-edge art from one of the world's thriving cultural capitals—London.

Enough Tate? Great. It's late.

TATE
MODERN
TOUR

Remember the 20th century? Accelerated by technology and fragmented by war, it was an exciting and chaotic time, with art as turbulent as the world that created it. The Tate Modern lets you walk through the last hundred years with a glimpse at the brave new art of this explosive century.

Orientation

Cost: Free for the permanent collection (but donations are appreciated). Varying costs for temporary exhibits.

Hours: Sun–Thu 10:00–18:00, Fri–Sat 10:00–22:00. This popular place is especially crowded on weekend days (crowds thin out on Fri and Sat evenings).

Getting There: Located on the South Bank, across from St. Paul's and near the Globe Theatre (Tube: Southwark or Blackfriars plus 10-min walk, or cross the Millennium Bridge from St Paul's).

Information: The museum is also known as "Tate Modern at Bankside" (tel. 020/7887-8000, recorded information tel. 020/7887-8008, www.tate.org.uk). On the ground floor, you'll find the information desk, baggage check, audioguide rentals, and tickets for temporary exhibits. Three audioguide tours (£1 apiece) are available: Director's Tour (highlights of the permanent collection), Collections Tour (all of the permanent collection), and a Children's Tour (geared for 8–12-year-olds). Free children's programs include Start, a variety of games and crafts (Sun 11:00–13:00 & 14:30–17:00), and Artmixx, an interactive workshop that includes drawing exercises and discussions for kids ages five and older (Sat 11:00–12:30 & 14:00–17:30, booking required, tel. 020/7887-8888).

Photography: Photos are permitted only in the entrance hall.

Cuisine Art: View coffee shops are on the fourth and seventh floors. Some fine restaurants are outside along the Cut (near Southwark Tube stop).

Starring: Picasso, Matisse, Dalí, and all the "classic" modern artists, plus the Tate Modern's specialty—British and American artists of the last half of the 20th century.

Orien-Tate-ing

The main permanent collection is on the third and fifth floors. Temporary exhibits are on the fourth. (Note: Modern British artists are divided between the Tate Modern and Tate Britain.)

The Tate Modern is (controversially) displayed by genre—nudes, landscapes, still lifes, and history—rather than by artist and chronology. Unlike the Tate Modern, this chapter will be neatly chronological. Read this chapter for a general introduction, then take advantage of the Tate's excellent audioguides to focus on specific works.

Entrance Hall

The massive empty space of the former industrial powerhouse dwarfs the art it houses. (A metaphor for the triumph of 20th-century technology, perhaps?)

1900—VICTORIA'S LEGACY

Anno Domini 1900, a new century dawns. Europe is at peace, Britannia rules the world. Technology is about to usher in a golden age.

Claude Monet

Monet captures the relaxed, civilized spirit of belle époque France and Victorian England with Impressionist snapshots of peaceful landscapes and middle-class family picnics. But the true subject is the shimmering effect of reflected light, rendered with rough brush strokes and bright paints that look messy up close, but blend at a distance. The newfangled camera made camera-eye realism obsolete. Artists began placing more importance on *how* something was painted than on *what* was painted.

1905—COLONIAL EUROPE

Europe ruled a global empire, tapping its dark-skinned colonials for raw materials, cheap labor, and bold new ways to look at the world. The cozy Victorian world was shattering. Nietzsche murdered God. Darwin stripped off Man's robe of culture and found a naked ape. Primitivism was Modern. Ooga-booga.

Henri Matisse (1869–1954)

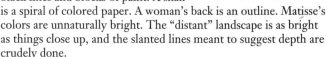

Matisse was one of the Fauves, or "wild beasts," who tried to inject a bit of the jungle into civilized European society. Inspired by "primitive" African and oceanic masks and voodoo dolls, the Fauves made modern art that looked primitive: long, mask-like faces with almond eyes, bright, clashing colors, simple figures, and "flat," two-dimensional scenes.

Matisse simplifies. A man is a few black lines and blocks of paint. A snail is a spiral of colored paper. A woman's back is an outline. Matisse's colors are unnaturally bright. The "distant" landscape is as bright as things close up, and the slanted lines meant to suggest depth are crudely done.

Traditionally, the canvas was like a window that you looked "through" to see a slice of the real world stretching off into the distance. With Matisse, you look "at" the canvas, like wallpaper, to appreciate the decorative pattern of colors and shapes.

Though fully modern, Matisse built on 19th-century art—the bright colors of van Gogh, the primitive figures of Gauguin, the colorful designs of Japanese prints, and the Impressionist patches of paint that only blend together at a distance.

Paul Cézanne (1839–1906)

Cézanne brings Impressionism into the 20th century. While Monet used separate dabs of different-colored paint to "build" a figure, Cézanne "builds" a man with somewhat larger slabs of paint, giving it a kind of 3-D chunkiness. It's not hard to see the progression from Monet's dabs to Cézanne's slabs to Picasso's cubes—Cubism.

1910—THE MODERNS

The modern world was moving fast, with automobiles, factories, and mass communication. Motion pictures caught the fast-moving world, while Einstein further explored the fourth dimension, time.

Cubism: Pablo Picasso (1881–1973)

Picasso's Cubist works show the old European world shattering to bits. He pieces the fragments back together in a whole new way,

showing several perspectives at once
(looking up the left side of a woman's
body, and down at her right, for example).
    While newfangled motion pictures
could capture several perspectives in
succession, Picasso does it on a canvas
with overlapping images. A single "cube"
might contain both an arm (in the foreground) and the window behind (in the
background), both painted the same
color. The foreground and background
are woven together so that the subject
dissolves into a pattern.

    Born in Spain, Picasso moved to Paris as a young man.
He worked with Georges Braque in poverty so dire they often
didn't know where their next bottle of wine was coming from.
    Picasso, the most famous and—OK, I'll say it—the greatest
artist of the 20th century, constantly explored and adapted his style
to new trends. He made collages, tried his hand at "statues" out of
wood, wire, or whatever, and even made art out of everyday house-
hold objects. These multimedia works, so revolutionary at the
time, have become stock-in-trade today. Scattered throughout the
museum are works from the many periods of Picasso's life.

Futurism: Fernand Leger (1881–1955) and Umberto Boccioni (1882-1916)

The Machine Age is approaching, and the whole world gleams
with promise in cylinder shapes ("Tubism"), like an internal-
combustion engine. Or is it the gleaming barrel of a cannon?

1914—WORLD WAR I

A soldier—shivering in a trench, ankle-deep in mud, waiting to
be ordered "over the top," to run through barbed wire, over fallen
comrades, and into a hail of machine-gun fire, only to capture a
few hundred yards of meaningless territory that would be lost
the next day. This soldier was not thinking about art.
    World War I left nine million dead. (England sometimes
lost more men in a single day than America lost in all of Vietnam.)
The war also killed the optimism and faith in mankind that had
guided Europe since the Renaissance.

Expressionism: Grosz, Kirchner, Beckmann, Soutine, Dix, Kokoschka

Cynicism and decadence settled over postwar Europe. Artists
"expressed" their disgust by showing a distorted reality that

emphasized the ugly. Using the lurid colors and simplified figures of the Fauves, they slapped paint on in thick brush strokes, depicting a hypocritical, hard-edged, dog-eat-dog world, a civilization watching its Victorian moral foundations collapse.

Dada: Duchamp's Urinal (1917)

When they could grieve no longer, artists turned to grief's giddy twin, laughter. The war made all old values a joke, including artistic ones. The Dada movement, choosing a purposely childish name, made art that was intentionally outrageous: a moustache on the Mona Lisa, a shovel hung on the wall, or a modern version of a Renaissance "fountain"— a urinal (by Marcel Duchamp ... or was it I. P. Freeley?).

It was a dig at all the pompous prewar artistic theories based on the noble intellect of Rational Women and Men. While the experts ranted on, Dadaists sat in the back of the class and made cultural fart noises.

Hey, I love this stuff. My mind says it's sophomoric, but my heart belongs to Dada.

1920—ANYTHING GOES

In the Jazz Age, the world turned upside down. Genteel ladies smoked cigarettes. Gangsters laid down the law. You could make a fortune in the stock market one day and lose it the next. You could dance the Charleston with the opposite sex, and even say the word "sex," talking about Freud over cocktails. It was almost ... surreal.

Surrealism: Dalí, Ernst, Magritte

Artists caught the jumble of images on a canvas. A telephone made from a lobster, an elephant with a heating-duct trunk, Venus sleepwalking among skeletons. Take one mixed bag of reality, jumble in a blender, and serve on a canvas—Surrealism.

The artist scatters seemingly unrelated things on the canvas, leaving us to trace the connections in a kind of connect-the-dots without numbers.

Further complicating the modern world was Freud's discovery of the "unconscious" mind that thinks dirty thoughts while we sleep. Surrealists let the id speak. The canvas is an uncensored, stream-of-consciousness "landscape" of these deep urges, revealed in the bizarre images of dreams.

Salvador Dalí (1904–1989)

Salvador Dalí, the most famous surrealist, combined an extraordinarily realistic technique with an extraordinarily twisted mind. He could paint "unreal" scenes with photographic realism, making us believe they could really happen. Dalí's  images—crucifixes, political and religious figures, and naked bodies—pack an emotional punch.

1930—DEPRESSION

As capitalism failed around the world, governments propped up their economies with vast building projects. The architecture style was modern, stripped-down (i.e., cheap), and functional. Propaganda campaigns champion noble workers in the heroic Social Realist style.

Piet Mondrian (1872–1944)

Like blueprints for modernism, Mondrian's T-square style boils painting down to its basic building blocks—black lines, a white 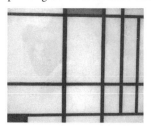 canvas, and the three primary colors—red, yellow, and blue— arranged in orderly patterns. (When you come right down to it, that's all painting ever has been. A schematic drawing of, say, the *Mona Lisa* shows that it's less about a woman than about the triangles and rectangles she's composed of.)

Mondrian started out painting realistic landscapes of the orderly fields in his native homeland of Holland. Increasingly, he simplified his style into horizontal and vertical patterns. For Mondrian, who was heavy into Eastern mysticism, "up versus down" and "left versus right" were the perfect metaphors for life's dualities: good versus evil, body versus spirit, Fascism vs. Communism, man versus woman. The canvas is a bird's-eye view of Mondrian's personal landscape.

1940—WORLD WAR II

World War II was a global war (involving Europe, the Americas, Australia, Africa, and Asia) and a total war (saturation bombing of civilians and ethnic cleansing). It left Europe in ruins.

Abstract Art

Abstract art simplifies. A man becomes a stick figure. A squiggle is a wave. A streak of red expresses anger. Arches make you want a cheeseburger. These are universal symbols  that everyone from a caveman to a banker understands. Abstract artists capture the essence of reality in a few lines and colors, even things a camera can't—emotions, abstract concepts, musical rhythms, and spiritual states of mind.

With Abstract art, you don't look "through" the canvas to see the visual world, but "at" it to read the symbolism of lines, shapes, and colors. Most 20th-century paintings are a mix of the real world (representation) and colorful patterns (abstraction).

Alberto Giacometti (1901–66)

Giacometti's skinny statues have the emaciated, haunted, and faceless look of concentration-camp survivors. In the sweep of world war and overpowering technology, man is frail and fragile. All he can do is stand at attention and take it like a man.

Francis Bacon (1909–92)

Bacon's caged creatures speak for all of war-torn Europe when they scream, "Enough!" (✪ For more on Bacon, see the Tate Britain Tour, page 161.)

1950—AMERICA THE GLOBAL SUPERPOWER

As converted war factories turned swords into kitchen appliances, America helped rebuild Europe, while pumping out consumer goods for a booming population. Prosperity, a stable government, national television broadcasts, and a common fear of Soviet Communism threatened to turn America into a completely homogeneous society.

Some artists, centered in New York, rebelled against conformity and superficial consumerism. (They'd served under

Eisenhower in war and now had to in peace, as well.) They created
art that was the very opposite of the functional, mass-produced
goods of the American marketplace.

Art was a way of asserting your individuality by creating a
completely original and personal vision. The trend was toward
bigger canvases, abstract designs, and experimentation with new
materials and techniques. It was called "Abstract Expressionism"—
expressing emotions and ideas using color and form alone.

Jackson Pollock (1912–56)

"Jack the Dripper" attacks convention with a can of paint, drip-
ping and splashing a dense web onto the canvas. Picture Pollock
in his studio, jiving to the hi-fi, bouncing off the walls, throwing
paint in a moment of enlightenment. Of course, the artist loses
some control this way—over the paint flying in midair and over
himself in an ecstatic trance. Painting becomes a whole-body
activity, a "dance" between the artist and his materials.

The intuitive act of creating is what's important, not the final
product. The canvas is only a record of that moment of ecstasy.

Big, Empty Canvases

With all the postwar prosperity, artists could afford bigger
canvases. But what reality are they trying to show?

In the modern world, we find ourselves insignificant specks
in a vast and indifferent universe. Every morning, each of us
must confront that big, blank, existentialist canvas and decide
how we're going to make our mark on it.

Another influence was the simplicity of Japanese landscape
painting. A Zen master studies and meditates for years to achieve
the state of mind where he can draw one pure line. These canvases, again, are only a record of that state of enlightenment.
(What is the sound of one brush painting?)

On more familiar ground, postwar painters were following in
the footsteps of artists such as Mondrian. The geometrical forms
here reflect the same search for order, but these artists painted to
the 5/4 symmetry of "Take Five."

Patterns and Textures

Enjoy the lines and colors, but also a new element: texture. Some
works have very thick paint piled on, where you can see the brush
strokes clearly. Some have substances besides paint applied to the
canvas, or the canvas is punctured so the fabric itself (and the hole)
becomes the subject. Artists show their skill by mastering new materials. The canvas is a tray, serving up a delightful array of different
substances with interesting colors, patterns, shapes, and textures.

Mark Rothko (1903–70)

Rothko makes two-toned rectangles, laid on their sides, that seem to float in a big, vertical canvas. The edges are blurred, so if you get close enough to let the canvas fill your field of vision (as Rothko intended), the rectangles appear to rise and sink from the cloudy depths like answers in a Magic Eight Ball.

Serious students appreciate the subtle differences in color between the rectangles. Rothko experimented with different bases for the same color, and used a single undercoat (a "wash") to unify them. His early works are warmer, with brighter reds, yellows, and oranges; the later works are maroon and brown, approaching black.

Still, these are not intended to be formal studies in color and form. Rothko was trying to express the most basic human emotions in a pure language. (A "realistic" painting of a person is inherently fake because it's only an illusion of the person.) Staring into these windows onto the soul, you can laugh, cry, or ponder just as Rothko did when he painted them.

Rothko, the last century's "last serious artist," believed in the power of art to express the human spirit. When he found out that his eight large Seagrams canvases were to be hung in a corporate restaurant, he refused to sell them (and they ended up in the Tate).

In his last years, Rothko's canvases—always rectangles—got bigger, simpler, and darker. When Rothko finally slashed his wrists in his studio, one nasty critic joked that what killed him was the repetition. The "Minimal" style was painting itself into a blank corner.

1960—"THE '60s"

The decade began united in idealism—young John F. Kennedy pledged to put a man on the moon; newly launched satellites signaled a united world, the Beatles sang exuberantly, peaceful race demonstrations championed equality, and the Vatican II council preached liberation. By decade's end, there were race riots, assassinations, student protests, and America's floundering war in distant Vietnam. In households around the world, parents screamed, "Turn that down . . . and get a haircut!"

Culturally, every postwar value was questioned by a rising, wealthy, populous, Baby-Boom generation. London—producer of rock-and-roll music, film actors, mod fashions, and Austin-Powers joie de vivre—once again became a world cultural center.

20th-Century British Artists

Since 1960, London has rivaled New York as a center for the visual arts. You'll find British artists displayed in both the Tate Modern and Tate Britain. Check out the Tate Britain chapter (page 149) for more on the following artists: David Hockney, Stanley Spencer, Jacob Epstein, Gilbert and George, Henry Moore, Francis Bacon, and Barbara Hepworth.

While government-sponsored public art was dominated by big, abstract canvases and sculptures, other artists pooh-poohed the highbrow seriousness of abstract art. Instead, they mocked lowbrow, "pop"-ular culture by embracing it in a tongue-in-cheek way (Pop art), or they attacked authority with absurd performances to make a political statement (conceptual art).

Pop Art: Andy Warhol (1930–1987)

America's postwar wealth made the consumer king. Pop art is created from the popular objects of that throwaway society—a soup can, car fender, tacky plastic statues, movie icons. Take a Sears product, hang it in a museum, and you have to ask, Is this art? Are mass-produced objects beautiful? Or crap? Why do we work so hard to acquire them? Pop art, like Dadaism, questions our society's values.

Andy Warhol (who coined "15 minutes of fame") concentrated on another mass-produced phenomenon—celebrities. He took publicity photos of famous people and repeated them. The repetition—like the constant bombardment we get from repeated images on TV—cheapens even the most beautiful things.

Roy Lichtenstein (1923–97)

Take a comic strip, blow it up, hang it on a wall and charge a million bucks— wham, Pop art. Lichtenstein suppos- edly was inspired by his young son, who  challenged him to do something as good as Mickey Mouse. The huge newsprint dots never let us forget that the painting—like all commercial art—is an illusionistic fake. The work's humor comes from portraying a lowbrow subject (comics and ads) on the epic scale of a masterpiece.

Op Art: Bridget Riley (1931–)

Optical illusions play tricks with your eyes, like the way a spiral starts to spin when you stare at it. These obscure scientific experiments in color, line, and optics suddenly became trendy in the psychedelic '60s.

1970—THE "ME DECADE"

All forms of authority—"The Establishment"—seemed bankrupt. America's president resigned in the Watergate scandal, corporations were polluting the earth, and capitalism nearly ground to a halt when Arabs withheld oil.

Artists attacked authority and institutions, trying to free individuals to discover their full human potential. Even the concept of "modernism"—that art wasn't good unless it was totally original and progressive—was questioned. No single style could dictate in this postmodern period.

"Earth Art"

Fearing for the health of earth's ecology, artists rediscovered the beauty of rocks, dirt, trees, even the sound of the wind, using them to create natural art. A rock placed in a museum or urban square is certainly a strange sight.

Joseph Beuys (1921–1986)

The Tate Modern's collection of "sculptures" by Beuys—assemblages of steel, junk, wood, and, especially, felt and animal fat—only hint at his greatest artwork: Beuys himself.

Imagine Beuys (pron. boyss) walking through the museum, carrying a dead rabbit, while he explains the paintings to it. Or taking off his clothes, shaving his head, and smearing his body with fat.

This charismatic, ex-Luftwaffe, art shaman did ridiculous things to inspire others to break with convention and be free. He choreographed "Happenings"—spectacles where people did absurd things while others watched—and pioneered performance art, in which the artist presents himself as the work of art. Beuys inspired a whole generation of artists to walk on stage, cluck like a chicken, and stick a yam up themselves. Beuys will be Beuys.

New Media

Minimalist painting and abstract sculpture were old hat, and there was an explosion of new art forms. Performance art was the most controversial, combining music, theater, dance, poetry, and the visual arts. New technologies brought video, assemblages, installations, artists' books (paintings in book form), and even (gasp!) realistic painting.

Conceptual Art
Increasingly, artists are not creating an original work (painting a canvas or sculpting a stone) but assembling one from premade objects. The *concept* of which object to pair with another to produce maximum effect ("Let's stick a crucifix in a jar of urine," to cite one notorious example) is the key.

1980—MATERIAL GIRL
Ronald Reagan in America, Margaret Thatcher in Britain, and corporate executives around the world ruled over a conservative and materialistic society. On the other side were starving Ethiopians, gays with the new disease of AIDS, people of color, and women demanding power. Intelligent, peaceful, straight, white males assumed a low profile.

The art world became big business, with a van Gogh fetching $54 million. Corporations paid big bucks for large, colorful, semiabstract canvases. Marketing became an art form. Gender and sexual choice were popular themes. Many women picked up paintbrushes, creating bright-colored abstract forms hinting at vulva and penis shapes. Visual art fused with popular music, bringing us installations in dance clubs and fast-edit music videos. The crude style of graffiti art demanded to be included in corporate society.

1990—MULTICULTURAL DIVERSITY
The Soviet-built Berlin Wall was torn down, ending four decades of a global Cold War between capitalism and communism. The new battleground was the "Culture Wars," the struggle to include all races, genders, and lifestyles within an increasingly corporate-dominated, global society.

Artists looked to Third World countries for inspiration and championed society's outsiders against government censorship and economic exclusion. A new medium arose, the Internet, allowing instantaneous audiovisual communication around the world through electronic signals carried by satellites and telephone lines.

2000—?
A new millennium dawns, with Europe and America at a peak of prosperity unmatched in human history....

BRITISH LIBRARY TOUR

The British Empire built its greatest monuments out of paper. It's with literature that England has made her lasting contribution to history and the arts. These national archives of Britain include more than 12 million books, 180 miles of shelving, and the deepest basement in London. But everything that matters for your visit is in one delightful room labeled "the Treasures." We'll concentrate on a handful of documents—literary and historical—that changed the course of history. Start with the top stops (described in this tour), then stray according to your interests.

Orientation

Cost: Free.

Hours: Mon–Fri 9:30–18:00 (until 20:00 on Tue), Sat 9:30–17:00, Sun 11:00–17:00.

Getting There: Take the Tube to King's Cross. Leaving the station, turn right and walk a block to 96 Euston Road.

Information: Tel. 020/7412-7000, www.bl.uk.

Tours: One-hour tours are usually offered on Mon, Wed, and Fri–Sun at 15:00, plus Tue at 18:30, Sat at 10:30, and Sun at 11:30 (£5; to confirm schedule and to reserve, call 020/7412-7332). Tuesday and Sunday tours include an additional visit to the reading room (£6). A £3.50 audioguide is available at the information desk (photo ID and £10 deposit required).

Length of Our Tour: One hour.

Cloakroom: Free (£3 donation requested). Lockers require £1 coin deposit (no large bags).

No-no's: No photography, smoking, or chewing gum.

Cuisine Art: A great cafeteria/restaurant is upstairs (serving good hot meals) above the ground-floor café (which is next to a vast and fun pull-out stamp collection). The 50-foot-tall wall of 65,000

British Library Tour

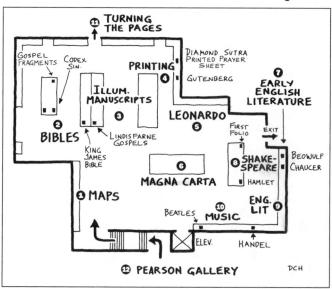

books within the cafés was given to the people by King George IV in 1823. This high-tech mother of all bookshelves is behind glass and has movable lifts.

Starring: Magna Carta, Bibles, Shakespeare, English Lit 101, and the Beatles.

The Tour Begins

Entering the library courtyard, you'll see a big statue of a naked Isaac Newton bending forward with a compass to measure the universe. The statue symbolizes the library's purpose: To gather all knowledge and promote our endless search for truth.

Stepping inside, you'll see the information desk and café. The cloakroom and WC are down a short staircase to the right. The reading rooms upstairs are not open to the public. Our tour is in the tiny but exciting area to the left, under the sign marked Exhibitions.

The priceless literary and historical treasures of the collection are in this one carefully designed and well-lit room. The "Turning the Pages" computer room (where you can electronically leaf through several rare manuscripts) is in an adjoining room. Down a few steps you'll find the Pearson Gallery, with temporary exhibits usually requiring an admission charge.

1. Maps

Navigate the wall of historic maps from left to right. "A Medieval Map of Britain," from 1250, puts medieval man in an unusual position—looking down on his homeland from 50 miles in the air. "Charting the Seas" from 1325 shows a well-defined west coast of Europe as European sailors ventured cautiously out of the Mediterranean. By 1564, you could plan your next trip to Britain with the map of "Mercator's Europe." "The End of... (1688)" has the world well-mapped, except that the United States has a Miami Beach perspective: Florida plus a lot of unexplored interior inhabited by strange beasts.

2. Bibles

My favorite excuse for not learning a foreign language is: "If English was good enough for Jesus Christ, it's good enough for me!" I don't know what that has to do with anything, but obviously Jesus didn't speak English—nor did Moses or Isaiah or Paul or any other Bible authors or characters. As a result, our present-day English Bible is not directly from the mouths and pens of these religious figures, but the fitful product of centuries of evolution and translation.

The Bible is not a single book; it's an anthology of books by many authors from different historical periods writing in different languages (usually Hebrew or Greek). So there are three things that editors must consider in compiling the most accurate Bible: 1) deciding which books actually belong, 2) finding the oldest and most accurate version of each book, and 3) translating it accurately.

Codex Sinaiticus (c. A.D. 350)

The oldest complete "Bible" in existence (along with one in the Vatican), this is one of the first attempts to collect various books together into one authoritative anthology. It's in Greek, the language in which most of the New Testament was written. The Old Testament portions are Greek translations from the original Hebrew. This particular Bible, and the nearby *Codex Alexandrus* (A.D. 425), contain some books not included in most modern English Bibles. (Even today, Catholic Bibles contain books not found in Protestant Bibles.)

Gospel Fragments

These gospels (an account of the life of Jesus of Nazareth) are about as old as any in existence, but they weren't written until several generations after Jesus died. Today, Bible scholars pore diligently over every word in the New Testament, trying to separate Jesus' authentic words from those that seem to have been added later.

The King James Bible (1611)

This Bible is in the same language you speak, but try reading it. The strange letters and archaic words clearly show how quickly languages evolve.

Jesus spoke Aramaic, a form of Hebrew. His words were written down in Greek. Greek manuscripts were translated into Latin, the language of medieval monks and scholars. By 1400, there was still no English version of the Bible, though only a small percentage of the population understood Latin. A few brave reformers risked death to make translations into English and print them using Gutenberg's new invention. Within two centuries, English translations were both legal and popular.

The King James version (done during his reign) has been the most widely used English translation. Fifty scholars worked for four years, borrowing heavily from previous translations, to produce the work. Its impact on the English language was enormous, making Elizabethan English something of the standard, even after all those "thees" and "thous" fell out of fashion in everyday speech.

Many of the most recent translations are both more accurate (based on better scholarship and original manuscripts) and more readable, using modern speech patterns. The late-20th-century debates over God's gender highlight the problems of translating old phrases to fit contemporary viewpoints.

3. Lindisfarne Gospels (A.D. 698) and Illuminated Manuscripts

Throughout the Middle Ages, Bibles had to be reproduced by hand. This was a painstaking process, usually done by monks for a rich patron. This beautifully illus-trated ("illuminated") collection of the four Gospels is the most magnificent of medieval British monk-uscripts. The text is in Latin, the language of scholars ever since the Roman Empire, but the illustrations—with elaborate tracery and interwoven decoration— mix Irish, classical, and even Byzantine forms. (Read an electronic copy in the adjacent "Turning the Pages" computer room.)

These Gospels are a reminder that Christianity almost didn't make it in Europe. After the fall of Rome (which had established Christianity as the official religion), much of Europe reverted to its pagan ways. This was the time of *Beowulf*, when people worshiped woodland spirits and terrible Teutonic gods. It took dedicated Irish missionaries 500 years to reestablish the faith on the Continent. Lindisfarne, an obscure monastery of Irish monks on an island off the east coast of England, was one of the few beacons of light after the fall of Rome, tending the embers of civilization through the long night of the Dark Ages.

Browse through more illuminated manuscripts (in the cases behind the Lindisfarne Gospels). This is some of the finest art from what we call the "Dark Ages." The little intimate details offer a rare and fascinating peek into medieval life.

4. Printing

Printing was invented by the Chinese (what wasn't?). The *Printed Prayer Sheet* (c. 618–907) was made seven centuries before the printing press was "invented" in Europe. A bodhisattva (an incarnation of Buddha) rides

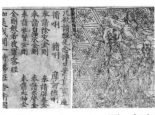

a lion, surrounded by a prayer in Chinese characters. The faithful gained a blessing by saying the prayer, and so did the printer by reproducing it. Texts such as this were printed using wooden blocks carved with Chinese characters that were dipped into paint or ink.

The Gutenberg Bible (c. 1455)

It looks like just another monk-made Latin manuscript, but it's the first book printed in Europe using movable type. Printing

is one of the most revolutionary inventions in history.

Johann Gutenberg (c. 1397–1468), a German silversmith, devised a convenient way to reproduce written materials quickly, neatly, and cheaply—by printing with movable type. You scratch each letter onto a separate metal block, then arrange them into words, ink them up, and press them onto paper. When one job was done you could reuse the same letters for a new one.

This simple idea had immediate and

revolutionary consequences. Knowledge became cheap and accessible to a wide audience, not just the rich. Books became the "mass medium" of Europe, linking people by a common set of ideas. And, like a drug, this increased knowledge only created demand for still more.

Suddenly, the Bible was available for anyone to read. Church authorities, more interested in "protecting" than spreading the word of God, passed laws prohibiting the printing of Bibles. As the Church feared, when people read the Bible they formed their own opinions of God's message, which was often different from the version spoon-fed to them by priests. In the resulting Reformation, Protestants broke away from the Catholic Church.

5. Leonardo da Vinci's Notebook

Books also spread secular knowledge. Renaissance men turned their attention away from heaven, to the nuts and bolts of the material world around them. These pages from Leonardo's notebook show his powerful curiosity, his genius for invention, and his famous backward and inside-out handwriting.

One person's research inspired another's, and books allowed knowledge to accumulate. Galileo championed the counter-commonsense notion that the Earth spun around the sun, then Isaac Newton perfected the mathematics of those moving bodies.

6. Magna Carta (1215)

How did Britain, a tiny island with a few million people, come to rule a quarter of the world? Not by force, but by law. The Magna Carta was the basis for England's constitutional system of government. Though historians talk about "The" Magna Carta, there are several different versions of the document on display.

In 1215, England's barons rose in revolt against the slimy King John. After losing London, John was forced to negotiate. The barons presented him with a list of demands (The Articles of the Barons). John, whose rule was worthless without the support of the barons, had no choice but to affix his seal to it.

This was a turning point in the history of government. Before, kings had ruled by God-given authority. They were above the laws of men, acting however they pleased. Now, for the first time, there were limits—in writing—on how a king could treat his subjects. More generally, it established the idea of "due process"—that is, the government can't infringe on people's freedom without a legitimate legal reason. This small step became the basis for all constitutional governments, including yours.

A few days after John agreed to this original document, it was rewritten in legal form, and some 35 copies of this final

version of the "Great Charter" were distributed around the kingdom ("Magna Carta" and "Burnt Magna Carta").

So what did this radical piece of paper actually say? Not
much by today's standards. The specific demands had to do with
things such as inheritance taxes, the king's duties to widows and
orphans, and so on. It wasn't the specific articles that were important, but the simple fact that the king had to abide by them as law.

Around the corner there are many more historical documents in the library—letters by Queen Elizabeth I, Isaac Newton,
Wellington, Gandhi, and so on. But for now, let's trace the
evolution of…

7. Early English Literature

Four out of every five English words have been borrowed from
other languages. The English language, like English culture
(and London today), is a mix derived from foreign invaders.
Some of the historic ingredients that make this cultural stew:

1. The original Celtic tribesmen
2. Latin-speaking Romans (A.D. 1–500)
3. Germanic tribes called Angles and Saxons (making
   English a Germanic language and naming the island
   "Angle-land"—England)
4. Vikings from Denmark (A.D. 800)
5. French-speaking Normans under William the
   Conqueror (1066–1250).

Beowulf (c. 1000)

This Anglo-Saxon epic poem, written in
Old English, the early version of our language, almost makes the hieroglyphics
on the Rosetta Stone look easy. The manuscript here is from A.D. 1000, although
the poem itself dates to about 750. This is
the only existing medieval manuscript of
this first English literary masterpiece.

In this epic story, the young hero
Beowulf defeats two half-human monsters
threatening the kingdom. Beowulf symbolizes England's emergence from Dark
Age chaos and barbarism.

The Canterbury Tales (c. 1410)

Six hundred years later, England was Christian, but it was hardly
the pious, predictable, Sunday-school world we might imagine.
Geoffrey Chaucer's bawdy collection of stories, told by pilgrims

on their way to Canterbury, gives us the full range of life's experiences—happy, sad, silly, sexy, and pious. (Late in life, Chaucer wrote an apology for those works of his "that tend toward sin.")

While most serious literature of the time was written in scholarly Latin, *The Canterbury Tales* were written in Middle English, the language that developed after the French invasion (1066) added a Norman twist to Old English.

8. Shakespeare (1564–1616)

William Shakespeare is the greatest author in any language. Period. He expanded and helped define modern English. In one fell swoop, he made the language of everyday people as important as Latin. In the process, he gave us phrases like "one fell swoop" that we quote without knowing it's Shakespeare.

Perhaps as important was his insight into humanity. With his stock of great characters—Hamlet, Othello, Macbeth, Falstaff, Lear, Romeo, and Juliet—he probed the psychology of human beings 300 years before Freud. Even today, his characters strike a familiar chord.

Shakespeare in Collaboration

Shakespeare co-wrote a play titled *The Booke of Sir Thomas More*. Some scholars have wondered if maybe Shakespeare had help on other plays as well. After all, they reasoned, how could a journeyman actor, with little education, have written so many masterpieces? Modern scholars, though, unanimously agree that Shakespeare did indeed write the plays ascribed to him. This particular manuscript is likely in Shakespeare's own handwriting. The crossed-out lines indicate that even geniuses need editing.

The Good and Bad Quarto of Hamlet

Shakespeare wrote his plays to be performed, not read. He published a few, but as his reputation grew, unauthorized "bootleg" versions also began to circulate. Some of these were written out by actors, trying (with faulty memories) to recreate a play they'd been in years before. Here are two different versions of *Hamlet:* "good" and "bad."

The Shakespeare First Folio (1623)

It wasn't until seven years after his death that this complete-works collection of Shakespeare's plays came out. The editors were friends and fellow actors.

The engraving of Shakespeare on the title page is one of only two portraits done during his lifetime. Is this what he really looked like? No one knows. The best answer probably comes from his friend and fellow poet Ben Jonson in the introduction on the facing page. He concludes, "Reader, look not on his picture, but his book."

9. Other Greats in English Literature

The rest of the "Beowulf/Chaucer wall" is a greatest-hits sampling of British literature featuring works that have enlightened and brightened our lives for centuries. Look for the writings of Wordsworth, Blake, Dickens, Joyce, and many others (a rotating collection). Recently on display were the following:

Coleridge—Xanadu, an Earthly Paradise from "Kubla Khan"

One day, Samuel Taylor Coleridge took opium. He fell asleep while reading about the fantastic palace of the Mongol emperor, Kubla Khan. During his three-hour drug-induced sleep, he composed in his head a poem of "from two to three hundred lines." When he woke up, he grabbed a pen and paper and "instantly and eagerly wrote down the lines that are here preserved." But just then, a visitor on business knocked at the door and kept Coleridge busy for an hour. When Coleridge finally kicked him out, he discovered that he'd forgotten the rest! The poem "Kubla Khan" is only a fragment, but it's still one of literature's masterpieces.

Coleridge (aided by his muse in the medicine cabinet) was one of the Romantic poets. Check out his fellow Romantics—Keats, Shelley, and Wordsworth—nearby.

Dickens

In 1400, few people could read. By 1850, almost everyone in England could and did. Charles Dickens gave them their first taste of "literature." Periodicals serialized his books, and the increasingly educated masses read them avidly. Stories recount mobs of enthusiastic American fans waiting at the docks for the latest news of their favorite character.

Dickens also helped raise social concern for the underprivileged—of whom England had more than her share. When Dickens was 12 years old, his father was thrown into debtor's prison, and young Charles was put to work to support the family. The ordeal of poverty scarred him for life, but gave depth to his books such as *Oliver Twist* and *David Copperfield*.

Lewis Carroll—The Original
Alice in Wonderland

I don't know if Charles L. Dodgson (Lewis Carroll) ever dipped into Coleridge's medicine jar or not, but his series of children's books makes "Kubla Khan" read like the phone book. Dodgson was a stammerer, which made him uncomfortable around everyone but children. For them he created a fantasy world where grown-up rules and logic were turned upside down.

10. Music

The Beatles

Future generations will have to judge whether this musical quartet ranks with artists such as Dickens and Keats, but no one can deny their historical significance. The Beatles burst onto the scene in the early 1960s to unheard-of popularity. With their long hair and loud music, they brought counterculture and revolutionary ideas to the middle class, affecting the values of a whole generation. Look for the photos of John Lennon, Paul McCartney, George Harrison, and Ringo Starr before and after their fame.

Most interesting are the manuscripts of song lyrics written by Lennon and McCartney, the two guiding lights of the group. "I Wanna Hold Your Hand" was the song that launched them to superstardom. John's song "Help" was the quickly written title song for one of the Beatles' movies. Some call "A Ticket to Ride" the first heavy-metal song. "Yesterday," by Paul, was recorded with guitar and voice backed by a string quartet—a touch of sophistication by producer George Martin. Also glance at the rambling, depressed, cynical, but humorous letter by John on the left. Is that a self-portrait at the bottom?

Handel's *Messiah* (1741) and other Music Manuscripts

Kind of an anticlimax after the Fab Four, I know, but here are manuscripts by Mozart, Beethoven, Schubert, and others, including George Frideric Handel's famous oratorio. Hallelujah.

11. Turning the Pages—Virtual-Reality Room

For a chance to page through a few of the most precious books in the collection, drop by the "Turning the Pages" room. Touch a computer screen and let your fingers do the walking.

WESTMINSTER ABBEY TOUR

Westminster Abbey is the greatest church in the English-speaking world. England's kings and queens have been crowned and buried here since 1066. The histories of Westminster Abbey and England are almost the same. A thousand years of English history—3,000 tombs, the remains of 29 kings and queens, and hundreds of memorials to poets, politicians, and warriors—lie within its stained-glass splendor and under its stone slabs.

Orientation

Cost: £6. Praying is free, thank God, but you must inform the marshal at the door of your purpose. Or, for a free peek inside and a quiet sit in the nave, you can tell a guard at the west end (where the tourists exit) that you'd like to pay your respects to Britain's Unknown Soldier, and he may let you slip in.

Hours: Mon–Fri 9:00–16:45, Wed also 18:00–19:45, Sat 9:30–14:45, last admission 60 min before closing, closed Sun to sightseers but open for services. The main entrance, on the Big Ben side, often has a sizable line; visit early or late to avoid tourist hordes. Mid-mornings are most crowded. On weekdays after 15:00 it's less crowded; come then and stay for the 17:00 evensong (see below).

Getting There: Near Big Ben and Houses of Parliament (Tube: Westminster or St. James' Park).

Information: To confirm the times of guided tours, concerts, and services, call 020/7222-7110. Since special events and services can shut out sightseers, it's wise to call ahead simply to confirm the Abbey is open. For more information and concert listings, see www.westminster-abbey.org.

Music: Evensong, a stirring experience in a nearly empty church, is on Mon, Tue, Thu, and Fri at 17:00, Sat and Sun at 15:00.

Westminster Abbey Tour

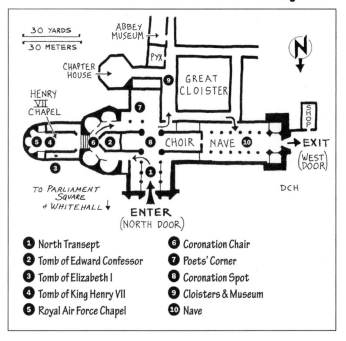

- ❶ North Transept
- ❷ Tomb of Edward Confessor
- ❸ Tomb of Elizabeth I
- ❹ Tomb of King Henry VII
- ❺ Royal Air Force Chapel
- ❻ Coronation Chair
- ❼ Poets' Corner
- ❽ Coronation Spot
- ❾ Cloisters & Museum
- ❿ Nave

Inexpensive organ recitals are held Sun at 17:45 (40 min, look for posted signs with schedules).

Tours: Vergers, the church equivalent of docents, give entertaining guided tours for £3 (up to 6/day, 90 min). Tour themes are the historic church, the personalities buried here, and the great coronations. Informative audioguide tours cost £2 (available weekdays until 15:00, Sat until 13:00, pick up at the information desk at the north door). Many prefer the audioguide to the vergers' tour because it is self-paced. Both live and audioguide tours include entry to the small museums by the cloister (otherwise £1).

Length of Our Tour: 90 minutes.

Photography: Photos are prohibited.

Starring: Edwards, Elizabeths, Henrys, Annes, Richards, Marys, and the Poets' Corner.

The Tour Begins

You'll have no choice but to follow the steady flow of tourists circling clockwise through the church—in through the north entrance, behind the altar, into Poets' Corner in the south transept, detouring through the cloisters, and finally, back out through the west end of the nave. It's all one-way, and the crowds can be a real crush. Here are the abbey's top 10 stops:

• *Walk straight in, pick up the map flier that locates the most illustrious tombs, and belly up to the barricade in the center.*

1. North Transept

Look down the long and narrow center aisle of the church. Lined with the praying hands of the Gothic arches, glowing with light from the stained glass, it's clear that this is more than a museum. With saints in stained glass, heroes in carved stone, and the bodies of England's greatest under the floor stones, Westminster Abbey is the religious heart of England.

You're standing at the center of a cross-shaped church. The main altar (with cross and candlesticks) sits on the platform up the five stairs in front of you. To the right stretches the long, high-ceilinged nave. Nestled in the nave is the elaborately carved wooden seating of the choir (or "quire").

The abbey was built in 1065. Its name, Westminster, means Church in the West (west of St. Paul's Cathedral). For the next 250 years, the abbey was redone and remodeled to become essentially the church you see today, notwithstanding an extensive resurfacing in the 19th century. Thankfully, later architects—ignoring building trends of their generation—honored the vision of the original planner, and the building was completed in one relatively harmonious style.

The abbey's 10-story nave is the tallest in England. The chandeliers, 10 feet tall, look small in comparison (16 were given to the abbey by the Guinness family).

The north transept (through which you entered) is nicknamed "Statesmen's Corner" and specializes in famous prime ministers. Find the rival prime ministers, proud William Gladstone and goateed Benjamin Disraeli, who presided over England's peak of power under Queen Victoria.

• *Now turn left and follow the crowd. Walk under Robert ("Bob") Peel, the prime minister whose policemen were nicknamed "bobbies," and stroll a few yards into the land of dead kings and queens. Stop at the wooden staircase on your right.*

2. Tomb of Edward the Confessor

The holiest part of the church is the raised area behind the altar (where the wooden staircase leads—sorry, no tourist access). Step back and peek over the dark coffin of Edward I to see the green-and-gold wedding-cake tomb of King Edward the Confessor—the man who built Westminster Abbey.

God had told pious Edward to visit St. Peter's Basilica in Rome. But with Normans thinking conquest, it was too dangerous for him to leave England. Instead, he built this grand church and dedicated it to St. Peter. It was finished just in time to bury Edward and to crown his foreign successor, William the Conqueror, in 1066. After Edward's death, people prayed at his tomb and, after getting fine results, canonized him. This elevated, central tomb is surrounded by the tombs of eight kings and queens.

• *Continue on. At the top of the stone staircase, detour left into the private burial chapel of Queen Elizabeth I.*

3. Tomb of Queen Elizabeth I and Mary I

Although there's only one effigy on the tomb (Elizabeth's), there are two queens buried beneath it, both daughters of Henry VIII (by different mothers). Bloody Mary—meek, pious, sickly, and Catholic—enforced Catholicism during her short reign (1553–58) by burning "heretics" at the stake and executing young Lady Jane Grey, a rival to the throne.

Elizabeth—strong, clever, "virginal," and Protestant—steered England on an Anglican course. She holds a royal orb symbolizing that she's queen of the whole globe. Her long reign (1559–1603) was one of the greatest in English history, a time when England ruled the seas and Shakespeare explored human emotions. Elizabeth's face, modeled after her death mask, is considered a very accurate take on this hook-nosed, virgin queen.

The two half-sisters disliked each other in life—Mary even had Elizabeth locked up in the Tower of London. Now they lie side by side for eternity—with a prayer for Christians of all persuasions to live peacefully together.

• *Continue into the ornate, flag-draped room behind the main altar.*

4. Chapel of King Henry VII (a.k.a. the Lady Chapel)

The light from the stained-glass windows, the colorful banners overhead, and the elaborate tracery in stone, wood, and glass give this room the festive air of a medieval tournament. The prestigious Knights of Bath meet here, under the magnificent ceiling studded with gold pendants. The ceiling is the finest English Perpendicular Gothic and fan vaulting you'll see (unless you're going to Cambridge's King's College Chapel). The brilliant stone ceiling was built in 1509, capping the Gothic period and signaling the vitality of the coming Renaissance.

The knights sit in the wooden stalls with churches on their heads, capped by their own insignia. When the queen worships here, she sits in the corner chair under the carved wooden throne with the lion crown.

Behind the small altar is an iron cage housing tombs of the old warrior Henry VII of Lancaster and his wife, Elizabeth of York. Their love and marriage finally settled the Wars of the Roses between the two clans. The combined red-and-white rose symbol decorates the ironwork. Henry VII, the first Tudor king, was the father of Henry VIII and grandfather of Elizabeth I. This exuberant chapel heralds a new optimistic, postwar era as England prepares to step onto the world stage.

• *At the far end of the chapel, stand at the banister in front of the modern set of stained-glass windows.*

5. Royal Air Force Chapel

Saints in robes and halos mingle with pilots in bomber jackets and parachutes in this tribute to WWII flyers who earned their angel wings in the Battle of Britain. Hitler's air force ruled the skies in the early days of the war, bombing at will, threatening to snuff Britain out without a fight. But while determined Londoners hunkered down underground, British pilots in their Spitfires took advantage of a new invention—radar—to get the jump on the more powerful Luftwaffe. These were the fighters about whom Churchill said, "Never has so much been owed by so many to so few."

The abbey survived the blitz virtually unscathed. As a memorial, a bit of bomb damage has been left—the little glassed-over hole in the wall below the windows in the lower left-hand corner. The book of remembrances lists each casualty of the Battle of Britain.

Hey. Look down at the floor. You're standing on the grave of Oliver Cromwell, leader of the rebel forces in England's Civil War. Or rather, Cromwell was buried here from 1658 to 1661. Then his corpse was exhumed, hanged, drawn, quartered, and decapitated, and the head displayed on a stake as a warning to anarchists.

• *Exit the Chapel of Henry VII. To your left (if you're interested) is a door to a side chapel with the tomb of Mary Queen of Scots (beheaded by Elizabeth I). Ahead of you, at the foot of the stairs, is the Coronation Chair. Behind the chair, again, is the tomb of the church's founder, Edward the Confessor.*

6. Coronation Chair

The gold-painted wooden chair waits here—with its back to the high altar—for the next coronation. For every English coronation

since 1296 (except two), it's been moved to its spot before the high altar to receive the royal buttocks. The chair's legs rest on lions, England's symbol. The space below the chair originally held a big rock from Scotland called the Stone of Scone (pron. skoon), symbolizing Scotland's unity with England's king. Recently, however, Britain gave Scotland more sovereignty, its own parliament, and the stone.
• *Continue on. Turn left into the south transept. You're in Poets' Corner.*

7. Poets' Corner

England's greatest artistic contributions are in the written word. Here lie buried the masters of arguably the world's most complex and expressive language. (Many writers are honored with plaques and monuments; relatively few are actually buried here.)
• *Start with Chaucer, buried in the wall under the blue windows. The plaques on the floor before Chaucer are memorials to other literary greats.*

Geoffrey Chaucer (c.1343–1400) is often considered the father of English literature. Chaucer's *Canterbury Tales* told of earthy people speaking everyday English. He was the first great writer buried here. Later, Poets' Corner was built around his tomb.

Lord Byron, the great lover of women and adventure: "Though the night was made for loving,/And the day returns too soon,/Yet we'll go no more a roving/By the light of the moon."

Dylan Thomas, alcoholic master of modernism, with a Romantic's heart: "Oh as I was young and easy in the mercy of his means,/Time held me green and dying/Though I sang in my chains like the sea."

W. H. Auden: "May I, composed like them/Of Eros and of dust/Beleaguered by the same/Negation and despair/Show an affirming flame."

Lewis Carroll, creator of *Alice in Wonderland*: "'Twas brillig, and the slithy toves/Did gyre and gimble in the wabe . . ."

T. S. Eliot, the dry voice of modern society: "This is the way the world ends/Not with a bang but a whimper."

Alfred, Lord Tennyson, conscience of the Victorian Age: "'Tis better to have loved and lost/Than never to have loved at all."

Robert Browning: "Oh, to be in England/Now that April's there."
• *Farther out in the south transept, you'll find . . .*

William Shakespeare: Although he's not buried here, this greatest of English writers is honored by a fine statue that stands near the end of the transept, overlooking the others: "All the world's a stage/And all the men and women merely players./They have their exits and their entrances/And one man in his time plays many parts."

George Handel: High on the wall opposite Shakespeare is the man famous for composing the *Messiah* oratorio: "Hallelujah, hallelujah, hallelujah." Musicians can read the vocal score in his hands for "I Know That My Redeemer Liveth." His actual tomb is on the floor next to...

Charles Dickens, whose serialized novels brought literature to the masses: "It was the best of times, it was the worst of times."

On the floor near Shakespeare, you'll also find the tombs of Samuel Johnson (who wrote the first English dictionary) and the great English actor Laurence Olivier. (Olivier disdained the "Method" style of experiencing intense emotions in order to portray them. When co-star Dustin Hoffman stayed up all night in order to appear haggard for a scene, Olivier said, "My dear boy, why don't you simply try acting?")

And finally, near the center of the transept, find the small white floor plaque of Thomas Parr. Check the dates of his life (1483–1635) and do the math. In his (reputed) 152 years, he served 10 sovereigns and was a contemporary of Columbus, Henry VIII, Elizabeth I, Shakespeare, and Galileo.

• *Walk to the center of the church in front of the high altar.*

8. The Coronation Spot

Here is where every English coronation since 1066 has taken place. Imagine the day when Prince William becomes king:

The nobles in robes and powdered wigs look on from the carved wooden stalls of the choir. The Archbishop of Canterbury stands at the high altar (table with candlesticks, up five steps). The coronation chair is placed in the center of the church, directly below the design-work cross on the ceiling high in the middle of the central tower. Surrounding the whole area are temporary bleachers for 7,000 VIPs, going halfway up the rose windows of each transept, creating a "theater."

Long silver trumpets hung with banners sound a fanfare as the monarch-to-be enters the church. The congregation sings, "I will go into the house of the Lord," as William parades slowly down the nave and up the steps to the altar. After a church service, he sits in the chair, facing the nobles in the choir. William receives a ceremonial sword, ring, and cup. The royal scepter is placed in his hands, and—dut, dutta dah—the archbishop lowers the Crown of St. Edward the Confessor onto his royal head. Finally, King William stands up, descends the steps, and is presented to the people. As cannons roar throughout the city, the people cry, "God save the king!"

• *Royalty are also given funerals here. Princess Diana's coffin lay here before her funeral service. She was then buried on her family estate. Exit the church (temporarily) at the south door, which leads to ...*

9. Cloisters and Museum

The buildings that adjoin the church housed the monks. (The church is known as the "abbey" because it was the headquarters of the Benedictine order—until Henry VIII kicked them out in 1540.) Cloistered courtyards gave them a place to meditate on God's creations.

Look back at the church exterior and meditate on the flying buttresses—the stone bridges that push in on the church walls—that allowed Gothic architects to build so high.

Historians should pay £1 extra to cover admission to three more rooms (covered by audioguide or live tour). The Chapter House, where the monks had daily meetings, features fine architecture with faded but well-described medieval art. The tiny Pyx Chamber has an exhibit about the King's Treasury. The Abbey Museum, formerly the monks' lounge with a cozy fireplace and snacks, now has fascinating exhibits on royal coronations, funerals, abbey history, and a close-up look at medieval stained glass. Look into the impressively realistic eyes of Henry VII's funeral effigy, one of a compelling series of wax-and-wood statues that, for three centuries, graced royal coffins during funeral processions.

• *Go back into the church for the last stop.*

10. Nave

On the floor near the west entrance of the abbey is the flower-lined Tomb of the Unknown Warrior, one ordinary WWI soldier buried in soil from France with lettering made from melted-down weapons from that war. Think about that million-man army from the Empire and Commonwealth and all those who gave their lives. Hanging on a column next to the tomb is the U.S. Congressional Medal of Honor, presented to England's WWI dead by General Pershing in 1921. Closer to the door is a memorial to the hero of WWII, Winston Churchill.

Find the stained-glass window (third from the left on the north side) of St. Edward the Confessor with crown, scepter, and ring, and thank him for the abbey. Look back down the nave, filled with the remains of the people who made Britain great—saints, royalty, poets, musicians, soldiers, politicians. Now step back outside into a city filled with the same kind of poets, saints, and heroes.

ST. PAUL'S TOUR

No sooner was Christopher Wren selected to refurbish Old St. Paul's Cathedral than the Great Fire of 1666 incinerated it. Within a week, Wren had a plan for a whole new building...and for the city around it, complete with some 50 new churches. For the next four decades he worked to achieve his vision—a spacious church, topped by a dome, surrounded by a flock of Wrens.

St. Paul's is England's national church. There's been a church on this spot since 604. It was the symbol of London's rise from the Great Fire of 1666 and of the city's survival of the Blitz of 1940.

Orientation

Cost: £6 (free on Sun but open only to worshipers); includes dome climb—allow an hour for the climb up and down (dome closed Sun).

Hours: Mon–Sat 8:30–16:30, last entry at 16:00, closed Sun except for worship.

Getting There: Located in the City in east London, Tube: St. Paul's.

Information: Sunday services are at 8:00, 10:15, 11:30 (sung Eucharist), 15:15 (evensong), and 18:00. Free organ recitals are held Sunday at 17:00. Weekday communion is at 8:00 and 12:30. Evensong occurs Mon–Sat at 17:00 and Sun at 15:15 (40 min, free to anyone, though visitors who haven't paid the £6 admission to the church aren't allowed to linger after the service; tel. 020/7236-4128). Major events can cause closures.

Tours: Guided £2.50 90-min "super tours" of the cathedral and crypt are offered Mon–Sat at 11:00, 11:30, 13:30, and 14:00 (confirm schedule at church or call 020/7236-4128). Audioguide tours cost £3.50 (available Mon–Sat 8:45–15:00, CC).

Length of Our Tour: One hour (2 if you climb dome).

St. Paul's Tour

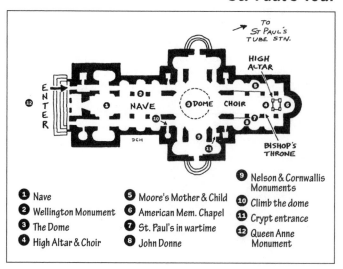

Photography: Photos are forbidden.
Cuisine Art: Good, cheap, and cheery café in the crypt.
Starring: Christopher Wren, Wellington, and World War II.

The Tour Begins

Even now, as skyscrapers encroach, the 365-foot dome of St. Paul's
rises majestically above the rooftops of the neighborhood. The tall
dome is set on classical columns, capped with a lantern, topped by
a six-foot ball, and iced with a cross. As the first Anglican cathedral
built in London after the Reformation, it is Baroque: St. Peter's in
Rome filtered through clear-eyed English reason.

• *Enter, buy your ticket, and stand at the back of the nave.*

1. Nave

Look down the nave through the choir stalls to the stained glass at
the far end. This big church feels big. It's Europe's fourth-largest,
after St. Peter's, Seville, and Milan. The spaciousness is accentuated by the relative lack of decoration. The simple, cream-colored
ceiling and the clear glass in the windows light everything evenly.
Wren wanted this: a simple, open church with nothing to hide.
Unfortunately, only this entrance area keeps his original vision—
the rest was crusted with Baroque decoration after his death.

• *Glance up and behind. The organ trumpets say, "Come to the 17:00
evensong." Ahead and on the left is the towering . . .*

The Anglican Communion

St. Paul's Cathedral is the nucleus of Earth's 70 million Anglicans. The Anglican Communion is a loose association of churches—including the Church of England and the Episcopal Church in the United States—with common beliefs. The rallying point is The Book of Common Prayer, their handbook for worship services.

Forged in the fires of Europe's Reformation, Anglicans see themselves as a "middle way" between Catholics and Protestants. They retain much of the pomp and ceremony of traditional Catholic worship but with Protestant elements such as married priests (and, recently, female priests), attention to Scripture, and a less-hierarchical, more-consensus approach to decision-making. Among Anglicans there are divisions, from Low Church congregations (more evangelical and "Protestant") to High Church (more traditional and "Catholic").

The Church of England, the largest single body, is still the official religion of state, headed by the archbishop of Canterbury (who lives in London). In 1982, Pope John Paul II and the archbishop of Canterbury met face to face, signaling a new ecumenical spirit.

2. Wellington Monument

It's so tall that even Wellington's horse has to duck to avoid bumping his head. Wren would have been appalled, but his church has become so central to England's soul that many national heroes are buried here (in the basement crypt). General Wellington, Napoleon's conqueror at Waterloo and the embodiment of British stiff-upper-lippedness, was honored here in a funeral packed with 13,000 fans.

• *Stroll up the same nave Prince Charles and Lady Diana walked on their 1981 wedding day. Imagine how they felt making the hike to the altar with the world watching. Grab a chair underneath the dome.*

3. The Dome

The dome you see, painted with scenes from the life of St. Paul, is only the innermost of three. From the painted interior of dome #1, look up through the tunnel to see the inside of the cone-shaped dome #2, which is capped by the light-filled lantern. Finally, the whole thing is covered on the outside by dome #3, the shell of lead-covered wood that you saw from the street.

Wren's ingenious three-in-one design was psychological as well as functional—he wanted a low inner dome so the worshiper wouldn't feel dwarfed.

You'll see tourists walking around the base of the dome in the Whispering Gallery. The dome is constructed with such precision that whispers from one side of the dome are heard on the other side, 170 feet away.

Christopher Wren (1632–1723) was the right man at the right time. Though the 31-year-old astronomy professor had never built a major building in his life when he got the commission for St. Paul's, his reputation for brilliance and unique ability to work with others carried him through. The church has the clean lines and geometric simplicity of the age of Newton, when reason was holy and God set the planets spinning in perfect geometrical motion.

For over 40 years, Wren worked on this site, overseeing every detail of the church and the 65,000-ton dome. At age 75, he got to look up and see his son place the cross on top of the dome, completing the masterpiece.

On the floor directly beneath the dome is a brass grate—part of a 19th-century attempt to heat the church. Encircling it is Christopher Wren's name and epitaph, written in Latin: *Lector, si monumentum requiris circumspice* (Reader, if you seek his monument, look around you).

Now review the ceiling: Behind is Wren simplicity and ahead is Baroque ornate.

• *The choir area blocks your way to the altar at the far end, but belly up to the entrance between two sets of organ pipes and look at the far end under a golden canopy.*

4. The Altar and Choir

The altar (the marble slab with crucifix and candlesticks—you'll get a close-up look later) was heavily damaged in World War II. Today it lies under a huge canopy with corkscrew columns. The canopy looks ancient but was actually built in 1958, according to sketches by Wren.

English churches, unlike most in Europe, often have a central choir area (or quire or chancel), where church officials and the singers sit. St. Paul's—a cathedral since 604—is home to the local

Anglican bishop, who presides in the chair nearest the altar on the south or right side (the carved bishop's hat hangs over the chair).

The ceiling above the choir is a riot of glass mosaic representing God and his creation.

• *Walk toward the altar, along the left side of the choir, pausing at a modern statue . . .*

5. Mother and Child—Henry Moore

Britain's (and the world's?) greatest modern sculptor, Henry Moore, rendered a traditional subject in an abstract, minimal way. This Mary-and-baby-Jesus was inspired by the sight of British moms nursing babies in World War II bomb shelters. After donating this to St. Paul's, Moore was rewarded with a burial spot in the crypt.

• *Continue to the far end of the church, where you'll find three bright and modern stained-glass windows.*

6. American Memorial Chapel

Each of the three windows has a central core of religious scenes, but the brightly colored panes that arch around them have some unusual iconography: American. Spot the American eagle (center window, to the left of Christ), George Washington (right window, upper right corner), and symbols of all 50 states (find your state seal). In the carved wood beneath the windows, you'll see birds and foliage native to the United States. And at the very far right, check out the tiny tree "trunk" (amid foliage, below the bird)— it's a U.S. rocket circa 1958, shooting up to the stars.

Britain is very grateful to its WWII saviors, the Yanks, and remembers them religiously here, immediately behind the altar, with the Roll of Honor. This 500-page book under glass lists the names of 28,000 U.S. servicemen based in Britain who gave their lives.

• *Take a close look at the high altar and the view back to the entrance from here, then continue around the altar, where you'll find a glass case of photographs.*

7. St. Paul's in Wartime

Nazi planes firebombed a helpless London in 1940. While The City around it burned to the ground, St. Paul's survived, giving hope to the citizens. The church took two direct hits—photos show a crumbled altar and a collapsed north transept. Another photo shows the incredible devastation in the neighborhood around the church, while the church rises above it, nearly intact. Some swear that many bombs bounced miraculously off Wren's dome, while others credit the heroic work of local firefighters. (There's a memorial chapel to the firefighters who kept watch

The Blitz and the Battle of Britain

Often used synonymously, the Blitz and the Battle of Britain are two different phases of the Nazi air raids of 1940–41. The Battle of Britain (June to September, 1940) pitted Britain's Royal Air Force against German planes trying to soften Britain up for a land-and-sea invasion. The Blitz (September 1940 to May 1941) was Hitler's punitive campaign of terror against civilian London.

In the early days of World War II, the powerful, technologically superior Nazi army quickly overran Poland, Belgium, and France. The British Army hightailed it out of France, crossing the Channel from Dunkirk, and Britain hunkered down, waiting to be invaded. Hitler bombed R.A.F. airfields while his ground troops massed along the Channel. Britain was hopelessly outmatched, but Prime Minister Winston Churchill vowed, "We shall fight on the beaches...we shall fight in the fields and in the streets.... We shall never surrender."

Britain fought back. Though greatly outgunned, they had a new, secret weapon—radar—allowing them to get the jump on puzzled Nazi pilots. Speedy Spitfires flown by a new breed of young pilots shot down 1,700 German planes. By September 1940 the German land invasion was called off, Britain counter-attacked with a daring raid on Berlin...and the Battle of Britain was won.

A frustrated Hitler retaliated with a series of punishing air raids on London itself, known as the Blitz. All through the fall, winter, and spring of 1940–41, including 57 straight nights, Goering's Luftwaffe pummeled a defenseless London, killing 20,000 and leveling half the city (mostly from St. Paul's eastward). Residents took refuge deep in the Tube stations. From his Whitehall bunker, Churchill radioed his people, exhorting them to give their all, their "blood, toil, sweat, and tears."

Late in the war (1944–45), Hitler ordered another round of terror-inducing attacks on London (sometimes called the "second Blitz") using car-sized V-1 and V-2 bombs, an early type of cruise missile. But Britain's resolve had returned, the United States had entered the fight, and the pendulum shifted. Churchill could say that even if the Empire lasted a thousand years, Britons would look back and say, "This was their finest hour."

over St. Paul's with hoses cocked.) Still, these photos make it clear St. Paul's was not fully blitz-proof.

After the war, St. Paul's was the site of a bittersweet remembrance of Britain's victory, when Winston Churchill's state funeral was held here.

• *Across the aisle, standing white in a black niche, is a statue of ...*

8. John Donne (1573–1631)

This statue survived the Great Fire of 1666. John Donne, shown here wrapped in a burial shroud, was a passionate preacher in Old St. Paul's, as well as a great poet.

Imagine hearing Donne deliver a funeral sermon here, with the huge church bell tolling in the background: "No man is an island.... Any man's death diminishes me, because I am involved in Mankind. Therefore, never send to know for whom the bell tolls—it tolls for thee."

• *And also for dozens of people who lie buried beneath your feet, in the crypt where you'll end your tour. But first, in the south transept, find the ...*

9. Horatio Nelson Monument (and Charles Cornwallis Monument)

Admiral Horatio Nelson (1758–1805) leans on an anchor, his coat draped discreetly over the arm he lost in battle.

In October 1805 England trembled in fear as Napoleon—bent on world conquest—prepared to invade England across the Channel. Meanwhile, hundreds of miles away off the coast of Spain, the daring Lord Nelson sailed HMS *Victory* into battle against the French and Spanish navies. His motto: England expects that every man shall do his duty.

Nelson's fleet smashed the enemy at Trafalgar, and Napoleon's hopes for a naval invasion of Britain sank. Unfortunately, Nelson took a sniper's bullet in the spine and died, gasping, "Thank God I have done my duty." The lions at Nelson's feet groan sadly, and two little boys gaze up—one at Nelson, one at Wren's dome. You'll find Nelson's tomb directly beneath the dome, downstairs in the Crypt.

Opposite Nelson is a monument to another great military man, **Charles Cornwallis** (1738–1805), honored here for his service as Governor General of Bengal (India). Yanks know him better as the general who lost the "American War" (the American Revolutionary War) when George Washington—aided by French ships—forced his surrender at Yorktown in 1780.

10. Climb the Dome

There are no elevators, but the 530-step climb is worthwhile. First you get to the Whispering Gallery (with views of the church interior). Have fun in the gallery and whisper sweet nothings into the wall; your partner (and anyone else) on the far side can hear you. Then, after another climb, you're at the Stone Gallery (views of London, high enough if you're exhausted). Finally a long, tight, metal, 150-step staircase takes you to the very top of the cupola for stunning unobstructed views of the city. A tiny window allows you to peek directly down—350 feet—to the church floor.

11. Crypt

Grand tombs of Admiral Nelson (who wore Napoleon down) and General Wellington (who finished him off) dominate the center of the crypt. Christopher Wren's tomb is in the far right corner (right of chapel altar). Also find painters Turner, Reynolds, and others (near Wren); Florence Nightingale (near Wellington); and memorials to many others (including George Washington, who lies buried back in old Virginny). There are models of the dome and interesting exhibits about the building of the cathedral, as well as a fine gift shop, a WC, and the tasty if grim-sounding Crypt Café.

COURTAULD
GALLERY
TOUR

The Courtauld Gallery is just small enough that you can see it all in a single visit, which makes for a pleasant experience. The collection spans the history of Western painting, from medieval altarpieces through Italian Renaissance to the 20th century. But its highlight is Impressionist and Post-Impressionist works, some of which you'll recognize when you see them. To me, the van Gogh self-portrait alone is worth the price of admission.

Orientation

Cost: £5 (free on Mon until 14:00). By buying a ticket here, you get £1 off the admission to either or both of the other museums contained within the Somerset House: the Gilbert Collection, featuring decorative art (normally £5, free after 16:30), and the Hermitage Rooms with Russian art (normally £6).

Hours: Daily 10:00–18:00 (last entry 17:15); same hours for Gilbert Collection and Hermitage Rooms.

Getting There: The Courtauld is one of three museums housed in the Somerset House along the Strand. Tube: Temple or Covent Garden, or catch bus #6, #9, #11, #13, #15, or #23 from Trafalgar Square.

Information: Tel. 020/7848-2589, www.somerset-house.org.uk.

Cloakroom: Lockers, checkroom, and WCs are in the basement.

Cuisine Art: The cafeteria is in the basement.

Photography: It's allowed if you ask when entering, but no flash or tripods.

Starring: A roomful of Manet, Monet, Degas, Renoir, etc.

Overview

The collection is roughly chronological, from ground-floor altarpieces to first-floor Renaissance to second-floor

Impressionism and Post-Impressionism. Besides the handful of paintings I've selected to describe, look for a Botticelli Crucifixion (Room 2), several of Rubens' works (Room 5), a Gainsborough portrait (Room 7), and Cranach's befuddled Adam getting an apple from a saucy Eve (Room 4).

The second floor is a *Who's Who* of 19th-century art—Monet, Seurat, Sisley, Degas, Toulouse-Lautrec, and Renoir.

Manet—*Le Dejeuner sur l'Herbe* (1863)

This is a smaller, cruder version Manet did of his famous painting (now in Paris' Orsay Museum) that launched the Impressionist revolution. The nude woman in a classical pose wasn't shocking. It was the presence of the fully clothed men in everyday dress that suddenly made the nude naked. Manet and the Impressionists rejected goddesses and romance for the landscapes, café scenes, and still lifes of the real world.

Manet—*A Bar at the Folies-Bergère* (1881–82)

While we look at the barmaid and her wares, Manet also shows us the barmaid's-eye-view of the crowded nightclub, reflected in the (slightly tilted) mirror behind her. We see the glittering chandeliers rendered in Impressionist smudges, the bottles of wine, the swirl of activity, and even a trapeze artist (upper left). From the barmaid's own smudgy reflection, we see that she's facing a moustached man in a top hat. This may be a self-portrait, but whoever he is, he's standing right where we are.

Manet, in his last major painting, places us in the center of the scene, surrounded with glitter. Reflected in the mirror, the gaiety all looks a bit fake, and, judging from her blank expression, that's the way the barmaid sees it.

Gauguin—*Nevermore* (1897)

A Tahitian nude lies daydreaming. The horizontal lines of the bed and the verticals of the wall are softened by the curve of her body and of the headboard.

Gauguin, who quit his stockbroker job, abandoned his wife and family, and moved to Tahiti, paints in the primitive style he found there. Like a child, he draws the girl with a thick outline (so different from Impressionists who "built" a figure with a mosaic of brushstrokes), then fills it in with solid Crayola colors. Gauguin emphasizes only the two dimensions of height and width, so the women and clouds in the "background" blend into the flowery wallpaper in the "foreground." Gauguin rejected the camera-eye literalness of Western art for a simpler style that required the viewer's imagination to fill in the blanks, perhaps evoking the romance of a bygone world that is… nevermore.

By the way, Gauguin insisted that the title and the raven were not from Poe's poem, but "a bird of the devil who watches." Hmm.

Van Gogh—*Self-Portrait with Bandaged Ear* (1888–89)

The night of December 23, 1888, Vincent van Gogh went ballistic. Drunk, self-doubting, clinically insane, and enraged at his friend Gauguin's smug superiority, he waved a knife in Gauguin's face, then cut off a piece of his own ear and gave it to a prostitute. Gauguin hightailed it back to Paris, and the locals in Arles persuaded the mad Dutchman to get help. A week later, just released from the hospital, Vincent stood in front of a blank canvas and looked at himself in the mirror.

What he saw looking back was a calm man with an unflinching gaze, dressed in a heavy coat (painted with thick, vertical strokes of blue and green) and fur-lined hat. The slightly stained bandage over his ear is neither hidden in shame nor worn as a badge of honor—it's just another accessory. The scene is evenly lit with no melodramatic shadows.

Vincent must have been puzzled and unnerved by his "artist's fit," as he called it. Does this man suspect it was only the first of many he'd suffer over the next year and a half before finally taking his own life?

THEATRE MUSEUM TOUR

Yes, the ancient Greeks invented theater, but London took the art form and refined it more than any other people on earth. For five centuries, Londoners from every social level have watched actors pretending to be real people in made-up situations. Theater can express mankind's deepest emotions, elicit belly laughs, or simply titillate the senses.

The Theatre Museum—using paintings, photos, costumes, props, and models—chronicles the great writers, actors, and trends of London's theater scene. True theater fans with low expectations will love this place—for the rest, hey, it's free.

Orientation

Cost: Free.
Hours: Tue–Sun 10:00–18:00, closed Mon.
Getting There: It's a block east of Covent Garden's marketplace down Russell Street (Tube: Covent Garden).
Information: Tel. 020/7943-4700, www.theatremuseum.org. If interested, call about makeup demos and costume workshops. The helpful staff is also in tune with London's contemporary theater scene.
Tours: Free guided tours are offered at 11:00, 12:00, and 16:00.
Length of Our Tour: 45 minutes.
Starring: Shakespeare, Gilbert and Sullivan, Coward, and Olivier.

Overview

The main level houses temporary exhibits, and there are often workshops, performances, and special displays scattered throughout the building.

This chapter describes the permanent collection (Main Gallery) in the basement.

• *Circle the room counter-clockwise for a chronological display of British theater.*

William Shakespeare (1564–1616) and the Globe Theatre (left wall)

The alpha and omega of English-language theater, Shakespeare hit the London stage just as it became a popular phenomenon. Shakespeare's early comedies, mid-career tragedies, and final fantasies set the tone of dramatic realism that is Britain's forte. In four centuries, his plays have never really fallen out of fashion.

The Globe Theatre (see Bankside Walk, page 64) seated 3,000 for open-air, daylight performances, and featured a British specialty—a "thrust" stage, jutting out into the audience.

Large Paintings of Brussels's Ommegang Procession (right wall)

First developed by the ancient Greeks and Romans, theater slumbered during the Middle Ages. But in medieval religious festivals, you'd see miniplays on portable stages dramatizing, say, Moses cursing Pharaoh, Saint Anthony wrestling Satan, or Christ healing a leper.

Eleanor "Nell" Gwyn, 1642–87 (left wall)

After Shakespeare, secular theater was banned by puritanical Puritans. It was "Restored" along with the monarchy, starring "pretty, witty" Nell Gwyn. Raised in a Covent Garden brothel, she sold oranges (tasty snack and harmless missile) and her female charms at rowdy Drury Lane Theatre (2 blocks east of here) before landing a part onstage. Nell was among the first generation of women to portray women onstage. Small, impish, and saucy, her comic characters epitomized the joyous decadence of the post-Puritan years. Nell became King Charles II's favorite mistress, birthing several royal bastards.
• *Turn the corner.*

George Frideric Handel, 1685–1729 (right wall)

A German writing Italian opera in London, his smash hit *Rinaldo* brought music to the London stage. But high opera was never as popular in England as it was in Italy. Londoners preferred a show where the storyline paused for a big musical number ... the style that developed into the modern "musical." Still, opera has a strong tradition in London at the Royal Opera House (a block away).

John Gay's *Beggar's Opera*, 1728 (right wall)

Gay's smash hit—a comic, social satire with hummable tunes— was a forerunner of blockbuster musicals.

David Garrick, 1717–79 (left wall)

In 1741, Garrick walked onstage as Richard III—his performance
made the unknown actor-playwright an overnight sensation.
His direct, understated realism was a breath of fresh air after the
pompous bombast of actors in the French style. Phenomenally
popular, Garrick bought the Drury Lane Theatre (where they're
currently showing *My Fair Lady*) and for the next 30 years he slowly
taught the eating-drinking-jeering vaudeville crowd to shut up and
love Shakespeare. He also introduced oil-lamp footlights and side-
lights. Garrick is buried in Poets' Corner in Westminster Abbey.

Edmund Kean, 1787–1833 (left wall)

England's greatest tragic actor, his off-stage life was also troubled.
He grew up on London's streets with one goal in life—to be a star.
After 10 years of obscurity with a traveling company, he debuted
at age 27 at Drury Lane Theatre as Shylock in *The Merchant of
Venice*. With flashing eyes, dramatic changes of mood, and magnetic
intensity, he oozed evil. Always the heavy—when he once played
Romeo, he drew laughs—Kean specialized in Shakespeare's villains
and tragic leads (Macbeth, Othello, Hamlet). Kean, who drank
heavily, channeled his offstage rage into perfectly choreographed
onstage passion. He died onstage playing Othello at Covent Garden.
His son, Charles (who was Iago in that last performance), carried
on the family tradition with a triumphant tour of America.

Jenny Lind, 1820–87 (left wall)

Born in Sweden and trained for opera, the "Swedish Nightingale"
wowed London and the United States with her singing. She could
do all the vocal acrobatics, but it was her pure presentation of
simple songs that created a sensation—"Jenny Lind Mania."

Music Halls of the 1800s (in the corner)

A night at the theater was usually a raucous affair, where the main
play or entertainment was interspersed with music, dancing, skits,
slapstick, and circus acts while the audience ate, drank, and chatted.
(In the United States, it's what we'd call vaudeville.)
• *Turn the corner.*

W. S. Gilbert, 1836–1911, and
Arthur Sullivan, 1842–1900 (right wall)

Though they reportedly disliked each other, this lyricist and com-
poser teamed up to create sophisticated comic operas (or "operettas,"
since it's intended as light entertainment). The characters spoofed
Victorian pompousness and operatic clichés, the words were witty,
and the songs tuneful and memorable. Even today, American

amateur companies stage *The Pirates of Penzance, The Mikado, and H.M.S.* Pinafore.

Henry Irving, 1838–1905 (right wall)

The Victorian era's most famous actor, Irving brought realism to acting, technical innovations to stage sets, and respectability to London theater, becoming the first actor to be knighted. Gaunt, brooding, and haunted-looking, he burst on the scene playing a guilt-ridden murderer in *The Bells* at the Lyceum Theatre (where *The Lion King* currently roars). As director of the Lyceum, he staged middle-brow melodramas fueled by his star-power and awe-inspiring sets. Irving recycled all profits into the latest stage technology—electric lights, machines to rearrange sets quickly between scenes, and devices that could create indoor thunderstorms and supernatural FX. Despite unheard-of popularity (except among highbrows), Irving died broke. (See Irving's statue just southeast of Leicester Square.)

• *Turn the corner.*

Noel Coward, 1899–1973 (left wall)

The generation that lived through World War I—disillusioned and world-weary, but dressing elegantly and sipping cocktails to forget—found comic expression in multitalented Noel Coward. His comedies (*Private Lives*, 1930) and songs ("Mad About the Boy") featured loving-but-bickering couples engaged in sophisticated banter and loose, Roaring '20s morality.

John Gielgud, 1904–2000; Laurence Olivier, 1907–89; Ralph Richardson, 1902–83 (left wall)

Three superb actors associated with the Old Vic Theatre (across the Thames, Tube: Waterloo) brought the serious Shakespearean tradition to the wider world of motion pictures. Picture young, handsome Gielgud as Romeo, onstage with Olivier as Mercutio—then the next night they'd switch parts. Olivier's versatility ranged from the original production of Coward's *Private Lives* to the Oscar-winning film *Hamlet* (1948, which he produced, directed, and starred in), to over-the-top Nazi villainy in the movie *Marathon Man* (1976).

Look Back in Anger, 1956, by John Osborne, 1924–94 (left wall)

The so-called Angry Young Men of the 1950s—the twentysomethings who had been too young to fight in World War II—were frustrated with a postwar society still dominated by traditional, small-minded, working-class values. Osborne's characters ranted in long tirades perfectly suited to a new breed of angry young British actors, such as Richard Burton and Peter O'Toole.

Recent British Opera (right wall)
London today is one of the world's most vibrant and progressive cities for opera, transforming musty old scores into visually interesting, edgy spectacles. The Royal Opera House productions are expensive, but by day you can visit parts of the recently refurbished complex (entrances on Covent Garden and Bow Street).

Royal Shakespeare Company (left wall)
Peter Brook's influential book, *The Empty Space* (1968), stated that you could do riveting theater with just good actors and a bare stage. As director of the Royal Shakespeare Company, he pioneered challenging productions with minimal trappings. After 400 years, Shakespeare lives.

Today's Theater Scene
It's upstairs and out the door—you're right in the thick of it.

TOWER OF LONDON TOUR

William I, still getting used to his new title of "the Conqueror," built the stone "White Tower" (1077–97) to keep the Londoners in line. The Tower served as an effective lookout for invaders coming up the Thames. His successors enlarged it to its present 18-acre size. Because of the security it provided, it has served over the centuries as the Royal Mint, the Royal Jewel House, and, most famously, as the prison and execution site of those who dared oppose the crown.

Today, while its military purpose is history, it's still home to a beefeating community of 120 (and host to three million visitors a year). The Tower's hard stone and glittering jewels represent the ultimate power of the king. So does the executioner's block. You'll find more bloody history per square inch in this original Tower of power than anywhere else in Britain.

Orientation

Cost: £11.50, family-£34, £19 for one-day combo-ticket with Hampton Court Palace.

Hours: March–Oct Mon–Sat 9:00–18:00, Sun 10:00–18:00; Nov–Feb Tue–Sat 9:00–17:00, Sun–Mon 10:00–17:00; last entry one hour before closing; closed Dec 24–26 and Jan 1.

Upon arrival, pick up the free little map/guide and check the schedule for a list of events and special demonstrations (like knights in armor explaining medieval fighting techniques). The audioguide is not worthwhile (£3 plus £10 deposit). And, considering how well-described everything is, neither is the Tower guidebook.

The crowd hits after the 9:30 cheap Tube passes start (worst on Sun). Even though the ticket line moves fast, it can be loooong. To avoid this line, buy your ticket at Tower Hill Tube stop (upon arrival) or at any London TI (in advance) at no extra cost. You can

Tower of London Tour

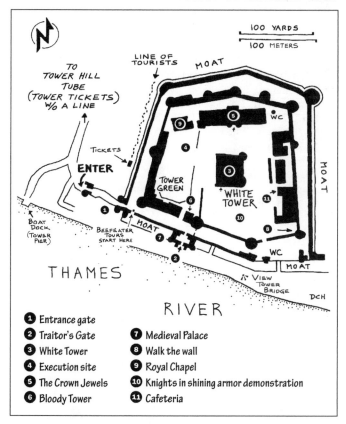

1 Entrance gate
2 Traitor's Gate
3 White Tower
4 Execution site
5 The Crown Jewels
6 Bloody Tower
7 Medieval Palace
8 Walk the wall
9 Royal Chapel
10 Knights in shining armor demonstration
11 Cafeteria

also book online at www.hrp.org.uk (£3 fee). There's a second line-up inside for the crown jewels, the best on earth. For fewer crowds, arrive when the Tower opens and go straight for the crown jewels, doing the Beefeater tour and White Tower later (or see the jewels after 16:30).

On Sunday, visitors are welcome on the grounds to worship in the Royal Chapel (free, 11:00 service with fine choral music, you get in with no lines and can probably stay after the service). For information on participating in the evening Ceremony of Keys, see page 43 (advance booking required).

Getting There: The Tower is located in East London (Tube: Tower Hill). For speed, take the Tube there; for romance, take the boat back. Boats run between the Tower of London and

Westminster Pier near Big Ben (£5, included with Big Bus London tour; £6 round-trip; daily 9:00–21:00, Nov–March until 15:45, 2/hr, 30 min, tel. 020/7930-9033).

Information: Tel. 020/7709-0765, recorded info: tel. 020/7680-9004, booking: tel. 0870/756-7070.

Yeoman Warder (Beefeater) Tours: The free, worthwhile, 60-minute Beefeater tours leave every 30 minutes from inside the gate (first one usually at 9:30, last one usually at 15:30, 14:30 off-season). The boisterous Beefeaters are great entertainers. While groups can be huge, the guides are easy to hear and fun to follow. Their talks include lots of bloody anecdotes about the Tower and its history.

Length of Our Tour: Two hours.

Photography: Photos are allowed, but not of the jewels.

Cuisine Art: The New Armouries Café, inside and beyond the White Tower, is a big, efficient cafeteria.

Starring: Crown jewels, Beefeaters, William the Conqueror, and Henry VIII.

1. Entrance Gate

Even an army the size of the ticket line couldn't storm this castle. After they pulled the drawbridge up and slammed the iron portcullis down, you'd have to swim a moat; cross an island prowled by tigers, elephants, and polar bears; then swim a second, 40-yard-wide inner moat (eventually drained to be a military parade ground); toss a grappling hook onto the wall and climb up while

the enemy poured boiling oil on you. Yes, it was difficult to get into the Tower... but it was almost impossible to get out.

• *The entertaining 50-minute tours by the Yeoman Warders (nicknamed "Beefeaters" for the rations of beef they earned) begin just inside the entrance gate (see "Orientation," above). The information booth is nearby, and toilets are 100 yards straight ahead. Otherwise, go 50 yards straight ahead to the...*

2. Traitor's Gate

This entrance to the Tower was a waterway from the Thames. Princess Elizabeth I, who was a prisoner here before she became Queen, was poled through this gate on a barge, thinking about her mom, Anne Boleyn, who had been decapitated inside just a few

years earlier. Many English leaders who fell from grace entered through here—Elizabeth was one of the lucky few to walk out.
• *Pass underneath the "Bloody Tower" into the inner courtyard. The big white tower in the middle is the . . .*

3. White Tower

This is the tower that gives this castle complex of 20 towers its name. William the Conqueror built it 900 years ago to put 15 feet of stone between himself and his conquered. Over the centuries, the other walls and towers were built around it.

The keep was a last line of defense. The original entry (on south side) is above ground level so that the wooden approach (you'll climb its modern successor to get in) could be removed, turning the Tower into a safe refuge. Originally, there were even fewer windows—the lower windows were added during a Christopher Wren–ovation in 1660. In the 13th century, the Tower was painted white.

Standing high above the rest of old London, the White Tower provided a gleaming reminder of the king's absolute power over his subjects. If you made the wrong move here, you could be feasting on roast boar in the banqueting hall one night and chained to the walls of the prison the next. Torture ranged from stretching on the rack to the full monty: hanging by the neck until nearly dead, then "drawing" (cut open to be gutted), and finally quartering, with your giblets displayed on the walls as a warning. (Guy Fawkes, who tried to blow up Parliament, got this treatment.) Any cries for help were muffled by the thick stone walls—15 feet at the base, a mere 11 feet at the top.

Inside the Tower today, you can see models of the Tower and exhibits re-creating medieval life, as well as suits of armor (including that of Henry VIII, other kings, and a 6-foot, 9-inch giant), guns, swords, and the actual ax and chopping block. The rare and lovely Norman chapel (St. John's Chapel, 1080), where Lady Jane Grey offered up a last unanswered prayer, is simple, plain, and moving.
• *Left of the Tower is the Tower Green, where you'll find a granite-paved square marked "Site of Scaffold."*

4. Execution Site

Here, enemies of the crown would kneel before the king for the final time and, with their hands tied behind their backs, say a final prayer, then lay their heads on a block, and—*shlit*—the blade would slice through their necks as their heads tumbled to the ground.

The headless corpses were buried in unmarked graves in

the Tower Green or under
the floor of the stone church
ahead of you. The heads were
stuck on a stick and displayed
at London Bridge. Passersby
did not see heads but spheres
of parasites.

Henry VIII axed a couple
of his exes here—Anne Boleyn,
whom he called a witch and an
adulteress, and the forgettable
Catherine Howard. Next.

Henry even beheaded his friend, Thomas More (a Catholic),
because he refused to recognize (Protestant) Henry as head of
the Church of England. (Thomas died at the less-prestigious
Tower Hill site just outside the walls—near the Tube stop—
where most Tower executions took place.)

The most tragic victim was 17-year-old Lady Jane Grey,
a simple girl who was manipulated into claiming the crown
during the scramble for power after Henry's death. When
"Bloody" Mary took control, she forced Jane to kneel at the
block. Jane's young husband, locked in the nearby Beauchamp
Tower, could vent his grief only by scratching "Jane" into the
Tower's stone (in the upstairs room find graffiti #85—"IANE").

A Beefeater, tired of what he called "Hollywood coverage"
of the Tower, grabbed my manuscript, read it, and told me that
in over 900 years as a fortress, palace, and prison, the place held
8,500 prisoners. But only 120 were executed, and of those, only
six were executed inside the Tower. Stressing the hospitality of
the Tower, he added, "Torture was actually quite rare here."

• *Look past the White Tower on the left to the line leading to the crown
jewels. Like a Disney ride, the line is still very long once you get inside.
But great videos help pass the time pleasantly. First, you'll pass through a
room of wooden chairs and coats of arms—one for every monarch who
wore jewels like these, from William the Conqueror (1066) to Elizabeth
I, with her lion-and-dragon crest, to Queen Elizabeth II. Next, you'll
see a film of Elizabeth's 1953 coronation—a chance to see the jewels in
action. You'll also see video close-ups of the jewels. (Get here before 10:00
to avoid the wait, but even if there's no crowd, take your time for the
videos about the jewels.) Finally, you pass into a huge vault and reach ...*

5. The Crown Jewels

In the first display case, notice the 12th-century coronation
spoon for anointing (used in 1953). Since most of the original
crown jewels were lost during the 1648 revolution, this is the

most ancient object here. After scepters, robes, trumpets, and wristlets, a moving sidewalk takes you past the most precious of the crown jewels.

• *The crowns are all facing you as you approach them (ride the nearest walkway). You're welcome to circle back and glide by the back side and hang out on the elevated viewing area with the guard. Chat with a guard—they're actually here to provide information. Ask him or her what they'd do if you shot a photo.*

These are the most important pieces (in cases 1, 2, 4, and 5):

• **St. Edward's Crown,** in the first glass case, is placed by the archbishop upon the head of each new monarch in Westminster Abbey on coronation day. It's worn for 20 minutes, then locked away until the next coronation. Although remodeled, this crown is older than the Tower itself, dating back to 1061, the time of King Edward the Confessor, "the last English king" before William the Conqueror invaded (1066). Since the gold and 443 precious and semiprecious stones weigh five pounds, weak or frail monarchs have opted not to actually wear it.

• **The Sovereign's Scepter and Orb:** The scepter, in the second case, is encrusted with the world's largest cut diamond—the 530-carat Star of Africa, as beefy as a quarter-pounder. This was one of nine stones cut from the original 3,106-carat diamond. The orb (in the same case) symbolized how Christianity rules over the earth and is a reminder that even a "divine monarch" is not above God's law. Since the king or queen is head of both the church and the state in Britain, the coronation is a kind of marriage between the church and state, celebrating the monarch's power to do good.

• **The Crown of the Queen Mother** (Elizabeth's famously old mom), the highest crown in the fourth case, has the 106-carat Koh-i-Noor diamond glittering on the front. The Koh-i-Noor diamond is considered unlucky for male rulers and therefore only adorns the crown of the king's wife. If Charles becomes king and has a wife...she'll wear this. This crown was remade in 1937 and given an innovative platinum frame.

The tiny crown to the left was Queen Victoria's. She suffered from migraine headaches, and the last thing someone with a migraine needs is a big crown. This four-ounce job was made in 1870 for £50,000—personally paid for by the queen.

• **The Imperial Crown,** in the fifth and last case, is for when the monarch slips into something a little less formal—for coronation festivities and the annual opening of Parliament. Among its 3,733 jewels are Queen Elizabeth I's former earrings (the hanging pearls), a stunning 13th-century ruby in the center, and Edward the Confessor's ring (the blue sapphire on top). When Edward's tomb was exhumed—a hundred years after he was buried—his body was "incorrupted." The ring on his saintly finger featured this sapphire and ended up on the crown of all future monarchs.

• *Leave the jewels. Back near the Traitor's Gate you'll find sights #6 and #7 . . .*

6. Bloody Tower

Not all prisoners died at the block. During the Wars of the Roses, the 13-year-old future king Edward and his kid brother were kidnapped by their uncle Richard III ("Now is the winter of our discontent . . .") and locked in the Bloody Tower, never to be seen again (until two centuries later, when two children's bodies were discovered).

Sir Walter Raleigh—poet, explorer, and political radical—was imprisoned here for 13 years. In 1603, the English writer and adventurer was accused of plotting against King James and sentenced to death. The king commuted the sentence to life imprisonment in the Tower. While in prison, Raleigh wrote the first volume of his *History of the World*. Check out his rather cushy bedroom, study, and walkway (courtesy of the powerful tobacco lobby?). Raleigh promised the king a wealth of gold if he would release him to search for El Dorado. The expedition was a failure. Upon Raleigh's return, the displeased king had him beheaded in 1618.

More recent prisoners in the complex include Rudolf Hess, Hitler's henchman, who parachuted into Scotland in 1941 (kept in bell tower). Hess claimed to have dropped in to negotiate a separate peace between Germany and Britain. Hitler denied any such plan.

7. Medieval Palace

The Tower was a royal residence as well as a fortress. These well-described rooms are furnished as they might have been during the reign of Edward I in the 13th century and come with an actor in medieval garb who explains lifestyles of the medieval rich and royal.

• *Enter near where you leave the Medieval Palace to . . .*

8. Walk the Wall

The Tower was defended by state-of-the-art walls and fortifications in the 13th century. This walk offers a good look. From the walls, you also get a good look at . . .

Tower Bridge

The famous bridge strad-
dling the Thames with the
twin towers and blue spans
is not London Bridge
(which is the nondescript
bridge just upstream), but
Tower Bridge. It looks
medieval, but this draw-
bridge was built in 1894

of steel and concrete. Sophisticated steam engines raise and lower
the bridge, allowing tall-masted ships to squeeze through.

Gaze out at the bridge, the river, and life-filled London,
then turn back and look at the stern stone walls of the Tower.
Be glad you can leave.

DAY TRIPS
IN ENGLAND

Greenwich • Windsor • Cambridge • Bath

Greenwich, Windsor, Cambridge, and Bath (listed from nearest to farthest) are four of the best day-trip possibilities near London. Greenwich is England's maritime capital; Windsor has the famous castle; Cambridge is England's best university town; and Bath is an elegant spa town dating from Roman times.

You could fill a book with the many easy and exciting day trips from London (Earl Steinbicker did: *Daytrips London: 50-One Day Adventures by Rail or Car, in and around London and Southern England*).

Getting Around

By Bus Tour: Several tour companies take London-based travelers out and back every day. If you're going to Bath and want to stay overnight, consider taking a day tour to Bath and skipping the trip back to London (for details, see page 312 in the Transportation Connections chapter).

By Train: The British rail system uses London as a hub and normally offers round-trip fares (after 9:30) that cost virtually the same as one-way fares. For day trips, "day return" tickets are best (and cheapest). You can save a little money if you purchase Super Advance tickets before 18:00 on the day before your trip.

By Train Tour: Original London Walks offers a variety of Explorer day trips year-round via train for about £10 plus transportation costs (see their walking-tour brochure, tel. 020/7624-3978, www.walks.com).

GREENWICH

The palace at Greenwich was favored by the Tudor kings. Henry VIII was born here. Later kings commissioned Inigo Jones and Christopher Wren to beautify the town and palace. In spite of

Greenwich's architectural and royal treats, this is England's maritime capital, and visitors go for things salty. Greenwich hosts historic ships, nautical shops, and hordes of tourists.

Planning Your Time

See the two ships—*Cutty Sark* and *Gipsy Moth IV*—upon arrival. Then walk the shoreline promenade, with a possible lunch or drink in the venerable Trafalgar Tavern, before heading up to the National Maritime Museum and the Royal Observatory Greenwich.

The town throbs with day-trippers on weekends because of its arts-and-crafts and antique markets. To avoid crowds, visit on a weekday.

Tourist Information

The TI, facing the riverside square a few paces from the *Cutty Sark*, has a café, WC, fast Internet connections (£1/20 min), and displays that provide a brief history of the town (daily 10:00–17:00, 2 Cutty Sark Gardens, Pepys House, tel. 0870/608-2000, www.greenwich.gov.uk). Guided walks cover the big sights (£4, daily 12:15 and 14:15). A shuttle bus runs from Greenwich Pier to the observatory on top of the hill (£1.50, ticket good all day, daily 11:00–17:00, every 15 min, erratic in winter).

Sights—Greenwich

▲▲*Cutty Sark*—The Scottish-built *Cutty Sark* was the last of the great China tea clippers. Handsomely restored, she was the queen of the seas when first launched in 1869. With 32,000 square feet of sail, she could blow with the wind 300 miles in a day. Below deck, you'll see the best collection of merchant-ship figureheads in Britain and exhibits giving a vivid peek into the lives of Victorian sailors back when Britain ruled the waves. Stand at the big wheel and look up at the still-rigged main mast towering 150 feet above. You may meet costumed storytellers spinning yarns of the high seas and local old salts giving knot-tying demonstrations (£3.90, daily 10:00–17:00, tel. 020/8858-3445, www.cuttysark.org.uk).

▲*Gipsy Moth IV*—Tiny next to the *Cutty Sark*, the 54-foot *Gipsy Moth IV* is the boat Sir Francis Chichester used for the first solo circumnavigation of the world in 1966 and 1967. Upon Chichester's return, Queen Elizabeth II knighted him in Greenwich, using the same sword Elizabeth I had used to knight Francis Drake in 1581 (free, viewable anytime, but interior not open to public).

Stroll the Thames to Trafalgar Tavern—From the *Cutty Sark* and *Gipsy Moth*, pass the pier and wander east along the Thames on Five Foot Walk (the width of the path) for grand views in front of the Old Royal Naval College (see below). Founded by William

Greenwich

III as a naval hospital and designed by Wren, the college was split in two because Queen Mary didn't want the view from Queen's House blocked. The riverside view is good, too, with the twin-domed towers of the college (one giving the time, the other the direction of the wind) framing Queen's House, and the Royal Observatory Greenwich crowning the hill beyond.

Continuing downstream, just past the college, you'll see the Trafalgar Tavern. Dickens knew the pub well and even used it as the setting for the wedding breakfast in *Our Mutual Friend*. Built in 1837 in the Regency style to attract Londoners downriver, the

tavern is still popular with Londoners (and tourists) for its fine
lunches. The upstairs Nelson Room is still used for weddings.
Its formal moldings and elegant windows with balconies over the
Thames are a step back in time (Mon–Sat 12:00–23:00, Sun from
12:00, lunch 12:00–15:00, £6–10 dinners Tue–Sat 17:00–22:00,
no dinner Sun–Mon, CC, Park Row, tel. 020/8858-2437). From
the pub, enjoy views of the white-elephant Millennium Dome a
mile downstream.

From the Trafalgar Tavern, you can walk the two long
blocks up Park Row and turn right onto the park leading up to
the Royal Observatory Greenwich.

Old Royal Naval College—Now that the Royal Navy has moved
out, the public is invited in to see the elaborate Painted Hall and
Chapel, grandly designed by Wren and completed by other architects in the 1700s (free, Mon–Sat 10:00–17:00, Sun 12:30–17:00,
in the 2 college buildings farthest from river, choral service Sun
at 11:00 in chapel—all are welcome).

Queen's House—This building, the first Palladian-style villa in
Britain, was designed in 1616 by Inigo Jones for James I's wife,
Anne of Denmark. All traces of the queen are now gone, and the
Great Hall and Royal Apartments serve as an art gallery for rotat-
ing exhibits (free, daily 10:00–17:00, June–Aug daily 10:00–18:00,
tel. 020/8858-4422).

▲▲National Maritime Museum—Great for anyone remotely
interested in the sea, this museum holds everything from *Titanic*
tickets and Captain Scott's reindeer-hide sleeping bag (from his
1910 Antarctic expedition) to the uniform Admiral Nelson wore
when he was killed at Trafalgar. Under a big glass roof, accompanied by the sound of creaking wooden ships and crashing waves,
slick, modern displays depict lighthouse technology, a whaling
cannon, and a Greenpeace "survival pod." The Nelson Gallery,
while taking up just a fraction of the floor space, deserves at least
half your time here. It offers an intimate look at Nelson's life,
the Napoleonic threat, Nelson's rise to power, and his victory
and death at Trafalgar. Don't miss Turner's *Battle of Trafalgar*—
his largest painting and only royal commission. Kids love the
All Hands Gallery, where they can send secret messages by
Morse code and operate a miniature dockside crane (free, daily
10:00–17:00, June–Aug daily 10:00–18:00, look for the events
board at entrance: singing, treasure hunts, storytelling, particularly on weekends, tel. 020/8312-6565, www.nmm.ac.uk).

▲▲The Royal Observatory Greenwich—Located on the
prime meridian (0 degrees longitude), the observatory is the point
from which all time is measured. However, the observatory's early
work had nothing to do with coordinating the world's clocks to

Greenwich Mean Time (GMT). The observatory was founded in 1675 by Charles II to find a way to determine longitude at sea. Today the Greenwich time signal is linked with the BBC (which broadcasts the "pips" worldwide at the top of the hour). In the courtyard, set your wristwatch to the digital clock showing GMT to a tenth of a second and straddle the prime meridian (called the "Times meridian" at the observatory, in deference to the *London Times*, which paid for the courtyard sculpture and the inset meridian line that runs banner headlines of today's *Times*—I wish I were kidding). Nearby, outside the courtyard, see how your foot measures up to the foot where the public standards of length are cast in bronze. Look up to see the orange Time Ball, also visible from the Thames, which drops daily at 13:00. Inside, check out the historic astronomical instruments and camera obscura. Listen to costumed actors tell stories about astronomers and historical observatory events (may require small fee, daily July–Sept, Easter, and bank holidays). Finally, enjoy the view: the symmetrical royal buildings; the Thames; the square-mile City of London, with its skyscrapers and the dome of St. Paul's Cathedral; the Docklands, with its busy cranes; and the huge Millennium Dome. At night (17:00–24:00), look for the green laser beam the observatory shines in the sky (best viewed in winter), extending along the prime meridian for 15 miles (free, daily 10:00–17:00, tel. 020/8858-4422, www.rog .nmm.ac.uk). Planetarium shows twinkle on weekdays at 14:30 and 15:30 and on Saturday and Sunday at 13:30, 14:30, and 15:30 (£4; buy tickets at observatory, a 2-min walk from planetarium).

Greenwich Town—Save time to browse the town. Covered markets and outdoor stalls make weekends lively. The arts-and-crafts market is an entertaining mini–Covent Garden between College Approach and Nelson Road (Thu–Sun 10:00–17:00, biggest on Sun), and the antique market sells old ends and odds at high prices on Greenwich High Road near the post office. Wander beyond the touristy Church Street and Greenwich High Road to where flower stands spill into the side streets and antique shops sell brass nautical knickknacks. King William Walk, College Approach, Nelson Road, and Turnpin Lane are all worth a look.

Transportation Connections—Greenwich

Getting to the town of Greenwich is a joy by boat or a snap by Tube. From London, you can cruise down the Thames from central London's piers at Westminster, Embankment, or Tower of London; or take the Tube to Cutty Sark in Zone 2 (free with Tube pass). Trains also go from London's Charing Cross, Waterloo East, and London Bridge stations several times each hour.

WINDSOR

The pleasant pedestrians-only shopping zone of Windsor litters the approach to its famous palace with fun temptations. You'll find the **TI** on 24 High Street (April–Sept daily 10:00–17:00, Oct–March daily 10:00–16:00, tel. 01753/743-900, www.windsor.gov.uk).

▲▲**Windsor Castle**—Windsor Castle, the official home of England's royal family for 900 years, claims to be the largest and oldest occupied castle in the world. The queen considers this sprawling and fortified palace her primary residence. Thankfully, touring it is simple: You'll see immense grounds, lavish state-rooms, a crowd-pleasing dollhouse, an art gallery, and the chapel.

Immediately upon entering, you pass through a simple modern building housing a historical overview of the castle. This excellent intro is worth a close look, since you're basically on your own after this. Inside you'll find the motte (artificial mound) and bailey (fortified stockade around it) of William the Conqueror's castle still visible. Dating from 1080, this was his first castle in England.

Follow the signs to the staterooms/gallery/dollhouse. Queen Mary's Dollhouse—a palace in miniature (1/12 scale from 1923) and "the most famous dollhouse in the world"—comes with the longest wait. You can skip that line and go immediately into the lavish staterooms. Strewn with history and the art of a long line of kings and queens, it's the best I've seen in Britain—and well restored after the devastating 1992 fire. The adjacent gallery is a changing exhibit featuring the royal art collection (and some big names, such as Michelangelo and Leonardo). Signs direct you (downhill) to St. George's Chapel. Housing ten royal tombs, it's a fine example of Perpendicular Gothic, with classic fan vaulting spreading out from each pillar (about 1500). Next door is the sumptuous 13th-century Albert Memorial Chapel, redecorated after the death of Queen Victoria's beloved Prince Albert in 1861 and dedicated to his memory. (Admission: £11.50, £29/family, £3 audioguide is better than official guidebook for help through-out, March–Oct daily 9:45–17:15, last entry 16:00, Nov–Feb closes at 16:15, changing of the guard most days at 11:00, even-song in the chapel at 17:15, recorded info tel. 01753/831-118, live info tel. 020/7321-2233, www.royal.gov.uk).

Legoland Windsor—This huge, kid-pleasing park next to Windsor Palace has dozens of tame but fun rides (often with very long lines) scattered throughout its 150 acres. An impressive Mini-Land has 28 million Lego pieces glued together to create 800 tiny buildings and a mini-tour of Europe. The place is fun for Legomaniacs under 12 (£19, children-£16, under 3 free, £10 if you enter during last 2 hrs, CC, April–Oct daily 10:00–17:00,

18:00, or 19:00 depending upon season and day, closed most Tue–Wed in Sept–Oct, closed Nov–March except Dec 21–Jan 5, £2.50 round-trip shuttle bus runs from Windsor's Parish Church, 2/hr, clearly signposted, easy free parking, next to Windsor Castle, tel. 08705/040-404, www.legoland.co.uk).

Transportation Connections—Windsor

By Train: Windsor has two train stations: Windsor Central (5-min walk to palace and TI) and Windsor & Eton Riverside (10-min walk to palace and TI). Thames Trains run between London's Paddington Station and Windsor Central (2/hr, 40 min, change at Slough, www.thamestrains.co.uk). South West Trains run between London's Waterloo Station and the Windsor & Eton Riverside station (2/hr, 50 min, www.swtrains.co.uk).

By Bus: Green Line buses #700 and #702 run hourly between London's Victoria Colonnade (between the Victoria train and coach stations) and Windsor, where the bus stops in front of Legoland and near the castle—the stop is "Parish Church" (1.5 hrs). Bus info tel. 0870/608-7261.

By Car: Windsor, 20 miles from London and just off Heathrow airport's landing path, is well signposted from the M4 motorway. It's a convenient stop for anyone arriving at Heathrow, picking up a car, and not going into London.

CAMBRIDGE

Cambridge, 60 miles north of London, is world-famous for its prestigious university. Wordsworth, Isaac Newton, Tennyson, Darwin, and Prince Charles are a few of its illustrious alumni. This historic town of 100,000 people is more pleasant than its rival, Oxford. Cambridge is the epitome of a university town, with busy bikers, stately residence halls, plenty of bookshops, and proud locals who can point out where DNA was modeled, the first atom split, and electrons discovered.

In medieval Europe, higher education was the domain of the Church and was limited to ecclesiastical schools. Scholars lived in "halls" on campus. This scholarly community of residential halls, chapels, and lecture halls connected by peaceful garden courtyards survives today in the colleges that make the universities at Cambridge and Oxford. By 1350 (Oxford is roughly 100 years older), Cambridge had eight colleges, each with a monastic-type courtyard and lodgings. Today, Cambridge has 31 colleges. While a student's life revolves around his or her independent college, the university organizes lectures, presents degrees, and promotes research.

The university dominates—and owns—most of Cambridge.

The approximate term schedule is late January to late March (called Lent term), mid-April to mid-June (Easter term), and early October to early December (Michaelmas term). The colleges are closed to visitors during exams, from mid-April until late June, but King's College Chapel and the Trinity Library stay open, and the town is never sleepy.

Planning Your Time

Cambridge is worth most of a day but not an overnight. The cheap day-return train plan makes Cambridge easy and economical as a side trip from London (from London's King's Cross Station, £15.20 round-trip, 2/hr, 50 min, fast trains depart at :15 and :45 past each hr each way; the budget ticket requires a departure after 9:30 except Sat–Sun). You can arrive in time for the 11:30 walking tour—an essential part of any visit—and spend the afternoon touring King's College and Fitzwilliam Museum (closed Mon) and simply enjoying the ambience of this stately old college town.

Orientation

Cambridge is small but congested. There are two main streets, separated from the river by the most interesting colleges. The town center, brimming with tearooms, has a TI and a colorful open-air market (daily 9:30–16:00, on Market Hill Square; arts and crafts Sun 10:30–16:30, clothes and produce rest of week). Also on the main square is a Marks & Spencer grocery (Mon–Sat 8:30–20:00, Sun 11:00–17:00). A J. Sainsbury supermarket, with longer hours and a better deli, is three blocks north on Sidney Street. A good picnic spot is Laundress Green, a grassy park on the river, at the end of Mill Lane near the Silver Street punts. Everything is within a pleasant walk.

Tourist Information: At the station, a City Sightseeing/ Guide Friday office dispenses free city maps and sells fancier ones. The official TI is well signposted and just off Market Hill Square (40p maps, Mon–Fri 10:00–17:30, Sat 10:00–17:00, Sun 11:00– 16:00, closed Sun Nov–Easter, books rooms, tel. 01223/322-640).

Arrival in Cambridge: To get to downtown Cambridge from the train station, take a 20-minute walk (the City Sightseeing/ Guide Friday map is fine for this), a £4 taxi ride, or bus #C1 or #C3 (£1, every 5 min). Drivers can follow signs to any of the handy and central Short Stay Parking Lots.

Tours of Cambridge

▲▲Walking Tour of the Colleges—A walking tour is the best way to understand Cambridge's mix of "town and gown." Walks give a good rundown on the historic and scenic highlights of the

Cambridge

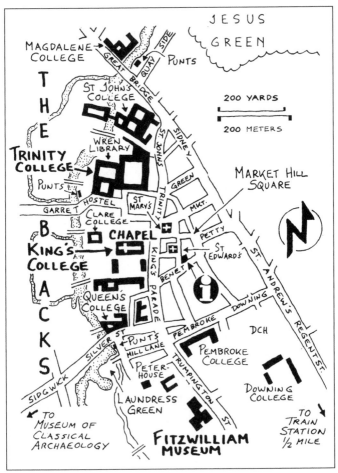

university as well as some fun local gossip. Walks are run by and leave from the TI. From mid-June through August, tours start at 10:30, 11:30, 13:30, and 14:30. In September they start at 10:30, 11:30, and 13:30. The rest of the year they often leave at 11:30 and always at 13:30. Tours cost £7.25 and include admission to King's College Chapel. Drop by the TI one hour early to snare a spot. Particularly if you're coming from London, call the TI (tel. 01223/322-640) at least to confirm that a tour is scheduled and not full. Private guides are also available (tel. 01223/457-574).

Bus Tours— City Sightseeing/Guide Friday hop-on, hop-off bus tours are informative and cover the outskirts, including the American Cemetery (£8.50, departing every 15 min, can use CC to buy tickets in their office in the train station). Walking tours go where the buses can't—right into the center.

Sights—Cambridge

▲▲**King's College Chapel**—Built from 1446 to 1515 by Henrys VI through VIII, England's best example of Perpendicular Gothic is the single most impressive building in town. Stand inside, look up, and marvel, as Christopher Wren did, at what was the largest single span of vaulted roof anywhere—2,000 tons of incredible fan vaulting. Wander through the Old Testament with the 25 16th-century stained-glass windows (the most Renaissance stained glass anywhere in one spot; it was taken out for safety during World War II then painstakingly replaced). Walk to the altar and admire Rubens' masterful *Adoration of the Magi* (£3.50, erratic hours depending on school and events, but usually daily 10:00–17:00). During term, you're welcome to enjoy an evensong service (Mon–Sat at 17:30, Sun at 15:30, tel. 01223/331-447).

▲▲**Trinity College**—Half of Cambridge's 63 Nobel Prize winners came from this richest and biggest of the town's colleges, founded in 1546 by Henry VIII. Don't miss the Wren-designed library, with its wonderful carving and fascinating original manuscripts (£2, 10p leaflet, Mon–Fri 12:00–14:00, also Sat 10:30–12:30 during term, always closed Sun; or visit the library for free during the same hours from the riverside entrance by the Garret Hostel Bridge). Just outside the library entrance, Sir Isaac Newton, who spent 30 years at Trinity, clapped his hands and timed the echo to measure the speed of sound as it raced down the side of the cloister and back. In the library's display cases (covered with brown cloth that you flip back), you'll see handwritten works by Newton, Milton, Byron, Tennyson, and Housman, alongside Milne's original *Winnie the Pooh* (the real Christopher Robin attended Trinity College).

▲▲**Fitzwilliam Museum**—Britain's best museum of antiquities and art outside of London is the Fitzwilliam. Enjoy its wonderful paintings (Old Masters and a fine English section featuring Gainsborough, Reynolds, Hogarth, and others, plus works by all the famous Impressionists), old manuscripts, and Greek, Egyptian, and Mesopotamian collections (free, £3 guided tour at 14:30 on Sun only, Tue–Sat 10:00–17:00, Sun 14:15–17:00, closed Mon, tel. 01223/332-900, www.fitzmuseum.cam.ac.uk).

Museum of Classical Archaeology—While this museum contains no originals, it offers a unique chance to see accurate copies (19th-century casts) of virtually every famous ancient Greek and Roman statue. More than 450 statues are on display (free, Mon–Fri 10:00–17:00, sometimes also Sat 10:00–13:00 during term, always closed Sun, Sidgwick Avenue, tel. 01223/335-153). The museum is a five-minute walk west of Silver Street Bridge; after crossing the bridge, continue straight until you reach a sign reading Sidgwick Site (museum is on your right; the entrance is away from the street).

▲**Punting on the Cam**—For a little levity and probably more exercise than you really want, try hiring one of the traditional (and inexpensive) flat-bottom punts at the river and pole yourself up and down (around and around, more likely) the lazy Cam. Once you get the hang of it, it's a fine way to enjoy the scenic side of Cambridge. After 17:00 it's less crowded and less embarrassing. Three places, one at each bridge, rent punts (£60 deposit required, can use CC) and offer £10 50-minute punt tours. Trinity Punt, at Garrett Hostel Bridge near Trinity College, has the best prices (£10/hr rental, ask for free short lesson). Scudamore's runs two other locations: the central Silver Street (£12/hr rentals) and the less-convenient Quayside at Great Bridge, at the north end of town (£12/hr, tel. 01223/359-750, www.scudamores.com). Depending on the weather, punting season runs daily March through October, with Silver Street open weekends year-round.

Transportation Connections—Cambridge

By Train: To London's **King's Cross Station** (fast train departures at :15 and :45 past each hr, 50 min, one-way £15.10, cheap day-return for £15.20), to York (about £62, 1/hr, 2.5 hrs, transfer in Petersborough). Tel. 08457-484-950.

By Bus: To **Heathrow** (1 bus/hr, 2.5 hrs). Tel. 08705-757-747.

BATH

The best city to visit within easy striking distance of London is Bath—just a 75-minute train ride away. Two hundred years ago, this city of 80,000 was the trendsetting Hollywood of Britain. If ever a city enjoyed looking in the mirror, Bath's the one. It has more "government-listed" or protected historic buildings per capita than any other town in England. The entire city, built of the creamy, warm-tone limestone called "Bath stone," beams in its cover-girl complexion. An architectural chorus line, it's a triumph of the Georgian style. Proud locals remind visitors that the town is routinely banned from the "Britain in Bloom" contest to give other towns a chance to win. Bath's narcissism is justified. Even with its mobs of tourists (2 million per year), it's a joy to visit.

Long before the Romans arrived in the first century, Bath was known for its hot springs. What became the Roman spa town of Aquae Sulis has always been fueled by the healing allure of its 116-degree mineral hot springs. The town's importance carried through Saxon times, when it had a huge church on the site of the present-day Abbey and was considered the religious capital of Britain. Its influence peaked in 973, with the sumptuous coronation of King Edgar the Peaceful in the Abbey. Bath prospered as a wool town.

Bath then declined until the mid-1600s, when it was just a huddle of huts around the Abbey and some hot springs, with 3,000 residents oblivious to the Roman ruins 18 feet below their dirt floors. Then, in 1687, Queen Mary, fighting infertility, bathed here. Within 10 months she gave birth to a son...and a new age of popularity for Bath.

The town boomed as a spa resort. Ninety percent of the buildings you'll see today are from the 18th century. Local architect John Wood was inspired by the Italian architect Palladio to build a "new Rome." The town bloomed in the neoclassical style, and streets were lined not with scrawny sidewalks but with wide "parades," upon which the women in their stylishly wide dresses could spread their fashionable tails.

Beau Nash (1673–1762) was Bath's "master of ceremonies." He organized both the daily regimen of the aristocratic visitors and the city, lighting and improving street security, banning swords, and opening the Pump Room. Under his fashionable baton, Bath became a city of balls, gaming, and concerts and the place to see and be seen in England. This most civilized place became even more so with the great neoclassical building spree that followed.

With a new spa tapping Bath's soothing hot springs, the town will once again attract visitors in need of a cure or a soak.

Planning Your Time

Bath needs at least two nights. There's plenty to do, and it's a delight to do it. On a one-week trip to London, consider spending two nights in Bath with one entire day for the city. Ideally, use Bath as your jet-lag recovery pillow and do London at the end of your trip.

Consider starting a London vacation this way:

Day 1: Land at Heathrow. Catch the National Express bus to Bath (11/day, 2.5 hrs).

Day 2: 9:00–Tour the Roman Baths, 10:30–Catch the free city walking tour, 12:30–Picnic on the open deck of a City Sightseeing/Guide Friday bus, 14:30–Free time in the shopping center of old Bath, 16:00–Tour the Costume Museum. Take an evening walk or see a play.

Day 3: Early train into London.

Orientation

Bath's town square, three blocks in front of the bus and train station, is a bouquet of tourist landmarks, including the Abbey, Roman and medieval baths, and the royal Pump Room.

Tourist Information: The TI is in the Abbey churchyard (Mon–Sat 9:30–18:00, Sun 10:00–16:00, Oct–April Mon–Sat until 17:00, tel. 01225/477-101, www.visitbath.co.uk, e-mail: tourism@bathnes.gov.uk). Pick up the 50p Bath miniguide (includes a map) and the free, info-packed *This Month in Bath*. Browse through scads of fliers, books, and maps. Skip their room-finding service (£5) and book direct. The TI sells a **Bath Pass** that gives you free entry to all the sights in town, but you have to work pretty hard to make it pay (£19/1 day, £29/2 days, £39/3 days). If you have a cell phone and are traveling with kids, ask the TI about "Texting Trails," a fun text-message scavenger hunt through Bath. An American Express office is tucked into the TI (decent rates, no commission on any checks, open same hrs as TI).

Arrival in Bath: The Bath train station is a pleasure (small-town charm, an international tickets desk, and a City Sightseeing/Guide Friday office masquerading as a TI). The bus station is immediately in front of the train station. To get to the TI, walk two blocks up Manvers Street from either station and turn left at the triangular "square," following the small TI arrow on a signpost. My recommended B&Bs are all within a 10- or 15-minute walk or a £3.50 taxi ride from the station.

Helpful Hints

Festivals: The International Music Festival bursts into song from May 16 to June 1 in 2003 (classical, folk, jazz, contemporary; tel. 01225/462-231), overlapped by the eclectic Fringe Festival from late May to mid-June (theater, walks, talks, bus trips; tel. 01225/480-079, www.bathfringe.co.uk, e-mail: admin@bathfringe.co.uk). Bath's box office sells tickets for most every event and can tell you exactly what's on tonight (2 Church Street, tel. 01225/463-362, www.bathfestivals.org.uk). Bath's local paper has a "What's On" event listing (www.thisisbath.com).

Internet Access: The Click Café is across from the train station on Manvers Street (£3/hr, daily 10:00–22:00, tel. 01225/481-008, www.click-cafe.com). Other places offering Internet access are the Itchy Feet Café & Travel Store (4 Bartlett Street, near Costume Museum) and the Bath Backpackers Hostel (13 Pierrepont Street; coming from train station, you pass hostel on way to TI).

Bath

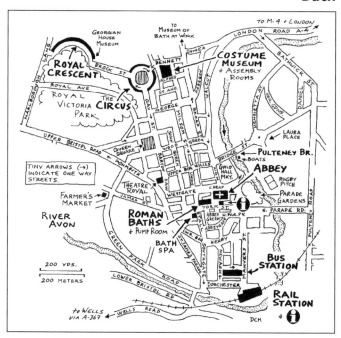

Tours of Bath

▲▲**City Bus Tours**—The City Sightseeing/Guide Friday green-and-cream open-top tour bus makes a 70-minute figure-eight circuit of Bath's main sights with an exhaustingly informative running commentary. For one £8.50 ticket (buy from driver), tourists can hop on and off at will for a whole day. The buses cover the city center and the surrounding hills (17 signposted pick-up points, 3/hr spring and fall—runs 9:30–17:00, 6/hr in summer—9:15–18:15, 1/hr in winter—9:30–15:30, tel. 01225/444-102). This is great in sunny weather and a feast for photographers. You can munch a sandwich, work on a tan, and sightsee at the same time. Several competing hop-on, hop-off tour-bus companies offer basically the same tour, but in 45 minutes and without the swing through the countryside, for a couple pounds less. Generally, the City Sightseeing/Guide Friday guides are better. (These tour buses are technically "public service vehicles"—a loophole they use to be able to run the same routes as transit buses. Consequently, tour buses are required to take passengers across town for the normal £1 fare. Nervy tourists have the right to hop on, ask for a "single fare," and pay £1.) Note that ticket stubs for any of the bus tours usually get you discounts at some sights. Pick up the various brochures at the TI and see what sights are currently discounted; if you want to see those sights, take the bus tour first.

▲▲▲Walking Tours—These free two-hour tours, offered by "The Mayor's Corps of Honorary Guides"—volunteers who want to share their love of Bath with its many visitors—are a chatty, historical, gossip-filled joy, essential for your understanding of this town's amazing Georgian social scene. How else will you learn that the old "chair ho" call for your sedan chair evolved into today's "cheerio" farewell? Tours leave from in front of the Pump Room (year-round daily at 10:30 plus Sun–Fri at 14:00; evening walks offered May–Sept at 19:00 on Tue, Fri, and Sat). For Ghost Walks and Bizarre Bath Comedy Walks, see "Nightlife," below. For a private walking tour, call the local guide's bureau (£46/2 hrs, tel. 01225/337-111).

Tours from Bath

"Mad Max" Minibus Tours—Maddy's tours are thoughtfully organized and informative. Operating daily from Bath, they run with a maximum group size of 16 people and cost £17.50 per person (no CC). Tours depart from Bath at 8:45 (at the statue on Cheap Street, next to London Camera Exchange) and end at 16:30, covering 110 miles with stops at Stonehenge, Avebury Stone Circles, and two cute villages—Lacock and Castle Combe. Castle Combe, the southernmost Cotswold village, is as cute as they come. Book ahead for this popular tour by phone (Bath YMCA tel. 01225/460-471) or e-mail (maddy@madmax.abel .co.uk, www.madmaxtours.com). Please honor or cancel your seat reservation.

If Mad Max is booked up, don't fret. Plenty of companies in Bath offer tours of varying lengths, prices, and destinations. Leaflets are available at the Bath TI, where you can also book some of these tours directly.

Consider the **Cotswold Experience** (tel. 01225/477-101, www.cotswold-tours.co.uk), **Danwood Tours** (cellular 07977-929-486, e-mail: dantour@hotmail.com), or **Andrews Country Tours** (tel. 01761/416-362, www.andrewstours.co.uk, e-mail: c.andrew@talk21.com, Chris Andrews).

Sights—Bath

▲▲▲Roman and Medieval Baths—In ancient Roman times, high society enjoyed the mineral springs at Bath. From Londinium, Romans traveled so often to Aquae Sulis, as the city was called, to "take a bath" that finally it became known simply as Bath.

Today, a fine museum surrounds the ancient bath. It's a one-way system leading you past well-documented displays, Roman artifacts, mosaics, a temple pediment, and the actual mouth of the spring, piled high with Roman pennies. Enjoy some quality time looking into the eyes of Minerva, goddess of the hot springs. The included self-guided tour audioguide makes the visit easy and plenty informative. For those with a big appetite for Roman history, in-depth 40-minute tours leave from the end of the museum at the edge of the actual bath (included, on the hour, a poolside clock is set for the next departure time). You can revisit the museum after the tour (£8.50, £11.50 combo-ticket includes Costume Museum at a good savings, family combo-£28, combo-tickets good for 1 week; April–Sept daily 9:00–18:00, July–Aug until 22:00—last entry at 21:00, Oct–March until 17:00, tel. 01225/477-784, www.romanbath.co.uk). After visiting the Roman Baths, drop by the attached Pump Room for a spot of tea.

▲**Pump Room**—For centuries, Bath was forgotten as a spa. Then, in 1687, the previously barren Queen Mary bathed here, became pregnant, and bore a male heir to the throne. Word of its wonder waters spread, and Bath was back on the aristocratic map. High society soon turned the place into one big pleasure palace. The Pump Room, an elegant Georgian hall just above the Roman baths, offers the visitor's best chance to raise a pinky in this Chippendale elegance. Drop by to sip coffee or tea or enjoy a light meal (9:30–12:00 morning coffee, 12:00–14:30 lunch—£12 2-course menu, 14:30–17:30 traditional high tea—£8, 17:30–20:30 dinner, £7 tea/coffee and pastry available anytime except during lunch, string trio or live pianist plays sporadically between 10:00 and 17:00, tel. 01225/444-477). Above the newspaper table and sedan chairs, a statue of Beau Nash himself sniffs down at you. Now's your chance to have a famous (but forgettable) "Bath bun" and split (and spit) a 50p drink of the awfully curative water. Convenient public WCs are in the entry hallway that connects the Pump Room with the Baths.

Thermae Bath Spa—Bath's natural thermal springs are once again being used for bathing and treatments, in a complex combining restored old buildings and a new, state-of-the-art leisure spa. Opened in early 2003, this is the only natural thermal spa in the United Kingdom This hedonistic marvel includes an open-air rooftop thermal pool and all the "pamper thyself" extras—Jacuzzi, steam room, massage room, solarium, and lots of healing-type treatments and classes. Swimwear is obligatory, but you can buy suits and footwear at the spa (£17/2 hrs, £23/4 hrs, £35/full day, these prices do not include treatments, massage, or solarium, reservations recommended for these extra services, 100 meters

from Roman and medieval baths on Beau Street, tel. 01225/
780-308, fax 01225/780-294, www.thermaebathspa.co.uk).

▲**Abbey**—Bath town wasn't much in the Middle Ages, but an
important church has stood on this spot since Anglo-Saxon times.
In 973, Edgar the Peaceful was crowned here. Dominating the
town center, the present church—the last great medieval church
of England—is 500 years old and a fine example of Late Perpendicular Gothic, with breezy fan vaulting and enough stained
glass to earn it the nickname "Lantern of the West" (worth the
£2 donation, Mon–Sat 9:00–18:00, Sun usually 13:00–14:30 &
15:30–17:30, closes at 16:30 in winter, handy flier narrates a self-
guided 19-stop tour). The schedule for concerts, services, and
evensong (Sun at 15:30 year-round, plus most Sat in Aug at 17:00)
is posted on the door. Take a moment to really appreciate the
Abbey's architecture from the Abbey Green square.

The Abbey's **Heritage Vaults,** a small but interesting
exhibit, tell the story of Christianity in Bath since Roman times
(£2, Mon–Sat 10:00–16:00, last entry 15:30, closed Sun, entrance
just outside church, south side).

▲**Pulteney Bridge, Parade Gardens, and Cruises**—Bath is
inclined to compare its shop-lined Pulteney Bridge to Florence's
Ponte Vecchio. That's pushing it. To best enjoy a sunny day,
pay £1.20 to enter the Parade Gardens below the bridge (daily
10:00–19:00, until 20:00 June–Aug, free after 20:00, includes deck
chairs, ask about concerts held some Sun at 15:00 in summer).

Across the bridge at Pulteney Weir, tour boats run cruises
from under the bridge (£5, up to 7/day if the weather's good,
50 min to Bathampton and back, WCs on board). Just take whatever
boat is running. Avon Cruisers stop in Bathampton if you'd like to
walk back; Pulteney Cruisers come with a sundeck ideal for picnics.

▲▲**Royal Crescent and the Circus**—If Bath is an architectural
cancan, these are the kickers. These first elegant Georgian "condos"
by John Wood (the Elder and the Younger) are well explained in
the city walking tours. "Georgian" is British for "neoclassical," or
dating from the 1770s. As you cruise the Crescent, pretend you're
rich. Pretend you're poor. Notice the "ha ha fence," a drop in the
front yard offering a barrier, invisible from the windows, to sheep
and peasants. The round Circus is a coliseum turned inside out.
Its Doric, Ionic, and Corinthian capital decorations pay homage
to its Greco-Roman origin.

▲▲**Georgian House at #1 Royal Crescent**—This museum (on the
corner of Brock Street and the Royal Crescent) offers your best look
into a period house. It's worth the £4 admission to get behind one of
those classy exteriors. The volunteers in each room are determined
to fill you in on all the fascinating details of Georgian life . . . like

how high-class women shaved their eyebrows and pasted on carefully trimmed strips of furry mouse skin in their place (Tue–Sun 10:30–17:00, closed Mon, closes at 16:00 in Nov, closed Dec–mid-Feb, "no stiletto heels, please," tel. 01225/428-126).

▲▲▲**Costume Museum**—One of Europe's great museums, displaying 400 years of fashion—one frilly decade at a time—is housed within Bath's Assembly Rooms. Follow the included, excellent audioguide tour. Special for 2003 is a *Modern Times* exhibit on fashions of the 1920s (£5.50, a £11.50 combo-ticket covers Roman Baths, family combo-£28, daily 10:00–17:00, tel. 01225/477-789). The Assembly Rooms, which you'll see en route to the museum, are big, elegant, empty rooms where card games, concerts, tea, and dances were held in the 18th century, before the advent of fancy hotels with grand public spaces made them obsolete.

▲▲▲**Museum of Bath at Work**—This is the official title for Mr. Bowler's Business, a 1900s engineer's shop, brass foundry, and fizzy-drink factory with a Dickensian office. It's just a pile of meaningless old gadgets until a volunteer guide lovingly resurrects Mr. Bowler's creative genius. Fascinating hour-long tours go regularly; just join the one in session upon arrival (£3.50, April–Oct daily 10:00–17:00, last entry at 16:00, weekends only in winter, 2 blocks up Russell Street from Assembly Rooms, call to be sure a volunteer is available to give a tour, café upstairs, tel. 01225/318-348).

Jane Austen Centre—This exhibition focuses on Jane Austen's five years in Bath (around 1800) and the influence Bath had on her writing. While the exhibit is thoughtfully done and a hit with "Jane-ites," there is little of historic substance here. You'll walk through a Georgian townhouse that she didn't live in and see mostly enlarged reproductions of things associated with her writing. After a live intro explaining how this romantic but down-to-earth girl dealt with the silly, shallow, and arrogant aristocrat's world where "the doing of nothings all day prevents one from doing anything," you see a 13-minute video and wander through the rest of the exhibit (£4.50, Mon–Sat 10:00–17:30, Sun 10:30–17:30, 40 Gay Street between Queen's Square and the Circus, tel. 01225/443-000, www.janeausten.co.uk).

The Building of Bath Museum—This offers a fascinating look behind the scenes at how the Georgian city was actually built. It's just one large room of exhibits, but those interested in construction find it worth the £4 (Tue–Sun 10:30–17:00, closed Mon, near the Circus on a street called "the Paragon," tel. 01225/333-895).

Views—For the best views of Bath, try Alexander Park (south of city, 10-min walk from train station), Camden Crescent (10–15 min walk north), or Becksford Tower (steep 20-min walk north up Lansdown Road, www.bath-preservation-trust.org.uk).

▲**American Museum**—I know, you need this in Bath like you
need a Big Mac. But this museum offers a fascinating look at
colonial- and early-American lifestyles. Each of 18 completely
furnished rooms (from the 1600s to the 1800s) is hosted by an
eager guide waiting to fill you in on the candles, maps, bedpans,
and various religious sects that make domestic Yankee history
surprisingly interesting. One room is a quilter's nirvana (£6,
April–Oct Tue–Sun 14:00–17:00, closed Mon and Nov–March,
at Claverton Manor, tel. 01225/460-503). The museum is outside of town and a headache to reach if you don't have a car
(15-min walk from the nearest City Sightseeing/Guide Friday
stop or a 10-min walk from bus #18).

Nightlife in Bath

This Month in Bath (free, available at TI) lists events.
Plays—The Theatre Royal, newly restored and one of England's loveliest, offers a busy schedule of London West End–
type plays, including many "pre-London" dress-rehearsal runs
(£11–25, cheaper matinees as low as £5, tel. 01225/448-844,
www.threatreroyal.org.uk). Forty standby tickets per evening
show go on sale starting at 12:00 on the day of the performance
(either pay cash at box office or call and book with CC, 2 tickets
maximum). Or you can buy a £10 last-minute seat 30 minutes
before "curtain up."
Evening Walks—Take your choice: comedy, ghost, or history.
For an immensely entertaining walking comedy act "with absolutely no history or culture," follow J. J. or Noel Britten on their
creative and entertaining **Bizarre Bath** walk. This 90-minute
"tour," which plays off local passersby as well as tour members,
is a belly laugh a minute (£5, April–Sept nightly at 20:00, smaller
groups Mon–Thu, heavy on magic, careful to insult all minorities
and sensitivities, just racy enough but still good family fun; leave
from Huntsman pub near the Abbey, confirm at TI or call 01225/
335-124, www.bizarrebath.co.uk). **Ghost Walks** are another way
to pass the after-dark hours (£5, 20:00, 2 hrs, unreliably Mon–Sat
April–Oct; in winter Fri only; leave from Garrick's Head pub near
Theatre Royal, tel. 01225/463-618, www.ghostwalksofbath.co.uk).
The TI offers **free evening walks** in summer (May–Sept at 19:00
on Tue, Fri, and Sat, 2 hrs, leave from Pump Room, confirm at TI);
for more information, see the Tours of Bath chapter, page 231.

Sleeping in Bath

To help you easily sort through these listings, I've divided the
rooms into three categories, based on the price for a standard
double room with bath:

Higher Priced—Most rooms more than £90.
Moderately Priced—Most rooms £90 or less.
Lower Priced—Most rooms £60 or less.
Sleep Code: S = Single, **D** = Double/Twin, **T** = Triple,
Q = Quad, **b** = bathroom, **s** = shower only, **CC** = Credit Cards
accepted, **no CC** = Credit Cards not accepted.

Bath is a busy tourist town. To get a good B&B, make a telephone reservation in advance. Competition is stiff, and it's worth
asking any of these places for a weekday, three-nights-in-a-row, or
off-season deal. Friday and Saturday nights are tightest, especially
if you're staying only one night, since B&Bs favor those staying
longer. If staying only Saturday night, you're very bad news. At
B&Bs (and cheaper hotels), expect lots of stairs and no lifts.

Launderettes: The Spruce Goose Launderette is around
the corner from Brock's Guest House on the pedestrian lane called
Margaret's Buildings (self-service or full-service on same day if
dropped off at 8:00, Sun–Fri 8:00–20:00, Sat 8:00–21:00, tel. 01225/
483-309). Anywhere in town, Speedy Wash can pick up your laundry for same-day service (£9/bag, most hotels work with them, tel.
01225/427-616). East of Pulteney Bridge, the humble Lovely Wash
is on Daniel Street (daily 9:00–21:00, self-service only).

Sleeping in B&Bs near the Royal Crescent

These listings are all a 15-minute uphill walk or an easy £3.50
taxi ride from the train station. Or take the City Sightseeing/
Guide Friday bus tour from the station and get off at the stop
nearest your B&B (for Brock's: Assembly Rooms; for Marlborough
listings: Royal Avenue; confirm with driver), check in, then finish
the tour later in the day. All of these B&Bs are non-smoking.

MODERATELY PRICED
Brock's Guest House will put bubbles in your Bath experience.
Marion and Geoffrey Dodd have redone their Georgian town-
house (built by John Wood in 1765) in a way that would make
the famous architect proud. It's located between the prestigious
Royal Crescent and the elegant Circus (Db-£65–75, 1 deluxe
Db-£75–82, Tb-£85–90, Qb-£99–110, CC, reserve with CC
number far in advance, little library on top floor, 32 Brock Street,
Bath BA1 2LN, tel. 01225/338-374, fax 01225/334-245, www
.brocksguesthouse.co.uk, e-mail: marion@brocksguesthouse.co.uk).

Elgin Villa, also thoughtfully run and a fine value, has five
comfy, well-maintained rooms (Ss-£32, Sb-£45, Ds-£45, Db-£65,
Tb-£85, Qb-£105, CC, more expensive for 1 night, discounted
for 3 nights, continental breakfast served in room, parking,
6 Marlborough Lane, Bath BA1 2NQ, tel. & fax 01225/424-557,

Bath Hotels

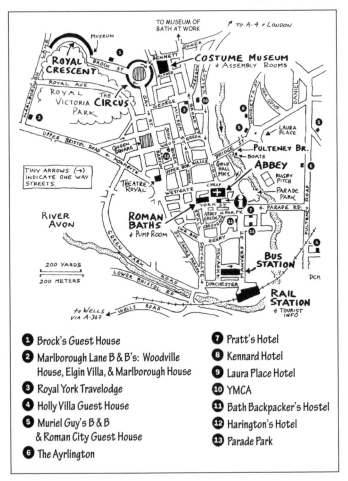

1. Brock's Guest House
2. Marlborough Lane B & B's: Woodville House, Elgin Villa, & Marlborough House
3. Royal York Travelodge
4. Holly Villa Guest House
5. Muriel Guy's B & B & Roman City Guest House
6. The Ayrlington
7. Pratt's Hotel
8. Kennard Hotel
9. Laura Place Hotel
10. YMCA
11. Bath Backpacker's Hostel
12. Harington's Hotel
13. Parade Park

www.elginvilla.co.uk, e-mail: stay@elginvilla.co.uk, Alwyn and Carol Landman).

Marlborough House Hotel is both Victorian and vegetarian, with seven comfortable rooms—well furnished with antiques—and optional £15 organic-veggie dinners (Sb-£45–75, Db-£65–85, Tb-£75–95, price depending on season, CC, varied breakfast menu, room service, 1 Marlborough Lane, Bath BA1 2NQ, tel. 01225/318-175, fax 01225/466-127, www.marlborough-house.net, Americans Laura and Charles).

LOWER PRICED

The **Woodville House** is run by Anne and Tom Toalster.
This grandmotherly little house has three tidy, charming
rooms, one shared shower/WC, an extra WC, and a TV
lounge. Breakfast is served at a big, family-style table (D-
£40, minimum 2 nights, no CC, strictly non-smoking, some
parking, below the Royal Crescent at 4 Marlborough Lane,
Bath BA1 2NQ, tel. & fax 01225/319-335, e-mail: toalster
@compuserve.com).

Prior House B&B, with four well-kept rooms, friendly
German shepherd Toby, and thoughtful touches such as
robes for guests who use the bathroom down the hall, is run
by helpful Lynn and Keith Shearn (D-£54, Db-£50, CC,
3 Marlborough Lane, Bath BA1 2NQ, tel. 01225/313-587,
fax 01225/443-543, www.greatplaces.co.uk/priorhouse/, e-mail:
priorhouse@greatplaces.co.uk).

Parkside Guest House has four Edwardian rooms
and a spacious back garden (Db-£67, CC, small breakfast,
11 Marlborough Lane, BA1 2NQ, tel. & fax 01225/429-444,
e-mail: parkside@lynall.freeserve.co.uk, Erica and Inge Lynall).

Sleeping in B&Bs East of the River

These listings are about a 10-minute walk from the city center.

HIGHER PRICED

The Ayrlington, next door to a lawn-bowling green, has attrac-
tive rooms that hint of a more genteel time. Though this well-
maintained hotel fronts a busy street, its double-paned windows make it feel tranquil inside. Rooms in the back have
pleasant views of sports greens and Bath beyond. For the best
value, request a standard double with a view of Bath (standard
Db-£99–120, superior Db-£110–135, deluxe Db with Jacuzzi-
£120–155, high prices on Fri, Sat, and Sun, no Sat night only,
CC, access to garden in back, easy parking, 24/25 Pulteney
Road, Bath BA2 4EZ, tel. 01225/425-495, fax 01225/469-029,
Simon and Mee-Ling).

MODERATELY PRICED

In Sydney Gardens: The **Sydney Gardens Hotel** is a classy
Casablanca-type place with six tastefully decorated rooms, an
elegant breakfast room, garden views, and an entrance to Sydney
Gardens park (Db-£75, Tb-£100, CC, request garden view, easy
parking, located on busy road between park and canal, Sydney
Road, Bath BA2 6NT, tel. 01225/464-818, fax 01225/484-347,
www.sydneygardens.co.uk, Rory).

LOWER PRICED

Near North Parade Road: The **Holly Villa Guest House,** with a cheery garden, six bright rooms, and a cozy TV lounge, is enthusiastically and thoughtfully run by Jill and Keith McGarrigle (Ds-£45, Db-£50–55, Tb-£75–80, no CC, strictly non-smoking, easy parking, 8-min walk from station and city center: Walk over North Parade Bridge, take the first right, and then take the second left, 14 Pulteney Gardens, Bath BA2 4HG, tel. 01225/310-331, e-mail: hollyvilla.bb@ukgateway.net).

Near Pulteney Road: Muriel Guy's B&B is another good value, mixing Georgian elegance with homey warmth and artistic taste (5 rooms, S-£25, Db-£55, Tb-£60, no CC, serves mostly organic foods, go over bridge on North Parade Road, left on Pulteney Road, cross to church, Raby Place is first row of houses on hill, 14 Raby Place, Bath BA2 4EH, tel. 01225/465-120, fax 01225/465-283, e-mail: no way).

Roman City Guest House, down the street from Muriel Guy's B&B, is a recently restored 1810 home with large bright rooms, some with views, and a welcoming lounge (Db-from £50, parking available, 18 Raby Place, Bath BA2 4EH, tel. & fax, 01225/463-668, www.romancityguesthouse.co.uk, e-mail: romancityguesthse@amserve.net).

Sleeping East of Pulteney Bridge

These are just a few minutes' walk from the city center.

HIGHER PRICED

Kennard Hotel is comfortable, with 14 charming Georgian rooms and a dazzling breakfast room. Richard Ambler runs this place warmly, giving careful attention to guests (S-£48, Db-£88–118 depending upon size, CC, no kids under 12, just over Pulteney Bridge, turn left at Henrietta, 11 Henrietta Street, Bath BA2 6LL, tel. 01225/310-472, fax 01225/460-054, www.kennard.co.uk, e-mail: reception@kennard.co.uk).

Laura Place Hotel is another elegant Georgian place (8 rooms, 2 on the ground floor, rooftop D-£62, Db-£70–95 from small and high up to huge and palatial, CC, 2-night minimum stay, family suite, easy parking, just over Pulteney Bridge, 3 Laura Place, Great Pulteney Street, Bath BA2 4BH, tel. 01225/463-815, fax 01225/310-222, Patricia Bull).

Villa Magdala, with 18 rooms in a freestanding Vic-torian townhouse opposite a park, is formal and hotel-esque (Db-£85–105, depending on size, type of bed, and plumbing; no CC, non-smoking, in quiet residential area, inviting lounge, parking, Henrietta Road, Bath BA2 6LX, tel. 01225/466-329, fax 01225-483-207, www.villamagdala.co.uk, e-mail: office@villamagdala.co.uk).

MODERATELY PRICED
Henrietta Hotel, with simple basic rooms and lots of stairs, gives you a budget-hotel option in this elegant neighborhood (10 rooms, Db-£50–75, discount with 3-night stay Sun–Thu, CC, 32 Henrietta Street, Bath BA2 6LR, tel. 01225/447-779, fax 01225/444-150, Jill).

Sleeping in the City Center
HIGHER PRICED
Harington's of Bath Hotel, with 13 newly renovated rooms on a quiet street in the town center, is run by Susan and Desmond Pow (Db-£88–118, Tb-£118–138, prices decrease midweek and increase Fri–Sat, 10 percent discount with this book for 2-night minimum stays Sun–Thu except on public holidays, CC, non-smoking, lots of stairs, attached restaurant/bar serves simple meals and pastries all day, extremely central at 10 Queen Street, Bath BA1 1HE, tel. 01225/461-728, fax 01225/444-804, www .haringtonshotel.co.uk).

    Pratt's Hotel is as proper and old English as you'll find in Bath. Its creaks and frays are aristocratic. Its public places make you want to sip a brandy, and its 46 rooms are bright, spacious, and come with all the comforts (Sb-£80, Db-£110, advanced reservations get highest rate, drop-ins after 16:00 often enjoy substantial discount, dogs-£4.95 but children free, breakfast extra, CC, attached restaurant/bar, elevator, 2 blocks immediately in front of the station on South Parade, Bath BA2 4AB, tel. 01225/460-441, fax 01225/448-807, www.forestdale.com, e-mail: pratts@forestdale.com).

    Best Western–style **Abbey Hotel** has 60 decent rooms, some on the ground floor, a super location, and a rare elevator (standard Db-£125, deluxe Db-£140, CC, attached restaurant, non-smoking rooms, North Parade, Bath BA1 1LF, tel. 01225/461-603, fax 01225/447-758, e-mail: ahres@compasshotels.co.uk).

MODERATELY PRICED
Parade Park Hotel, in a Georgian building, has a central location, helpful owners, and comfortable basic rooms decorated in a modern style (35 rooms, S-£35, D-£50, Db-£60–80, Tb-£90, Qb-£120, CC, non-smoking, beaucoup stairs, 10 North Parade, Bath BA2 4AL, tel. 01225/463-384, fax 01225/442-322, www.paradepark.co.uk, e-mail: info@paradepark.co.uk).

LOWER PRICED

The **Royal York Travelodge** offers American-style, characterless, comfortable rooms—worrying B&Bs and hotels alike with its reasonable prices (Db-£60, £70 on Fri–Sun, breakfast extra, CC, non-smoking rooms available, 1 York Bldg, George Street, Bath BA1 3EB, tel. 0870-191-1718, central reservation tel. 08700-850-950, www.travelodge.co.uk).

Henry Guest House is a plain, simple, old, vertical, eight-room, family-run place two blocks in front of the train station on a quiet side street. Nothing matches—not the curtains, wallpaper, carpeting, throw rugs, or bedspreads—but it is the cheapest hotel in the center (S-£25, D-£50, T-£65, no CC, lots of narrow stairs, 3 showers and 2 WCs for all, 6 Henry Street, Bath BA1 1JT, tel. 01225/424-052, fax 01225/316-669, www.thehenry.com, e-mail: enquiries@thehenry.com, Sue and Derek).

Sleeping in Lower-Priced Dorms

The **YMCA,** central on a leafy square down a tiny alley off Broad Street, has 208 beds in industrial-strength rooms with tired carpeting (S-£18, D-£32, T-£48, Q-£64, beds in big dorms-£12, includes meager continental breakfast, CC, families offered a day nursery for kids under 5, cheap dinners, no lockers, dorms closed 10:00–16:00, Broad Street Place, Bath BA1 5LH, tel. 01225/460-471, fax 01225/462-065, e-mail: reservation@ymcabath.co.uk).

White Hart Hostel is a simple, new place offering adults and families good cheap beds in two- to six-bed dorms (£12.50/bed, Db-£40–50, family rooms, breakfast-£2.50, CC, smoke free, kitchen, small cafe/bar, 5-min walk behind train station at Widcombe—where Widcombe Hill hits Claverton Street, Bath BA2 6AA, tel. 01225/313-985, www.whitehartbath.co.uk, e-mail: sue@whitehartinn.freeserve.co.uk, run by Mike and Sue).

Bath Backpackers Hostel bills itself as a totally fun-packed, mad place to stay. This youthfully run dive/hostel rents bunk beds in 6- to 10-bed rooms (£12/bed, 2 D-£30, T-£45, lockers, Internet access for nonguests as well, bar, kitchen, a couple of blocks toward city center from train station, 13 Pierrepont Street, Bath BA1 1LA, tel. 01225/446-787, e-mail: bath@hostels.co.uk).

Eating in Bath

While not a great pub-grub town, Bath is bursting with quaint and stylish eateries. There's something for every appetite and budget—just stroll around the center of town. A picnic dinner of deli food or take-out fish 'n' chips in the Royal Crescent Park is ideal for aristocratic hobos.

Eating between the Abbey and the Station

Three fine and popular places share North Parade Passage, a block south of the Abbey: **Tilley's Bistro,** popular with locals, serves healthy French, English, and vegetarian meals with candlelit ambience. Their fun menu lets you build your meal choosing from an interesting array of £6 starters (Mon–Sat 12:00–14:30 & 18:30–23:00, closed Sun, CC, reservations smart, non-smoking, North Parade Passage, tel. 01225/484-200). **Sally Lunn's House** is a cutesy, quasi-historic place for expensive doily meals, tea, pink pillows, and lots of lace (£15–20, nightly, CC, smoke-free, 4 North Parade Passage, tel. 01225/461-634). It's fine for tea and buns (£7–10,served until 18:00), and customers get a free peek at the basement Kitchen Museum (otherwise 30p). **Demuth's Vegetarian Restaurant** serves good £16 meals (daily 10:00–22:00, CC, vegan options available, reservations wise, tel. 01225/446-059).

Crystal Palace Pub, with typical pub grub under rustic timbers or in the sunny courtyard, is a handy standby (£6 meals, Mon–Fri 11:30–20:00, Sat 11:00–16:00, Sun 12:00–15:30, children welcome on patio but not indoors, 11 Abbey Green, tel. 01225/482-666).

Evans is decent for fish 'n' chips (Mon–Fri 11:30–15:00, Sat 11:30–17:00, closed Sun, on Abbeygate, near Marks & Spencer). Also greasy is **Seafoods** (daily 12:00–23:00, last seating 22:30, last take-out 23:00; try the mushy peas, cup of tea, and fish and chips special for £4; 27 Kingsmeads Street, just off Kingsmead Square). For more cheap meals, try **Spike's Fish and Chips** (open very late) and the neighboring café just behind the bus station.

Eating between the Abbey and the Circus

George Street is lined with cheery eateries: Thai, Italian, wine bars, and so on. The hopping **Martini Restaurant** is purely Italian with class and jovial waiters (£12 entrées, £7 pizzas, daily 12:00–14:30 & 18:00–22:30, CC, reservations smart, smoke-free section, 9 George Street, tel. 01225/460-818, Nunzio, Franco, and Luigi).

Bengal Brasserie, a Bangaladeshi place specializing in Tandoori and curries, is unpretentious with good food at good prices (12:00–14:00 & 18:00–23:00, 32 Milsom Street, tel. 01225/447-906).

Jamuna makes a mean curry (daily 12:00–14:30 & 18:00–24:00, 10 percent discount for take-out, Abbey views, 9-10 High Street, tel. 01225/464-631).

The **Old Green Tree Pub** on Green Street is a rare pub with good grub, locally brewed real ales, and a non-smoking room (lunch only, served 12:00–14:30, no children, live jazz Sun–Mon 20:30 until closing, tel. 01225/448-259).

Bath Restaurants

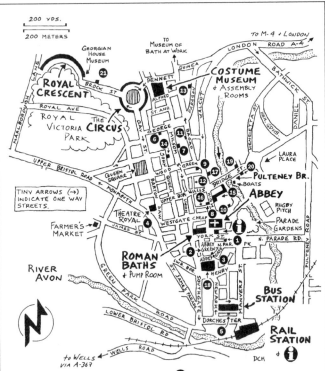

1 Tilley's Bistro, Sally Lunn's, Demuth's Veg. Rest.	**11** The Moon and Sixpence
2 Crystal Palace Pub	**12** Devon Savouries
3 Evans Fish & Chips	**13** Star Pub
4 Seafoods Fish & Chips	**14** Firehouse Rotisserie
5 Spike's Fish & Chips	**15** Guildhall Market
6 Martini Rest.	**16** Cornish Bakehouse
7 Bengal Brasserie	**17** Waitrose Supermarket
8 Jamuna Rest.	**18** Marks & Spencer Supermarket
9 Old Green Tree Pub	**19** No. 5 Bistro, Rajpoot Tandoori
10 Browns Rest.	**20** Cappeti's Italian Rest. & The Boater Pub
	21 Circus Rest.

Browns, a popular, modern chain, offers affordable—though not great—English food throughout the day (Sun–Fri 12:00–23:30, Sat 10:00–23:00, CC, kid-friendly, half block east of the Abbey, Orange Grove, tel. 01225/461-199).

The Moon and Sixpence, prized by locals, offers "modern English fusion" cuisine, giving British cooking a needed international flair and flavor (£7 2-course lunch, £21 3-course dinner menu, daily 12:00–14:30 & 17:30–22:30, CC, indoor/outdoor seating, 6a Broad Street, tel. 01225/460-962).

Devon Savouries serves greasy-but-delicious take-out pasties, sausage rolls, and vegetable pies (Mon–Sat 9:00–17:30, hours vary on Sun, cheaper if you get it to go, on Burton Street, the main walkway between New Bond Street and Upper Borough Walls).

If you're missing California, try the popular **Firehouse Rotisserie** (Mon–Sat 12:00–14:30 & 18:00–23:00, closed Sun, make reservations, near Queen Square on John Street, tel. 01225/482-070).

Guildhall Market, across from Pulteney Bridge, is fun for browsing and picnic shopping, with an inexpensive Market Café if you'd like to sip tea surrounded by stacks of used books, bananas on the push list, and honest-to-goodness old-time locals (Mon–Sat 9:00–17:00, closed Sun, a block north of the Abbey, main entrance on High Street).

The **Cornish Bakehouse,** near the Guildhall Market, has good take-away pasties (open until 17:30, 11a The Corridor, off High Street, tel. 01225/426-635).

Supermarkets: **Waitrose,** at the Podium shopping center, is great for groceries (Mon–Fri 8:30–20:00, Sat 8:30–19:00, Sun 11:00–17:00, salad bar, just west of Pulteney Bridge and across from post office on High Street). **Marks & Spencer,** near the train station, has a good grocery at the back of its department store (Mon–Sat 9:00–17:30, Sun 11:00–17:00, Stall Street).

Eating East of Pulteney Bridge

For a stylish, intimate setting and "new English" cuisine worth the splurge, dine at **No. 5 Bistro** (£13–16 main courses with vegetables, Mon–Sat 18:30–22:00, closed Sun, Mon–Tue are "bring your own bottle of wine" nights—no corkage fee, smart to reserve, CC, just over Pulteney Bridge at 5 Argyle Street, tel. 01225/444-499). **Rajpoot Tandoori,** next door to No. 5, serves good Indian food. You'll hike down deep into a cellar where the classy Indian atmosphere and award-winning cooking makes paying the extra pounds OK, (12:00–14:00 & 18:00–23:00, 4 Argyle Street, tel. 01225/466-833). **Cappeti's Italian Restaurant** is a checkered-tablecloth place in another deep cellar serving good Italian (Tue–Sat 12:00–14:00

& 18:30–22:30, closed Sun–Mon, CC, 12 Argyle Street, tel.
01225/442-299). Two doors down, the popular **Boater Pub**
offers a good selection of ales and pub grub and a pleasant beer
garden overlooking the river (Mon-Sat 11:00–23:00, Sun 12:00-
20:30, 9 Argyle Street, tel. 01225/464-211).

Eating near the Circus and Brock's Guest House
Circus Restaurant is intimate and a good value, with Mozartian
ambience and candlelit prices: £17 for a three-course dinner
special including great vegetables and a selection of fine desserts
(daily 12:00–14:00 & 18:30–22:00, reservations smart, CC,
34 Brock Street, tel. 01225/318-918, run by Felix Rosenow).

For real ale (but no food), try the **Star Pub** (top of
Paragon Street).

Transportation Connections—Bath
Bath's train station is called Bath Spa. The National Express bus
office (Mon–Sat 8:00–17:30, closed Sun) is one block in front
of the train station.

To London: By train to Paddington Station (2/hr, 75 min,
£32 one-way after 9:30), or cheaper by National Express bus to
Victoria Station (nearly 1/hr, a little over 3 hrs, £13 one-way,
£21 round-trip, www.gobycoach.com). To get from London to
Bath and see Stonehenge to boot, consider an all-day organized
bus tour from London (see page 312 in the Transportation
Connections chapter). Train info: tel. 08457-484-950.

To London's airports: By National Express bus to
Heathrow Airport and continuing on to London (10/day, 2.5 hrs,
£13, tel. 08705/808-080) and to **Gatwick** (approx 2/hr, 4.5 hrs,
£20). Trains are faster but more expensive (1/hr, 2.5 hrs, £29.20).

DAY TRIP
TO PARIS

The most exciting single day trip from London is Paris, just a three-hour journey by Eurostar train. Paris offers sweeping boulevards, sleepy parks, world-class art galleries, chatty crêpe stands, sleek shopping malls, the Eiffel Tower, and people-watching from outdoor cafés. Climb Notre-Dame and the Eiffel Tower, master the Louvre, and cruise the grand Champs-Elysées. Many fall in love with Paris, one of the world's most romantic cities. (This chapter is excerpted from *Rick Steves' France 2003*, by Rick Steves and Steve Smith.)

Getting to Paris

You can order tickets for the Eurostar train from London to Paris by phone or online with a credit card through a U.S. company (U.S. tel. 800/EUROSTAR, www.raileurope.com; add charge for FedEx mailing) or a British company (tel. 08705-186-186, www.eurostar.co.uk; pick up tickets at London's Waterloo station an hour before the Eurostar departure). In Europe, you can buy Eurostar tickets at any major train station. Note that Britain's time zone is one hour earlier than the Continent's; the departure and arrival times listed on Eurostar tickets are local times. For more information, see the Transportation Connections chapter.

Planning Your Time

Ideally, spend the night in Paris, but if all you have is a day, here's the plan: about 7:10–Depart London; about 11:20–Arrive in Paris, take a taxi or the Métro to Notre-Dame; 12:00–Explore Notre-Dame and Sainte-Chapelle; 14:00–Taxi or Métro to the Arc de Triomphe; 14:30–Walk down the Champs-Elysées and through the Tuileries Gardens; 16:00–Tour the Louvre (open until 18:00, until 21:45 Wed, closed Tue, only Denon wing open until 21:45 Mon,

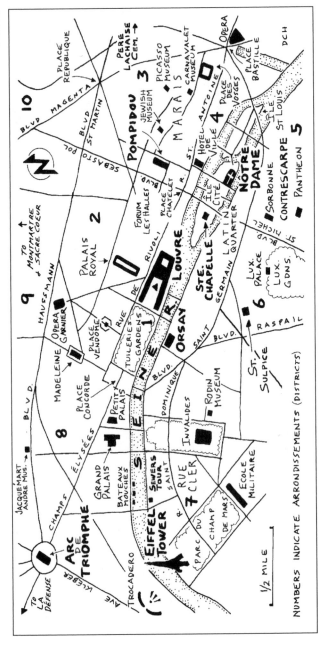

Paris

after 15:00 it's cheaper and not crowded); 18:00–Taxi or Métro to Trocadero, walk to Eiffel Tower (if you ascend, allow plenty of time for delays); take a taxi or the Métro back to Paris' Gare du Nord train station one hour before departure; catch late train back to London (usually 20:07 or 21:13); arrive in London (usually 22:13 or 23:16). Confirm train times when you purchase ticket.

Note: For a trip of more than one day, it's worth getting *Rick Steves' Paris 2003*, which includes extensive museum tours and interesting walks, along with great places to eat and sleep.

Arrival in Paris
(€1 = about $1)

Paris has six major train stations, each serving a different region. The Eurostar train from London zips you to Paris' Gare du Nord train station. You'll find handy train information booths near tracks 8 and 18. Change offices, the Métro, and taxis are easy to find. You'll need currency in euros to function in Paris.

Passengers departing for London on the Eurostar must check in on the second level, opposite track 6. A peaceful waiting area overlooks the tracks.

Orientation

Paris is split in half by the Seine River. You'll find Paris easier to navigate if you know which side of the river you're on, and which subway stop (abbreviated "Mo") you're closest to. If you're north of the river (above on any city map), you're on the Right Bank *(rive droite)*. If you're south of it, you're on the Left Bank *(rive gauche)*.

Tourist Information

Avoid the Paris TIs—long lines, short information, and a charge for maps. This chapter and a map (cheap at newsstands or free from any hotel) are all you need for a short visit. If you're staying longer than a day, pick up a copy of *Pariscope* (or one of its clones, €0.50 at any newsstand, in French), which lists museum hours, concerts, plays, movies, nightclubs, and art exhibits.

If you really need a TI, try the main office at 127 avenue des Champs-Elysées (daily 9:00–20:00, tel. 08 36 92 31 12, www.paris-touristoffice.com) or the small office at the Louvre (Wed–Mon 10:00–19:00, closed Tue).

Getting around Paris

By Taxi: Two people with only one day should taxi everywhere. You'll save lots of time and spend only a few bucks per ride (a 10-min ride costs about €8). Parisian cabs are comfortable, have hassle-free meters, and are easy to flag down (or ask for a nearby taxi stand).

By Métro: In Paris, you're never more than a 10-minute walk from a Métro station. One ticket takes you anywhere in the system with unlimited transfers for €1.40. These are your essential Métro words: *direction*, *correspondance* (transfer), *sortie* (exit), *carnet* (cheap set of 10 tickets for €10), and *Donnez-moi mon porte-monnaie!* (Give me back my wallet!). Thieves thrive in the Métro.

Helpful Hints

On Monday, the Orsay Museum, Rodin Museum, and Versailles are closed. The Louvre is more crowded because of this. On Tuesday, when the Louvre is closed, Versailles, the Eiffel Tower, and the Orsay Museum can be jammed.

Paris Museum Pass: Serious sightseers save time (less time in lines) and money by getting this pass. Sold at museums, major Métro stations, and TIs, it pays for itself in two admissions and gets you into nearly all the sights (major exceptions: Eiffel Tower and Disneyland Paris). The pass allows you to skip to the front of lines at many sights, saving hours of waiting in summer—though everyone must pass through the slow-moving metal-detector lines at some sights, and a few places, such as Notre-Dame's tower, can't accommodate a bypass lane (1 day-€15, 3 consecutive days-€30, 5 consecutive days-€45; no youth discounts, and not worth buying for kids, as most museums are free for those under 18, note that kids can skip lines with passholder parents).

Sights—Paris

Start your visit where the city began—on the Ile de la Cité (the island of the city), facing the Notre-Dame.

▲▲**Notre-Dame Cathedral**—This 700-year-old cathedral is packed with history and tourists. Study its sculpture (Notre-Dame's forte) and windows, eavesdrop on guides, and walk all around the outside of the church dedicated to Our Lady (Notre-Dame). The facade is worth a close look. Mary, cradling Jesus and surrounded by the halo of the rose window, is center stage. Adam is on the left, and Eve is on the right. Below Mary and above the arches is a row of 28 statues known as the Kings of Judah. During the French Revolution, these Biblical kings were mistaken for the hated French kings. The citizens stormed the church, crying, "Off with their heads." All were decapitated but have since been recapitated (cathedral free, daily 8:00–18:45; treasury-€2.50, not covered by museum pass; daily 9:30–17:30; free English tours usually offered Wed and Thu at 12:00 and Sat at 14:30, Mo: Cité). Climb to the top for a great gargoyle's-eye view of the city; you get 400 steps for only €5.50 (covered by museum pass, entrance on outside, north tower open daily April–Sept

Heart of Paris

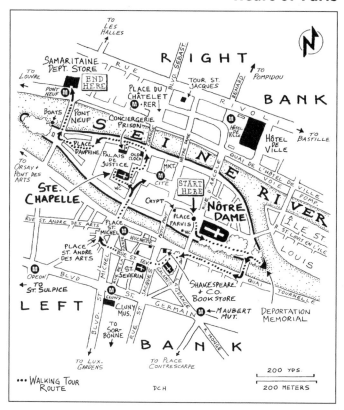

9:30–19:30, Oct–March 10:00–17:30). Clean €0.50 toilets are
in front of the church near Charlemagne's statue.

Two blocks west of Notre-Dame is the . . .

▲▲▲**Sainte-Chapelle**—The triumph of Gothic church architecture is a cathedral of glass like no other. It was speedily built from
1242 to 1248 for St. Louis IX (the only French king who is now a
saint) to house the supposed Crown of Thorns. Its architectural
harmony is due to the fact that it was completed under the direction of one architect in only six years—unheard of in Gothic times.
(Notre-Dame took more than 200 years to build.) Climb the spiral
staircase to the *Chapelle Haute* and "let there be light." There are
15 huge stained-glass windows (two-thirds of them 13th-century
originals) with more than 1,100 different scenes, mostly from
the Bible (€5.50, covered by museum pass, daily April–Sept

9:30–18:30, Oct–March 10:00–17:00, concerts nearly nightly year-round, Mo: Cité, tel. 01 48 01 91 35 for concert information).

▲▲▲**Arc de Triomphe**—Napoleon had the magnificent Arc de Triomphe commissioned to commemorate his victory at the battle of Austerlitz. There's no triumphal arch bigger (164 feet high, 130 feet wide). And, with 12 converging boulevards, there's no traffic circle more thrilling to experience—either behind the wheel or on foot (take the underpass). An elevator or a spiral staircase leads to a cute museum about the arch, and a grand view from the top, even after dark (€7, covered by museum pass, April–Sept daily 9:30–23:00, Oct–March daily 9:30–22:00, Mo: Etoile, tel. 01 55 37 73 77).

▲▲**Champs-Elysées and Place de la Concorde**—This famous boulevard, which carries the city's greatest concentration of traffic, came about because Catherine de Medici wanted a place to drive her carriage. She had the swamp that would become this boulevard drained. Napoleon put on the final touches, and it's been the place to be seen ever since. The Tour de France bicycle race ends here, as do all parades (French or foe) of any significance. While the boulevard has become a bit hamburgerized, a walk here is a must. Take a taxi or the Métro to the Arc de Triomphe (Mo: Etoile) and saunter down the Champs-Elysées (Métro stops are located every few blocks along the boulevard: Etoile, George V, FDR). The Champs-Elysées leads to the city's largest square, Place de la Concorde. Here the guillotine took the lives of thousands—including King Louis XVI and Marie-Antoinette. Back then it was called Place de la Révolution. Continuing past this square and through the Tuileries Garden brings you to the . . .

▲▲▲**Louvre**—This is Europe's oldest, biggest, greatest, and possibly most crowded museum. It's packed with ancient Greek and Roman masterpieces, medieval jewels, Michelangelo statues, and paintings by the greatest artists from the Renaissance to the Romantic movement of the mid-1800s. A security check with metal detectors creates a line in front of the pyramid; although there is no grander entry than through the pyramid, there are quicker ways to get in (see "Getting to the Louvre," below).

Pick up the free English-language *Louvre Handbook* at the information desk under the pyramid as you enter. Don't try to cover the museum thoroughly. The 90-minute English-language tours (for €3 plus your entry ticket), which leave three times daily except Sunday (normally at 11:00, 14:00, and 15:45), boil this overwhelming museum down to size (tour tel. 01 40 20 52 63, www.louvre.fr). Clever €5 digital audioguides (after ticket booths, at top of stairs) give you a receiver and a directory of about 130 masterpieces, allowing you to dial a rather dull commentary on included works as you stumble upon them. The books *Rick Steves'* *Mona Winks* and *Rick Steves' Paris* (buy in the United States) include a self-guided tour of the Louvre.

If you're without a guide, start in the Denon wing and visit these highlights, in this order: Ancient Greek and Roman art (Parthenon frieze, Venus de Milo, Pompeii mosaics, Etruscan sarcophagi, Roman portrait busts, Nike of Samothrace); French and Italian paintings in the Grand Gallery (a quarter-mile long and worth the hike); the *Mona Lisa* and her Italian Renaissance room-mates; the neoclassical collection (J. L. David's *Coronation of Napoleon*); the Romantic collection (Delacroix's *Liberty at the Barricades* and Géricault's *Raft of the Medusa*); and Michelangelo's *Slaves*.

Cost: €7.50, €5 after 15:00 and all day Sun, covered by museum pass; free on the first Sun of the month and any time for those under 18.

Hours: Wed–Mon 9:00–18:00, closed Tue; Denon wing open Mon until 21:45, all wings open Wed until 21:45 (tel. 01 40 20 51 51 or 01 40 20 53 17 for recorded information).

Getting to the Louvre: There are several ways you can avoid the line at the pyramid.

1) If using the Métro, get off at the Palais-Royal/Musée du Louvre Métro stop (not the Louvre Rivoli stop, which is farther away). Exiting the Métro, follow Musée du Louvre signs and head for the inverted pyramid, where you'll uncover a handy TI, glitter-ing boutiques, a dizzying assortment of good-value eateries (up the escalator), and the underground entrance to the Louvre.

2) If approaching the Louvre aboveground, museum-pass holders can use the group entrance in the pedestrian passageway between the pyramid and rue de Rivoli (facing the pyramid with your back to the Tuileries Gardens, go to your left, which is north; under the arches you'll find the entrance and escalator down).

3) You can enter the Louvre underground from the Carrousel shopping mall, which connects with the museum; enter the mall at 99 rue de Rivoli (the door with the red awning).

▲▲▲**Eiffel Tower**—It may be crowded and expensive, but it's worth the trouble. The Eiffel Tower is 1,000 feet tall (6 inches taller in hot weather), covers two and one-half acres, and requires 50 tons of paint. Its 7,000 tons of metal are spread out so well at the base that it's no heavier per square inch than a linebacker on tiptoes.

Built a hundred years after the French Revolution (and in the midst of an industrial one), the tower served no function but to impress. To a generation hooked on technology, the tower was the marvel of the age, a symbol of progress and of human ingenuity.

There are three observation platforms, at 200, 400, and 900

feet; the higher you go, the more you pay. Each requires a separate elevator (and a line), so plan on at least 90 minutes if you want to go to the top and back. The view from the 400-foot-high second level is plenty. It costs €4 to go to the first level, €7 to the second, and €10 to go all the way for the 1,000-foot view (not covered by museum pass, March–Sept daily 9:00–24:00, Oct–Feb daily 9:30–23:00, Mo: Trocadero, tel. 01 44 11 23 23). Go early (arrive by 8:45) or late in the day (after 18:00, after 20:00 in summer) to avoid most crowds; weekends are worst. The Pilier Nord (the north pillar) has the biggest elevator and, therefore, the fastest-moving line.

The best place to view the tower is from Trocadero Square to the north (a 10-min walk across the river and a happening scene at night). Arrive at the Trocadero Métro stop for the view, then walk toward the tower. However impressive it may be by day, it's an awesome thing to see at twilight, when the tower becomes engorged with light, and virile Paris lies back and lets night be on top.

More Sights—Paris

▲▲▲Orsay Museum—Paris' 19th-century art museum (actually, art from 1848 to 1914) includes Europe's greatest collection of Impressionist works. The museum is housed in a former train station (Gare d'Orsay) across the river and a 15-minute walk downstream from the Louvre (Métro stop Solferino is 3 blocks south of the Orsay). Until the summer of 2003, the main entrance to the Orsay will be closed for renovation, and visitors must enter through the temporary entrance that faces the river.

Start on the ground floor. The "pretty" conservative-establishment art is on the south side. The north side contains the brutally truthful and, at that time, very shocking art of the realist rebels and Manet. Then ride the escalators at the far end (detouring at the top for a grand museum view) to the series of Impressionist rooms (Monet, Renoir, Dégas, et al.). On the mezzanine level, don't miss the Grand Ballroom (room 52, *Arts et Décors de la IIIème République*) and the elegant restaurant, Le Salon de Thé du Musée (peek in or enjoy the €9 salad bar and a cup of coffee).

Cost: €7; €5 after 16:15, on Sun, and for ages 18–25; covered by museum pass; free on first Sun of month and for under 18. Ask for a free floor plan in English. English-language tours usually run daily except Sun at 11:30, cost €6, take 90 minutes, and are also available on audioguide (€5). Tickets are good all day. Museum-pass holders can enter to the left of the main entrance (during the renovation, they can walk to the front of the line and show their passes, tel. 01 40 49 48 48).

Hours: June 20–Sept 20 Tue–Sun 9:00–18:00, Sept 21–June 19 Tue–Sat 10:00–18:00, Sun 9:00–18:00, Thu until 21:45 all year, always closed Mon. Last entrance 45 min before closing. Galleries start closing 30 min early.

▲▲**Napoleon's Tomb and Les Invalides Army Museum**— The emperor lies majestically dead inside several coffins under a grand dome—a goose-bumping pilgrimage for historians. Napoleon is surrounded by the tombs of other French war heroes and Europe's greatest military museum in the Hôtel des Invalides. Follow signs to the crypt, where you'll find Roman Empire–style reliefs listing the accomplishments of Napoleon's administration. The restored dome glitters with 26 pounds of gold (€6, students-€5, under 18 free, covered by museum pass, daily April–Sept 10:00–18:00, Oct–March 10:00–17:00, open 30 min longer Sun, Napoleon's Tomb open June 15–Sept 15 until 18:45, Mo: La Tour Maubourg, Varennes, or Invalides, tel. 01 44 42 37 72, www.invalides.org).

▲▲**Rodin Museum**—This user-friendly museum is filled with works by the greatest sculptor since Michelangelo. See *The Kiss, The Thinker, The Gates of Hell,* and many more. Don't miss the room full of work by Rodin's student and mistress, Camille Claudel (€5, €3 on Sun and for students, free first Sun of month and for those under 18, covered by museum pass; €1 for gardens only—perhaps Paris' best deal, as many works are well displayed in the beautiful gardens, April–Sept Tue–Sun 9:30–17:45, closed Mon, gardens close 18:45, Oct–March Tue–Sun 9:30–17:00, closed Mon, gardens close 16:45, near Napoleon's Tomb, 77 rue de Varennes, Mo: Varennes, tel. 01 44 18 61 10, www.musee-rodin.fr). A good cafeteria and idyllic picnic spots are in the family-friendly back garden.

▲**Latin Quarter**—The Left Bank neighborhood just opposite Notre-Dame is the Latin Quarter. This was a center of Roman Paris, but its touristic fame relates to the Latin Quarter's intriguing artsy, bohemian character. This was Europe's leading university district in the Middle Ages—home, since the 13th century, to the prestigious Sorbonne College. Back then, Latin was the language of higher education. And since students here came from all over Europe, Latin served as their linguistic common denominator. Locals referred to the quarter by its language: Latin. In more recent times, this was the center of Paris' café culture. The neighborhood's main boulevards (St. Michel and St. Germain) are lined with cafés—once the haunts of great poets and philosophers, but now just places where tired tourists can hang out. While still youthful and artsy, the area has become a tourist ghetto filled with cheap North African eateries.

▲▲**Sacré-Coeur and Montmartre**—This Byzantine-looking church, while only 130 years old, is impressive. It was built as a "praise the Lord anyway" gesture after the French were humiliated by the Germans in a brief war in 1871. The church is open daily until 23:00. One block from the church, the square called the Place du Tertre was the haunt of Toulouse-Lautrec and the original bohemians. Today, it's mobbed by tourists and unoriginal bohemians, but it's still fun. Either use the Anvers Métro stop (plus 1 Métro ticket for the funicular to avoid stairs) or the closer but less scenic Abbesses stop. A taxi to the top of the hill saves time and avoids sweat.

Sights—Near Paris

▲▲▲**Palace of Versailles**—Every king's dream, Versailles was the residence of the French king, and the cultural heartbeat of Europe, for about 100 years—until the Revolution of 1789 ended the notion that God deputized some people to rule for Him on earth. Louis XIV spent half a year's income of Europe's richest country turning his dad's hunting lodge into a palace fit for a divine monarch. Louis XV and Louis XVI spent much of the 18th century gilding Louis XIV's lily. In 1837, about 50 years after the royal family was evicted, King Louis Philippe opened the palace as a museum. Europe's next-best palaces are Versailles wannabes.

Ticket Options: The self-guided one-way romp through the State Apartments, including the Hall of Mirrors, costs €7.50 (covered by museum pass; €5.50 after 15:30; under 18 free). Admission is payable at entrances A, C, and D. If you want a guided tour through the other sections, you need to pay the €7.50 base price, then pay extra for the tour.

Hours: April–Oct Tue–Sun 9:00–18:30, Nov–March Tue–Sun 9:00–17:30, closed Mon (last entry 30 min before closing). In summer, Versailles is especially crowded around 10:00 and 13:00, and all day Tue and Sun. To minimize crowds, either arrive by 9:00 or after 15:30 (admission is cheaper after 15:30, but you'll miss the last guided tours of the day, which generally depart around 15:00); tour the gardens after the palace closes. The palace is great late. On my last visit, at 18:00, I was the only tourist in the Hall of Mirrors...even on a Tuesday.

Getting There: Take the **RER-C train** (€5 round-trip, 30 min one-way) from these RER stops: Gare d'Austerlitz, St. Michel, Musée d'Orsay, Invalides, Pont de l'Alma, and Champ de Mars. Trains named "Vick" leave about five times an hour for the palace. Any train named Vick goes to Versailles; don't board other trains. Get off at the last stop (Versailles R.G. or "Rive Gauche"—not Versailles C.H., which is farther from the palace),

Versailles

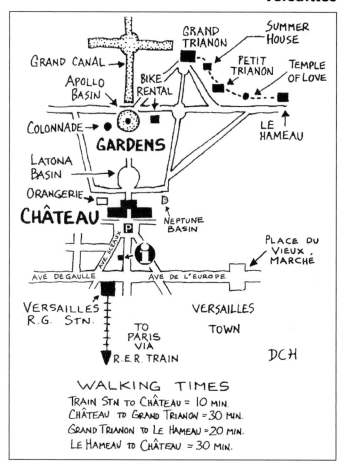

GRAND TRIANON

SUMMER HOUSE

GRAND CANAL →

PETIT TRIANON

TEMPLE OF LOVE

APOLLO BASIN

BIKE RENTAL

COLONNADE →

LE HAMEAU

GARDENS

LATONA BASIN

ORANGERIE →

CHÂTEAU

NEPTUNE BASIN

PLACE DU VIEUX MARCHÉ

AVE DE GAULLE

AVE DE L'EUROPE

VERSAILLES R.G. STN.

VERSAILLES TOWN

TO PARIS VIA R.E.R. TRAIN

DCH

WALKING TIMES
TRAIN STN TO CHÂTEAU = 10 MIN.
CHÂTEAU TO GRAND TRIANON = 30 MIN.
GRAND TRIANON TO LE HAMEAU = 20 MIN.
LE HAMEAU TO CHÂTEAU = 30 MIN.

turn right out of the station, and turn left at the first boulevard. It's a 10-minute walk to the palace.

When returning from Versailles, look through the windows past the turnstiles for the departure board. Any train leaving Versailles serves all downtown Paris RER line C stops (they're marked *toutes les gares jusqu'à Austerlitz*, meaning "all stations until d'Austerlitz").

Taxis for the 30-minute ride between Versailles and Paris cost about €25. To cut your park walking by 50 percent, consider having the taxi drop you at the Hamlet *(Hameau)*.

Versailles' Entrances

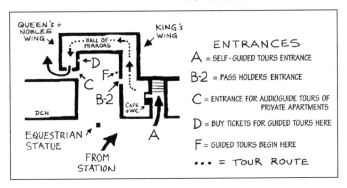

ENTRANCES

A = SELF-GUIDED TOURS ENTRANCE

B-2 = PASS HOLDERS ENTRANCE

C = ENTRANCE FOR AUDIOGUIDE TOURS OF PRIVATE APARTMENTS

D = BUY TICKETS FOR GUIDED TOURS HERE

F = GUIDED TOURS BEGIN HERE

••• = TOUR ROUTE

Information: A helpful TI is just past the Hôtel Sofitel on your way from the station to the palace (May–Sept daily 9:00–19:00, Oct–April daily 9:00–18:00, tel. 01 39 24 88 88, www.chateauversailles.fr). You'll also find information booths inside the château (at doors A, B-2, and C). The useful brochure *Versailles Orientation Guide* explains your sightseeing options.

Tours: You may select a one-hour guided tour from a variety of themes, such as the daily life of a king or the lives of such lesser-known nobles as the well-coifed Madame de Pompadour (€4, join first English tour available). Or consider the 90-minute tour (€6) of the King's Private Apartments (Louis XV, Louis XVI, and Marie-Antoinette), the Chapel, and the Opera House. For a live tour, make reservations immediately upon arrival, at entrance D, as tours can sell out by 13:00 (first tours generally begin at 10:00, last tours depart at 15:00 or 16:00). Guided tours begin at entrance F. Two informative but dry audioguide tours are available. One covers the State Apartments (€4, includes Hall of Mirrors and Queen's Bedchamber; start at entrance A or, if you have a museum pass, at entrance B-2). The other includes more of the King's Private Apartments (Louis XIV) and a sampling of nobles' chambers (€4, entrance C). Both audioguide tours are sold until one hour before closing. If you have extra time before your tour, wander through the State Apartments or gardens.

Self-Guided Tour: For the basic self-guided tour, join the line at entrance A if you need to pay admission. Those with a museum pass are allowed in through entrance B-2 without a wait. Enter the palace and take a one-way walk through the State Apartments from the King's Wing, through the magnificent Hall of Mirrors, and out via the Queen's and Nobles' Wing.

The Hall of Mirrors was the ultimate hall of the day—

250 feet long, with 17 arched mirrors matching 17 windows with royal-garden views, 24 gilded candelabra, eight busts of Roman emperors, and eight classical-style statues (7 are ancient originals). The ceiling is decorated with stories of Louis XIV's triumphs. Imagine this place filled with silk gowns and powdered wigs, lit by thousands of candles. The mirrors—a luxurious rarity at the time—were a reflection of a time when aristocrats felt good about their looks and their fortunes. In another age altogether, this was the room in which the Treaty of Versailles was signed, ending World War I.

Before going downstairs at the end, take a stroll clockwise around the long room filled with the great battles of France murals. In addition to *Rick Steves' Paris* and *Rick Steves' Mona Winks*, the guidebook called *The Châteaux, the Gardens, and Trianon* gives a room-by-room rundown.

Time to Allow: Six hours round-trip from Paris (1 hour each way in transit, 2 hours for palace, 2 for gardens).

Getting around the Gardens: It's a 30-min hike from the palace, down the canal, past the two minipalaces to the Hamlet. You can rent bikes (€6/hr). The pokey tourist train runs between the canal and château (€5, 4/hr, 4 stops, you can hop on and off as you like; nearly worthless commentary).

Garden Hours: Daily from 7:00 to sunset (as late as 21:30). There's a sandwich kiosk and a decent restaurant at the canal. The gardens cost €3, more on splashy summer weekends (see below).

Fountain Spectacles: Classical music fills the king's backyard, and the garden's fountains are in full squirt, on Sat July–Sept and on Sun early April–early Oct (schedule for both days: 11:00–12:00 & 15:30–17:00 & 17:20–17:30). On these "spray days," the gardens cost €5.50 (not covered by museum pass, ask for a map of fountains). Louis had his engineers literally reroute a river to fuel these fountains. Even by today's standards, they are impressive. Pick up the helpful brochure of the fountain show ("Les Grandes Eaux Musicales") at any information booth for a guide to the fountains. Also ask about the impressive *Les Fêtes de Nuit* nighttime spectacle (some Sat, July–mid-Sept).

Palace Gardens: The gardens offer a world of royal amusements. Outside the palace is L'Orangerie. Louis XIV, the only one who could grow oranges in Paris, had an orange grove on wheels that could be wheeled in and out of his greenhouses according to the weather. A promenade leads from the palace to the Grand Canal, an artificial lake that, in Louis' day, was a miniature sea with nine ships, including a 32-cannon warship. France's royalty used to float up and down the canal in Venetian gondolas.

While Louis XIV cleverly used palace life at Versailles to "domesticate" his nobility, turning otherwise meddlesome nobles into groveling socialites, all this pomp and ceremony hampered the royal family as well. For an escape from the public life at Versailles, the king and his successors built more intimate palaces as retreats in the garden. Before the Revolution there was plenty of space to retreat—the grounds were enclosed by a 25-mile-long fence.

The beautifully restored **Grand Trianon Palace** is as sumptuous as the main palace, but much smaller. With its pastel-pink colonnade and more human scale, this is a place you'd like to call home. The nearby **Petit Trianon,** which has a fine neoclassical exterior and a skippable interior, was Marie-Antoinette's favorite residence (€5 for both, €3 after 15:30, covered by museum pass, April–Oct Tue–Sun 12:00–18:00, Nov–March Tue–Sun 12:00–17:00, closed Mon).

You can almost see princesses bobbing gaily in the branches as you walk through the enchanting forest, past the white marble temple of love (1778), to the queen's fake peasant **Hamlet** (*Hameau*; interior not tourable). Palace life really got to Marie-Antoinette. Sort of a back-to-basics queen, she retreated further and further from her blue-blooded reality. Her happiest days were at the Hamlet, under a bonnet, tending her perfumed sheep and her manicured gardens in a thatch-happy wonderland.

▲▲**Disneyland Paris**—Europe's Disneyland is a remake of California's, with most of the same rides and smiles. The main difference is that Mickey Mouse speaks French (and you can buy wine with your lunch). My kids went ducky. It's easy to get to and worth a day if Paris is handier than Florida or California. Saturday, Sunday, Wednesday, public holidays, and July and August are most crowded. After dinner, crowds are gone. Food is fun and not outrageously priced. (Still, many smuggle in a picnic.) The free FASTPASS system is a worthwhile timesaver (get FASTPASS card at entry, good for 5 most popular rides, at ride insert card in machine to get a window of time to enter—often within about 45 min). You'll also save time by buying your tickets ahead (at airport TIs, more than 100 Métro stations, or along the Champs-Elysées at the TI, Disney Store, or Virgin Megastore). Disney brochures are in every Paris hotel (Disneyland Paris tel. 01 60 30 60 30, www.disneylandparis.com). See prices under Walt Disney Studios below.

Walt Disney Studios—The new zone, opened in 2002 next to the original 10-year-old amusement park, has the same hours, contact information, and admission prices (but you must pay separately to enjoy both parks; see below). Aimed at an older crowd, its Hollywood focus is on animation, special effects, and movie magic "rides." The Aerosmith Rock 'n' Roller Coaster is nothing special. The highlight is the Stunt Show Spectacular, filling a huge back-lot stadium five times a day for 45 minutes of car chases and thriller filming tips. An actual movie sequence is filmed with stunt drivers, audience bit players, and brash MTV-style hosts.

Cost: Each park charges the same and you pay separately. Only the three-day passes (called "Hopper" tickets) include entry to both parks. From March 31 through November 5, adults pay €38 for one day (€72 for 2 days, €99 for 3-day Hopper ticket) and kids ages 3–11 pay €29 for one day (€56 for 2 days, €80 for 3-day Hopper ticket). Regular prices are about 25 percent less off-season. Kids under 3 are always free. On summer evenings (17:00–23:00) at the Disneyland Park only, everyone pays €19. The only budget deal (and, I think, the only way the Walt Disney Studios are worth visiting) is to pay for a full-price Walt Disney Studios ticket, which gets you into the Disneyland Park for free during the last three hours of that day.

Hours: Both parks are open April–June daily 9:00–20:00, July–Aug daily 9:00–23:00, Sept–March Mon–Fri 10:00–20:00, Sat–Sun 9:00–20:00.

Getting to Disneyland Paris/Walt Disney Studios: The slick one-hour RER trip is the best way to Disneyland from downtown Paris. Take RER line A-4 to Marne-la-Vallée-Chessy (from Etoile, Auber/Opéra, Chatelet, and Gare de Lyon stations, about €7.50 each way, hrly, drops you 1 hour later right in the park). The last train back to Paris leaves shortly after midnight. Be sure to get a ticket that is good on both RER and Métro; returning, remember to use your RER ticket for your Métro connection in Paris.

Sleeping in Paris
(€1 = about $1)

Sleep Code: S = Single, **D** = Double/Twin, **T** = Triple, **Q** = Quad, **b** = bathroom, **s** = shower only, **CC** = Credit Cards accepted, **no CC** = Credit Cards not accepted, * = French hotel rating system (0–4 stars).

To help you easily sort through these listings, I've divided the rooms into three categories, based on the price for a standard double room with bath:

Higher Priced—Most rooms more than €140.
Moderately Priced—Most rooms €140 or less.
Lower Priced—Most rooms €100 or less.

If you're calling Paris from the United States, dial 011-33 (from Britain dial 00-33) and then dial the local number without the initial zero.

Sleeping in the Rue Cler Neighborhood
(7th district, Mo: Ecole Militaire, zip code: 75007)

Rue Cler, a village-like pedestrian street, is safe, tidy, and makes me feel like I must have been a poodle in a previous life. How such coziness lodged itself between the high-powered government/business district and the expensive Eiffel Tower area, I'll never know. Living here ranks with the top museums as one of the city's great experiences.

The street called rue Cler is the glue that holds this pleasant neighborhood together. On rue Cler, you can eat and browse your way through a street full of tart shops, cheeseries, and colorful outdoor produce stalls.

HIGHER PRICED

Hôtel Relais Bosquet*** is modern, spacious, and a bit upscale, with snazzy, air-conditioned rooms, electric darkness blinds, and big beds. Gerard and his staff are politely formal and friendly (Sb-€125–146, standard Db-€140, spacious Db-€160, extra bed-€30, CC, parking-€14, 19 rue de Champ de Mars, tel. 01 47 05 25 45, fax 01 45 55 08 24, www.relaisbosquet.com).

MODERATELY PRICED

Hôtel Beaugency***, on a quieter street a short block off rue Cler, has 30 small but comfortable air-conditioned rooms, a lobby you can stretch out in, and friendly Chantal in charge. When I have tour groups in Paris, this is my first choice for their home base (Sb-€104, Db-€111, Tb-€127, CC, buffet breakfast, 21 rue Duvivier, tel. 01 47 05 01 63, fax 01 45 51 04 96, www.hotel-beaugency.com).

LOWER PRICED

Warning: The first two hotels listed here—while the best value—are overrun with my readers (reserve long in advance . . . or avoid).

Hôtel Leveque** is ideally located, with a helpful staff (Pascale and Christophe SE), a singing maid, and a Starship Enterprise elevator. It's a classic old hotel with well-designed rooms that have all the amenities (S-€53, Db-€84–91, Tb-€114, breakfast-€7, first breakfast free for readers of this book, CC, air-con, 29 rue Cler, tel. 01 47 05 49 15, fax 01 45 50 49 36, www.hotel-leveque.com, e-mail: info@hotelleveque.com).

Hôtel du Champ de Mars**, with charming pastel rooms and helpful English-speaking owners Françoise and Stephane and right-hand man Slim, is a cozier rue Cler option. This plush little hotel has a Provence-style, small-town feel from top to bottom. Rooms are small, but comfortable and a good value. Single rooms can work as tiny doubles (Sb-€66, Db-€72–76, Tb-€92, CC, 30 meters off rue Cler at 7 rue de Champ de Mars, tel. 01 45 51 52 30, fax 01 45 51 64 36, www.hotel-du-champ-de-mars.com, e-mail: stg@club-internet.fr).

Hôtel la Motte Piquet**, at the end of rue Cler, is reasonable and spotless, and comes with a cheery welcome from Daniele. Most of its 18 homey rooms face a busy street, but the twins are on the quieter rue Cler (Ss-€57, Sb-€60–64, Db-€73–81, CC, 30 avenue de la Motte Piquet, tel. 01 47 05 09 57, fax 01 47 05 74 36).

Transportation Connections—Paris

To London: The sleek Eurostar train makes the trip in just three hours, with 15 departures daily in each direction. For details and prices, see the end of the Transportation Connections chapter.

To Other Destinations: Paris is Europe's transportation hub. The city has six central rail stations, each serving a different region. You'll find trains (day and night) to almost any French or European destination. For schedule information, call 08 36 35 35 35 (€0.50/min, English sometimes spoken).

SLEEPING

I favor accommodations (and restaurants) handy to your sight-seeing activities. Rather than list hotels scattered throughout London, I've chosen several favorite neighborhoods and recommend the best accommodations values for each.

I look for places that are friendly (enjoy Americans); clean, with firm beds; a good value; located in a central, safe, quiet neighborhood; and not mentioned in other guidebooks (therefore, filled mostly with English travelers). I'm more impressed by a handy location and a fun-loving philosophy than hair dryers and shoe-shine machines.

London is expensive. For £50 ($75), you'll get a double with breakfast in a safe, cramped, and dreary place with minimal service. For £75 ($115), you'll get a basic, clean, reasonably cheery double in a usually cramped, cracked-plaster building, or a soulless but comfortable room without breakfast in a huge Motel 6–type place. My London splurges, at £100–150 ($150–230), are spacious, thoughtfully appointed places you'd be happy to entertain or make love in. Hearty English or generous buffet breakfasts are included unless otherwise noted, and TVs are standard in rooms.

Hotels and B&Bs

I've described my recommended hotels and B&Bs with a standard code (see below). Prices listed are for one-night stays in peak season and assume you're booking directly and not through a TI. Prices may be soft for off-season and longer stays. Some fancy £120 rooms rent for a third off if you arrive late on a slow day and ask for a deal. "Twin" means two single beds, and "double" means one double bed. If you'll take either one, let them know, or you might be needlessly turned away. Most hotels offer family deals, which means that parents with young children can easily get a

Sleep Code

To help you easily sort through these listings, I've divided the rooms into three categories, based on the price for a double room with bath:

Higher Priced—Most rooms more than £100.
Moderately Priced—Most rooms £100 or less.
Lower Priced—Most rooms £70 or less.

To give maximum information with a minimum of space, I use this code to describe accommodations listed in this book. Prices in this book are listed per room, not per person. Breakfast is included.

S = Single room, or price for one person in a double.
D = Double or twin room. (I specify double- and twin-bed rooms only if they are priced differently, or if a place has only one or the other. When reserving, you should specify.)
T = Three-person room (often a double bed with a single).
Q = Four-person room (adding an extra child's bed to a T is usually cheaper).
b = Private bathroom with toilet and shower or tub.
s = Private shower or tub only. (The toilet is down the hall.)
CC = Accepts credit cards (Visa and MasterCard, rarely American Express).
no CC = Does not accept credit cards; pay in local cash.

According to this code, a couple staying at a "Db-£60, CC" hotel would pay a total of £60 (about $90) per night for a room with a private toilet and shower (or tub). The hotel accepts credit cards or cash.

room with an extra child's bed or a discount for larger rooms. Call to negotiate the price. Teenage kids are generally charged as adults. Kids under five sleep almost free.

Most places listed have three floors of rooms and steep stairs. Elevators are rare except in the larger hotels. If you're concerned about stairs, call and ask about ground-floor rooms or pay for a hotel with a lift (elevator).

Many places now offer non-smoking rooms (listed in descriptions). Breakfast rooms are nearly always smoke-free.

Most rooms have sinks. Any room without a bathroom has access to a free bath or shower on the corridor. Rooms with private plumbing are called "en suite"; rooms that lack private plumbing are "standard." As more rooms go en suite, the hallway bathroom is shared with fewer standard rooms. If money's tight, request standard rooms.

Phone Codes and Exchange Rate

To phone London, you'll need to know Britain's country code: 44. To call from the United States or Canada, dial 011-44-20 (area code without its intial zero)-local number. If calling from another European country, dial 00-44-20-local number. If calling from within Britain but outside London, dial 020-local number.

The exchange rate: 1 British pound (£1) = about $1.50.

Making Reservations

Reserve your London room by phone or e-mail as soon as you can commit to a date. It's possible to visit London any time of year without reservations, but given the high stakes, erratic accommodations values, and the quality of the gems we've listed, I recommend calling ahead.

A few national holidays jam things up (especially "bank holiday" Mondays) and merit reservations long in advance. Mark these dates in red on your travel calendar: New Year's Day, Good Friday, Easter Monday, the first and last Monday in May, the last Monday in August, Christmas, and December 26 (Boxing Day). Just like at home, Monday holidays are preceded by busy weekends, so book the entire weekend in advance.

It's easy to reserve by phone. I've taken great pains to list telephone numbers with long-distance instructions (see "Telephones" in the introduction). You can also reserve by e-mail, fax, or letter. E-mail is preferred when possible. To fax, use the fax form in the appendix (online at www.ricksteves.com/reservation). If you're writing, add the zip code and confirm the need and method for a deposit. A two-night stay in August would be "two nights, 16/8/03 to 18/8/03" (Europeans write the date day/month/year, and hotel jargon uses your day of departure).

Some places will trust you and hold a room until 16:00 without a deposit, although most places will ask you for a credit-card number. Many inexpensive places don't take credit cards and require a cash deposit (generally a personal check if 6 weeks in advance, otherwise a bank draft in pounds). The pricier ones sometimes have expensive cancellation policies (you might lose, say, a deposit if you cancel within two weeks of your reserved stay, or you might be billed for the entire visit if you leave early); ask about their policies before you book. If your credit card is the deposit, you can pay with your card or cash when you arrive.

Honor (or cancel by phone) your reservations. If you don't show up, you'll be billed for one night. Reconfirm your reservations a day in advance for safety. Also, don't just assume you can extend. Consider carefully—and well in advance—how long you'll stay.

Sleeping in Victoria Station Neighborhood, Belgravia

The streets behind Victoria Station teem with budget B&Bs. It's a safe, surprisingly tidy, and decent area without a hint of the trashy, touristy glitz of the streets in front of the station. Here in Belgravia, your neighbors include Andrew Lloyd Webber and Margaret Thatcher (her policeman stands outside 73 Chester Square). Decent eateries abound (see the Eating chapter). Cheaper rooms are relatively dumpy. Don't expect £90 cheeriness in a £50 room. Off-season, it's possible to save money by arriving late without a reservation and looking around. Competition softens prices, especially for multinight stays. On hot summer nights, request a quiet back room. All are within a five-minute walk of the Victoria Tube, bus, and train stations. There's a £15-per-day (with a hotel voucher) garage, a nearby **launderette** (daily 8:00–20:30, do self-service and avoid unpredictable full service, past Warwick Square at 3 Westmoreland Terrace, tel. 020/7821-8692), and a little dance club (Club D'Jan, £5 includes drink, Wed–Sat, 63 Wilton Road).

HIGHER PRICED

Lime Tree Hotel, enthusiastically run by David and Marilyn Davies, comes with spacious and thoughtfully decorated rooms and a fun-loving breakfast room. While priced a bit steep, the place has character, and there are plans in the works for more improvements (Sb-£80, Db-£110–120, Tb-£150, family room-£160, CC, possible discount with cash, all rooms non-smoking, David deals in slow times and is creative at helping travelers in a bind, 135 Ebury Street, London SW1W 9RA, tel. 020/7730-8191, fax 020/7730-7865, www.limetreehotel.co.uk).

Quality Hotel Eccleston is big, modern (but with tired carpets), well-located, and a fine value for no-nonsense comfort (Db-£125, on slow days drop-ins can ask for "saver prices"—33 percent off on first night, breakfast extra, CC, non-smoking floor, elevator, 82 Eccleston Square, London SW1V 1PS, tel. 020/7834-8042, fax 020/7630-8942, www.qualityinn.com/hotel/gb614, e-mail: admin@gb614.u-net.com).

MODERATELY PRICED

Winchester Hotel is family-run and perhaps the best value, with 18 fine rooms, no claustrophobia, and a wise and caring

Victoria Station Neighborhood

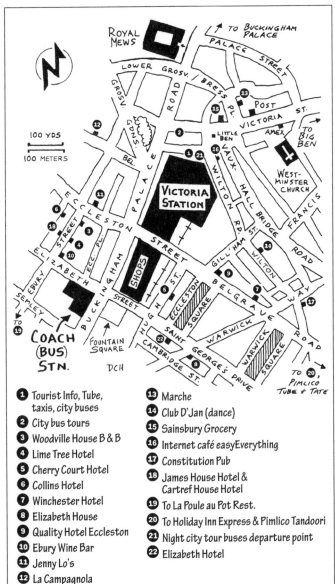

① Tourist Info, Tube, taxis, city buses
② City bus tours
③ Woodville House B & B
④ Lime Tree Hotel
⑤ Cherry Court Hotel
⑥ Collins Hotel
⑦ Winchester Hotel
⑧ Elizabeth House
⑨ Quality Hotel Eccleston
⑩ Ebury Wine Bar
⑪ Jenny Lo's
⑫ La Campagnola
⑬ Marche
⑭ Club D'Jan (dance)
⑮ Sainsbury Grocery
⑯ Internet café easyEverything
⑰ Constitution Pub
⑱ James House Hotel & Cartref House Hotel
⑲ To La Poule au Pot Rest.
⑳ To Holiday Inn Express & Pimlico Tandoori
㉑ Night city tour buses departure point
㉒ Elizabeth Hotel

management (Db-£85, Tb-£110, Qb-£140, no CC, no groups, no infants, 17 Belgrave Road, London SW1V 1RB, tel. 020/7828-2972, fax 020/7828-5191, www.winchester-hotel.net, e-mail: winchesterhotel17@hotmail.com, run by Jimmy). The Winchester also recently began renting well-appointed, spacious apartments—most with kitchens and sitting rooms—around the corner from the hotel on Warwick Way (£125–230).

James House and **Cartref House** are two nearly identical, well-run, smoke-free, 10-room places on either side of Ebury Street (S-£55, Sb-£65, D-£74, Db-£90, T-£100, Tb-£115, family bunkbed quad-£130, CC, 5 percent discount with cash, all rooms with fans, James House at 108 Ebury Street, London SW1W 9QD, tel. 020/7730-2511; Cartref House at 129 Ebury Street, London SW1W 9QU, tel. 020/7730-6176, fax for both: 020/7730-7338, www.jamesandcartref.co.uk, e-mail: jandchouse@aol.com).

Elizabeth Hotel is a stately old place overlooking Eccleston Square, with fine public spaces and 38 spacious and decent rooms that could use a minor facelift (D-£68, small Db-£83, big Db-£95, Tb-£108, Qb-£120, Quint/b-£125, CC, 37 Eccleston Square, London SW1V 1PB, tel. 020/7828-6812, fax 020/ 7828-6814, www.elizabeth-hotel.com, e-mail: info@elizabethhotel.com). Be careful not to confuse this hotel with the nearby Elizabeth House (listed below). This one is big and comfy, the other small and dumpy.

Holiday Inn Express fills an old building with 52 fresh, modern, and efficient rooms (Db-£97, Tb-£107, CC, family rooms-prices vary, up to 2 kids free, some discounts on Web site, non-smoking floor, elevator, Tube: Pimlico, 106 Belgrave Road, London SW1V 2BJ, tel. 020/7630-8888 or 0800/897-121, fax 020/7828-0441, www.hiexpress.com, e-mail: info@hiexpressvictoria.co.uk).

Collins House Hotel, clean, simple and efficiently-run, offers 12 basic rooms in a mid-Victorian style townhouse (Sb-£55, D-£68, Db-£82, T-£95, non-smoking rooms, 104 Ebury St, London SW1W 9QD, tel.& fax 020/7730-8031, www.collinhouse.co.uk)

LOWER PRICED

In **Woodville House,** the quarters are dollhouse tight and showers are down the hall. This well-run, well-worn place is a good value, with lots of travel tips and friendly chat—especially about the local rich and famous—from Rachel Joplin (S-£46, D-£68, bunky family deals-£85-115 for 3–5 people, CC, 107 Ebury Street, London SW1W 9QU, tel. 020/7730-1048, fax 020/7730-2574, www.woodvillehouse.co.uk, e-mail: woodville.house@cwcom.net).

Georgian House Hotel has 50 smallish rooms and a cheaper annex that works well for backpackers (tiny D on fourth floor-£44,

Db-£68, annex Db-£59, Tb-£86, Qb-£94, CC, Internet access, 35 St. George's Drive, London SW1V 4DG, tel. 020/7834-1438, fax 020/7976-6085, www.georgianhousehotel.co.uk, e-mail: reception@georgianhousehotel.co.uk).

Enrico Hotel, with 26 simple rooms, is basic, well worn, and affordable (S-£50, D-£60, Ds-£65, CC, non-smoking, 77 Warwick Way, London SW1V 1QP, tel. 020/7834-9538, fax 020/7233-9995, e-mail: enricohotel@hotmail.com).

Cherry Court Hotel, run by the friendly and industrious Patel family, offers small, basic rooms for good value in a central location (Sb-£42, Db-£48, Tb-£70, Qb-£90, Quint/b-£100, prices promised with this book through 2003, CC for 5 percent extra, fruit-basket breakfast in room, non-smoking, free Internet access, peaceful garden patio, 23 Hugh Street, London SW1V 1QJ, tel. 020/7828-2840, fax 020/7828-0393, www.cherrycourthotel.co.uk, e-mail: info@cherrycourthotel.co.uk).

Elizabeth House is a last resort. It feels institutional and bland—as you might expect from a former YMCA—but it's run-down and none too clean. Only the price is right (S-£30, D-£40, Db-£50, T-£60, Q-£70, plus extra £10/room for D or Db in July–Aug, CC, 118 Warwick Way, London SW1 4JB, tel. 020/7630-0741, fax 020/7630-0740, e-mail: elizabethhouse @ehlondonfsnet.co.uk).

Big, Cheap, Modern Hotels

These places—popular with budget tour groups—are well-run and offer elevators and all the modern comforts in a no-frills, practical package. The doubles for £65–94 are a great value for London. Mid-week prices are generally higher than weekend rates.

MODERATELY PRICED

Jurys Inn rents 200 modern, compact, and comfy rooms near King's Cross station (Db/Tb-£94, 2 adults and 2 kids—under age 12—can share 1 room, breakfast extra, CC, non-smoking floors, 60 Pentonville Road, London N1 9LA, Tube: Angel, tel. 020/7282-5500, fax 020/7282-5511, www.jurysdoyle.com).

London County Hall Travel Inn, literally down the hall from a $400-a-night Marriott Hotel, fills one end of London's massive former County Hall building. This place is wonderfully located near the base of the London Eye Ferris Wheel and across the Thames from Big Ben. Its 300 slick and no-frills rooms come with all the necessary comforts (Db-£77 for 2 adults and up to 2 kids under age 15, couples can request a bigger family room—same price, CC, breakfast extra, book in advance, no-show rooms are released at 16:00, elevator, some smoke-free and easy-access rooms, 500 yards from

Westminster Tube stop and Waterloo Station where the Chunnel train leaves for Paris, Belvedere Road, London SE1 7PB, you can call central reservations at 0870/242-8000 or 0870/238-3300 but you'll be put on hold, you can fax at 020/7902-1619 but you might not get a response, it's easiest to book online at www.travelinn.co.uk).

LOWER PRICED
Other London Travel Inns charging about £70 per room include **London Euston** (a big, blue, Lego-type building on a handy but noisy street packed with Benny Hill families on vacation, 141 Euston Road, London NW1 2AU, Tube: Euston, tel. 0870-238-3301), **Tower Bridge** (Tower Bridge Road, London SE1, Tube: London Bridge, tel. 0870-238-3303), and **London Putney Bridge** (farther out, 3 Putney Bridge Approach, London SW6 3JD, Tube: Putney Bridge, tel. 0870-238-3302). For any of these, call 0870/242-8000, fax 0870/241-9000, or best, book online at www.travelinn.co.uk.

Hotel Ibis London Euston, which feels classier than a Travel Inn, is located on a quiet street a block behind Euston Station (380 rooms, Db-£70, breakfast-£5, CC, no family rooms, breakfast extra, non-smoking floor, 3 Cardington Street, London NW1 2LW, tel. 020/7388-7777, fax 020/7388-0001, e-mail: h0921@accor-hotels.com).

Premier Lodge is near Shakespeare's Globe on the South Bank (55 rooms, Db for up to 2 adults and 2 kids-£70, Bankside, 34 Park Street, London SE1, tel. 0870-700-1456, www.premierlodge.co.uk).

"South Kensington," She Said, Loosening His Cummerbund

To live on a quiet street so classy it doesn't allow hotel signs, surrounded by trendy shops and colorful restaurants, call "South Ken" your London home. Shoppers like being a short walk from Harrods and the designer shops of King's Road and Chelsea. When I splurge, I splurge here. Sumner Place is just off Old Brompton Road, 200 yards from the handy South Kensington Tube station (on Circle Line, 2 stops from Victoria Station, direct Heathrow connection). There's a taxi rank in the median strip at the end of Harrington Road. The handy Wash & Dry **launderette** is on the corner of Queensberry Place and Harrington Road (daily 8:00–21:00, bring 20p and £1 coins).

HIGHER PRICED
Aster House, run by friendly and accommodating Simon and Leona Tan, has a sumptuous lobby, lounge, and breakfast room.

South Kensington Neighborhood

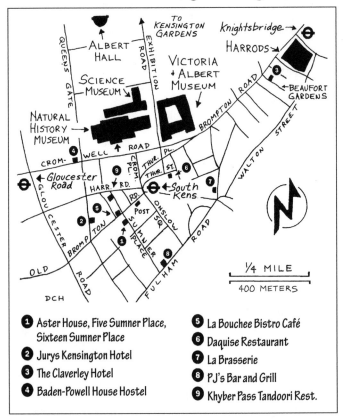

1 Aster House, Five Sumner Place, Sixteen Sumner Place
2 Jurys Kensington Hotel
3 The Claverley Hotel
4 Baden-Powell House Hostel
5 La Bouchee Bistro Café
6 Daquise Restaurant
7 La Brasserie
8 PJ's Bar and Grill
9 Khyber Pass Tandoori Rest.

Its newly renovated rooms are comfy and quiet, with TV, phone, and air-conditioning. Enjoy breakfast or just lounging in the whisper-elegant Orangery, a Victorian greenhouse (Sb-£75–99, Db-£135, bigger Db-£150, deluxe 4-poster Db-£180, CC, entirely non-smoking, 3 Sumner Place, London SW7 3EE, tel. 020/7581-5888, fax 020/7584-4925, www.asterhouse.com, e-mail: asterhouse@btinternet.com).

Five Sumner Place Hotel has received several "best small hotel in London" awards. The rooms in this 150-year-old building are tastefully decorated, and the breakfast room is a Victorian-style conservatory/greenhouse (13 rooms, Sb-£100, Db-£153, third bed-£22, CC, TV, phones, and fridge in rooms by request, non-smoking rooms, elevator, 5 Sumner Place, London SW7 3EE, tel. 020/7584-7586, fax 020/7823-9962, www.sumnerplace.com, e-mail: reservations@sumnerplace.com, run by Tom).

Sixteen Sumner Place, a lesser value for classier travelers, has over-the-top formality and class packed into its 39 unnumbered but pretentiously named rooms, plush lounges, and quiet garden (Db-£170, CC, breakfast in your room, elevator, 16 Sumner Place, London SW7 3EG, tel. 020/7589-5232, fax 020/7584-8615, U.S. tel. 800/533-6674, www.numbersixteenhotel.co.uk, e-mail: reservations@numbersixteenhotel.co.uk).

Jurys Kensington Hotel is big, stately, and impersonal, with a greedy pricing scheme (Sb/Db/Tb-£100–220 depending upon "availability," ask for a deal, breakfast extra, CC, piano lounge, non-smoking floor, elevator, Queen's Gate, London SW7 5LR, tel. 020/7589-6300, fax 020/7581-1492, www.jurysdoyle.com, e-mail: kensington@jurysdoyle.com).

The Claverley, two blocks from Harrods, is on a quiet street similar to Sumner Place. The 30 fancy, dark-wood-and-marble rooms come with all the comforts (S-£70, Sb-£85–120, Db-£120–190, sofa bed Tb-£190–215, prices may be flexible Dec–March, CC, plush lounge, non-smoking rooms, elevator, 13–14 Beaufort Gardens, London SW3 1PS, Tube: Knightsbridge, tel. 020/7589-8541, fax 020/7584-3410, U.S. tel. 800/747-0398).

MODERATELY PRICED
Baden-Powell House Hostel—open to anyone—is a huge, modern, institutional place built to inexpensively house Boy and Girl Scouts and their families in central London. Those with a relative in a scouting organization get about a 30 percent discount. It's a big, bright, smoke-free place that feels safe and is well-run (180 single beds, Sb-£65 Scout rate-£46, Db-£94 Scout rate-£70, Tb-£120 Scout rate-£96, extra bed-£12, dorm bed-£29 Scout rate-£22, CC, air-con, cheap meals served, rooms are spacious with yacht-type bathrooms, receive discount with a letter from your Boy or Girl Scout troop saying you're "family," across from Natural History Museum on corner of Cromwell Road and Queen's Gate at 65 Queen's Gate, London SW7 5JS, Tube: South Kensington, tel. 020/7584-7031, fax 020/7590-6902 and 020/7590-6900, www.scoutbase.org.uk, e-mail: bph.hostel@scout.org.uk).

Sleeping in Notting Hill Gate Neighborhood
Residential Notting Hill Gate has quick bus and Tube access to downtown, is on the A2 Airbus line from Heathrow, and, for London, is very "homely." It has two self-serve launderettes on Moscow Road, an artsy theater, a late-hours supermarket, and lots of fun budget eateries (see Eating chapter).

Notting Hill Gate Neighborhood

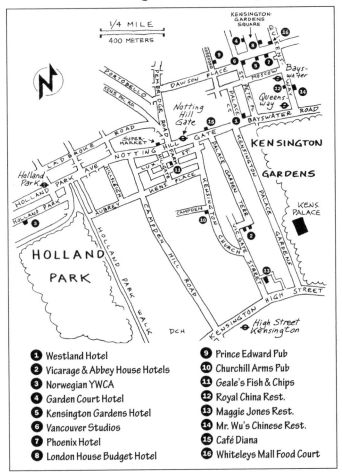

1 Westland Hotel
2 Vicarage & Abbey House Hotels
3 Norwegian YWCA
4 Garden Court Hotel
5 Kensington Gardens Hotel
6 Vancouver Studios
7 Phoenix Hotel
8 London House Budget Hotel

9 Prince Edward Pub
10 Churchill Arms Pub
11 Geale's Fish & Chips
12 Royal China Rest.
13 Maggie Jones Rest.
14 Mr. Wu's Chinese Rest.
15 Café Diana
16 Whiteleys Mall Food Court

HIGHER PRICED

Westland Hotel is comfortable, convenient, and hotelesque, with a fine lounge and spacious rooms (Sb-£80–90, Db-£95–105, cavernous deluxe Db-£110–125, sprawling Tb-£120–140, gargantuan Qb-£135–160, Quint/b-£150–170, CC, elevator, free garage with 7 spaces, between Notting Hill Gate and Queensway Tube stations, 154 Bayswater Road, London W2 4HP, tel. 020/7229-9191, fax 020/7727-1054, www.westlandhotel.co.uk, e-mail: reservations@westlandhotel.co.uk).

MODERATELY PRICED

Vicarage Private Hotel, understandably popular, is family-run and elegantly British in a quiet, classy neighborhood. It has 18 rooms furnished with taste and quality, a TV lounge, and facilities on each floor. Mandy, Richard, and Tere maintain a homey and caring atmosphere (S-£45, D-£74, Db-£98, T-£90, Q-£98, no CC, 6-min walk from the Notting Hill Gate and High Street Kensington tube stations, near Kensington Palace at 10 Vicarage Gate, London W8 4AG, tel. 020/7229-4030, fax 020/7792-5989, www.londonvicaragehotel.com, e-mail: reception@londonvicaragehotel.com).

Abbey House Hotel, next door, is similar but has a tea room (16 rooms, S-£45, D-£74, T-£90, Q-£100, Quint-£110, no CC, 11 Vicarage Gate, London W8 4AG, tel. 020/7727-2594, fax 020/7727-1873, www.abbeyhousekensington.com, Rodrigo).

LOWER PRICED

Norwegian YWCA (Norsk K.F.U.K.) is for women under 30 only (and men with Norwegian passports). Located on a quiet, stately street, it offers non-smoking rooms, a study, TV room, piano lounge, and an open-face Norwegian ambience. They have mostly quads, so those willing to share with strangers are most likely to get a place (July–Aug: Ss-£29, shared double-£27.50/bed, shared triple-£23/bed, shared quad-£20/bed, with breakfast; Sept–June: same prices include dinner; CC, 52 Holland Park, London W11 3RS, tel. 020/7727-9897, fax 020/7727-8718, www.kfuk.dial.pipex.com, e-mail: kfuk.hjemmet@kfuk-kfum.no). With each visit, I wonder which is easier to get—a sex change or a Norwegian passport?

Sleeping on Kensington Gardens

Several big old hotels line the quiet Victorian Kensington Gardens, a block off the bustling Queensway shopping street near the Bayswater Tube station. Popular with young international travelers, Queensway is a multicultural festival of commerce and eateries (such as Mr. Wu's Chinese Buffet and the Whiteleys Mall Food Court—see the Eating chapter). These hotels come with the least traffic noise of all my downtown recommendations. One of several laundrettes in the neighborhood is **Brookford Wash & Dry,** at Queensway and Bishop's Bridge Road (daily 7:00–19:30, service from 9:00–17:30, computerized pay point takes all coins).

HIGHER PRICED

Phoenix Hotel, a Best Western modernization of a 125-room hotel, offers American business-class comforts; spacious, plush public spaces; and big, fresh, modern-feeling rooms (Sb-£94,

Db-£120, Tb-£165, Qb-£185, flaky "negotiable" pricing list, CC, elevator, 1-8 Kensington Gardens Square, London W2 4BH, tel. 020/7229-2494, fax 020/7727-1419, U.S. tel. 800/528-1234, www.phoenixhotel.co.uk).

MODERATELY PRICED

Garden Court rents 34 comfortable rooms and is one of London's best accommodation values. It's friendly and has a garden (S-£39, Sb-£58, D-£58, Db-£88, T-£72, Tb-£99, Q-£82, Qb-£120, 5 percent discount with this book, CC, 30 Kensington Gardens Square, London W2 4BG, tel. 020/7229-2553, fax 020/7727-2749, www.gardencourthotel.co.uk, e-mail: info@gardencourthotel.co.uk, Edward Connolly).

Kensington Gardens Hotel laces 16 decent but worn rooms together in a tall, skinny place with peeling wallpaper, lots of stairs, and no lift (Ss-£55, Sb-£62, Db-£85, Tb-£105, CC, 9 Kensington Gardens Square, London W2 4BH, tel. 020/7221-7790, fax 020/7792-8612, www.kensingtongardenshotel.co.uk, e-mail: info@kensingtongardenshotel.co.uk).

Vancouver Studios offers 45 modern rooms with all the amenities, and gives you a fully-equipped kitchenette (utensils, stove, microwave, and fridge) rather than breakfast (small Sb-£55, big Sb-£75, small Db-£95, big Db-£110, Tb-£130, extra bed-£10, 10 percent discount with week or more stay CC, welcoming staff, homey lounge and private garden, 30 Prince's Square, London W2 4NJ, tel. 020/7243-1270, fax 020/7221-8678, www.vienna-group.co.uk, e-mail: vancouverstudios@vienna-group.co.uk, managed by Fiona).

LOWER PRICED

London House Budget Hotel is a threadbare, nose-ringed slumber mill renting 240 beds in 93 stark rooms (S-£40, Sb-£45, twin-£54, Db-£68, dorm bed-£15, includes continental breakfast, CC, lots of school groups, 81 Kensington Gardens Square, London W2 4DJ, tel. 020/7243-1810, fax 020/7243-1723, e-mail: londonhouse-hotel@yahoo.co.uk).

Sleeping in Other Neighborhoods

HIGHER PRICED

Covent Garden: Fielding House Hotel, located on a charming, quiet, pedestrian street just two blocks from Covent Garden, offers 24 clean, no-nonsense rooms, bright orange hallways, and lots of stairs (Db-£100–115, Db with sitting room-£130, CC, non-smoking, no kids under 13, 134 Broad Court, Bow St, London WC2B 5QZ, tel. 020/7497-8305, fax 020/7497-0064, www.the-fielding-hotel.co.uk).

Paddington Station: The Royal Norfolk Hotel is a 60-room place on a busy corner just one short block from the Paddington Station terminus of the Heathrow Express train (Sb-£99, Db-£109, superior Db-£120, Tb-£139, 25 percent discount for 3-night stay, CC, elevator, 25 London Street, London W2 1HH, tel. 020/7723-3386, fax 020/7724-8442, www.royalnorfolk.co.uk, e-mail: reservations@royalnorfolkhotel.co.uk).

Downtown near Baker Street: For a less hotelesque alternative in the center, consider renting one of the 18 stark, hardwood, comfortable rooms in **22 York Street B&B** (Db-£100, Tb-£141, CC, strictly smoke-free, inviting lounge, social breakfast, from Baker Street tube station walk 2 blocks down Baker Street and take a right, 22 York Street, London W1U 6PX, tel. 020/7224-3990, fax 020/7224-1990, www.myrtle-cottage.co.uk/callis.htm, energetically run by Liz and Michael).

MODERATELY PRICED
Near Buckingham Palace: Vandon House Hotel, formerly run by the Salvation Army, is now run by the Central University of Iowa. Filled with students most of the year, the 33 rooms are rented to travelers from late May through August at great prices. The rooms, while institutional, are comfy, and the location is excellent (S-£42, D-£66, Db-£82, Tb-£119, Qb-£149, prices promised with this book through 2003, CC, only single beds, non-smoking, elevator, on a tiny road 2 blocks west of St. James Park Tube station, near east end of Petty France Street at 1 Vandon Street, London SW1H OAH, tel. 020/7799-6780, fax 020/7799-1464, www.vandonhouse.com, e-mail: info@vandonhouse.com).

Euston Station: The **Methodist International Centre,** a modern, youthful, Christian residence, fills its lower floors with international students and its top floor with travelers. Rooms are modern and simple yet comfortable, with fine bathrooms, phones, and desks. The atmosphere is friendly, safe, clean, and controlled; also has a spacious lounge and game room (Sb-£48, Db-£71, 2-course buffet dinner-£8, CC, non-smoking rooms, elevator, on a quiet street a block west of Euston Station, 81–103 Euston Street, not Euston Road, London W1 2EZ, Tube: Euston Station, tel. 020/7380-0001, fax 020/7387-5300, www.micentre.com, e-mail: sales@micentre.com). In June, July, and August, when the students are gone, they rent simple £38 singles.

LOWER PRICED
Euston Station: Cottage Hotel is tucked away a block off the west exit of Euston Station. Established in 1950—a bit tired, cramped, and smoky—it feels like 1950. But it's cheap and quiet

(40 rooms, D-£55, Db-£65, T-£70, Tb-£80, Qb-£90, CC, 10 percent discount for 2-night cash-only stays, 67 Euston Street, London NW1 2ET, tel. 020/7387-6785, fax 020/7383-0859, managed by Ali).

Near St. Paul's: The **City of London Youth Hostel** is clean, modern, friendly, and well-run. You'll pay about £25 for a bed in their three- to eight-bed rooms, £28 for a single room (hostel membership required, 193 beds, CC, cheap meals, open 24 hrs, Tube: St. Paul's, 36 Carter Lane, London EC4V 5AD, tel. 020/7236-4965, fax 020/7236-7681, www.yha.org.uk, e-mail: city@yha.org.uk).

Sleeping near Gatwick and Heathrow Airports

LOWER PRICED

Near Gatwick Airport: The **London Gatwick Airport Travel Inn** rents cheap rooms at the airport (Db-£50, CC, tel. 0870-238-3305, www.travelinn.co.uk). The **Gatwick Travelodge,** also a budget hotel, is two miles from the airport (Db-£50, CC, breakfast extra, free shuttle from south terminal, Church Road, Lowfield Heath, Crawley, tel. 0870-905-6343, www.travelodge.co.uk).

Barn Cottage, a converted 17th-century barn, sits in the peaceful countryside, with a tennis court, small swimming pool, and a good pub within walking distance. It has two wood-beamed rooms, antique furniture, and a large garden that makes you forget Gatwick is 10 minutes away (S-£40–45, D-£55, no CC, can drive you to airport or train station for £6, Leigh, Reigate, Surrey, RH2 8RF, tel. 01306/611-347, warmly run by Pat and Mike Comer).

The **Wayside Manor Farm** is another rural alternative to a bland airport hotel. This four-bedroom countryside place is a 10-minute drive from Gatwick (Db-£60, Norwood Hill, near Charlwood, tel. 01293/862-692, www.wayside-manor.com, e-mail: info@wayside-manor.com).

Near Heathrow Airport: It's so easy to get to Heathrow from central London, I see no reason to sleep there. But for budget beds near the airport, consider **Heathrow Ibis** (Db-£65, Db-£40–45 on Fri–Sun nights, breakfast extra, CC, £2.50 shuttle bus to/from terminals except T-4, 112 Bath Road, tel. 020/8759-4888, fax 020/8564-7894, www.ibishotel.com, e-mail: h0794@accor-hotels.com).

EATING

I don't mind English food. But then, I liked dorm food. True, England isn't famous for its cuisine and probably never will be. Still, the sheer variety of foods in London—from every corner of the former empire—is astonishing.

If you want to dine (as opposed to eat), check out the extensive listings in the weekly entertainment guides sold at London news-stands (or catch a train for Paris). The thought of a £30 meal in Britain generally ruins my appetite, so my London dining is limited mostly to easygoing, fun, but inexpensive alternatives. I've listed places by neighborhood—handy to your sightseeing or hotel. Considering how expensive London can be, if there's any good place to cut corners to stretch your budget, it's in eating.

Tips on Budget Eating

Your £7 budget choices are pub grub, restaurant specials, bakeries, ethnic, cafeterias, fast food, picnics, fish and chips, greasy spoon cafes, or pizza.

Pub grub is the most atmospheric budget option. Many of London's 7,000 pubs serve fresh, tasty buffets under ancient timbers, with hearty lunches and dinners priced at £6–8 (see below).

At classier restaurants, look for **"early bird specials,"** allowing you to eat well and affordably, but early (around 17:30–19:00, last order by 19:00). A top-end, £25-for-dinner–type restaurant often serves the same quality two-course lunch deals for £10.

Ethnic restaurants from all over the world add spice to England's lackluster cuisine scene. Eating Indian or Chinese is cheap (even cheaper if you take it out). Middle-Eastern stands sell gyros sandwiches and *shwarmas* (lamb in pita bread sandwich).

Most large **museums** (and many churches) have inexpensive, cheery **cafeterias.**

Fast food places, both American and British, are everywhere.

Picnicking saves time and money. Fine park benches and polite pigeons abound in most neighborhoods. You can easily get prepared food to go. **Bakeries** sell yogurt, cartons of "semi-skimmed" milk, pastries, and pasties (pron. PAST-eez). Pasties are "savory" (not sweet) meat pies that originated in the mining country; they had big crust handles so miners with filthy hands could eat them and toss the crust.

Good **sandwich shops** (try curry-flavored "*tikka* chicken") and corner **grocery stores** are a hit with local workers eating on the run. Try boxes of orange juice (pure, by the liter), fresh bread, tasty English cheese, meat, a tube of Colman's English mustard, local eatin' apples, bananas, small tomatoes, a small tub of yogurt (they're drinkable), gorp or nuts, plain or chocolate-covered "digestive biscuits," and any local specialties. At **open-air markets** and **supermarkets**, you can get produce in small quantities (3 tomatoes and 2 bananas cost me 50p). Supermarkets often have good deli sections, even offering Indian dishes, and sometimes salad bars. Decent packaged sandwiches (£2–3) are sold everywhere.

I often munch a relaxed "meal on wheels" in a car, train, or open-top bus tour or river cruise to save 30 precious minutes for sightseeing.

Breakfast

The traditional "fry" is famous as a hearty way to start the day. Also known as a "heart attack on a plate," the breakfast is especially feasty if you've just come from the land of the skimpy continental breakfast across the Channel.

Your standard fry gets off to a healthy start with juice and cereal or porridge. (Try Weetabix, a soggy English cousin of Shredded Wheat.) Next, with tea or coffee, you get a heated plate with a fried egg, lean Canadian-style bacon, a bad sausage, a grilled tomato, and often a slice of delightfully greasy pan toast and sautéed mushrooms. Toast comes on a rack (to cool quickly and crisply) with butter and marmalade. Try kippers (herring filets smoked in an oak fire). This meal tides many travelers over until dinner. Order only what you'll eat. Hoteliers and B&B hostesses don't like to see food wasted. And there's nothing wrong with skipping the "fry"—few locals actually start their day with this heavy traditional breakfast.

These days, the best coffee is served in a *cafetière* (also called a "French press"). When your coffee has steeped as long as you like, plunge down the filter and pour. To revitalize your brew, pump the plunger again.

Going Local: Pubs...and Indian Food

Pubs

Pubs are a basic part of the British social scene, and, whether you're a teetotaler or a beer guzzler, they should be a part of your travel here. "Pub" is short for "public house." It's an extended living room where, if you don't mind the stickiness, you can feel the pulse of London. Unfortunately, many of London's pubs have been afflicted with an excess of brass, ferns, and video games. In any case, smart travelers use the pubs to eat, drink, get out of the rain, watch the latest sporting event, and make new friends.

Pub hours vary. The strict wartime hours (designed to keep the wartime working force sober and productive) finally ended a few years ago, and now pubs can serve beer daily 11:00–23:00 (Sun 12:00–22:30). As it nears 23:00, you'll hear shouts of "Last orders" to order a beer. Then comes the 10-minute warning bell. Finally, they'll call "Time!" to pick up your glass, finished or not, sometime before 23:25, when the pub closes. Children are served food and soft drinks in pubs, but you must be 18 to order a beer.

A cup of darts is free for the asking. People go to a "public house" to be social. They want to talk. Get vocal with a local. This is easiest at the bar, where people assume you're in the mood to talk (rather than at a table). The pub is the next best thing to having relatives in town. Cheers!

Pub Grub

Pub grub gets better each year. It's London's best eating value. For £6–8, you'll get a basic budget hot lunch or dinner in friendly surroundings. The *Good Pub Guide*, published annually by the British Consumers Union, is excellent. Pubs attached to restaurants often have fresher food and a chef who knows how to cook.

Pubs generally serve traditional dishes, like fish and chips, vegetables, "bangers and mash" (sausages and mashed potatoes), roast beef with Yorkshire pudding (batter baked in the oven), and assorted meat pies, such as steak-and-kidney pie or shepherd's pie (stewed lamb topped with mashed potatoes). Side dishes include salads (sometimes even a nice self-serve salad bar), vegetables (especially soggy peas), and—invariably—"chips" (French fries). "Crisps" are potato chips. A "jacket potato" (baked potato stuffed with fillings of your choice) can almost be a meal in itself. A "ploughman's lunch" is a modern "traditional English meal" of bread, cheese, and sweet pickles that nearly every tourist tries...once. These days, you'll likely find more Italian pasta, curried dishes, and quiche on the menu than "traditional" fare.

Meals are usually served from 12:00 to 14:00 and from 18:00 to

20:00, not throughout the day. There's usually no table service. Order at the bar, then take a seat and they'll bring the food when it's ready (or sometimes you pick it up at the bar). Pay at the bar (sometimes when you order, sometimes after you eat). Don't tip unless it's a place with full table service. Servings are hearty, service is quick, and you'll rarely spend more than £8. Your beer or cider adds another couple of pounds. (Free tap water is always available.) Pubs that advertise their food and are crowded with locals are less likely to be the kinds that serve only lousy microwaved snacks.

Beer

The British take great pride in their beer. Many Brits think that drinking beer cold and carbonated, as Americans do, ruins the taste. Most pubs will have **lagers** (cold, refreshing, American-style beer), **ales** (amber-colored, room-temperature beer), **bitters** (hop-flavored ale, perhaps the most typical British beer), and **stouts** (dark and somewhat bitter, like Guinness). At pubs, long hand pulls are used to pull the traditional, rich-flavored "real ales" up from the cellar. These are the connoisseur's favorites: fermented naturally, varying from sweet to bitter, often with a hoppy or nutty flavor. Notice the fun names. Short hand pulls at the bar mean colder, fizzier, mass-produced, and less interesting keg beers. Mild beers are sweeter, with a creamy malt flavoring. Irish cream ale is a smooth, sweet experience. Try the draft cider (sweet or dry)...carefully.

Order your beer at the bar and pay as you go, with no need to tip. An average beer costs £2.50. Part of the experience is standing before a line of "hand pulls," or taps, and wondering which beer to choose.

Drinks are served by the pint (20-ounce imperial size) or the half-pint. (It's almost feminine for a man to order just a half; I order mine with quiche.) Proper English ladies like a half-beer and half-lemonade **shandy.**

Besides beer, many pubs actually have a good selection of wines by the glass, a fully stocked bar for the gentleman's "G and T" (gin and tonic), and the increasingly popular bottles of alcohol-plus-sugar (such as Bacardi Breezers) for the younger, working-class set. Teetotalers can order from a wide variety of soft drinks.

Indian Food

Eating Indian food is "going local" in cosmopolitan, multiethnic London. Take the opportunity to sample food from Britain's former colony. Indian cuisine is as varied as the country itself. In general, they use more exotic spices than we're accustomed to—some hot, some sweet. (Step inside a restaurant and sniff to see if you'll like it.)

Here's a grunt-simple introduction to just a few popular dishes you'll find in London.

As with Chinese food, you build an Indian meal with several dishes. The portions are quite small, so you'll need at least two dishes per person. A typical meal for one might include **dal** (lentil soup) as a starter; one **meat dish** with sauce (for example, chicken curry, chicken *tikka masala* in a creamy tomato sauce, grilled chicken tandoori, or the spicy chicken vindaloo); one **vegetable dish** (in a similar sauce to the meat); **rice** (boiled white basmati rice, fried rice, or *pilau*—cooked in broth with meats); **nan** (a leavened, grilled tortilla, used by Indians to mop up food); and an Indian **beer** (wine and Indian food don't really mix).

A meal like this will set you back about £20. Many restaurants offer a fixed-price combination meal that's simpler and cheaper than ordering à la carte.

Desserts (Sweets)

Anyone care for a pud? (American translation: Would you like dessert?) To the British, the traditional word for dessert is **pudding**, although it's also referred to as **sweets** these days. Sponge cake, cream, fruitcake, and meringue are key players.

Trifle is the best-known British concoction, consisting of sponge cake soaked in brandy or sherry (or orange juice for children), then covered with jam and/or fruit and custard cream. Whipped cream can sometimes put the final touch on this "light" treat.

Castle puddings are sponge puddings cooked in small molds and topped with "Golden Syrup" (a popular brand and a cross between honey and maple syrup). **Bread and butter pudding** consists of slices of French bread baked with milk, cream, eggs, and raisins (similar to the American preparation), served warm with cold cream. **Hasty pudding,** supposedly the invention of people in a hurry to avoid the bailiff, is made from stale bread with dried fruit and milk. **Queen of puddings** is a breadcrumb pudding topped with warm jam, meringue, and cream. **Treacle pudding** is a popular steamed pudding whose "sponge" mixture combines flour, suet, butter, sugar, and milk. **Christmas pudding** (also called plum pudding) is a dense mixture with dried and candied fruit served with brandy butter or hard sauce.

Spotted Dick is a sponge pudding with currants. How did it get its name? Some say it looks like a spotted dog, and dogs were often called Dick. Another theory suggests that "Dick," "duff," and "dog" are all variants of the word "dough." One thing's for sure: The stuff isn't selling very well today, thanks to the name's connotation. Grocers are considering renaming it "Spotted Richard."

English Chocolate

My chocoholic readers are enthusiastic about English chocolates. Their favorites include Cadbury Wispa Gold bars (filled with liquid caramel), Cadbury Crunchie bars, Nestle's Lion bars, Cadbury's Boost bars (a shortcake biscuit with caramel in milk chocolate), and Galaxy chocolate bars (especially the ones with hazelnuts). Thornton shops (in larger train stations) sell a box of sweets called the Continental Assortment, which comes with a tasting guide. The highlight is the mocha white chocolate truffle. British M&Ms, called Smarties, are better than American ones. For a few extra pence, adorn your ice cream cone with a "flake"—a chocolate bar stuck right into the middle.

The English version of **custard** is a smooth, yellow liquid. Cream tops most everything custard does not. There's **single cream** for coffee. **Double cream** is really thick. **Whipped cream** is familiar, and **clotted cream** is the consistency of butter.

Fool is a dessert with sweetened pureed fruit (such as rhubarb, gooseberry, or black currants) mixed with cream or custard and chilled. Elderflower is a popular flavoring for sorbet.

In the north, **flitting dumpling** is a pudding made with dates, walnuts, and syrup. It is dense and easily sliced to take with you when you are "flitting along" from place to place. Scotland has its famous **shortbread** as well as other tasty biscuits (cookies), such as raisin and apple bars and jelly-filled **empire biscuits.**

Scones are tops, and many inns and restaurants have their secret recipes. Whether made with fruit or topped with clotted cream, scones take the cake.

Afternoon Tea

People of leisure punctuate their afternoon with a "cream tea" at a tearoom. You'll get a pot of tea, small finger foods (like cucumber sandwiches), homemade scones, jam, and thick clotted cream. For maximum pinkie-waving taste per calorie, slice your scone thin like a miniature loaf of bread. Tearooms, which often serve appealing light meals, are usually open for lunch and close around 17:00, just before dinner.

While tea-time is still going strong, the new phenomenon is coffee shops: Starbucks and its competitors have sprouted up all over town, providing cushy and social watering holes with comfy chairs, easy WCs, £2 lattes, and a nice break between sights.

Tipping

Tipping is an issue only at restaurants and fancy pubs that have waiters and waitresses. If you order your food at a counter, don't tip.

If the menu states that service is included, there's no need to tip beyond that. If service isn't included, tip about 10 percent by rounding up. The discreet English don't like "big deals" made of anything. Leave the tip on the table, or hand it to your server with your payment for the meal and say, "Keep the rest, please."

RESTAURANTS

Eating near Trafalgar Square

To locate restaurants, see map on page 287.

For a tasty meal on a monk's budget, sitting on somebody's tomb in an ancient crypt, descend into the **St. Martin-in-the-Fields Café in the Crypt** (£5–7 cafeteria plates, cheaper sandwich bar, Mon–Sat 10:00–20:00, Sun 12:00–20:30, profits go to the church, no CC, underneath St. Martin-in-the-Fields on Trafalgar Square, tel. 020/7839-4342).

Chandos Bar's Opera Room floats amazingly apart from the tacky crush of tourism around Trafalgar Square. Look for the pub opposite the National Portrait Gallery (corner of William Street and St. Martin's Lane) and climb the stairs to the Opera Room. They serve £6–7 pub lunches and dinners (kitchen open daily 11:00–19:00, tel. 020/7836-1401). This is a fine Trafalgar rendezvous point—smoky, but wonderfully local. Order and pay at the bar.

Gordon's Wine Bar is ripe with atmosphere. A simple, steep staircase leads into a 14th-century cellar filled with dusty old wine bottles, faded British memorabilia, local nine-to-fivers, and candlelight (hot meals only for lunch, fine plate of cheeses or various cold cuts with salad buffet all day until 21:00—1 plate of each feeds 2 for £7). While it's crowded, you can normally corral two chairs and grab the corner of a table (arrive before 18:00 to get a seat, Mon–Sat 11:00–23:00, Sun 12:00–22:00, 2 blocks from Trafalgar Square, bottom of Villiars Street at #47, Tube: Embankment, tel. 020/7930-1408).

Down Whitehall, a block south of Trafalgar Square toward Big Ben, you'll find the touristy but atmospheric **Clarence Pub** (lunch only, decent grub) and several cheaper cafeterias and pizza joints.

For a classy lunch in the National Gallery, treat your palate to the moderately priced light Mediterranean cuisine at **Crivelli's Garden** (daily 10:00–17:00, first floor of Sainsbury Wing).

Simpson's on the Strand serves a stuffy, aristocratic,

old-timey carver dinner—where the chef slices your favorite red meat from a fancy trolley at your table—in its elegant, smoky old dining room (£20, Mon–Sat 12:15–14:30 & 17:30–22:45, no tennis shoes or T-shirts, at 100 Strand, tel. 020/7836-9112).

Eating near Piccadilly

Hungry and broke in the theater district? Head for Panton Street (off Haymarket, 2 blocks southeast of Piccadilly Circus) for cheap Thai, Chinese, and two famous London eateries. **Stockpot** is a mushy-peas kind of place, famous and rightly popular for its edible, cheap meals (daily 7:00–22:00, 38 Panton Street). The **West End Kitchen** (across the street at #5, same hours and menu) is a direct competitor that's just as good. Vegetarians would prefer the **Woodland South Indian Vegetarian Restaurant,** across from the West End Kitchen.

The palatial **Criterion Brasserie** serves a special £15 two-course "Anglo-French" menu (or £18 for 3 courses) under gilded tiles and chandeliers in a dreamy Byzantine church setting from 1880. It's right on Piccadilly Circus but a world away from the punk junk. The house wine is great and so is the food (specials available Mon–Sat 12:00–14:30 & 17:30–18:30, dinner served until 23:00, closed Sun lunch, CC, tel. 020/7930-0488). Anyone can drop in for coffee or a drink.

The "Food Is Fun" Dinner Crawl:
From Covent Garden to Soho

London has a trendy generation-X scene that most Beefeater-seekers miss entirely. For a multicultural movable feast and a chance to sample some of London's most popular eateries, con-sider exploring these. Start around 18:00 to avoid lines, get in on early specials, and find waiters willing to let you split a meal. Prices, while reasonable by London standards, add up. Servings are large enough to share. All are open nightly.

Suggested nibbler's dinner crawl for two: Arrive before 18:00 at **Belgo Centraal** and split the early-bird dinner special: a kilo of mussels, fries, and dark Belgian beer. At **Yo! Sushi,** have beer or sake and a few dishes. Slurp your last course at **Wagamama Noodle Bar.** Then, for dessert, people-watch at Leicester Square, where the serf's always up.

Belgo Centraal is a space-station world overrun with Trappist monks serving hearty Belgian specialties. The classy restaurant section requires reservations, but just grabbing a bench in the boisterous beer hall (no reservations possible) is more fun. The same menu and specials work on both sides. Belgians claim they eat as well as the French and as heartily as the Germans.

From Covent Garden to Soho: Food is Fun

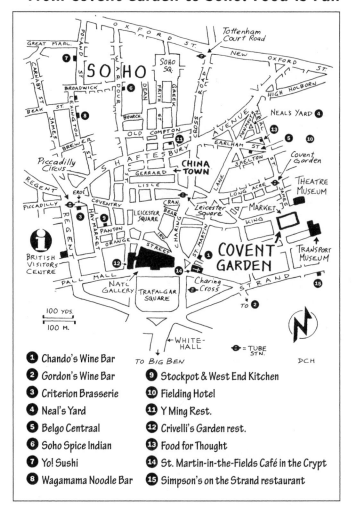

❶ Chando's Wine Bar

❷ Gordon's Wine Bar

❸ Criterion Brasserie

❹ Neal's Yard

❺ Belgo Centraal

❻ Soho Spice Indian

❼ Yo! Sushi

❽ Wagamama Noodle Bar

❾ Stockpot & West End Kitchen

❿ Fielding Hotel

⓫ Y Ming Rest.

⓬ Crivelli's Garden rest.

⓭ Food for Thought

⓮ St. Martin-in-the-Fields Café in the Crypt

⓯ Simpson's on the Strand restaurant

Specialties include mussels, great fries, and a stunning array of dark, blond, and fruity Belgian beers. Belgo actually makes things Belgian trendy—a formidable feat (£14 meals; open daily until very late, kitchen closes Fri–Sat at 24:00, Sun–Thu at 23:00; Mon–Fri 17:00–18:30 "beat the clock" meal specials cost only the time...£5–6.30, and you get mussels, fries, and beer; no meal-splitting after 18:30, and they are not licensed to serve

anyone just a beer; daily £5 lunch special 12:00–17:00; 1 block
north of Covent Garden Tube station at intersection of Neal
and Shelton Streets, 50 Earlham Street, tel. 020/7813-2233).

Yo! Sushi is a futuristic Japanese-food-extravaganza experience. With thumping rock, Japanese cable TV, a 195-foot-long
conveyor belt, the world's longest sushi bar, a robotic drink trolley,
and automated sushi machines, just sipping a sake on a bar stool
here is a trip. For £1 you get miso, or unlimited tea (on request) or
water (from spigot at bar, with or without gas). Grab dishes as they
rattle by (priced by color of dish; check the chart) and a drink off
the trash-talking robot (£12 meals, daily 12:00–24:00, 2 blocks
south of Oxford Street, where Lexington Street becomes Poland
Street, 52 Poland Street, tel. 020/7287-0443). For more serious
drinking on tatami mats, go downstairs into "Yo Below."

Wagamama Noodle Bar is a noisy, pan-Asian, organic slur-
pathon. As you enter, check out the kitchen and listen to the roar
of the basement, where benches rock with happy eaters. Everybody
sucks. Stand against the wall to feel the energy of all this "positive
eating" (daily 12:00–24:00, crowded after 20:00, non-smoking,
10A Lexington Street, tel. 020/7292-0990). If you like this place,
there are now branches all over town (including a handy one near
the British Museum on Streatham Street).

Soho Spice Indian is where modern Britain meets Indian
tradition—fine Indian cuisine in a trendy, jewel-tone ambience.
The £15 "tandoori selections" meal is the best "variety" dish and
big enough for two (Mon–Sat 11:30–24:00, Sun 12:30–22:30,
non-smoking section available Sun–Tue, CC, 5 blocks north of
Piccadilly Circus at 124 Wardour Street, tel. 020/7434-0808).

Y Ming Chinese Restaurant, across Shaftesbury Avenue
from the ornate gates, clatter, and dim sum of Chinatown,
has clean European decor, serious but helpful service, and
authentic Northern Chinese cooking (good £10 meal deal
offered 12:00–18:00, Mon–Sat 12:00–23:30, last order at 23:00,
closed Sun, CC, 35 Greek Street, tel. 020/7734-2721).

Andrew Edmunds Restaurant is a tiny, candlelit place
where you'll want to hide your camera and guidebook and act as
local as possible. The modern European cooking is worth the
splurge (3 courses for £25, daily 12:30–15:00 & 18:00–22:45,
reservations are generally necessary, 46 Lexington Street in
Soho, tel. 020/7437-5708).

For cheap, hip, and healthy near Covent Garden, the area
around Neal's Yard is busy with fun, hippie-type cafés. One of
the best is **Food for Thought,** packed with local health nuts
(good £5 vegetarian meals, Mon–Sat 12:00–20:30, Sun 12:00–
17:00, non-smoking, 2 blocks north of Covent Garden Tube

station, 31 Neal Street, tel. 020/7836-0239). **Neal's Yard** itself
is a food circus of trendy, healthy eateries.

Eating near Recommended Victoria Station Accommodations

Here are places a couple of blocks southwest of Victoria Station
where I've enjoyed eating (see map on page 268).

The small but classy **La Campagnola** is Belgravia's favorite
budget Italian restaurant (£12–16 plus 10 percent service charge,
Mon–Sat 12:00–15:00 & 18:00–23:30, closed Sun, CC, 10 Lower
Belgrave Street, tel. 020/7730-2057).

The **Ebury Wine Bar,** filled with young professionals, provides
a classy atmosphere and pricey but delicious meals (£15–18, Mon–
Fri 11:00–23:00, Sat 12:00–23:00, Sun 18:00–23:00, CC, 139 Ebury
Street, at intersection with Elizabeth Street, near bus station, tel. 020/
7730-5447). Several cheap places are around the corner on Elizabeth
Street (#23 for take-out or eat-in, super-absorbent fish and chips).

The **Duke of Wellington** pub is a good, if somewhat smoky,
neighborhood place for dinner (£6 meals, Mon–Sat 11:00–23:00,
Sun 12:00–22:30, 63 Eaton Terrace, at intersection with Chester
Row, tel. 020/7730-1782).

At **Constitution Pub,** a friendly local hangout, owner Lee
and his family offer a warm welcome and traditional pub grub
(£4–7, Mon–Sat 11:00–22:00, Sun 12:00–22:00, 42 Churton
Street, tel. 020/7834-3651).

Jenny Lo's Tea House is a simple, budget place serving
up £5–7 eclectic Chinese-style meals to locals in the know (Mon–
Fri 11:30–15:00 & 18:00–22:00, Sat 12:00–15:00 & 18:00–22:00,
closed Sun, no CC, 14 Eccleston Street, tel. 020/7259-0399 or
020/7823-6331).

La Poule au Pot, ideal for a romantic splurge, offers a classy,
candlelit ambience with well-dressed patrons and expensive but
fine Mediterranean and Provençal-style French food (£20–25
dinners, daily 12:30–14:30 & 18:45–23:00, Sun until 22:00, leafy
patio dining, reservations smart, CC, end of Ebury at intersection
with Pimlico, 231 Ebury Street, tel. 020/7730-7763).

Pimlico Restaurant serves quality Indian cuisine (daily
12:00–14:30 & 18:00–21:30, CC, 38 Moreton Street, just off of
Belgrave Street, tel. 020/7976-6331).

The **Marche** is an easy, moderately priced cafeteria a couple
of blocks north of Victoria Station at Bressenden Place (Mon–Sat
7:30–23:00, Sun 11:00–21:00, CC, tel. 020/7630-1733). If you miss
America, there's a mall-type food circus at Victoria Place, upstairs
in Victoria Station; **Café Rouge** offers the best food here (£8–11
dinners, daily 9:30–22:30).

Groceries: The late-hours **Whistle Stop** at the station has decent sandwiches, fresh fruit, snacks, and beverages (daily, 24 hrs). A larger grocery, **Sainsbury Local,** is on Victoria Street in front of the station, just past the buses (Mon–Fri 7:00–22:00, Sat 7:00–21:00, Sun 10:00–16:00).

Eating near Recommended Notting Hill Gate B&Bs and Bayswater Hotels

Queensway is lined with lively and inexpensive eateries. See map on page 274.

The exuberantly rustic and very English **Maggie Jones** serves my favorite £20 London dinner. You'll get solid English cuisine, including huge plates of crunchy vegetables—by candle-light (daily 12:30–14:30 & 18:30–23:00, much less expensive lunch menu, reservations recommended—request upstairs for noisy but less-cramped section, CC, friendly staff, 6 Old Court Place, just east of Kensington Church Street, near High Street Kensington Tube stop, tel. 020/7937-6462). If you eat well once in London, eat here (and do it quick, before it burns down).

The **Churchill Arms** pub is a local hangout, with good beer and old-English ambience in front and hearty £6 Thai plates in an enclosed patio in the back. You can bring the Thai food into the smoky but wonderfully atmospheric pub section. Arrive by 18:00 to avoid a line (Mon–Sat 12:00–14:30 & 18:00–21:30, Sun 12:00–14:30, 119 Kensington Church Street, tel. 020/7792-1246).

Prince Edward Pub serves good pub grub in a quintessential pub setting (£8 meals, Mon–Sat 12:00–15:00 & 18:00–22:00, Sun 12:00–18:00, indoor/outdoor seating, CC, 2 blocks north of Bayswater Road at the corner of Dawson Place and Hereford Road, 73 Prince's Square, tel. 020/7727-2221).

Café Diana is a healthy little eatery serving sandwiches and Middle Eastern food. It's decorated with photos of Princess Diana because she used to drop by for pita sandwiches (daily 8:00–22:30, 5 Wellington Terrace, on Bayswater Road, opposite Kensington Palace Garden Gates—where Diana once lived, tel. 020/7792-9606).

The Royal China Restaurant is filled with London's Chinese, who consider this one of the city's best eateries. It's black, white, and chrome, with candles, brisk waiters, and fine food (£7–9 dishes, dim sum until 17:00, Mon–Thu 12:00–23:00, Fri–Sat 12:00–23:30, Sun 11:00–22:00, CC, 13 Queensway, tel. 020/7221-2535).

Mr. Wu's Chinese Restaurant serves a 10-course buffet in a bright and cheery little place. Just grab a plate and help yourself (£4.50, daily 12:00–23:30, check quality of buffet—right inside entrance—before committing, pickings can get slim, across from Bayswater Tube station, 54 Queensway, tel. 020/7243-1017).

Whiteleys Mall Food Court offers a fun selection of ethnic and fast-food eateries in a delightful mall (good salads at Café Rouge, second floor, corner of Porchester Gardens and Queensway).

Supermarket: Europa is a half block from the Notting Hill Gate Tube stop (Mon–Fri 8:00–23:00, Sun 12:00–18:00, 112 Notting Hill Gate, near intersection with Pembridge Road).

Eating near Recommended Accommodations in South Kensington

Popular eateries line Old Brompton Road and Thurloe Street (Tube: South Kensington). See map on page 272.

La Bouchee Bistro Café is a classy, hole-in-the-wall touch of France serving early-bird, three-course £11 meals before 19:00 and *plats du jour* for £8 all *jour* (daily 12:00–23:00, Sun until 22:00, CC, 56 Old Brompton Road, tel. 020/7589-1929).

Daquise, an authentic-feeling Polish place, is ideal if you're in the mood for kielbasa and kraut. It's fast, cheap, family-run, and a part of the neighborhood (£10 meals, daily 11:00-23:00, non-smoking, CC, 20 Thurloe Street, tel. 020/7589-6117).

The **Khyber Pass Tandoori Restaurant** is a nondescript but handy place serving great Punjabi-style Indian cuisine. Locals in the know travel to eat here (£10 dinners, daily 12:00–14:30 & 18:00–23:30, CC, 21 Bute Street, tel. 020/7589-7311).

La Brasserie fills a big, plain room painted "nicotine yellow," with ceiling fans, a Parisian ambience, and good, traditional French cooking at reasonable prices (2-course £16 "regional menu," £13 bottle of house wine, nightly until 23:00, CC, 272 Brompton Road, tel. 020/7581-3089).

PJ's Bar and Grill is lively with the yuppie Chelsea crowd for a good reason. Traditional "New York Brasserie"–style, yet trendy, it has dressy tables surrounding a centerpiece bar. It serves pricey, cosmopolitan cuisine from a menu that changes with the seasons (£20 meals, nightly until 24:00, CC, 52 Fulham Road, at intersection with Sydney Street, tel. 020/7581-0025).

Eating Elsewhere in London

Near St. Paul's, in The City: The **Counting House,** formerly an elegant old bank, offers great £7 meals, nice homemade meat pies, fish, and fresh vegetables (Mon–Fri 12:00–20:00, closed Sat–Sun, gets really busy with the buttoned-down 9-to-5 crowd after 12:15, near Mansion House in the City, 50 Cornhill, tel. 020/7283-7123).

Near the British Library: Drummond Street (running just west of Euston Station) is famous in London for very cheap and good Indian and vegetarian food. Consider **Chutneys** and **Ravi Shankar** for a good *thali.*

LONDON
WITH
CHILDREN

The key to a successful family trip to London is making everyone happy, including the parents. My family-tested recommendations have this objective in mind.

Consider these tips:

- Take advantage of the local newsstand guides. *Time Out*'s family monthly is called *Kids Out*. *Time Out* and *What's On* also have handy kids' calendars listing activities and shows.
- Ask at London TIs about kids' events.
- London's big, budget chain hotels allow two kids to sleep for free in their already-inexpensive rooms (see page 264).
- Eat dinner early (around 18:00) to miss the romantic crowd. Skip the famous places. Look instead for relaxed cafés, pubs (kids are welcome—though sometimes restricted to restaurant section or courtyard area), or even fast-food restaurants where kids can move around. Picnic lunches and dinners work well.
- Public WCs can be hard to find. Try department stores, museums, and restaurants, particularly fast-food restaurants.
- Follow this book's crowd-beating tips. Kids get antsy standing in a line for a museum. At each sight, ask about a kids' guide or flier.
- Hamleys is the biggest toy store in Britain (Mon–Sat 10:00–20:00, Sun 12:00–18:00, 188 Regent Street, Tube: Oxford Circus, tel. 020/8752-2277, www.hamleys.co.uk).

TOP KIDS' SIGHTS
In East London
Tower of London—The crown jewels are awesome, and the Beefeater tour plays off kids in a memorable and fun way (£11.50, cheaper for kids, March–Oct Mon–Sat 9:00–18:00,

Sun 10:00–18:00, Nov–Feb Tue–Sat 9:00–17:00, Sun–Mon 10:00–17:00, last entry 60 min before closing, Tube: Tower Hill, tel. 020/7709-0765, recorded info: 020/7680-9004, booking: 0870/756-7070). ✪ For Tower of London Tour, see page 210.

Museum of London—A very kid-friendly presentation takes you from the Romans to the Blitz. Parents will learn something, too (free, Mon–Sat 10:00–18:00, Sun 12:00–18:00, Tube: Barbican or St. Paul's, tel. 020/7600-3699).

In Central London

Covent Garden—A great area for people-watching and candy-licking. Kids like the London Transport Museum (£6, kids under 16 free, Sat-Thu 10:00–18:00, Fri 11:00–18:00, 30 yards southeast of Covent Garden's marketplace, tel. 020/7379-6344); see page 34.

Trafalgar Square—The grand square is great fun for kids. Feed the pigeons and climb the lions. After that, munch lunch in a crypt and tour the National Gallery (below). See page 32.

National Gallery—Start your visit in the Micro Gallery computer room. Your child can list his or her interests (cats, naval battles, and so on) and print out a tailor-made tour map (free, daily 10:00–18:00, Wed until 21:00, on Trafalgar Square, Tube: Charing Cross or Leicester Square, tel. 020/7747-2885, www.nationalgallery.org). Ask about their Kids Trail. ✪ See National Gallery Tour on page 116.

St. Martin-in-the-Fields—This church on Trafalgar Square has a brass-rubbing center that's fun for kids who'd like a souvenir to show for their efforts (free, donations welcome, open daily, www.stmartin-in-the-fields.org). The affordable Café in the Crypt has just the right spooky, tables-on-tombstones ambience (Mon–Sat 10:00–20:00, Sun 12:00–20:30).

London Eye Ferris Wheel—This grand Ferris wheel is a delight for the whole family (opposite Big Ben, on the South Bank near Westminster Bridge). For details, see page 45.

Changing of the Guard—Kids enjoy the bands and pageantry of the Buckingham Palace Changing of the Guard, but little ones get a better view at the inspection: 11:00 at Wellington Barracks (see page 38). Horse-lovers enjoy the **Horse Guards'** colorful dismounting ceremony daily at 16:00 (on Whitehall, between Trafalgar Square and #10 Downing Street, Tube: Westminster); for details, see page 31.

Piccadilly Circus—This titillating district has lots of Planet Hollywood–type amusements, such as Segaworld and the Guinness Hall of World Records. Be careful of fast-fingered riffraff. For details on the district, see page 33. Hamleys toy store is just two blocks up Regent Street at #188 (hours listed above).

In West London

Natural History Museum—This wonderful world of dinosaurs, volcanoes, meteors, and creepy-crawlies offers creative interactive displays (free, possible fee for special exhibits, adults must accompany children under 12, Mon–Sat 10:00–17:50, Sun 11:00–17:50, last entrance 15:30, long tunnel leads directly from South Kensington Tube station to museum, tel. 020/7942-5000, exhibit info and reservations tel. 020/7942-5011, www.nhm.ac.uk). For details, see page 41.

In North London

Madame Tussaud's Waxworks—This is popular with kids (in spite of the lines) for its gory stuff, pop and movie stars, everyone's favorite royals, and more (£14.95, children-£10.50, under 5 free, tickets include entrance to the London Planetarium, Jan–Sept daily 9:00–17:30, Oct–Dec Mon–Fri 10:00–17:30, Sat–Sun 9:30–17:30, last entry 30 min before closing, Marylebone Road, Tube: Baker Street, tel. 0870/400-3000, www.madame-tussauds.com). For details and tips on crowd avoidance, see page 36.

London Zoo—This venerable zoo, with more than 8,000 animals, is one of the best in the world (£11, children-£8, family-£26, daily 10:00–17:30, last entry 16:30, in Regent's Park, Tube: Camden Town, then bus #274, tel. 020/7722-3333). Call for feeding and event times.

Fun Transportation

Thames Cruise—Young sailors delight in boats. Westminster Pier (near Big Ben) offers the most action, with boats to the Tower of London, Greenwich, and Kew Gardens. For details, see page 27.

Hop-on, Hop-off London Bus Tours—These two-hour double-decker bus tours, which drive by all the biggies, are fun for kids and stress-free for parents. You can stay on the bus the entire time, or "hop-on and hop-off" at any of the 20-plus stops and catch a later bus (4–6/hr in summer, 3/hr in winter). To find out how to get a special price with this book, see page 26. The Original London Sightseeing Tour's language bus (marked with lots of flags or a green triangle) has a kids' track on the earphones, but then you miss the live guide.

Day Trip

Legoland Windsor—If your kids are loopy over Legos, they'll love a day trip to Legoland Windsor (£19, children-£16, under 3 free, £10 if you enter during last 2 hrs, CC, April–Oct daily

10:00–17:00, 18:00, or 19:00 depending upon season and day, closed most Tue–Wed in Sept–Oct, closed Nov–March except Dec 21–Jan 5, easy train and bus connections from London, clearly signposted, easy free parking, next to Windsor Castle, tel. 08705/040-404, www.legoland.co.uk). For details, see page 223.

What to Avoid

The **London Dungeon**'s popularity with teenagers makes it one of London's most-visited sights. I enjoy gore and torture as much as the next boy, but this is lousy gore and torture, and I would not waste the time or money on it with my child.

SHOPPING

Consider five ways to shop in London:

1) If all you need are souvenirs, a surgical strike at any souvenir shop will do.

2) Large department stores offer relatively painless one-stop shopping. Consider the down-to-earth Marks & Spencer (Mon–Fri 9:00–20:00, Sat 9:00–21:00, Sun 12:00–18:00, 173 Oxford Street, Tube: Oxford Circus; another at 458 Oxford Street, Tube: Bond Street or Marble Arch).

3) Connect small shops with a pleasant walk (see "Oxford Circus to Piccadilly Walk," below).

4) For flea-market fun, try one of the many street markets.

5) Gawkers or serious bidders can attend auctions.

Most stores are open Monday through Saturday from roughly 10:00 to 18:00, with a late night (until 19:00 or 20:00) on Wednesday or Thursday, depending on the neighborhood. On Sunday, when some stores are closed, shoppers hit the street markets.

Fancy Department Stores in East London

Harrods—Filled with wonderful displays, Harrods is London's most famous and touristy department store. Big yet classy, Harrods has everything from elephants to toothbrushes. The food halls (ground floor) are sights to savor. If nothing else, ride the ornate Egyptian escalator (Mon–Sat 10:00–19:00, closed Sun, mandatory storage for big backpacks-£2.50, on Brompton Road, Tube: Knightsbridge, tel. 020/7730-1234). Many readers report that Harrods is overpriced (its £1 toilets are the most expensive in Europe), snooty, and teeming with American and Japanese tourists. Still, it's the palace of department stores. The nearby Beauchamp Place is lined with classy and fascinating shops.

Harvey Nichols—Once Princess Diana's favorite, "Harvey Nick's" remains the department store du jour (Mon, Tue, Sat 10:00–19:00, Wed–Fri until 20:00, Sun 12:00–18:00, near Harrods, Tube: Knightsbridge, 109 Knightsbridge, www.harveynichols.com). Want to pick up a little £20 scarf for the wife? You won't do it here, where they're more like £200. The store's fifth floor is a veritable food fest, with a gourmet grocery store, a fancy (smoky) restaurant, a Yo! Sushi bar, and a lively café. Consider a take-away tray of sushi to eat on a bench in the Hyde Park rose garden two blocks away. On Friday nights, the café hosts a popular "Film on Five" event: A three-course dinner followed by recently released films shown on big-screen televisions (£35, 20:00–24:00, for reservations call 020/7201-8562).

Oxford Circus to Piccadilly Walk

For this walk from Oxford Circus to Piccadilly Street, allow three-quarters of a mile (and only you know how much money and time). If you'd like to stop for high tea at Fortnum & Mason (Mon–Sat 15:00–17:30), start this walk after lunch. Many stores are open on Sunday from 12:00 to 18:00.

Starting from the Oxford Circus Tube stop, Regent Street leads past a diverse array of places to shop, all on the left-hand (east) side of the street. You'll find the following: the pricey **Laura Ashley;** then **Liberty,** a big, stately, locals' favorite department store (Mon–Wed 10:00–18:30, Thu until 20:00, Fri–Sat until 19:00, Sun 12:00–18:00, 214 Regent Street); the once-upon-a-decade hip **Carnaby Street** a block away (with cafés and boutiques selling clothes, shoes, handmade soap, and so on; turn left at first alley after Liberty onto Foubert's Place); and **Hamleys,** the biggest toy store in Britain—seven floors buzzing with 28,000 toys, managed by a staff of 200. At the "Bear Factory," kids can get a made-to-order teddy bear by picking out a "bear skin" and watch while it's stuffed and sewn (Mon–Sat 10:00-20:00, Sun 12:00–18:00, 188 Regent Street, tel. 020/8752-2277, www.hamleys.co.uk). Farther on is **Waterford Wedgwood** (at #158), **The Scotch House** (at #165, across the street from Waterford; knits, sweaters, woolens), and the **British Air Travel Shops,** with accessories, guidebooks, travel agents, a travelers' clinic, and a WC (Mon–Fri 9:30–18:00, Sat 10:00–16:00, tel. 020/7434-4700). Next comes the **Disney Store** (at #144), **Lush** (#80; stop in to sniff the earthy/fruity/spicy soap slabs), **Starbucks,** and Piccadilly Circus.

Sotheby's main gallery for bidders to review items for upcoming auctions is two blocks off Regent Street (down Maddox Street, left on New Bond Street; see description on page 300).

From Piccadilly Circus, turn right and wander down Piccadilly Street. On your left, escape from the frenzy of Piccadilly into the

Oxford Circus to Piccadilly Walk

1. Laura Ashley
2. Liberty department store
3. Carnaby Street
4. Hamleys Toy Store
5. Warner Brothers Studio Store
6. Waterford Wedgwood, British Air Travel Shops
7. Disney Store
8. The Scotch House & Starbucks
9. Sotheby's auction
10. St. James Church & flea market, Aroma Café
11. Fortnum & Mason, St. James Rest.
12. French Travel Center
13. Burlington Arcade
14. Ritz Hotel

quiet of **Waterstone's,** Europe's largest bookstore (housed in a former men's clothing store). Page through seven orderly floors. The fifth floor offers a hip bar with minimalist furniture and great views of the London Eye, Big Ben, and Westminster's towers (Mon–Sat 10:00–23:00, Sun 12:00–18:00, 203 Piccadilly, tel. 020/7851-2400). Next you'll pass Christopher Wren's **St. James Church** (with free lunchtime concerts at 13:00, the leafy **Aroma Café**, and a tiny all-day flea market: Tue—antiques, Wed–Sat—crafts, closed Sun–Mon) then **Fortnum & Mason,** an extremely classy department store. Fortnum—with lush, rich displays and deep red carpet—feels more sumptuous than Harrods. Consider a traditional tea in its **St. James Restaurant,** on the fourth floor (£18, Mon–Sat 15:00–17:30, closed Sun, dress up a bit for this, 181 Piccadilly, tel. 020/7734-8040 ext. 241). As you relax to piano music in plush seats under the elegant tearoom's chandeliers, you'll get the standard three-tiered silver tea tray: finger sandwiches on the bottom, fresh scones with jam and clotted cream on the first floor, and decadent pastries and "tartlets" on the top floor, with unlimited tea. Consider it dinner.

Just past Fortnum & Mason is the **French Travel Center,** across the street is the delightful **Burlington Arcade,** and a block farther down is the original **Ritz Hotel,** where the tea is much fancier.

Street Markets

Antique buffs, people-watchers, and folks who brake for garage sales love London's street markets. There's some good early-morning market activity somewhere any day of the week. The best are Portobello Road and Camden Market. Any London TI has a complete, up-to-date list. If you like to haggle, there are no holds barred in London's street markets. Warning: Markets attract two kinds of people—tourists and pickpockets.

Portobello Road Market—This flea market, with 2,000 stalls (open daily but hopping on Sat), has three sections: antiques at one end, produce in the middle, and clothing and books at the other end. Antiques are featured on Saturday (roughly Mon–Sat 10:00–17:00, Tube: Notting Hill Gate, near recommended B&Bs, tel. 020/7229-8354).

Camden Lock Market—This huge, trendy arts-and-crafts festival—London's fourth-most-popular tourist attraction—is held daily from 10:00 to 18:00 (Tube: Camden Town, tel. 020/7284-2084, www.camdenlock.net).

Brixton Market—Here the food, clothing, records, and hair-braiding throb with an Afro-Caribbean beat (Mon–Sat 9:00–18:00, closes at about 13:00 on Wed, Tube: Brixton).

Petticoat Lane Market—Expect budget clothing, leather, shoes, watches, jewelry, and crowds (Sun 9:00–14:00, sometimes later, Tube: Liverpool Street).

Spitalfields Market—This features a lively organic food market (with eateries), crafts, trendy clothes, bags, and an antique market (Mon–Fri 9:00–18:00, Sun 9:00–17:00, closed Sat, Tube: Liverpool Street, tel. 020/7377-1496).

Greenwich Market—You'll find homemade crafts, bric-a-brac, antiques, and clothing (Thu–Sun 9:30–17:00, biggest on Sun; Thu—antiques, Fri—bric-a-brac, Sat–Sun—crafts, www.greenwich-market.co.uk). See pages 219 and 222 for information on Greenwich's sights and transportation connections.

Famous Auctions

London's famous auctioneers welcome the curious public for viewing and bidding. For schedules, call **Sotheby's** (Mon–Fri 9:00–16:30, closed Sat–Sun, 34–35 New Bond Street, Tube: Oxford Circus, tel. 020/7293-5000, www.sothebys.com) or **Christie's** (Mon–Fri 9:00–16:30, Tue until 20:00, closed Sat–Sun, 8 King Street, Tube: Green Park, tel. 020/7839-9060, www.christies.com).

ENTERTAINMENT

London bubbles with top-notch entertainment seven days a week. Everything's listed in the weekly entertainment magazines (such as *Time Out*), available at newsstands. Choose from classical, jazz, rock, and far-out music, Gilbert and Sullivan, dance, comedy, Baha'i meetings, poetry readings, spectator sports, film, and theater. In Leicester Square, you'll find movies that have yet to be released in the States—if Hugh Grant is attending an opening-night premier in London, it will likely be at one of the big movie houses here.

Theater (a.k.a. "Theatre")

London's theater rivals Broadway's in quality and beats it in price. Choose from Shakespeare, musicals, comedy, thrillers, sex farces, cutting-edge fringe, revivals starring movie celebs, and more. London does it all well. I prefer big, glitzy—even bombastic—musicals over serious chamber dramas, simply because London can deliver the lights, sound, dancers, and multimedia spectacle I rarely get back home.

Most theaters, marked on tourist maps, are found in the West End between Piccadilly and Covent Garden. Box offices, hotels, and TIs offer a handy *Theatre Guide*. Performances are nightly except Sunday, usually with one or two matinees a week (Shakespeare's Globe is the rare theater that does offer performances on Sunday, mid-May–Sept). Tickets range from about £8 to £40. Matinees are generally cheaper and rarely sell out.

To book a seat, simply call the theater box office directly, ask about seats and available dates, and buy a ticket with your credit card. You can call from the United States as easily as from England (check www.officiallondontheatre.co.uk, the American magazine *Variety*, or photocopy your hometown library's London newspaper theater section). Pick up your ticket 15 minutes before the show.

What's On in the West End

Here are some of the perennial favorites that you're likely to find among the West End's evening offerings. Generally, you can book tickets for free in person at the box office or for a £1–2.50 fee by telephone or online. See map on page 304 for locations.

Musicals

Blood Brothers—Liverpudlian twins are separated at birth and cross paths again after living different lives (£15–38, Mon–Sat 19:45, matinees Thu 15:00 and Sat 16:00, Phoenix Theatre, Charing Cross Road, Tube: Tottenham Court Road or Leicester Square, box office tel. 020/7369-1733).

Chicago—A chorus-girl-gone-bad forms a nightclub act with another murderess to bring in the bucks (£11–38, Mon–Thu and Sat 20:00, Fri 20:30, matinees Fri 17:00 and Sat 15:00, Adelphi Theatre, Strand, Tube: Covent Garden or Charing Cross, booking tel. 020/7344-0055, www.chicagothemusical.com).

Lion King—In this Disney extravaganza featuring music by Elton John, Simba the lion learns about the delicately balanced circle of life on the savanna (£18–43, Tue–Sat 19:30, matinees Wed and Sat 14:00 and Sun 15:00, Lyceum Theatre, Wellington Street, Tube: Charing Cross or Covent Garden, booking tel. 0870-243-9000 or tel. 0161/228-1953, theater info tel. 020/7420-8112, www.disney.co.uk/MusicalTheatre/TheLionKing/).

Mamma Mia—A bride-to-be reminisces to the strains of ABBA (£19–40, Mon–Thu and Sat 19:30, Fri 20:30, matinees Fri 17:00 and Sat 15:00, Prince Edward Theatre, Old Compton Street, Tube: Leicester Square, booking tel. 020/7447-5400).

Les Miserables—Claude-Michel Schönberg's musical adaptation of Victor Hugo's epic follows the life of Jean Valjean as he struggles with the social and political realities of 19th-century France (£9–40, Mon–Sat 19:30, matinees Thu and Sat 14:30,

For a booking fee, you can reserve online (www.ticketmaster.co.uk or www.firstcalltickets.com) or call Global Tickets (U.S. tel. 800/223-6108). While booking through an agency is quick and easy, prices are inflated by a standard 25 percent fee. Ticket agencies (whether in the U.S., at London's TIs, or scattered throughout the city) are scalpers with an address. If you're buying from an agency, look at the ticket carefully (your price should be no more than 30 percent over the printed face value; the 15 percent VAT is already

Palace Theatre, Cambridge Circus, Tube: Leicester Square, box office tel. 020/7434-0909, www.lesmis.com).

Phantom of the Opera—A mysterious masked man falls in love with a singer in this haunting Andrew Lloyd Webber musical about life beneath the stage of the Paris Opera (£10–40, Mon–Sat 19:45, matinees Wed and Sat 15:00, Her Majesty's Theatre, Haymarket, Tube: Piccadilly Circus, booking tel. 0870-890-1106, or tel. 020/7494-5400, www.thephantomoftheopera.com).

Comedies

Complete History of America—The Reduced Shakespeare Company brings you the humorous history of America in two hours (£8–30, Tue 20:00, Criterion Theatre, Piccadilly Circus, Tube: Piccadilly Circus, box office tel. 020/7413-1437, www.reduced-shakespeare.co.uk).

Complete Works of William Shakespeare—Get your Cliffs Notes here: The bard's best all packed into one sitting (£8–30; Wed–Sat 20:00; matinees Thu 15:00, Sat 17:00, and Sun 16:00; Criterion Theatre, Piccadilly Circus, Tube: Piccadilly Circus, box office tel. 020/7413-1437, www.reduced-shakespeare.co.uk).

Thrillers

The Mousetrap—Agatha Christie's whodunit about a murder in a country house continues to stump audiences after 50 years (£11.50–30, Mon–Sat 20:00, matinees Tue 14:45 and Sat 17:00, St. Martin's Theatre, West Street, Tube: Leicester Square, box office tel. 020/7836-1443).

The Woman in Black—The chilling tale of a solicitor who is haunted by what he learns when he closes a reclusive woman's affairs (£10–30, Mon–Sat 20:00, matinees Tue 15:00 and Sat 16:00, Fortune Theatre, Russell Street, Tube: Covent Garden, box office tel. 020/7836-2238, www.thewomaninblack.com).

included in the face value) and understand where you're sitting according to the floor plan (if your view is restricted, it will state this on the ticket; for floor plans of the various theaters, see www.theatremonkey.com). Agencies are worthwhile only if a show you've got to see is sold out at the box office. They scarf up hot tickets, planning to make a killing after the show is sold out. U.S. booking agencies get their tickets from another agency, adding even more to your expense by involving yet another middleman.

London Theatres

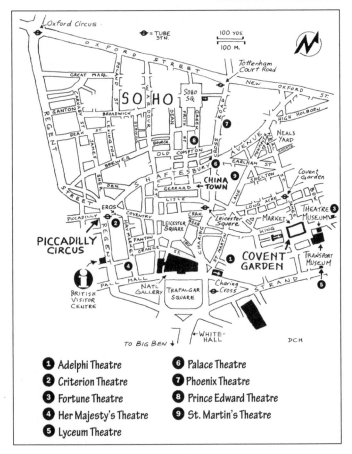

1 Adelphi Theatre
2 Criterion Theatre
3 Fortune Theatre
4 Her Majesty's Theatre
5 Lyceum Theatre

6 Palace Theatre
7 Phoenix Theatre
8 Prince Edward Theatre
9 St. Martin's Theatre

Many tickets sold on the streets are forgeries. With cheap international phone calls and credit cards, there's no reason not to book directly with the box office.

Theater Lingo: stalls (ground floor), dress circle (first balcony), upper circle (second balcony), balcony (sky-high third balcony), slips (cheap seats on the fringes). Many cheap seats have a restricted view (behind a pillar).

Cheap Theater Tricks: Most theaters offer cheap returned tickets, standing-room, matinee, and senior or student stand-by deals. These "concessions" are indicated with a "conc" or "s" in the listings. Picking up a late return can get you a great seat at a cheap-seat price. If a show is "sold out," there's usually a way to get a seat. Call the theater box office and ask how.

Half-Price Booth at Leicester Square: The famous half-price booth at Leicester (pron. LES-ter) Square sells discounted tickets for top-price seats to shows on the push list the day of the show only (Mon–Sat 10:00–19:00, Sun 12:00–15:00, matinee tickets from noon, cash only, lines often form early).

Here are some sample prices: A top-notch seat to the long-running *Les Miserables* (which rarely sells out) costs £40 bought directly from the theater, but only £22.50 at Leicester Square. The cheapest balcony seat (bought from the theater) is £15.

Half-price tickets can be a good deal, unless you want the cheapest seats or the hottest shows. But check the board; occasionally they sell cheap tickets to good shows. Note that the real half-price booth is a freestanding kiosk at the edge of the garden in Leicester Square. Several dishonest outfits nearby advertise "official half-price tickets." Avoid these.

Many theaters are so small that there's hardly a bad seat. After the lights go down, scooting up is less than a capital offense. Shakespeare did it.

West End Theaters—The commercial (non-subsidized) theaters cluster around Soho (especially along Shaftesbury Avenue) and Covent Garden. With a centuries-old tradition of pleasing the masses, these present London theater at its glitziest. See "What's On in the West End" sidebar.

Royal Shakespeare Company—If you'll ever enjoy Shakespeare, it'll be in Britain. The RSC performs at London's Barbican Centre from December through May and in Stratford year-round. To get a schedule, contact the RSC (Royal Shakespeare Theatre, Stratford-upon-Avon, CV37 6BB Warwickshire, tel. 01789/403-403, www.rsc.org.uk).

Tickets range in price from £10 to £30 (discounts for young and old). Book directly by telephone and credit card and pick up your ticket at the door at the Barbican Centre (office open daily 9:00–20:00, box office tel. 020/7638-8891 or 020/7628-2326, recorded information tel. 020/7628-9760, Silk Street, Tube: Barbican, book online at www.barbican.org.uk).

Shakespeare's Globe—To see Shakespeare in a replica of the theater for which he wrote his plays, attend a play at the Globe. This thatch-roofed, open-air round theater does the plays much as Shakespeare intended (with no amplification). The play's the thing from mid-May through September (usually Tue–Sat 14:00 and 19:30, Sun at either 13:00 and 18:30 or 16:00 only, no plays on Mon, tickets can be sold out months in advance). You'll pay £5 to stand and £12–27 to sit (usually on a backless bench; only a few rows and the pricier Gentlemen's Rooms have seats with backs). The £5 "groundling" tickets—while the only ones open to rain—are most fun. Scurry in early to stake out a spot on the stage's-edge leaning rail, where the most interaction with the actors occurs. You're a crude peasant. You can lean your elbows on the stage, munch a picnic dinner, or walk around. I've never enjoyed Shakespeare as much as here, performed as it was meant to be in the "wooden O." Plays can be long. Many groundlings leave before the end. If you like, hang out an hour before the finish and beg or buy a ticket from someone leaving early (groundlings are allowed to come and go).

The theater is on the South Bank directly across the Thames over the Millennium Bridge from St. Paul's Cathedral (Tube: Mansion House or London Bridge, tel. 020/7902-1500, box office tel. 020/7401-9919, www.shakespeares-globe.org). The Globe is inconvenient for public transport, but the courtesy phone in the lobby gets a minicab in minutes. (These have set fees—e.g., £8 to South Kensington—but generally cost less than a metered cab and provide fine and honest service.)

Fringe Theatre—London's rougher evening-entertainment scene is thriving, filling pages in *Time Out*. Choose from a wide range of fringe theater and comedy acts (generally £5).

Classical Music

For easy, cheap, or free concerts in historic churches, check the TIs' listings for lunch concerts (especially Wren's St. Bride's Church; St. James at Piccadilly—free lunch concerts on Mon, Wed, and Fri at 13:00, info tel. 020/7381-0441; and St. Martin-in-the-Fields—free lunch concerts on Mon, Tue, and Fri at 13:05, church tel. 020/7766-1100). St. Martin-in-the-Fields also hosts fine evening concerts by candlelight (£6–16, Thu–Sat at 19:30, CC, box office tel. 020/7839-8362).

At St. Paul's Cathedral, evensong is held Monday through Saturday at 17:00 and on Sunday at 15:15. At Westminster Abbey, it's sung weekdays at 17:00 (but not on Wed) and Saturday and Sunday at 15:00. Organ recitals are held on Sunday at Westminster Abbey (17:45, 40 min, small fee, tel. 020/7222-7110) and at St. Paul's (17:00, 30 min, free, tel. 020/7236-4128).

For a fun classical event (mid-July–early Sept), attend a "Prom Concert" during the annual festival at the Royal Albert Hall. Nightly concerts are offered at give-a-peasant-some-culture prices (£4 standing-room spots sold at the door, £7 restricted-view seats, most £22, depending on performance, CC, Tube: South Kensington, tel. 020/7589-8212, www.royalalberthall.com).

Some of the world's best opera is belted out at the prestigious

Royal Opera House, near Covent Garden (box office tel. 020/ 7304-4000, www.royalopera.org), and at the less-formal Sadler's Wells Theatre (Rosebery Avenue, Islington, Tube: Angel, box office tel. 020/7863-8000, www.sadlers-wells.com).

Evening Museum Visits
Many museums are open an evening or two during the week, offering fewer crowds. Here are the late nights for some of the major attractions:

Vinopolis: Mon until 21:00 and Sat until 20:00 (see page 48).

British Library: Tue until 20:00 (see tour on page 176).

National Gallery: Wed until 21:00 (see tour on page 116).

British Museum: Thu–Fri until 20:30, selected galleries and Reading Room only (see tour on page 94).

National Portrait Gallery: Thu–Fri until 21:00 (see tour on page 135).

Tate Modern: Fri–Sat until 22:00 (see tour on page 164).

Walks
Guided walks are offered several times a day. Original London Walks is the most established company (tel. 020/7624-3978, www.walks.com). Daytime walks vary: ancient London, museums, legal London, Dickens, Beatles, Jewish quarter, Christopher Wren, and so on. In the evening, expect a more limited choice: ghosts, Jack the Ripper, pubs, or a literary theme. Get the latest from a TI, fliers, or *Time Out.* Show up at the listed time and place, pay £5, and enjoy the two-hour tour.

Cruises
During the summer, boats sail as late as 21:00 between Westminster Pier (near Big Ben) and the Tower of London. (For details, see page 27.)

A handful of outfits run Thames River evening cruises with four-course meals and dancing. London Showboat offers the best value (£51, April–Oct Wed–Sun, departs 19:00 from Westminster Pier, Thu–Sat evening cruises through the winter, 3.5 hrs, tel. 020/7237-5134, www.citycruises.com). For more on cruising, get the Thames River Services brochure from a London TI.

TRANSPORTATION
CONNECTIONS

Flying into London's Heathrow Airport

Heathrow Airport is the world's fourth busiest. Think about it:
60 million passengers a year on 425,000 flights from 200 destinations riding 90 airlines...some kind of global maypole dance.
While many complain about it, I like it. It's user-friendly. Read
signs, ask questions. For Heathrow's airport, flight, and transfers
information, call the switchboard at 0870/000-0123. It has four
terminals: T-1 (mostly domestic flights, with some European),
T-2 (mainly European flights), T-3 (mostly flights from the
United States), and T-4 (British Air transatlantic flights and
BA flights to Paris, Amsterdam, and Athens). Taxis know which
terminal you'll need.

Each terminal has an airport information desk, car-rental
agencies, exchange bureaus, ATMs, a pharmacy, a VAT refund
desk (VAT info tel. 020/8910-3682; you must present the VAT
claim form from the retailer here to get your 15 percent tax
rebate on items purchased in Britain, see page 6 for details),
and a £3.50/day baggage-check desk (open 5:30–23:00). There
are post offices in T-2 and T-4. Each terminal has cheap eateries
(such as the cheery Food Village self-service cafeteria in T-3).
The American Express desk, in the Tube station at Terminal 4
(daily 7:00–19:00), has rates similar to the exchange bureaus
upstairs, but doesn't charge a commission (typically 1.5 percent)
for cashing any type of traveler's check.

Heathrow's small TI gives you all the help that London's
Victoria Station does, but with none of the crowds (daily 8:30–
18:00, 5-min walk from Terminal 3 in the tube station, follow
signs to Underground; bypass the queue for transit info to reach
the window for London questions). If you're riding the Airbus
into London, have your partner stay with the bags at the terminal

while you head over to the TI to get a free simple map and bro-
chures. If you're taking the Tube into London, buy a one-day
Travel Card pass to cover the ride (see below). Heathrow's
Internet Exchange provides Internet access 24 hours a day (T-3).

Transportation to London from Heathrow Airport

By Tube (Subway): For £3.60, the Tube takes you the 14 miles
to downtown London in 50 minutes (6/hr, depending on your
destination, may require a change). Even better, buy a £5 one-day
Travel Card that covers your trip into London and all your Tube
travel for the day (starting at 9:30). Buy it at the ticket window at
the Tube. You can hop on the Tube at any terminal.

By Airport Bus: The Airbus, running between the airport
and London's King's Cross station, serves the Notting Hill Gate
and Bayswater neighborhoods (£8, £12-round-trip, 2/hr, 60 min,
runs 5:00–21:15, departs from each terminal, buy ticket from
driver, tel. 0875/757-747). The Tube works fine, but with baggage I prefer the Airbus (assuming it serves my hotel neighborhood) because there are no connections underground and there's
a lovely view from the top of the double-decker bus. Ask the driver
to remind you when to get off. For people heading to the airport,
exact pickup times are clearly posted at each bus stop.

If you're staying in London's Victoria Station neighborhood, consider the National Express bus that runs between
Heathrow's central bus station and the Victoria Coach Station,
which is one block from Victoria Station (£7, kids go free, 2/hr,
45 min, 5:40–21:45 from Heathrow, 7:45–24:00 from Victoria,
tel. 08705/808-080).

By Taxi: Taxis from the airport cost about £40. For four
people traveling together, this can be a deal. Hotels can often
line up a cab back to the airport for £30. For the cheapest taxi to
the airport, don't order one from your hotel. Simply flag down a
few and ask them for their best "off-meter" rate. Another good
option is Hotelink, a door-to-door airport shuttle (Heathrow-
£15 per person, Gatwick-£22 per person, book the day before
departure, tel. 01293/532-244, www.hotelink.co.uk, e-mail:
reservations@hotelink.co.uk).

By Heathrow Express Train: This slick train service
zips you between Heathrow Airport and London's Paddington
Station. At Paddington Station, you're in the thick of the Tube
system, with easy access to any of my recommended neighborhoods—Notting Hill Gate is just two stops away. It's only
15 minutes to downtown from Terminals 1, 2, and 3 and
20 minutes from Terminal 4 (at the airport, you can use the
Express as a free transfer between terminals). Buy your ticket

to London before you board or pay a £2 surcharge to buy it on the train (£12, but ask about discount promos at Heathrow ticket desk, kids under 16 ride free if you buy your ticket before boarding, CC, covered by Britrail pass, 4/hr, daily 5:10–23:30, tel. 0845/600-1515, www.heathrowexpress.co.uk). A "Go Further" ticket (£13.50) includes one Tube ride from Paddington to get you to your hotel (valid only on same day and in Zone 1, saves time). For one person on a budget, combining the Heathrow Express with either a Tube or taxi ride (between your hotel and Paddington) is nearly as fast and half the cost of taking a cab directly to (or from) the airport.

Buses from Heathrow to Destinations beyond London
The **National Express Central Bus Station** offers direct bus connections to **Gatwick Airport** (4/hr, 70 min), departing just outside arrivals at all terminals; there are two services: Speedlink for £17 and Jetlink for £14. To **Bath,** direct buses run daily from Heathrow (11/day, 2.5 hrs, £13, tel. 08705-757-747). BritRail passholders may prefer the 2.5-hour Heathrow-Bath bus/train connection via Reading (£9 for bus, rail portion free with pass, otherwise £29.20 total, payable at desk in terminal, CC); first catch the twice-hourly RailAir Link shuttle bus to Reading (pron. RED-ding), then hop on the hourly express train to Bath. Most Heathrow buses depart from the common area serving Terminals 1, 2, and 3 (a 5-min walk from any of these terminals), although some depart from T-4 (bus tel. 08705-747-777).

Flying into London's Gatwick Airport
More and more flights, especially charters, land at Gatwick Airport, halfway between London and the southern coast (recorded airport info tel. 0870/000-2468). Express trains— clearly the best way into London from here—shuttle conveniently between Gatwick and London's Victoria Station (£11, £21 round-trip, children under 5 free, 4/hr during day, 1–2/hr at night, 30 min, runs 24 hrs daily, can purchase tickets on train at no extra charge, tel. 08705-301-530, www.gatwickexpress.co.uk). Or you can save a few pounds by taking South Central rail line's slower and less-frequent shuttle between Victoria Station and Gatwick (£8.20, 3/hr, 1/hr midnight–04:00, 45 min, tel. 08457-484-950, www.southcentraltrains.co.uk).

To get to Bath from Gatwick, catch a bus to Heathrow and the bus to Bath from there.

To make a flight connection between Heathrow and Gatwick (see "Buses," above), allow three hours between your arrival at one airport and departure at the other.

London's Other Airports

If you're flying into or out of **Stansted** (airport tel. 0870-0000-303), you can take the Airbus between the airport and downtown London's Victoria Coach Station (£8, 2/hr, 1.5 hrs, runs 4:00–24:00, picks up and stops throughout London, tel. 08705-747-777) or take the Stansted Airport Rail Link (£13, departs London's Liverpool Station, 40 min, 2–4/hr, 5:00–23:00, tel. 08705-301-530, www.stanstedexpress.com).

For **Luton** (airport tel. 01582/405-100, www.london-luton .com), take Green Line's bus #757, which runs between the airport and London's Victoria Station at Buckingham Palace Road—stop 6 (£8.50, £7.50 for easyJet passengers, 2/hr, 1–1.25 hrs depending on time of day, runs 4:30–24:00, tel. 0870-608-7261, www.greenline.co.uk).

Discounted Flights from London

Although **bmi british midland** has been around the longest, the others generally offer cheaper flights.

With **bmi british midland,** you can fly inexpensively to Edinburgh (8/day, 75 min, as little as £30 one-way or £60 round-trip); to Dublin, Ireland (8/day, 75 min, starting at £52 one-way, £104 round-trip); to Paris (from £36 one-way, £72 round-trip); to Brussels (from £45/£90), to Amsterdam (from £34/£68), and more. For the latest, call British tel. 0870-607-0555 or U.S. tel. 800/788-0555 (check www.flybmi.com and their subsidiary, bmi baby, at www.bmibaby.com). Book in advance. Although you can book right up until the flight departs, but the cheap seats will have sold out long before, leaving the most expensive seats for latecomers. With no frills and cheap fares, **easyJet,** flies mostly from Luton and Gatwick. Prices are based on demand, so the least popular routes make for the cheapest fares, especially if you book early (tel. 0870-600-0000, www.easyjet.com).

Ryanair is a creative Irish airline that prides itself on offering the lowest fares. It flies from London (mostly Stansted airport) to often obscure airports in Dublin, Glasgow, Frankfurt, Stockholm, Oslo, Venice, Turin, and many others. Sample fares: London–Dublin—£78 round-trip (sometimes as low as £25), London–Frankfurt—£67 round-trip (Irish tel. 01/609-7881, British tel. 0870-333-1231, www.ryanair.com). Because they offer promotional deals any time of year, it's not essential that you book long in advance to get the best deals.

Virgin Express is a British-owned company with good rates (book by phone and pick up ticket at airport an hour before your flight, tel. 020/7744-0004, www.virgin-express.com). Virgin

Express flies from London Heathrow and Brussels. From its hub in Brussels, you can connect cheaply to Barcelona, Madrid, Nice, Malaga, Copenhagen, Rome, or Milan (round-trip from Brussels to Rome for as little as £105). Their prices stay the same whether or not you book in advance.

Trains and Buses

London, Britain's major transportation hub, has a different train station for each region. Waterloo handles the Eurostar to Paris. King's Cross covers northeast England and Scotland (tel. 08457-225-225). Paddington covers west and southwest England (Bath) and South Wales (tel. 08457-000-125). For the others, call 08457-484-950. Also see the BritRail Routes map in this chapter. Note that for security reasons, stations offer a left-luggage service (£5/day) rather than lockers.

National Express' excellent bus service is considerably cheaper than trains. (For a busy signal, call 08705-808-080, or visit www.nationalexpress.co.uk or the bus station a block southwest of Victoria Station.)

To Bath: Trains leave London's Paddington Station every hour between 7:00 and 19:00 (at a quarter after) for the 75-minute ride to Bath (costs £32 if you leave after 9:30).

To get to Bath via Stonehenge, consider taking a guided bus tour from London to Stonehenge and Bath and abandoning the tour in Bath. Evan Evans' tour is fully guided for £52 (includes admissions). The tour leaves from the Victoria Coach station daily every morning at 9:00 (you can stow your bag under the bus), stops in Stonehenge (45 min), and then stops in Bath for lunch and a city tour before returning to London (offered year-round). You can book the tour at the Victoria Coach station, the Evan Evans' office (258 Vauxhall Bridge Road, near Victoria Coach station, tel. 020/7950-1777, www.evanevans.co.uk), or the Green Line Travel Office (4a Fountain Square, across from Victoria Coach station, tel. 020/7950-1777). Golden Tours also runs a fully guided Stonehenge–Bath tour for a similar price (departs from Fountain Square, located across from Victoria Coach Station, tel. 020/7233-6668, U.S. tel. 800/456-6303, www.goldentours.co.uk).

To Points North: Trains run hourly from London's King's Cross Station, stopping in York (2 hrs), Durham (3 hrs), and Edinburgh (5 hrs).

To Dublin, Ireland: The boat/rail journey takes between 10 and 11 hours and goes all day or all night (£24–35, 7/day, tel. 08705-143-219, www.eurolines.co.uk). Consider a cheap 70-minute Ryanair flight instead (see above).

BritRail Routes

KEY: ✳ MAP NOT TO SCALE

London Stations:

1 **VICTORIA** - S & S.E. ENG, CONN TO PARIS & BRUSSELS
2 **CHARING CROSS** - S.E. ENG
3 **WATERLOO** - S. ENGLAND, PARIS & BRUSS (CHUNNEL)
4 **LIVERPOOL ST.** - EAST ANGLIA, AMSTERDAM
5 **KING'S CROSS** - MIDLANDS, N.E. ENG., E. SCOTLAND
6 **ST. PANCRAS** - E. MIDLANDS
7 **EUSTON** - MIDLANDS, N.WALES, N.W.ENG., W.SCOT.
8 **PADDINGTON** - W ENG, S WALES

← RAIL --- BUS
⋯ FERRY WITH
(6H) CROSSING TIME
NOTE: FASTER ENGLISH
CHANNEL CROSSINGS WITH
HOVERCRAFT & HYDROFOIL
ON SOME RUNS CHECK!
THE CHUNNEL IS
FASTER STILL...

LONDON AIRPORTS: ✈
A - HEATHROW B - GATWICK
C - LUTON D - STANSTED

Crossing the Channel by Eurostar Train

The fastest and most convenient way to get from Big Ben to the Eiffel Tower is by rail. In London, advertisements claim "more businessmen travel from London to Paris on the Eurostar than on all airlines combined."

Eurostar is the speedy passenger train that zips you (and up to 800 others in 18 sleek cars) from downtown London to downtown Paris (15/day, last departure 19:23, 3 hrs) or Brussels (9/day, 3 hrs) faster and easier than flying. The train goes 80 mph in England and 190 mph on the Continent. (When the English segment gets up to speed, the journey time will shrink to 2 hours.) The actual tunnel crossing is a 20-minute, black, silent, 100-mile-per-hour non-event. Your ears won't even pop. You can go direct to Disneyland Paris (1/day, more frequent with transfer at Lille) or change at Lille to catch a TGV to Paris' Charles de Gaulle Airport.

Channel fares (essentially the same to Paris or Brussels) are reasonable but complicated. As with airfares, the most expensive and flexible option is a full-fare ticket with no restrictions on refundability. Cheaper tickets come with more restrictions— and sell out more quickly.

Prices vary depending on when you travel; whether you can live with restrictions; and whether you're eligible for any discounts (youth, seniors, and railpass holders all qualify). The various second-class Leisure Tickets are a good deal, but many require a round-trip purchase. Compare one-way fares with cheap round-trip fares (you can forget to return).

You can check and book fares by phone or online in the United States (U.S. tel. 800/EUROSTAR, www.eurostar.com or www.raileurope.com, prices listed in dollars) or in Britain (British tel. 08705-186-186, www.eurostar.co.uk, prices listed in pounds). These are two different companies, often with different prices and discount deals on similar tickets (see below)— if you order from the United States, check out both. (If you buy from the U.S. company, you'll pay a FedEx charge for ticket delivery in the United States; if you book with the British company, you'll pick up your ticket at Waterloo Station.) In Europe, you can get your Eurostar ticket at any major train station in any country or at any travel agency that handles train tickets (expect a booking fee).

Note that Britain's time zone is one hour earlier than the Continent's. Times listed on tickets are local times.

Here are typical fares available in 2002. For 2003 fares, check the Eurostar phone numbers and Web sites listed above. Notice that sometimes it's a better deal to buy your ticket in Britain instead of the United States—or vice-versa.

Building the Chunnel

The toughest obstacle to building a tunnel under the English Channel was overcome in 1986, when long-time rivals Britain and France reached an agreement to build it together. Britain began in Folkestone, France in Calais, planning a rendezvous in the middle.

By 1988, specially made machines three football fields long were boring 25-foot-long holes under the ground. The dirt they hauled out became landfill in Britain and a hill in France. Crews inched forward 100 feet a day until June 1991, when French and English workers broke through and shook hands midway across the Channel—the tunnel was complete. Rail service began in 1994.

The Chunnel is 31 miles long (24 miles of it underwater) and 26 feet wide. It sits 130 feet below the seabed in a chalky layer of sediment. It's segmented into three separate tunnels—two for trains (one in each direction) and one for service and ventilation. The walls are concrete panels and rebar fixed to the rock around it. Sixteen-thousand-horsepower engines pull 850 tons of railcars and passengers at speeds up to 100 mph through the tunnel.

The ambitious project—the world's longest undersea tunnel—helped to show the European community that cooperation between nations could benefit everyone.

Eurostar Full-Fare Tickets

Full-fare tickets are fully refundable even after the departure date. As with plane tickets, you'll pay more to have fewer restrictions. In 2002, one-way Business First cost £210 in Britain/$279 in the U.S. and included a meal (a dinner departure nets you more grub than breakfast). Full-fare second-class tickets (Standard Flexi) cost £170/$199.

Cheaper Tickets

Since full-fare, no-restrictions tickets are so expensive, most travelers sacrifice flexibility for a cheaper ticket with more restrictions. Second class is plenty comfortable, making first class an unnecessary expense for most; prices listed below are for second class unless otherwise noted. Some of these tickets are available only in Britain, others only in the United States. They are listed roughly from most expensive to cheapest (with more restrictions as you move down the list).

Leisure Flexi: £160 round-trip (round-trip purchase required, partially refundable before departure date, not available in U.S.).

U.S. Leisure: $139 one-way (partially refundable before departure date, not available in Britain).

Leisure: £120 round-trip (round-trip purchase required, nonrefundable, not available in U.S.).

Leisure Apex 7: £95 round-trip (round-trip purchase required, nonrefundable, purchase at least 7 days in advance, not available in U.S.).

Leisure Apex 14: £79/$178 round-trip (round-trip purchase required, nonrefundable, purchase at least 14 days in advance, stay 2 nights or over a Sat, available in U.S. and Britain).

Weekend Day Return: £60 for same-day round-trip on a Saturday or Sunday (round-trip purchase required, nonrefundable, not available in U.S.). Note that this round-trip ticket is cheaper than many one-way tickets.

Eurostar Discounts

For Railpass Holders: Discounts are available in the U.S. or Britain to travelers holding railpasses that include France, Belgium, or Britain (£50/$75 one-way for second-class, £100/$155 one-way for first). In Britain, passholder tickets can be issued only at the Eurostar office in Waterloo Station or the American Express office in Victoria Station—not at any other stations. You can also order them by phone, then pick them up at Waterloo Station.

For Youth and Seniors: Discounts are available in the U.S. and Britain for children under 12 (£30/$69 one-way for second class) and youths under 26 (£50/$79 one-way for second class). Only in the U.S. can seniors over 60 get discounts ($189 one-way for first class).

Crossing the Channel without Eurostar

By Bus and Boat or Train and Boat: The old-fashioned way of crossing the Channel is cheaper than crossing by Eurostar. It's also twice as romantic, complicated, and time-consuming. You'll get better prices arranging your trip in London than you would in the United States. Taking the bus is cheapest, and round-trips are a bargain.

By Bus: To Paris, Brussels, or Amsterdam from Victoria Coach Station (via boat or Chunnel): £32 one-way, £52 round-trip; 7 hrs to Paris—7/day; 7 hrs to Brussels—10/day; 11.25 hrs to Amsterdam—6/day; day or overnight, on Eurolines (tel. 08705/143-219, www.eurolines.co.uk).

The **Hoverspeed ferry** runs between Dover, England, and Calais, France (tel. 08705/240-241 or 0870/240-8070, www.hoverspeed.com). Hoverspeed sells London–Paris rail and ferry packages: £39 one-way; £49 round-trip with five-day return; and £58 round-trip over more than five days. You can buy this package deal in person at Waterloo and Charing Cross stations. If you book by phone (number listed above), you must book at least two weeks in advance, and the ticket will be mailed to you (no ticket pickup at station for bookings by phone).

By **P&O Stena Line ferry** from Dover to Calais: £26 one-way; £48 round-trip with five-day return; £52 round-trip over more than five days (tel. 0870-600-0613, www.posl.com). Prices are for the ferry only; you need to book your own train tickets— see P&O's Web site for details.

By Plane: Typical fares are £110 regular, less for student standby. Check with the budget airlines for cheap round-trip fares to Paris (see "Discounted Flights from London," page 311).

HISTORY

ENGLISH HISTORY—
FOUR MILLENNIA IN THREE PAGES
Invasions (2000 B.C.–A.D. 1000)

The mysterious Stonehenge builders were replaced by the Celts, whose Druid priests made human sacrifices and worshipped trees.

The Romans brought 500 years of peace and stability, establishing London (Londinium) as a major city. Then civilization fell for a thousand years, to German pirates (Angles and Saxons), Danish Vikings and, finally, William the Conqueror (A.D. 1066). During these "Dark Ages," Christians had to battle pagan gods for supremacy of the island.

> *People*: Boadicea, Julius Caesar, "King Arthur," "Beowulf," Alfred the Great
> *Sights*: Boadicea statue, Roman Wall, Lindisfarne Gospels

Wars with France, Wars of the Roses (1066–1500)

French-speaking kings ruled England, and English-speaking kings invaded France as the two budding nations defined their modern borders. In the 1400s, feuding English nobles duked it out for control of the country.

> *People*: Richard the Lionhearted, Robin Hood, Eleanor of Aquitaine, Chaucer, Joan of Arc
> *Sights*: Tower of London, Magna Carta, Westminster Abbey, Temple Church

1500s—The Tudor Renaissance

Powerful Henry VIII thrust England onto the world stage by defying the Pope and sparking a century of Protestant/Catholic warfare. His daughter, Elizabeth I, reigned over a cultural renaissance of sea exploration, scientific discovery and literature known as the "Elizabethan Age."

    People: Anne Boleyn, Thomas More, "Bloody Mary," William Shakespeare, Sir Francis Drake, Sir Walter Raleigh

    Sights: Shakespeare folios and Shakespeare's Globe, Tower of London execution site, Chapel of Henry VII and Elizabeth's tomb in Westminster Abbey, portraits of Henry VIII's wives and daughter Elizabeth

1600s—Catholic Kings vs. Protestant Parliament

The "Virgin Queen" Elizabeth died without heirs, and the crown passed to the Catholic Stuart family. Their arrogant, divine-right management style sparked a Civil War, led by the commoner Oliver Cromwell, who beheaded the king and briefly established a Commonwealth. The monarchy returned, along with back-to-back disasters—the Great Plague (1665) and Great Fire (1666) that leveled London.

    People: King James I (Bible), Charles I (headless), Christopher Wren (St. Paul's), Isaac Newton (apple)

    Sights: St. Paul's and other Wren churches, Fire Monument, City of London, Banqueting House, Crown Jewels, King James Bible

1700s—Colonial Expansion

Britannia ruled the waves and became a world power, exploiting the wealth of India, Africa, Australia and America ... at least, until the Yanks revolted in the "American War."

    People: King George III, James Cook, Handel, Lord Nelson, Duke of Wellington

    Sights: Portraits by Reynolds and Gainesborough in the Tate Britain

1800s—Victorian Gentility and the Industrial Revolution

Britain under Queen Victoria reigned supreme, steaming into the modern age with railroads, factories, electricity, telephones, and the first underground. Meanwhile, Romantic poets longed for the innocence of Nature, Charles Dickens questioned the social order, and Rudyard Kipling criticized the colonial system.

People: Byron-Wordsworth-Keats-Shelley-Coleridge-Blake, James Watt, Charles Darwin, Tennyson, "Sherlock Holmes," Jack the Ripper

Sights: Big Ben and Halls of Parliament, Buckingham Palace, The Mall, Hyde Park, the Tube, writers' manuscripts in the British Library, Poets' Corner in Westminster Abbey

20th Century—World Wars and Recovery

Two World Wars whittled Britain down from a world empire to an island chain struggling to compete in a global economy. The German Blitz in WWII leveled London. Colonies rebelled and gained their independence, then flooded London with immigrants. Longtime residents fled on the Tube for London's suburbs.

In the 1960s, "Swinging London" became a center for rock music, film, theatre, youth culture, and Austin Powers–style joie de vivre. The 1970s brought massive unemployment, and a conservative reaction in the 1980s and early 1990s.

People: T.E. Lawrence (of Arabia), Winston Churchill, Edward VIII and Wallis Simpson, T. S. Eliot, Dylan Thomas, John-Paul-George-Ringo (Beatles), The Rolling Stones, The Who, Elton John, David Bowie, Margaret Thatcher, John Major

Sights: Cabinet War Rooms, Cenotaph, Westminster Abbey tombs, Blitz photos at St. Paul's, Beatles memorabilia in British Library, Rock Circus at Piccadilly Circus

2003—London Today

London is one of the world's major cultural capitals, an exporter of art, science, and technology.

People: Tony Blair, Hugh Grant, Beck, Monty Python alumni,

Anthony Hopkins, Martin Amis, Tom Stoppard, Prince William

Sights: The London Eye Ferris Wheel, West End theaters, Tate Modern contemporary art exhibits

TIMELINE OF LONDON HISTORY

c. 1700 B.C. Stone slabs erected to create ceremonial site . . . Stonehenge.

A.D. 43 Romans defeat the Celtic locals and establish Londinium as a seaport. They build the original London Bridge and a city wall, encompassing one square mile, which sets the city boundaries for 1,500 years.

c. 60 Boadicea defies the Romans and burns Londinium before the revolt is squelched.

c. 200 London is the thriving, river-trading, walled, Latin-speaking capital of Roman-dominated England.

410 The city of Rome is looted by invaders, and the Europe-wide Roman infrastructure crumbles. England is soon overrun by "barbarian" Anglo-Saxon invaders from Germany. This begins 500 years of Viking invasions, poverty, ignorance, superstition, and hand-me-down leotards—the "Dark Ages."

886 King Alfred the Great liberates London from Danish Vikings; he helps reunite England, reestablish Christianity, and encourage learning.

1052 King Edward the Confessor builds his palace and abbey a mile and a half from London at Westminster.

1066 England is conquered by Norman invaders under William the Conqueror, beginning two centuries of rule by French-speaking kings. London reasserts itself as a trade center.

1215 King John, under pressure from barons and London's powerful trade guilds, signs the Magna Carta, establishing that even kings must follow the rule of law.

1209 London Bridge—the famous stone version, topped with houses—is built. It stands until 1832.

1280 Old St. Paul's Cathedral is finished.

1337 Start of the "Hundred Years' War" with France.

1348 The Black Plague kills half of London.

1415 British victory over the French at Battle of Agincourt.

1455–85 Prosperous London plays king-maker in the Wars of the Roses, helping determine which noble becomes king.

1500   London's population swells to 50,000.

1534   Henry VIII breaks with Rome and dissolves monasteries, bringing religious strife. Generally speaking, London leans to the Protestant side.

1558   Elizabeth I is crowned, with London's backing. Her reign brings a renaissance of theater (Shakespeare), literature, science, discovery, and manners to the city.

1588   England's navy defeats the powerful Spanish armada and now rules the waves. Overseas trade brings the world's wealth directly to London's wharves.

1600   London, population 200,000, is Europe's largest city, expanding beyond the medieval walls, stretching westward along the river to Charing Cross.

1649   King Charles I is beheaded outside Whitehall as London backs the Protestant Parliament in England's Civil War (1642–48). Oliver Cromwell heads a democratic Commonwealth (1649–53) and then becomes Lord Protector (1653–59).

1660   Charles II, the son of Charles I, is invited to restore the monarchy.

1665   The Great Plague kills 100,000.

1666   The Great Fire rages for four days, destroying the wooden city. The city is rebuilt in stone, including Christopher Wren's new St. Paul's Cathedral and other churches.

1700   London's population is 500,000 and growing fast. One in 10 Brits lives in London.

1702   London's first daily newspapers hit the streets.

1776   Britain fights one of its colonies in the American War of Independence (1775–83).

1789   The French Revolution sparks decades of war with France.

1805   Lord Nelson defeats the French navy at Trafalgar (Spain), ending the threat of invasion by Napoleon.

1815   The Duke of Wellington defeats Napoleon for good at Waterloo (Belgium). Britain becomes Europe's #1 power.

c. 1830   Railroads lace the country together. The Industrial Revolution kicks into high gear.

1837   Eighteen-year-old Victoria becomes Queen, soon marries Prince Albert, and presides over an era of peace and middle-class values.

1851   With Britain at the peak of prosperity from its worldwide colonial empire, London—population one million—hosts a Great Exhibition in Hyde Park, trumpeting the latest triumphs of science and technology.

1863   First Underground line is built.

1914–18   World War I. Britain, France, and other allies battle Germany from trenches dug in the open fields of France and Belgium. A million British men die.

1936   King Edward VIII abdicates to marry an American commoner.

1939–45   World War II.

1940–41   The Blitz—preparing to invade the Isle, Nazi Germany air bombs Britain, and particularly London. Despite enormous devastation, Britain holds firm.

1945   Postwar recovery begins, aided by the United States. Many cheap, concrete (ugly) buildings rise from the rubble. Britain begins granting independence to many foreign colonies.

1964   Rock band The Beatles tours America, spreading "Swinging London" hipness to the world.

1970s   Labor strikes, unemployment, recession.

1980s   Conservative government of Margaret Thatcher.

1981   Prince Charles marries Lady Diana Spencer.

1982   Britain battles Argentina over the Falkland Islands. Britain claims victory.

1992   Britain is part of the European Union but maintains her distance.

1994   Channel Tunnel opens, linking London with Paris and Brussels.

1994   Tony Blair becomes Prime Minister, signaling a shift toward moderate liberalism.

1997   Princess Di dies in a car crash in Paris. The nation and the world mourn.

2000   London hosts big millennium celebration, building a Ferris wheel, Millennium Bridge, and the Millennium Dome exhibition.

2002   Many E.U. nations adopt the euro currency, but Britain sticks with pounds sterling. Queen Elizabeth II celebrates her 50-year Jubilee.

2003   You visit Britain and make your own history.

London's History Is Britain's History

When Julius Caesar landed on the misty and mysterious isle of Britain in 55 B.C., England entered the history books. The primitive Celtic tribes he conquered were themselves invaders, who had earlier conquered the even more mysterious people who built

Royal Families: Past and Present

Royal Lineage

802–1066	Saxon and Danish kings
1066–1154	Norman invasion (William the Conqueror), Norman kings
1154–1399	Plantagenet
1399–1461	Lancaster
1462–1485	York
1485–1603	Tudor (Henry VIII, Elizabeth I)
1603–1649	Stuart (civil war and beheading of Charles I)
1649–1653	Commonwealth, no royal head of state
1653–1659	Protectorate, with Cromwell as Lord Protector
1660–1714	Restoration of Stuart monarchy
1714–1901	Hanover (four Georges, Victoria)
1901–1910	Edward VII
1910–present	Windsor (George V, Edward VIII, George VI, Elizabeth II)

The Royal Family Today

It seems you can't pick up a London newspaper without some mention of the latest scandal or oddity involving the Royal Family. Here they are:

Queen Elizabeth II wears the traditional crown of her great-great grandmother, Victoria. Her husband is **Prince Phillip** (he's not considered king).

Their son, **Prince Charles** (the Prince of Wales), is next in line to become king. In 1981, Charles married Lady Diana

Stonehenge. The Romans built towns and roads and established their capital at Londinium. The Celtic natives in Scotland and Wales, consisting of Gaels, Picts, and Scots, were not subdued so easily. The Romans built Hadrian's Wall near the Scottish border as protection against their troublesome northern neighbors. Even today, the Celtic language and influence are strongest in these far reaches of Britain.

As Rome fell, so fell Roman Britain, a victim of invaders and internal troubles. Barbarian tribes from Germany and Denmark, called Angles and Saxons, swept through the southern part of the island, establishing Angle-land. These were the days of the real King Arthur, possibly a Christianized Roman general fighting

Spencer (**"Princess Di"**) who, after their bitter divorce, died in a car crash in 1997. Their two sons, **William** and **Harry,** are next in line to the throne after their father.

The **Queen Mother** (or "Queen Mum") is the late mother of Queen Elizabeth II. Prince Charles' siblings are often in the news for their marital or dating escapades: **Princess Anne, Prince Andrew** (who married and divorced **Sarah "Fergie" Ferguson**), and **Prince Edward** (who married Di look-alike **Sophie Rhys-Jones**). **Camilla Parker Bowles** is Prince Charles' longtime girlfriend who is trying to gain respectability with the Queen and the public.

Royal Sightseeing

You can see the trappings of royalty at **Buckingham Palace** (the Queen's residence) with its Changing of the Guard; **Kensington Palace,** where members of the extended royal family rent apartments; **St. James' Palace,** the London home of Prince Charles and sons; **Althorp Estate** (80 miles from London), the childhood home and burial place of Princess Diana; **Windsor Castle,** a royal country home near London; and the **Crown Jewels** in the Tower of London.

Your best chances to actually see the Queen are on three public occasions: Opening of Parliament (late October), Remembrance Sunday (early November, at the Cenotaph), or Trooping the Colour (one Saturday in mid-June, parading down Whitehall and at Buckingham Palace).

Otherwise, check daily papers for the "Court Circular," which lists all public engagements of the royal family.

valiantly, but in vain, against invading barbarians. The island was plunged into 500 years of Dark Ages—wars, plagues, and poverty—lit only by the dim candle of a few learned Christian monks and missionaries trying to convert the barbarians. The sightseer sees little from this Saxon period.

Modern England began with yet another invasion. William the Conqueror and his Norman troops crossed the English Channel from France in 1066. William crowned himself king in Westminster Abbey (where all subsequent coronations would take place) and began building the Tower of London. French-speaking Norman kings ruled the country for two centuries. Then followed two centuries of civil wars, with various noble families vying for the crown. In one of the most bitter feuds, the York and Lancaster families fought the Wars of the Roses, so-called because of the white and red flowers the combatants chose as their symbols. Battles, intrigues, kings, nobles, and ladies imprisoned and executed in the Tower—it's a wonder the country survived its rulers.

England was finally united by the "third-party" Tudor family. Henry VIII, a Tudor, was England's Renaissance king. He was handsome, athletic, highly sexed, a poet, a scholar, and a musician. He was also arrogant, cruel, gluttonous, and paranoid. He went through six wives in 40 years, divorcing, imprisoning, or beheading them when they no longer suited his needs.

Henry also "divorced" England from the Catholic Church, establishing the Protestant Church of England (the Anglican Church) and setting in motion years of religious squabbles. He also "dissolved" the monasteries (around 1540), leaving just the shells of many formerly glorious abbeys dotting the countryside and pocketing their land and wealth for the crown.

Henry's daughter, Queen Elizabeth I, who reigned for 45 years, made England a great trading and naval power (defeating the Spanish armada) and presided over the Elizabethan era of great writers (such as Shakespeare) and scientists (such as Francis Bacon).

The long-standing quarrel between England's divine-right kings and the nobles in Parliament finally erupted into a civil war (1642). Parliament forces under the Protestant Puritan farmer Oliver Cromwell defeated—and beheaded—King Charles I. This civil war left its mark on much of what you'll see in England. Eventually, Parliament invited Charles' son to take the throne. This "restoration of the monarchy" was accompanied by a great colonial expansion and the rebuilding of London (including Christopher Wren's St. Paul's Cathedral), which had been devastated by the Great Fire of 1666.

Britain grew as a naval superpower, colonizing and trading with all parts of the globe. Admiral Horatio Nelson's victory over Napoleon's fleet at the Battle of Trafalgar secured her naval superiority ("Britannia rules the waves"). Ten years later, the Duke of Wellington stomped Napoleon on land at Waterloo. Nelson and Wellington—both buried in London's St. Paul's Cathedral—are memorialized by many arches, columns, and squares throughout England.

Economically, Britain led the world into the Industrial Age with her mills, factories, coal mines, and trains. By the time of Queen Victoria's reign (1837–1901), Britain was at the zenith of her power, with a colonial empire that covered one-fifth of the world.

The 20th century was not kind to Britain. Two world wars devastated the population. The Nazi blitzkrieg reduced much of London to rubble. The colonial empire dwindled to almost nothing, and Britain was no longer an economic superpower. The "Irish Troubles" were constant, as the Catholic inhabitants of British-ruled Northern Ireland fought for the independence their southern neighbors won decades ago. The war over the Falkland Islands in 1982 showed how little of the British Empire was left— and how determined the British were to hang on to what remains.

But the tradition (if not the substance) of greatness continues, presided over by Queen Elizabeth II, her husband Prince Philip, and their son Prince Charles. With economic problems, the turmoil between Charles and the late Princess Diana, and a relentless popular press, the royal family has had a tough time. But the queen has stayed above it all, and most British people still jump at an opportunity to see royalty. The massive outpouring of grief over the death of Princess Diana made it clear that the concept of royalty is still alive and well as Britain enters the third millennium.

Queen Elizabeth marked her 50th year on the throne in 2002 with a flurry of Golden Jubilee festivities. While many wonder who will succeed her, the case is fairly straightforward: The queen sees her job as a lifelong position, and legally, Charles (who wants to be king) cannot be skipped over for his son William. Given the longevity in the family (the Queen's mum, born in August of 1900 made it to 101 before she died in April 2002), Charles is in for a long wait.

Thumbnail Sketches of Famous Brits

Albert, Prince (1819–61)—German-born husband of Queen Victoria whose support of the arts and sciences enriched London. (See National Portrait Gallery Tour.)

Arthur, King (c. 600?)—A character of legend, perhaps based on a Roman Christian general battling barbarians after the Fall of Rome.

Boadicea (d. 61)—A queen of the isle's indigenous people, who defied Roman occupation, burning Londinium to the ground before being defeated. (See Westminster Walk.)

Beatles (1960s)—Rock music quartet (John Lennon, Paul McCartney, George Harrison, Ringo Starr) whose worldwide popularity brought counterculture ideas to the middle class. (See British Library Tour.)

Charles I (1600–49)—King beheaded after England's Civil War, which pitted a Catholic aristocracy against a Protestant Parliament. Parliament won. (See Westminster Walk, National Gallery Tour, and National Portrait Gallery Tour.)

Charles II (1630–85)—Son of Charles I who was invited to restore the monarchy under supervision by the Parliament. (See National Portrait Gallery Tour.)

Cromwell, Oliver (1599–1658)—Leader of the Protestant Parliament that deposed the king in England's Civil War, briefly establishing a Parliament-run Commonwealth. (See National Portrait Gallery Tour and Westminster Walk.)

Chaucer, Geoffrey (c. 1340–1400)—Poet, author of *The Canterbury Tales*, which popularized common English. (See Westminster Abbey Tour and Bankside Walk.)

Churchill, Sir Winston (1874–1965)—As prime minister during World War II, his resolve and charismatic speeches rallied Britain during its darkest hour. (See Westminster Walk, St. Paul's Tour, and The City Walk.)

Constable, John (1776–1837)—Painter of the English countryside, specializing in cloudy skies. (See Tate Britain Tour and National Gallery Tour.)

Dickens, Charles (1812–70)—Popular novelist, bringing literature to the masses and educating them about Britain's harsh social and economic realities. (See Bankside Walk and Westminster Abbey Tour.)

Edward the Confessor (c. 1002–66)—The English king who built Westminster Abbey, his death prompted the Norman invasion by William the Conqueror. (See Westminster Abbey Tour.)

Elizabeth I (1533–1603)—Daughter of Henry VIII and Anne Boleyn, she ruled England when its navies gained mastery of the seas, bringing prosperity and a renaissance of the arts (Shakespeare). (See National Portrait Gallery Tour and Tower of London Tour.)

Garrick, David (1717–79)—Actor and theater manager whose naturalism on the stage and business sense off it greatly enhanced the blossoming theater scene. (See National Portrait Gallery Tour, Theatre Museum Tour, and The City Walk.)

Henry VIII (1491–1547)—Charismatic king during an era of expansion whose marital choices forced a break with the pope in Rome, leading to centuries of religious division. (See National Portrait Gallery Tour and Tower of London Tour.)

Hogarth, William (1697–1764)—Painter of realistic slices of English life. (See Tate Britain Tour.)

Holmes, Sherlock (late 1800s)—Fictional detective living at fictional 221-B Baker Street, who solved fictional crimes that the real Scotland Yard couldn't.

Jack the Ripper (late 1800s)—Serial killer of prostitutes in east London; his or her identity remains unknown.

Johnson, Dr. Samuel (1709–84)—Writer of a magazine column on everyday London life, compiler of the first great English dictionary, known to us today for witty remarks captured by his friend and biographer, James Boswell. (See The City Walk.)

Keats, John (1795–1821)—Romantic poet (in the company of Percy Shelley, Lord Byron, and William Wordsworth) who pondered mortality before dying young. (See National Portrait Gallery Tour.)

Nelson, Horatio (1758–1805)—Admiral who defeated the French navy at Trafalgar (Spain), ending Napoleon's plans to invade England. (See Westminster Walk, National Portrait Gallery Tour, and St. Paul's Tour.)

Pepys, Samuel (1633–1701)—Not a famous man himself, Pepys (pron. "Peeps") kept a diary chronicling London life and the Great Fire that, even today, makes that time come alive.

Richard the Lionhearted (1157–99)—Not a great king, he preferred speaking French and spent his energy on distant Crusades.

Robin Hood (1100s)—Fictional (or perhaps real) bandit.

Shakespeare, William (1564–1616)—Earth's greatest playwright. Born in Stratford, he lived most of his adult life in

London, writing and acting. (See Bankside Walk, British Library Tour, Westminster Abbey Tour.)

Thatcher, Margaret (b. 1925)—Prime minister during the conservative 1980s, known as the "Iron Lady." (See Westminster Walk and National Portrait Gallery Tour.)

Victoria, Queen (1819–1901)—During her 64-year reign, the worldwide British Empire reached its height of power and prosperity. "Victorian" has come to describe the middle-class morality of the time. (See National Portrait Gallery Tour.)

Wellington, Duke of (1769–1852)—General who defeated Napoleon at Waterloo and later served as a domineering prime minister. (See National Portrait Gallery Tour and St. Paul's Tour.)

William the Conqueror (c. 1027–87)—Duke of Normandy in northern France, he invaded England (1066), built the Tower of London, and initiated two centuries of rule by French-speaking kings. (See Tower of London Tour.)

Wren, Christopher (1632–1723)—Architect who rebuilt London after the Great Fire of 1666, designing more than 50 churches, including his masterpiece, St. Paul's Cathedral. (See St. Paul's Tour and The City Walk.)

What's So Great about Britain?

Regardless of the revolution we had 200 years ago, many American travelers feel that they "go home" to Britain. This most popular tourist destination has a strange influence and power over us. The more you know of Britain's roots, the better you'll get in touch with your own.

Geographically, the Isle of Britain is small (about the size of Uganda or Idaho)—600 miles long and 300 miles at its widest point. Its highest mountain is 4,400 feet, a foothill by our standards. The population is a quarter that of the United States. At its peak in the mid-1800s, Britain owned one-fifth of the world and accounted for more than half the planet's industrial output. Today, the Empire is down to the Isle of Britain itself and a few token, troublesome scraps, such as the Falklands, Gibraltar, and Northern Ireland.

Economically, Great Britain's industrial production is about five percent of the world's total. For the first time in history, Ireland has a higher per-capita income than Britain. Still, the

Get It Right

Americans tend to use "England," "Britain," and "United Kingdom" interchangeably, but they're not quite the same:

- **England** is the country occupying the southeast part of the island.
- **Britain** is the name of the island.
- **Great Britain** is the political union of the island's three countries, England, Scotland, and Wales.
- The **United Kingdom** adds a fourth country, Northern Ireland.
- The **British Isles** (not a political entity) also includes the independent nation of Ireland.
- The **British Commonwealth** is a loose association of possessions and former colonies (including Canada, Australia, and India) that profess at least symbolic loyalty to the Crown.
- You can call the modern nation either the United Kingdom ("the U.K.") or simply "Britain."

economy is booming, and inflation, unemployment, and interest rates are all low.

Culturally, Britain is still a world leader. Her heritage, her culture, and her people cannot be measured in traditional units of power. London is a major exporter of actors, movies, and theater, of rock and classical music, and of writers, painters, and sculptors.

Ethnically, the British Isles are a mix of the descendants of the early Celtic natives (like Scots and Gaels, in Scotland, Ireland, and Wales), descendants of the invading Anglo-Saxons who took southeast England in the Dark Ages, and descendants of the conquering Normans of the 11th century. Cynics call the United Kingdom an English Empire ruled by London, whose dominant Anglo-Saxon English (46 million) far outnumber their Celtic brothers and sisters (10 million).

Politically, Britain is ruled by the House of Commons, with some guidance from the mostly figurehead Queen and House of Lords. Just as the United States Congress is dominated by Democrats and Republicans, Britain's Parliament is dominated by two parties: Labor and Conservative ("Tories"). (George W. Bush would fit the Conservative Party and Bill Clinton the Labor Party like political gloves.)

The prime minister is the chief executive. He's not elected

directly by voters; rather, he assumes power as the head
of the party that wins a majority in Parliamentary elections.

In the 1980s, Conservatives were in charge under
Prime Minister Margaret Thatcher and Prime Minister
John Major. As proponents of traditional, Victorian values—
community, family, hard work, thrift, and trickle-down econom-
ics—they took a Reaganesque approach to Britain's serious
social and economic problems.

In 1994, a huge Labor victory brought Tony Blair to
the prime ministership. Labor began shoring up a social service
system (health care, education, the minimum wage) undercut by
years of Conservative rule. Blair's Labor Party is "New Labor"—
akin to Clinton's "New Democrats"—meaning they're fiscally
conservative but attentive to the needs of the people. Conservative
Party fears of old-fashioned, big-spending, bleeding-heart, Union-
style liberalism have proved unfounded. The Liberal Parliament is
more open to integration with Europe.

Tony Blair—relatively young, family-oriented, personable,
easy-going, and forever flashing his toothy grin—is the most popular PM in memory. After the Labor landslide victory in June of
2001, it looks like Britain is in for a long period of Labor rule.

APPENDIX

Let's Talk Telephones

Here's a primer on making phone calls. For information specific to Britain, see "Telephones" in the introduction.

Making Calls within a European Country: About half of all European countries—including Britain—use area codes; the other half uses a direct-dial system without area codes.

In countries that use area codes (such as Austria, Britain, Finland, Germany, Ireland, the Netherlands, and Sweden), you dial the local number when calling within a city, and you add the area code if calling long-distance within the country.

To make calls within a country that uses a direct-dial system (Belgium, the Czech Republic, Denmark, France, Italy, Portugal, Norway, Spain, and Switzerland), you dial the same number whether you're calling across the country or across the street.

Making International Calls: You always start with the international access code (011 if you're calling from America or Canada, or 00 from Europe), then dial the country code of the country you're calling (see chart below).

What you dial next depends on the phone system of the country you're calling. If the country uses area codes, drop the initial 0 of the area code, then dial the rest of the number.

Countries that use direct-dial systems (no area codes) vary in how they're accessed internationally by phone. For instance, if you're making an international call to the Czech Republic, Denmark, Italy, Norway, Portugal, or Spain, simply dial the international access code, country code, and phone number. But if you're calling Belgium, France, or Switzerland, drop the initial 0 of the phone number. Example: To call a Paris hotel (tel. 01 47 05 49 15) from London, dial 00, 33 (France's country code), then 1 47 05 49 15 (phone number without the initial 0).

European Calling Chart

Just smile and dial, using this key:
AC = Area Code, LN = Local Number.

European Country	Calling long distance within...	Calling from the U.S.A./ Canada to...	Calling from another European country to...
Austria	AC (Area Code) + LN (Local Number)	011 + 43 + AC (without the initial zero) + LN	00 + 43 + AC (without the initial zero) + LN
Belgium	LN	011 + 32 + LN (without initial zero)	00 + 32 + LN (without initial zero)
Britain	AC + LN	011 + 44 + AC (without initial zero) + LN	00 + 44 + AC . (without initial zero) + LN
Czech Republic	LN	011 + 420 + LN	00 + 420 + LN
Denmark	LN	011 + 45 + LN	00 + 45 + LN
Estonia	LN	011 + 372 + LN	00 + 372 + LN
Finland	AC + LN	011 + 358 + AC (without initial zero) + LN	00 + 358 + AC (without initial zero) + LN
France	LN	011 + 33 + LN (without initial zero)	00 + 33 + LN (without initial zero)
Germany	AC + LN	011 + 49 + AC (without initial zero) + LN	00 + 49 + AC (without initial zero) + LN
Gibraltar	LN	011 + 350 + LN	00 + 350 + LN From Spain: 9567 + LN
Greece	LN	011 + 30 + LN	00 + 30 + LN

European Country	Calling long distance within...	Calling from the U.S.A./ Canada to...	Calling from another European country to...
Ireland	AC + LN	011 + 353 + AC (without initial zero) + LN	00 + 353 + AC (without initial zero) + LN
Italy	LN	011 + 39 + LN	00 + 39 + LN
Morocco	LN	011 + 212 + LN (without initial zero)	00 + 212 + LN (without initial zero)
Nether-lands	AC + LN	011 + 31 + AC (without initial zero) + LN	00 + 31 + AC (without initial zero) + LN
Norway	LN	011 + 47 + LN	00 + 47 + LN
Portugal	LN	011 + 351 + LN	00 + 351 + LN
Spain	LN	011 + 34 + LN	00 + 34 + LN
Sweden	AC + LN	011 + 46 + AC (without initial zero) + LN	00 + 46 + AC (without initial zero) + LN
Switzer-land	LN	011 + 41 + LN (without initial zero)	00 + 41 + LN (without initial zero)
Turkey	AC (if no initial zero is included, add one) + LN	011 + 90 + AC (without initial zero) + LN	00 + 90 + AC (without initial zero) + LN

- The instructions above apply whether you're calling a fixed phone or cell phone.
- The international access codes (the first numbers you dial when making an international call) are 011 if you're calling from the U.S.A./Canada, or 00 if you're calling from virtually anywhere in Europe. Finland and Lithuania are the only exceptions. If calling from either of these countries, replace the 00 with 990 in Finland and 810 in Lithuania.
- To call the U.S.A. or Canada from Europe, dial 00 (unless you're calling from Finland or Lithuania), then 1 (the country code for the U.S.A. and Canada), then the area code and number. In short, 00 + 1 + AC + LN = Hi, mom!

International Access Codes
When dialing direct, first dial the international access code. If you're calling from the United States or Canada, it's 011. Virtually all European countries use 00 as their international access code; the only exceptions are Finland (990) and Lithuania (810).

Country Codes
After you've dialed the international access code, then dial the code of the country you're calling.

Austria—43	Greece—30
Belgium—32	Ireland—353
Britain—44	Italy—39
Canada—1	Morocco—212
Czech Republic—420	Netherlands—31
Denmark—45	Norway—47
Estonia—372	Portugal—351
Finland—358	Spain—34
France—33	Sweden—46
Germany—49	Switzerland—41
Gibraltar—350	U.S.A.—1

Useful Numbers in Britain
Emergency (police and ambulance): 999
Operator Assistance: 100
Directory Assistance: 192 (20p from phone booth, otherwise expensive)
International Info: 153 (20p from phone booth, £1.50 otherwise)
International Assistance: 155
United States Embassy: 020/7499-9000
Eurostar (Chunnel Info): 08705-186-186 (www.eurostar.com)
Trains to all points in Europe: 08705-848-848 (www.raileurope.com)
Note: Understand the various prefixes—09 numbers are telephone sex–type expensive. The prefixes 0845 (4p/min, 2p evenings and weekends) and 0870 (8p/min, 4p evenings and weekends) are local calls nationwide. And 0800 numbers are toll-free. If you have questions about a prefix, call 100 for free help.

London's Airports and Airlines
Airports
For online information on the first three airports, check www.airwise.com/airports/europe or www.baa.co.uk.

Heathrow (switchboard): 0870-000-0123
Gatwick (general info): 0870-000-2468 for all airlines,
  except British Airways—0870-551-1155 (flights) or
  0845-773-3377 (booking)
Stansted (general info): 0870-000-0303.
Luton (general info): 01582/405-100
  (www.london-luton.com)

Airlines
Aer Lingus: 0845-084-4777, 0845-084-4444 (www.aerlingus.ie)
Air Canada: 0870-524-7226, 020/8751-1331 (www.aircanada.ca)
Alitalia: reservations 0870-544-8259, Heathrow
  020/8745-5812, (www.alitalia.it)
American: 020/8750-1048 (www.aa.com)
British Airways: reservations 0845-773-3377, flight info
  0870-551-1155 (www.britishairways.com)
bmi british midland: reservations 0870-607-0555,
  info 020/8745-7321 (www.flybmi.com)
Continental Airlines: 0800-776-464, 01293/511-581
  (www.continental.com)
easyJet (cheap fares): 0870-600-0000, at Luton 01582/445-354
  (www.easyjet.com)
KLM Royal Dutch Airlines: 0870-507-4074 (www.klm.com)
Lufthansa: 020/8750-3300 (www.lufthansa.co.uk)
Ryanair (cheap fares): 0870-333-1231 (www.ryanair.com)
Scandinavian Airlines System (SAS): 020/8990-7122
  (www.scandinavian.net)
United Airlines: 0845-844-4777, 07626/915-500 (www.ual.com)
Virgin Express: 020/7744-0004 (www.virgin-express.com)

London Heathrow Car Rental Agencies
Avis: 0870-606-0100, 020/8899-1000
Budget: 0800-181-181, 020/8750-2520
Europcar: 0870-607-5000, 020/8897-0811
Hertz: 0870-599-6699, 020/8897-2072
National: 0870-600-6666, 020/87502-800

Numbers and Stumblers
- Europeans write a few of their numbers differently than we do.
  1 = 1, 4 = 4, 7 = 7. Learn the difference or miss your train.
- In Europe, dates appear as day/month/year, so Christmas is
  25/12/03.
- Commas are decimal points and decimals commas. A dollar
  and a half is 1,50, and there are 5.280 feet in a mile.
- When pointing, use your whole hand, palm down.

- When counting with fingers, start with your thumb. If you hold up your first finger to request one item, you'll probably get two.
- What Americans call the second floor of a building is the first floor in Europe.
- Europeans keep the left "lane" open for passing on escalators and moving sidewalks. Keep to the right.

Climate

The first line is the average low, the second line is the average high, and the third line is number of days with no rain.

J	F	M	A	M	J	J	A	S	O	N	D
LONDON											
36°	36°	38°	42°	47°	53°	56°	56°	52°	46°	42°	38°
43°	44°	50°	56°	62°	69°	71°	71°	65°	58°	50°	45°
16	15	20	18	19	19	19	20	17	18	15	16

Metric Conversion (approximate)

1 inch = 25 millimeters
1 foot = 0.3 meter
1 yard = 0.9 meter
1 mile = 1.6 kilometers
1 centimeter = 0.4 inch
1 meter = 39.4 inches
1 kilometer = .62 mile

32 degrees F = 0 degrees C
82 degrees F = about 28 degrees C
1 ounce = 28 grams
1 kilogram = 2.2 pounds
1 quart = 0.95 liter
1 square yard = 0.8 square meter
1 acre = 0.4 hectare

British–Yankee Vocabulary

advert advertisement

afters dessert

anticlockwise counterclockwise

aubergine eggplant

banger sausage

bangers and mash sausage and mashed potatoes

bank holiday legal holiday

bap hamburger-type bun

billion a thousand of our billions (a million million)

biro ballpoint pen

biscuit cookie

black pudding sausage made from dried blood

bloody damn

bobby police officer ("copper" is more common)

Bob's your uncle there you go (with a shrug), naturally

bomb success

bonnet car hood

boot car trunk

braces suspenders

bridle way path for walkers, bikers, and horse riders

brilliant cool

bubble and squeak cold meat fried with cabbage and potatoes

bum bottom or backside

candy floss cotton candy

car boot sale temporary flea market with car trunk displays (a good place to buy back your stolen goods)

caravan trailer

cat's eyes road reflectors

ceilidh (pron. KAY-lee) informal evening of song and folk fun

cheap and nasty cheap and bad quality

cheerio good-bye

cheers Originally a toast, now it's used as a general polite word: "You're welcome," "Enjoy," "Have a nice day."

chemist pharmacist

chicory endive

chips french fries

chock-a-block jam-packed

cider alcoholic apple cider

clearway road where you can't stop

coach long-distance bus

concession discounted admission

cotton buds Q-tips

courgette zucchini

cos romaine lettuce

craic (pron. crack) good conversation (Irish and spreading to England)

crisps potato chips

cuppa cup of tea

dear expensive

dicey iffy, risky

digestives round graham crackers

dinner lunch or dinner

diversion detour

donkey's years until the cows come home

draughts checkers

draw marijuana

dual carriageway divided highway (four lanes)

elvers baby eels

face flannel washcloth

fag cigarette

fagged exhausted

faggot meatball

fanny vagina

fell hill or high plain

first floor second floor

football soccer

force waterfall (Lake District)

fortnight two weeks
Frogs French people
full monty the whole shebang, everything
gallery balcony
gammon ham
gangway aisle
gaol jail (same pronunciation)
give way yield
glen narrow valley (Scot.)
goods wagon freight truck
grammar school high school
half eight 8:30 (not 7:30)
heath open treeless land
holiday vacation
homely likable or cozy
hoover vacuum cleaner
ice lolly Popsicle
interval intermission
ironmonger hardware store
jacket potato baked potato
jelly Jell-O
Joe Bloggs John Doe
jumble sale, rummage sale
jumper sweater
just a tick just a second
keep your pecker up be brave
kipper smoked herring
knackered exhausted (Cockney: cream crackered)
knickers ladies' panties
knocking shop brothel
knock up wake up or visit
ladybird ladybug
lady fingers okra
left luggage baggage check
lemon squash lemonade
let rent
loo toilet or bathroom
lorry truck
mac mackintosh coat
mate buddy (boy or girl)
mean stingy
mews courtyard stables, often used as cottages

minced meat hamburger
mobile (pron. MOH-bile) cell phone
nappy diaper
natter talk and talk
neep turnip (Scot.)
nought zero
noughts & crosses tic-tac-toe
off license store selling take-away liquor
pasty crusted savory (usually meat) pie
pavement sidewalk
petrol gas
pissed (rude), paralytic, bevvied, wellied, popped up, ratted, pissed as a newt drunk
pillar box postbox
pitch playing field
plaster Band-Aid
poppers snaps
publican pub manager
public convenience toilets
public school private "prep" school (e.g., Eton)
punter partygoer
put a sock in it shut up
queue line
queue up line up
quid pound (money, worth about $1.50)
randy horny
redundant, made fired
Remembrance Day Veterans' Day
return ticket round-trip
ring up call (telephone)
roundabout traffic circle
rubber eraser
sanitary towel sanitary pad
sausage roll sausage wrapped in a flaky pastry
Scotch egg hard-boiled egg wrapped in sausage meat
self-catering apartment with kitchen

sellotape Scotch tape
serviette napkin
single ticket one-way ticket
sleeping policeman speed bump
smalls underwear
snogging kissing, cuddling
solicitor lawyer
starkers buck naked
starters appetizers
stone 14 pounds (weight)
subway underground pedestrian
   passageway
sultanas golden raisins
surgical spirit rubbing alcohol
suss out figure out
swede rutabaga
ta thank you
taxi rank taxi stand
telly TV
theatre live stage
tick a check mark
tight as a fish's bum cheapskate
   (watertight)
tights panty hose
tipper lorry dump truck

tin can
to let for rent
top hole first rate
topping excellent
top up refill a drink
torch flashlight
towpath path along a river
Tube subway
twee quaint, cute
underground subway
vegetable marrow summer
squash
verge grassy edge of road
verger church official
way out exit
Wellingtons, wellies rubber boots
wee urinate
whacked exhausted
witter on gab and gab
yob hooligan
zebra crossing crosswalk
zed the letter *Z*

Faxing Your Hotel Reservation

Use this handy form for your fax or find it online at
www.ricksteves.com/reservation. Photocopy and fax away.

One-Page Fax

To: _____ @ _____
                    hotel   *fax*

From: _____ @ _____
                    name   *fax*

Today's date: ____ / ____ / ____
                  day   *month* *year*

Dear Hotel _____,

Please make this reservation for me:

Name: _____

Total # of people: _____   # of rooms: _____   # of nights: _____

Arriving: ____ / ____ / ____   My time of arrival (24-hr clock): _____
               day *month* *year*   (I will telephone if I will be late)

Departing: ____ / ____ / ____
               day *month* *year*

Room(s): Single___ Double___ Twin___ Triple___ Quad___

With: Toilet___ Shower___ Bath___ Sink only___

Special needs: View___ Quiet___ Cheapest___ Ground Floor___

Credit card: Visa___ MasterCard___ American Express___

Card #: _____

Expiration date:_____

Name on card: _____

You may charge me for the first night as a deposit. Please fax, e-mail, or
mail me confirmation of my reservation, along with the type of room
reserved, the price, and whether the price includes breakfast. Please also
inform me of your cancellation policy. Thank you.

_____
Signature

_____
Name

_____
Address

_____
City   *State*   *Zip Code*   *Country*

_____
E-mail Address

Road Scholar Feedback for LONDON 2003

We're all in the same travelers' school of hard knocks. Your feedback helps us improve this guidebook for future travelers. Please fill this out (or use the online version at www.ricksteves.com/feedback), attach more info or any tips/favorite discoveries if you like, and send it to us. As thanks for your help, we'll send you our quarterly travel newsletter free for one year. Thanks! **Rick**

Of the recommended accommodations/restaurants used, which was:

Best _____

      Why? _____

Worst _____

      Why? _____

Of the sights/experiences/destinations recommended by this book, which was:

Most overrated _____

      Why? _____

Most underrated _____

      Why? _____

Best ways to improve this book:

_____

_____

I'd like a free newsletter subscription:

_____ Yes   _____ No   _____ Already on list

_____
Name

_____
Address

_____
City, State, Zip

_____
E-mail Address

    Please send to: ETBD, Box 2009, Edmonds, WA 98020

INDEX

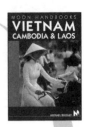

MOON HANDBOOKS®

The top choice for travelers seeking the most complete coverage of destinations in the Americas, Asia, and the Pacific.

www.moon.com

MOON METRO

Innovative city guides featuring pop-out neighborhood maps, color photos, and text written by local authors detailing the hottest sights, restaurants, and entertainment.

www.moon.com

Rick Steves

America's favorite guidebook writer offers best-selling guides to Europe for travelers who want to have more fun and spend less money.

www.ricksteves.com

Rick Steves' **Phrase Books**

Rick provides well-tested phrases and key words to cover every situation you're likely to encounter.

www.ricksteves.com

AVALON TRAVEL PUBLISHING
www.travelmatters.com

Avalon Travel Publishing guides are available at your favorite book or travel store

⑤OGHORN OUTDOORS®

Campers, hikers, boaters, and anglers agree:
With Foghorn, you'll spend less time planning and more time enjoying the outdoors.

www.foghorn.com

ROAD TRIP USA

Road Trip USA guides take you off
the beaten path, onto classic blacktop,
and into the soul of America.

www.roadtripusa.com

THE DOG LOVER'S COMPANION

A special breed of guidebook for
travelers and residents who don't want
to leave their canine pals behind.

www.dogloverscompanion.com

ADAPTER KIT

Adapter Kit helps travelers extend their journey
and live like the locals, with the help of authors
who have taken the plunge themselves.

www.adapterkit.com

AVALON TRAVEL PUBLISHING
www.travelmatters.com

Avalon Travel Publishing guides are available at your favorite book or travel store.

FREE-SPIRITED TOURS FROM

Rick Steves

Great Guides

Big Buses

Small Groups

No Grumps

Best of Europe ■ Village Europe ■ Eastern Europe ■ Turkey ■ Italy ■ Village Italy ■ Britain
Spain/Portugal ■ Ireland ■ Heart of France ■ South of France ■ Village France ■ Scandinavia
Germany/Austria/Switzerland ■ London ■ Paris ■ Rome ■ Venice ■ Florence ■ Prague

Looking for a one, two, or three-week tour that's run in the Rick Steves style? Check
out Rick Steves' educational, experiential tours of Europe.

Rick's tours include much more in the "sticker price" than mainstream tours.
Here's what you'll get with a Europe or regional Rick Steves tour ...

- **Group size:** Your tour group will be no larger than 26.

- **Guides:** You'll have two guides traveling and dining with you on your fully guided
  Rick Steves tour.

- **Bus:** You'll travel in a full-size bus, with plenty of empty seats for you to spread
  out and read, snooze, enjoy the passing scenery, get away from your spouse, or
  whatever.

- **Sightseeing:** Your tour price includes all group sightseeing. There are no hidden
  extra charges.

- **Hotels:** You'll stay in Rick's favorite small, characteristic, locally-run hotels in
  the center of each city, within walking distance of the sights you came to see.

- **Price and insurance:** Your tour price is guaranteed for 2003. Single travelers
  do not pay an extra supplement (we have them room with other singles).
  ETBD includes prorated tour cancellation/ interruption protection coverage at
  no extra cost.

- **Tips and kickbacks:** All guide and driver tips are included in your tour price.
  Because your driver and guides are paid salaries by ETBD, they can focus on
  giving you the best European travel experience possible.

Interested? Call (425) 771-8303 or visit www.ricksteves.com for a free copy of
Rick Steves' 2003 Tours booklet!

Rick Steves' Europe Through the Back Door

130 Fourth Avenue North, PO Box 2009, Edmonds, WA 98020 USA
Phone: (425) 771-8303 ■ Fax: (425) 771-0833 ■ www.ricksteves.com

FREE TRAVEL GOODIES FROM

Rick Steves

EUROPEAN TRAVEL NEWSLETTER

My *Europe Through the Back Door* travel company will help you travel better *because* you're on a budget—not in spite of it. To see how, ask for my 64-page *travel newsletter* packed full of savvy travel tips, readers' discoveries, and your best bets for railpasses, guidebooks, videos, travel accessories and free-spirited tours.

2003 GUIDE TO EUROPEAN RAILPASSES

With hundreds of railpasses to choose from in 2003, finding the right pass for your trip has never been more confusing. To cut through the complexity, visit www.ricksteves.com for my online *2003 Guide to European Railpasses.* Once you've narrowed down your choices, we give you unbeatable prices, including important extras with every Eurailpass, **free:** my 90-minute *Travel Skills Special* video or DVD and your choice of one of my 24 guidebooks.

RICK STEVES' 2003 TOURS

We offer 20 different one, two, and three-week tours (200 departures in 2003) for those who want to experience Europe in Rick Steves' Back Door style, but without the transportation and hotel hassles. If a tour with a small group, modest family-run hotels, lots of exercise, great guides, and no tips or hidden charges sounds like your idea of fun, ask for my 48-page 2003 Tours booklet.

YEAR-ROUND GUIDEBOOK UPDATES

Even though the information in my guidebooks is the freshest around, things do change in Europe between book printings. I've set aside a special section at my website (www.ricksteves.com/update) listing *up-to-the-minute changes* for every Rick Steves guidebook.

*Visit **www.ricksteves.com** to get your...*

☑ **FREE EUROPEAN TRAVEL NEWSLETTER**
☑ **FREE 2003 GUIDE TO EUROPEAN RAILPASSES**
☑ **FREE RICK STEVES' 2003 TOURS BOOKLET**

Rick Steves' Europe Through the Back Door

130 Fourth Avenue North, PO Box 2009, Edmonds, WA 98020 USA
Phone: (425) 771-8303 ■ Fax: (425) 771-0833 ■ www.ricksteves.com

Free, fresh travel tips, all year long.

Visit **www.ricksteves.com**
to get Rick's free
64-page newsletter... and more!